Counseling: Philosophy, Theory and Practice

COUNSELING:

Philosophy, Theory and Practice

Dugald S. Arbuckle
Boston University

Allyn and Bacon, Inc.
Boston

first printing . . . May 1965
second printing . . . July 1966

Library of Congress Catalog Card Number: 65–19244.

Printed in the United States of America.

PREFACE

THIS BOOK IS A REVISION of *Counseling: An Introduction,* but in many ways it is a new book. The new title is more appropriate to the new content, which in turn reflects certain changes in my attitudes, as well as, I hope, greater knowledge in the area. There is a much greater stress on the philosophical base of counseling, and although the clinical aspect of counseling is covered, there is an increased stress on the school counselor, and the functions he should and does perform. The book also reflects the tremendous changes and upheavals that have taken place in the field of counseling in the past few years. The increasing involvement of the federal government, the growth and the impact of the various professional organizations, the results of current research, environmental stresses and strains, the simple "growing up" of the profession of counseling—all of these have left their mark on this book.

"Revising" is an interesting procedure, in that it often spells out fairly well where one has moved, and where one remains the same. Much more now than in the past, I think of counseling as a total human involvement, in which methodology and technique pay little or no part. The understanding of the counselor by the counselor also looms as a more basic and crucial problem. I notice that I tend to write "counselor" more frequently now than I write "Client-centered counselor," probably not so much because I do not think there is such a fellow as a Client-centered counselor, but rather because the name carries the connotation of a "way," or a "method" or a "procedure," whereas I would think of it as describing a certain kind of person.

I have read with interest the words of the critics, and some of these words show their effect in this book. On the other hand, I cannot apologize for writing from my frame of reference, since this is the one I know best, and I do not see a book as a bloodless chronicle of what someone else has said and what someone else has done. I have tried, as best I can, to present various sides on various issues, but these other sides must be seen from my point of view. I also use the first person, since it seems rather pointless to write "it appears to the author" when what I mean is "I think. . . ."

Some readers will doubtless question the location of the various chapters, but, in keeping with my own feelings, I have placed the "why" chapter before the "what" and "how" chapters. Some may prefer to read Chapters 2, 3, and 4 before reading Chapter 1!

I have also been affected by the close human relationship I have had with a number of other people who have come to me as clients. Some of them, and some of their struggles, and their growth, and their movement toward greater freedom, appear in these pages.

Although the book is aimed at all of those individuals who may be considered to be students of counseling—therapists, teachers, clergymen, personnel directors, psychologists, psychiatrists—the major stress is on the one known as the counselor, especially the one known as the school counselor, and the environmental milieu in which he works.

My thanks to those individuals who provided me with excerpts from counseling tapes, especially Don Davis, Bill Cash, and Paul Munger, and a special word of thanks to Angelo Boy and Gerry Pine.

DSA

CONTENTS

Restrictions and Contradictions that Affect
the Counselor

The Client-Counselor Relationship

Chapter Seven

The Semantic Problem

Interpretation and Reflection of Feeling

Diagnosis

Eclecticism

Counselor Direction and Counselor Control

Advice and Information

Testing and Measurement in Counseling

Chapter Eight

The Values of Man

Ethical Issues that Face the Counselor

Examples of Ethical Issues

Chapter Nine

Reality

Cognition, Knowledge, Understanding, Insight

Empathy and Congruence

Transference and Counter-Transference

Part Four: The Counseling Experience

To Peg

PART ONE

THE PHILOSOPHY
OF COUNSELING

Chapter One

THE PHILOSOPHICAL BASE
OF COUNSELING

THE INDIVIDUAL who is known as "the counselor" might range all the way from someone who has just completed his several semester hours of training, and is thus considered to be "certified" by a state department of education, to someone whose name might happen to be Rogers or Freud or Menninger or May, but all would be likely to agree that whatever counseling might be, it at least involves two human beings, and thus man and his nature is a proper subject of concern. Counseling is also an expression of human values and human attitudes, and as the counselor is working and relating and experiencing with another person, he is giving a fairly clear picture of his own personal philosophical concept of man, his nature, and his function on earth. It would seem logical, then, that the first question that should be examined is the question of why we do what we do, rather than how we do it. The "why" is the philosophical rationale for whatever one does as a counselor, and this chapter will attempt to examine what would appear to be the major philosophical concepts that are currently affecting counseling and psychotherapy.

Man, for the greater part of his existence, has indicated his concept of man and his nature and his purpose through his religion, and it is only recently, in the pages of history, that science has become involved in the struggle with religion over the nature of man. Counseling is involved in this struggle, and the counselor must meditate on questions of science and religion when he looks at such current issues as humanism, determinism, phenomenology, existentialism, and Client-centered counseling. Indeed, it is difficult to discuss any of the latter terms without constant reference to science and (or) religion.

COUNSELING, RELIGION AND MAN

Man, in his present form (give or take a little), has been around for some time—about two million years, some anthropologists say, and it is likely that his living, for an important segment of that time, has had as a part of it what would be described today as religion. In that brief span of history which is recorded, man has had his gods, and he likely had them in some form in much of that greater part of his history which is unrecorded. On the more recent pages of history four great religious leaders appeared within less than two thousand years of each other. From an anthropological point of view, Moses, Mohammed, Christ, and Buddha were all born, and lived and died within the same day, and one must assume that man's development must have had something to do with their joint appearance on the earthly scene. In the several centuries since their day, a significant proportion of the world's organized religions have become centered around these four giant figures, and as long as man has need to differentiate and separate his identity from that of his brother, it is likely that "I am a Jew" and "I am a Christian" will be enough to separate one from another. It is likely too that the debate and the dissension and the violence that have centered around the attempt to answer the question of just who these men were, and what they believed, what they said, and what they did, will continue for some time. It may be just as well for organized religion that tape recorders were not available several thousand years ago. Human beings being what they are, we can assume that there would be some discrepancy between these people as they actually were and the images of them that have been developed.

The Greeks looked at life rationally, and the Greek citizen could have his religion and his reason. The Christian religion, however, was based on faith, and even more important for the future of man in the centuries that lay ahead, he *had* to believe or be guilty of heresy. For much of the Western world, philosophy became *religious* philosophy. It was concerned with the other world rather than with this world, and with man's relation to God rather than with man. Aquinas became the official Christian spokesman for the separation of reason from faith, and truth was that which came from God, rather than the product of reason.

Science, at least as we know it today, was a rather modern upstart, and it has been engaged in an almost constant struggle with organized religion. The counselor, particularly one of somewhat humanistic leanings, may periodically find himself in line of fire from both sides! In many ways, this struggle has been primarily one of faith (believe what I tell you) against reason (believe what your mind says is true); a struggle of truth against truths; a struggle of the absolute against the relative; a struggle of answers against questions. Ironically enough, both religion and science have expressed their love of man and their concern for him, yet both would appear to have been concerned generally with bits and pieces of him, although they may, of course, have felt that these bits and pieces were man. Thus, in the Western world, the Christian church has generally exerted no great social effort for the benefit of man, and has appeared more concerned with getting him into the next world than with helping him in the current world, which is the only one that man can know. The church has always been concerned about the soul of man, but it has too frequently ignored the rest of him. Religion and science have struggled against each other, and yet, so often, neither appeared to have known and understood the real existential living-in-being man. To the church he was a soul, preparing for the glory to come; to the scientist, he was a set of behaviors to be examined. For both, he was someone to be controlled and manipulated and directed for the good of someone other than himself. To both, he was one who could not be trusted. Freud was anti-religious, and yet the psychological body of man, as developed by Freud, bears a striking resemblance to the spiritual body of man of the church of the day.

Although Tillich [1] was later to argue that the man whose will is in bondage must have the power of self determination, since a being without the power of self determination has no capacity for decision at all, organized religion has generally shared with science a deterministic view of man. Thus while science may talk about natural laws' being lawful and determined, religion will talk about universal truths' being ultimately determined by some divine will or some supreme supernatural being. In both situations, man is obviously not in control; he is being controlled.

It would probably be safe to say that most religions—those of

1 Paul Tillich, *The Protestant Era* (Chicago: The University of Chicago Press, 1948).

Moses, and Buddha, and Christ, and Mohammed—were at least to some extent a protest of man against his suppression and his misery and his fear and his anxiety. They were movements, and all of the major original religious figures, known and unknown, were heretics against the current ruling order. Christ and Socrates shared the same fate, and they were guilty of the same offense, heresy against the state. It is ironic that the revolutionary individualism of Christ should have become symbolized so quickly by the dogma and conservatism of an organized church named after him. Kaufmann points this out when he says: [2]

> What is ironical . . . is that Jesus' dissatisfaction with all formulas and rules should have given way within one generation, to an attempt, not yet concluded, to determine the most precise dogmas.

And again: [3]

> The point is not just that religion tends to become repulsive when it prospers, or that religion is at its best in times of persecution . . . but whether religion is a pious name for conformity or a fighting name for non-conformity. The men who conducted the Greek heresy trials, the Inquisition, and the witch hunts, who went on crusades and to holy wars, were conformists, men of the crowd, true believers. The Hebrew prophets were not.

Religion and the church need not, of course, be synonymous, and one might pose a reasonable argument as to why "religious" and "religion" need not be synonymous. Most individuals, growing up in a "religious" culture, generally assume that if one is religious he must have a denominational title, and they would probably be disturbed if someone said, "Yes, I think I'm religious, but I don't know that I fit any particular title or name." For many citizens, agnostic and atheistic mean the same thing, and both are nasty words! Most, too, would probably think that one's devoutness is measured by the extent to which he accepts the dogma of the particular creed that he professes, although very rarely would this dogma have anything to do with man's relations with man. Affiliation with a particular denomination often tends to encourage and facilitate withdrawal and segregation, and the building of parochial walls. This, in turn, tends to make it more difficult to see all men as one's brothers, just as does the stress on any

[2] Walter Kaufmann, *The Faith of a Heretic* (New York: Doubleday & Co., 1961), p. 233.
[3] *Ibid.*, p. 264.

differences between men. There is no particular difference in the element of the denial of one's fellows when one is told, "Don't ever forget you are an American, not an Indian," or "a white man, not a Negro," or "a Jew, not a Baptist." They are all equally vicious, and it is particularly tragic when, in the name of religion, one must learn to spurn and suspect, and if necessary to kill, one's fellows. "Love" is a word that organized religions have used profusely, but they have practiced love less frequently.

On the other hand, man as seen by various people who probably consider themselves religious, in a current cultural sense, is by no means the same fellow. We may contrast, for example, this somewhat broad perspective of religion of Progoff: [4]

> The psychological dimension of religion is the dimension of lived experience in which religion is not a dogma but a fact of life and of accomplishment for persevering effort. . . .

with this astonishingly parochial version of one who happens to be a psychoanalyst: [5]

> The historical defect in human psychological understanding has been spanned by the vision of religion; the historical inadequacy of human responsibility has been remedied by the heroic in military life. Without religion, society would have lost its capacity for faith; without military life men would have failed to give embodiment to hope and its accompanying social morality.

The continual tying together, throughout Rosenfels' book, of religion and war, is most fascinating. Living and killing would seem to be rather odd boon companions!

On the other hand, Curran, who is a man of the cloth, also feels that man must search for his own answers.[6]

> It would restore again the possibility of starting out . . . on a thrilling personal pursuit of oneself in a fierce and independent search for reasonable self values and yet allow that one would ultimately come, by this process, not to violent rebellion and anarchy, but to ancient and secure traditional values.

[4] Ira Progoff, "The Psychological Dimension of Religion," *Journal of Existential Psychiatry* 3:166–178 (Fall, 1962).
[5] Paul Rosenfels, *Psychoanalysis and Civilization* (New York: Library Publishers, Inc., 1962), pp. 34–35.
[6] Charles A. Curran, "Some Ethical and Scientific Values in the Counseling Therapeutic Process," *Personnel and Guidance Journal* 39:15–20 (September, 1960).

Curran is existential in that he would see man taking the lonely road of choice in search of his self, and the measure of his existentialism might be seen in the extent to which he would freely allow man to make his search, and to move in directions that might not be toward those "ancient values" that Curran apparently feels *must* be there.

It is often difficult too, to try to determine just what is meant by the often vague and somewhat amorphous term "God." In much of the culture, God has become a requisite, and for many Americans, God is something of a status symbol. Fromm has a related thought when he says: [7]

> If there is anything to be taken seriously in our profession of God, it is to recognize the fact that God has become an idol. Not an idol of wood or stone like our ancestors worshiped, but an idol of words, phrases, doctrines. . . . We consider people to be "religious" because they say that they believe in God. Is there any difficulty in *saying* this?

Many counselors would see God as being in the person, and of the person. Wheelis comments: [8]

> But freedom is not fortuity, does not war with continuity, means only that we make out of past and present something new, something which is not a mechanical unfolding, and cannot have been foretold, that no law limits how far we may go, how wide, how deep. We are gods because we create.

Sartre, who could hardly be considered to be denominationally "religious," says:

> The best way to conceive of the fundamental project of human reality is to say that man is the being whose project is to be God. . . . To be man means to reach toward being God. Or, if you prefer, man fundamentally is the desire to be God.[9]

Gary describes vividly some of the gods (many would say devils) that reside within all of us. Probably all of us have heard their voices: [10]

[7] Eric Fromm, *Beyond the Chains of Illusion* (New York: Pocket Books, Inc., 1962), p. 169.
[8] Allen Wheelis, "To Be a God," *Commentary* 36:125–134 (August, 1963).
[9] Jean-Paul Sartre, *Existentialism and Human Emotions* (New York: The Wisdom Library, 1957), p. 63.
[10] Romain Gary, *Promise at Dawn* (New York: Harper & Row, Publishers, 1961), pp. 5–6.

First comes Totoche, the god of Stupidity, with his scarlet monkey's behind, the swollen head of a doctrinaire and a passionate love for abstractions; he has always been the Germans' pet, but today he prospers almost everywhere, always ready to oblige; he is now devoting himself more and more to pure research and technology, and can be seen frequently grinning over the shoulders of our scientists; with each nuclear explosion his grin grows wider and wider and his shadow looms larger over the earth; his favorite trick is to hide his stupidity under the guise of scientific genius, and to enlist support among our great men to ensure our own destruction.

Then there is Merzavka, the god of Absolute Truth and Total Righteousness, the lord of all true believers and bigots; whip in hand, a Cossack's fur cap over one eye, he stands knee-deep in a heap of corpses, the eldest of our lords and masters, since time immemorial the most respected and obeyed; since the dawn of history he has had us killed, tortured and oppressed in the name of Absolute Truth, Religious Truth, Political Truth, Moral Truth; always with a capital "T" raised high above our heads, like a scaffold. One half of the human race obsequiously licks his boots, and this causes him immense amusement, for well he knows that there is no such thing as absolute truth, the oldest trick to goad us into slavery or to drive us at each other's throats; and even as I write these words, I can hear above the barking of the seals and the cries of the cormorants the sound of his triumphant laughter rolling toward me from the other end of the earth, so loud that even my brother the ocean cannot raise his voice above it.

Then there is Filoche, the god of Mediocrity, full of bilious scorn and rabid prejudice, of hatred and petulance, screaming at the top of his voice, "You dirty Jew! You nigger! Jap! Down with the Yanks! Kill the yellow rats! Wipe out capitalists! Imperialists! Communists!" —lover of holy wars, a Great Inquisitor, who is always there to pull the rope at a lynching, to command a firing squad, to keep the jails full; with his mangy coat, his hyena's head and his deadly breath, he is one of the most powerful of the gods and the most eagerly listened to; he is to be found in every political camp, from right to left, lurking behind every cause, behind every ideal, always present, rubbing his hands whenever a dream of human dignity is stamped into the mud.

And Trembloche, the god of Acceptance and Servility, of survival at all costs, shaking with abject fear, covered with goose flesh, running with the hare and hunting with the hounds; a skilled persuader, he knows how to worm his way into a tired heart, and his white reptilian snout always appears before you when it is so easy to give up and to remain alive takes only a little cowardice.

The more one feels that counseling is related to, or aligned with, philosophy, the more likely it is that he feels it is also related to religion; whereas the more he feels that counseling is an empirical science, the more likely it is that he will question the necessity of counseling's becoming involved with religion. On the other hand, most counselors would agree with Becker when he writes: [11]

> Thus psychology and religion, which entered into a state of legal separation during the early part of this century in order to allow psychology to thrive as a science unfettered by doctrinal restraints, have fallen in love again, and are at least cohabiting if not fully married to each other because of the influence of psychotherapy on psychology.

Certainly the basic principles of operation of the counselor often appear to bear a remarkable resemblance to the basic principles of the operation of the Christian and Jewish cultures. Statements regarding the integrity and rights of the individual are found as often in religious literature as they are in counseling literature. It was not a professional counselor who first uttered such words as "Love your enemy," "Turn the other cheek," "Who will throw the first stone"; nor, however, we must add, was it a professional counselor who first said, "Vengeance is mine." In fact, it would almost seem that if John Smith, Christian, and Mart Cohen, Jew, were to *practice* to the *n*th degree the basic principles of their religions as regards their relationship with their fellow men of all faiths and sizes and colors, then there might not be much difference between their relationship with another human being and the relationship between a counselor and a client. It is when one gets to what people actually do, in the name of their religion, or supposedly because of their religion, or for their religion, that one might say "Well, if this is what you must be or if this is what you must do—and if this is synonymous with your religion, then there is a big gap between the practice of your religion and the practice of counseling."

In an article on this subject Cole has this to say: [12]

> If this interest in psychotherapy does no more than muzzle the minister its worth will be beyond measure. The contrast between the approaches of parson and psychiatrist to troubled human beings is sharp and cutting. The psychotherapist, even if he is a psychoanalyst, the most directive of the new secular priesthood, listens and listens and listens, with an angelic fear of treading too heavily on an already trampled psyche. He waits for weeks before he essays a highly tentative diagnosis and he allows the patient to come to his own insights into the nature of

[11] Russell J. Becker, "Links Between Psychology and Religion," *The American Psychologist* 13:566–568 (October, 1958).
[12] William Graham Cole, "Couch and Confessional," *The Nation,* September 20, 1958, pp. 147–150.

his problems and their solution. The minister, dealing with the same individual, talks and talks and talks!

The minister wants to persuade the troubled parishioner to see his problem in terms of a particular theological formulation. And that is precisely what the analyst does not want. . . .

Thus, if the psychotherapeutic binge now being enjoyed by the clergy does no more than influence them to talk less and listen more, the results will be startling. Further, if ministers can learn the importance of focusing on how people feel rather than on what they say, then counseling will be more effective. For the Bible is at one with the new depth psychology in regarding all human behavior, including conversation, as symptomatic, as springing from the inner wells of emotion. "As a man thinketh in his heart, so is he."

What Cole is saying here is not that religion is in the way of counseling, but rather that some individuals who are called clergymen operate, in the name of religion, in ways that could hardly be called therapeutic.

Mann stresses another problem of the religious counselor when he says: [13]

In the meantime, the clergyman employed in clinical work will have to stand guard against his own need to trespass upon the apparent theological insufficiencies of the patient. Otherwise, he will reap the bitter fruits of his compulsion: a rebellious patient who will not return for counseling, or a submissive devotee who has temporarily buried his pathology under the superficial signs and symbols of religion.

Because in recent years the role of the clergyman as a counselor has been increasingly stressed, counseling is becoming a familiar term to the clergyman, rabbi, and priest-to-be. On the other hand, if the counselor is primarily a clergyman it means that he may view his function as a counselor in a somewhat different light than does the professional secular counselor. On the Catholic side of this question, for example, Bier says: [14]

As a Catholic, I consider this care to be first of all of a spiritual nature and to be exercised through the spiritual ministrations of the priest. . . . a clergyman would think of himself as being dedicated principally to the religious care of those entrusted to him.

13 Kenneth W. Mann, "Religious Factors and Values in Counseling: A Symposium," *Journal of Counseling Psychology* 6:255–274 (Winter, 1959).
14 William C. Bier, "Goals in Pastoral Counseling," *Pastoral Psychology* 10:10 (February, 1959).

And Moynihan has this to say: [15]

Pastoral counseling primarily involves education and re-education, a realization of how a problem may be solved through the means at hand in a given religion, be it prayer, the sacraments, conferences and re-treats, whereby a new outlook on life is reached, new motivations are reached, and the basis of character modification through a change of will is developed. The primary function of the pastoral counselor is the care of the souls entrusted by ecclesiastic jurisdiction to his ministration, and since this is a spiritual function, the means he employs will be primarily spiritual.

Judaism has not moved into the area of pastoral counseling to the same degree as has Christianity, one of the reasons being that a rabbi is viewed somewhat differently from the priest or the clergyman. First and foremost they are teachers. This is the essence of their being. In light of this situation, the obvious problem of the rabbi as a counselor is expressed by Schnitzer.[16]

The usual and accepted role of the rabbi may not be readily adapted to the requirement of the professional counselor who listens and helps people to help themselves.

It is in the Protestant area that pastoral counseling has probably found its greatest support. Fairly typical of the comments of Protestant clergymen would be those of Hiltner.[17]

Broadly speaking, the special aim of pastoral counseling may be stated as the attempt by a pastor to help people help themselves through the process of gaining understanding of their inner conflicts. Counseling is sometimes referred to as emotional re-education, for in addition to its attempting to help people with a problem immediately confronting them, it should teach people to help themselves with other problems.

And Wise adds the thought: [18]

Counseling is essentially communication and as such it is essentially a two directional process. It is not what the counselor does for or to the counselee that is important; the important thing is what happens be-

[15] James F. Moynihan, "The Counselor and His Religion," *Personnel and Guidance Journal* 36:328 (January, 1958).
[16] Jeshaia Schnitzer, *New Horizons for the Synagogue* (New York: Bloch Publishing Co., 1956), p. 16.
[17] Seward Hiltner, *Pastoral Counseling* (New York: Abingdon Press, 1949), p. 19.
[18] Carrol A. Wise, *Pastoral Counseling—Its Theory and Practice* (New York: Harper & Row, Publishers, 1951), p. 63.

tween them. The pastor needs to know himself as well as the dynamic processes of personality as they find expression in the counselee.

Even in these few examples of the expressed attitudes of clergymen who are leaders in the area of pastoral counseling, there are noticeable differences between the secular counselor and the clerical counselor.

There are many traits and characteristics that are usually associated with organized religion, and, to a greater or lesser degree, with those who are the spokesmen for religion. Let us look at some of these traits that would appear to be somewhat contradictory to a philosophy of counseling, and that might be considered to hinder the development of a therapeutic relationship between counselor and client.

(1) The desire to convert and to change—usually to the religion of the counselor, and to his particular denomination of that religion— is generally a trait of many clergymen, if not an outright obligation that the clergyman has to his particular church. Many religious denominations even have particular orders whose primary purpose is to convert people to see the truth and the light. "The truth and the light," of course, are the way the particular denomination sees them, even though quite a different truth and light from those accepted by another religion. Whether an individual who feels within him a burning responsibility to persuade all people to feel and to think the way he does could be considered a counselor (much less a Client-centered counselor) is a question. Such a setting would surely contradict the concept of the acceptance of the right of the individual to be as he is and to hold the values that he holds, the right to be a free man and to develop his own system of values. It may be a moot theological question whether the "true" Christian, or whether the X denomination— which, in its own mind, represents the "true" Christianity—can operate in a philosophical area such that they would, in effect, be saying that other Christian denominations, or other non-Christian religions, might have the true answers. If this is the case, one might push a little further and say, "Well, since, you do not *know* if you have answers, and since others might be just as right as you, then what difference does it make what denomination of Christian I might be, or whether I am a Christian at all, or instead a Jew or a Buddhist?" What it boils down to might be the simple question: can a good and devout Christian say that he might, in later years, in a later period of the world's history, be shown to be quite wrong in his religious beliefs? With this general question in mind I wrote to the leaders of nine different de-

nominations in the New England area, a fairly representative sampling of Catholic, Jewish, and Protestant points of view, and asked this question: "Is it possible that in a later period of the world's history the church that you represent might be shown to be wrong in some of its religious beliefs which it makes reference to as 'God's law,' and which, therefore, are 'eternal and unchanging'?" Answers were received from all of the leaders, and there was general agreement that while God's laws are unchanging, what might be referred to as God's laws were man's interpretation of them, and as such, they would be subject to change. Thus these leaders appear to find no problem in disagreeing with the church's earlier pronouncements regarding, say, Galileo and Bruno, the question of the sun or the earth as the center of the universe, and the question of evolution.

Actually, there would appear to be little difference between those who would speak of relative truths and the more theologically oriented who feel that there is a God's truth, but are willing to accept the possibility that the current version of *the* truth may not be the correct Godly version. If the church of earlier years had accepted this philosophy, there would have been little reason for it to jail Galileo and burn Bruno. This too, of course, would remove from the church the major reason for the existence of heresy; at least one could hypothesize that the doubter might be closer to God's truth than the devout! The acceptance of the possibility of human (if not Godly) error also removes the major reason for the existence of different branches and denominations of religions. Thus, as the leaders of the Eastern and the Western branches of the Catholic church meet and talk with each other, and cautiously say, "We should not be so far apart—we are not *that* different," they are doing what is also being done by various Protestant denominations, by Protestants and Catholics, and by Christians and Jews. And the closer they become, of course, the more absurd their centuries-long self-segregation becomes. And it may be, eventually, that there will be no point in saying, "I am a Methodist" or "I am a Catholic" or "I am a Jew." All one will need to say is, "I am a human being, and you are my brother."

Certainly many of the concepts of religion are quite akin to those of counseling. The Judeo-Christian heritage stresses the worth and the dignity of the individual man, and it puts on the shoulders of man the responsibility for his actions.

Curran [19] describes some of the relationships between counseling

[19] Charles A. Curran, "Religious Factors and Values in Counseling: A Symposium," *Journal of Counseling Psychology* 6:266–270 (Winter, 1959).

and religion as "parallels." The first parallel is the commitment of self of both the counselor and the religious person. The second parallel has to do with communion—the religious person "communes" with God, whereas the client and the counselor "communicate" together. A third parallel relates to the urge of the religious person to "do better" for himself because of the love and acceptance and understanding of him by God; so too the client is urged to movement and growth because he knows he is understood and accepted, and is thus freer to become.

White speaks much like a counselor when he says: [20]

> We Catholics ask of psychotherapy, not to make us good, not to tell us what to do or not to do in order to be good, nor to make us "normal" in accord with any given norm, however estimable; but only to help us to achieve greater freedom through a better knowledge of our necessities and compulsions. We must decline to be "made" anything by psychotherapy; we want to be helped to be able to make or mar ourselves.

On the other hand, the *meaning* of religion, like that of every other aspect of living, must be measured by what it does rather than by what it says. If the Christian counselor who, when some topic about religion is being discussed, feels toward his Jewish client, "*I* am right," then he is probably saying not only "*You* must be wrong," but also, "*I* must be right." The problem then, rests: is it possible to be accepted by your church as a good and devout and faithful member, and be able to say to yourself, "I think I'm right, but it doesn't really matter too much if it turns out that I am wrong, and you are right, as well you might be." If he can feel this way, then it might be possible for him to be completely acceptant of an individual whose value system, as well as religion, differed sharply from his own. If he cannot feel this way, it would be rather difficult for him to accept another individual when he is saying to himself, "You are, of course, quite wrong."

(2) Another area where counseling and religion might find themselves to be uneasy bedfellows is in dealing with the question of sin, original or otherwise. A generally accepted psychological tenet is that it is not so much the actual "sinning," but the acceptance of the belief that we have sinned that causes problems and troubles of the mind. A person may become neurotic not because of his sins, but because he feels that he has sinned. Is the person who wears a hair shirt, or scourges himself, or pays penance, indicating the depth of his religious

[20] Victor White, *God and the Unconscious* (London: Harvill Press, 1953), p. 166.

belief, or is he rather indicating his lack of capacity to accept himself as he is? And does he thus appease himself by doing something to atone for his sins, and, in the meantime, do nothing whatsoever to really change this self that is such that he must continue to sin, and to punish himself for sinning?

It might be, too, that one should distinguish between the social and the religious mores of a Judeo-Christian society. Can we compare the feeling of sinfulness that the Jew might have in committing adultery (which would also be breaking a social law), and that which he might feel because he did not eat Kosher foods (which would be a religious custom, limited only to those Jews who accepted this particular concept)? Every counselor has had as clients individuals who are highly disturbed because they cannot intellectually accept some of the "sinful" acts of their religion as being sinful, and yet who cannot dismiss them. They may be torn between being what they feel is intellectually dishonest but secure, or being intellectually honest and uneasy. The Jew who does not eat Kosher foods, the Catholic who uses contraceptive devices, the Mormon who drinks coffee, the Seventh Day Adventist who works on Saturday—these individuals are sinning according to their religion, but not according to their society. If a person accepts such acts easily or rejects them easily, then he has no problem; but the unhappy one is the person who can do neither.

There are even good citizens who almost seem to be being scared into Heaven because they are afraid that if they do what they want to do, then they will go to Hell. Preparing for Heaven in this manner seems a most unhappy way of spending one's years on earth; and yet there is a strong segment in nearly every religious denomination—more in some than others, of course—where a basic tenet seems to be "You have sinned, and only by living the life that we say you should live will you have any chance of ever seeing the promised land." Surely, this is rather a negative way to do good. Are we good to our neighbors only because of our guilt feelings? It would seem that an ideal and realistic society will be one where such authoritarian and autocratic means for control are not necessary. We know, as a matter of fact, that such means of control are actually useless, and in the long run no control at all. In a free and democratic society, the individual accepts his responsibility for his own behavior without any pressures, subtle or otherwise. He does not steal his neighbor's belongings because he has *no need to steal,* even though he may have a very real need for his neighbor's belongings.

As long as a person can be acceptant, however, of his particular religion's "sins," and not do what he is not supposed to do, or if he can, on the other hand easily reject them as sins, then he has no psychological trouble. If, however, these sins begin to be imposed as sins on others who do not see them as sins, what then? Laws preventing the sale of merchandise on Sunday or preventing the dissemination of information on contraceptive devices are good examples of supposedly "social" laws that are actually religious laws, and are imposed on some who do not accept them as religious laws.

If a person believes too that he is basically a sinful creature, through no fault of his own other than having been born, then he begins his life as a guilty creature. This too would seem to be an insecurity-breeding way of introducing the young to life—the idea that a person must somehow get off his back sins for which he has no responsibility, other than by being a human being. Does man have potential for good and a tendency to evil, or does he have, to start, potential for good and potential for evil, but tendency, if there must be tendency one way or the other, for good rather than evil? This latter point, however, would be in the realm of belief. The empiricist might well say that man, at the beginning, has his various potentialities, but he has no tendencies until he is born, or at least, to play it safe, until he is conceived.

The problem of sins and sinning may also raise problems for the theologian as a counselor, since a client, in talking with a clergyman about sins he has committed, knows that the clergyman must consider them sins, and therefore cannot be acceptant to them. Hence the client will assume, almost certainly, that the clergyman cannot be acceptant of him as a person. This situation is illustrated by a statement by Moynihan,[21] who says, "While the pastoral counselor cannot permit anything which is contrary to the laws of God and nature, what he may legitimately permit is the opportunity for the client to talk out any kind of situation or motivation which may have led him to contemplate such a course of action." This point of view indicates that the pastoral counselor must surely be in a somewhat conflicting situation, and that his acceptance is of the most limited type. If the Catholic pastoral counselor does not feel free as an individual to accept the decision of the Catholic client to use contraceptive devices, if the Jewish pastoral counselor does not feel free as an individual to accept the decision of his Jewish client to eat non-Kosher foods, if the Methodist pastoral counselor does not feel free as an individual to accept the

---

21 James F. Moynihan, "Symposium: The Counselor and His Religion," *The Personnel and Guidance Journal* 36:327–331 (January, 1958).

decision of his Methodist client to use alcoholic beverages, if the Mormon pastoral counselor does not feel free as an individual to accept the decision of his Mormon client to drink coffee, and if all four feel that as the arm of their respective churches they must be non-acceptant of the client's right to do these things, then surely their acceptance is most limited, and surely, as therapists, they are handicapped.

Such a situation, of course, occurs to some extent with every counselor, since clients frequently discuss various deviations which are not acceptable, and might even be considered criminal, by their culture; and the client may have some beginning uneasiness as to the extent to which the counselor will be acceptant of him and his actions. Thus a Lesbian client once said to me, "I feel okay talking to you like this when I think of you as a counselor, but when I think of your title as Professor of Education, I don't feel so good!" At least the client does not know how the lay counselor feels about these things; but he does know, in his own mind at least, that the theological counselor is the arm of a powerful organization that says, "This is a sin that you should not have committed."

It is of some interest to note that this issue of sin and counseling appeared as a topic at the 1959 meetings of the American Psychological Association in Cincinnati, when Mowrer, Ellis, and Curran took part in a symposium entitled "The Role of the Concept of Sin in Psychotherapy." It is of interest, too, to note that an article on this meeting appeared in *Time* magazine (September 14, 1959) under the heading "Medicine," while in *Newsweek* (September 14, 1959) it appeared under the main heading "Science," with the subheading "Psychology"!

Mowrer also has spoken out in defense of sin as being of therapeutic value: [22]

> Therefore, we can and should show him all the love and charity within our souls, and do not need in the least to play a punitive role. But this is very different from saying that we should dispute or brush aside his assertions of guilt or minimize the reality of his need for deliverance. Several members of the group expressed the conviction that much of our present would-be therapeutic effort is useless and even harmful because we so actively *oppose* the patient's own most substantial psychological realities and his brightest prospects for change and recovery, i.e., his conviction of guilt and sense of sin. Perhaps the patient is not so wrong, not so "crazy" as some of our own theories have been!

22 O. Hobart Mowrer, "Judgment and Suffering: Contrasting Views," *Faculty Forum* No. 10, October, 1959.

In a later, thought-provoking article, Mowrer has discussed at length the problems of sin and psychotherapy.[23]

(3) Another problem that finds its way into any discussion of religion and counseling is that concerned with morality and virtue. If religion thinks of itself, as it appears to, as the custodian of man's moral values, then it is speaking in terms of absolutes, a stand that poses a knotty set of problems in a nation where there are many religions, and therefore many sets of values, each set being somebody's "absolutes." Roessler has some interesting comments on this subject. In comparing a personal morality with a "codified" morality, he writes as follows: [24]

> Personal morality is defined in positive terms. Feelings become a reliable guidance to action which enhances and enriches both self and others. . . . By contrast, codified moralities are most often preponderantly prohibitions, because they are frequently based on a pessimistic view of man's nature. . . .
>
> Like good law, such morality is centered in the needs of men rather than in the sometimes arbitrary demands of institutionalized codes. Because it is so centered, it is tailor-made. . . .
>
> It is a morality of dynamic rather than static quality, changing with ever-changing circumstances and the ever-changing person. It is ceaselessly fluid, completely or almost completely adapted to the requirements of the complex moment. . . .
>
> Personal morality is morality without absolutes. . . . Another characteristic of personal morality is its tolerance for the behavior of others. . . .
>
> The person capable of choice . . . does not function in spite of circumstances but because of them and in concert with them. . . .
>
> It seems to me that codified moralities may have a predominantly negative effect on self-realization and thereby on society. If they are characterized preponderantly by an absence of "roots in man's nature," if they are inherently inflexible and narrow, if they are absolute—then they will serve neither the needs of the individual nor those of the society comprised of individuals. Fortunately for man, such systems either die because of their lack of pragmatic value, or they are ignored in action as they deserve to be.

[23] O. Hobart Mowrer, " 'Sin', the Lesser of Two Evils," *The American Psychologist* 15:301–304 (May, 1960).
[24] Robert Roessler, "A Psychiatrist's View of Morality," *The Humanist* 18:333–339 (November-December, 1958).

This probably points to one of the dilemmas that religion faces when it begins to be involved in the problems of man's behavior. Neither man nor his society, nor the needs of the individual man nor those of the collective society, have much resemblance to what they were several thousands of years ago. The "moralities" of then do not fit the "moralities" of today any more than the sins of yesterday are the sins of today. We may argue that they should be, but if we go on the basis of the way man operates, then he simply does not accept them. If we assume that there should be some relationship between a man's behavior and his morality, then those individuals who are most closely related to a religion or to a church should be our most moral citizens (in the sense of being acceptant of their responsibility toward their neighbors, their love of their fellow man, and their defense of the rights of others). I know of no evidence to indicate that this is so. Theoretically, one might assume that among the graduates of religious schools there should be less in the way of immoral behavior, but there is no evidence to indicate that this is so. We might assume that the person who goes to his synagogue or church every Sunday should be a better man than the one who does not; but, again, there is no evidence that this is so.

The counselor is very much concerned with love and acceptance, and his love and acceptance of an individual client is not of a limited nature. The client finds in the counselor an individual who may gradually help him to feel, "I *really* am being accepted—me—as I am." Although he may not say it to himself, somewhere in his feelings may possibly come a sense that he is experiencing a non-wanting and a non-demanding love, from a counselor who wants nothing from the client, not even for him to be anybody else other than the person he himself wants to be. This is surely the love that was preached by the great and original men of many religions, and it is the love that must encompass man's morality. But is it the love that man over the centuries has really believed that he was getting from his religion; or did he feel rather that he was being measured and judged, and then possibly forgiven, but not loved? It might even be that what we are saying is: has the Christian, over the centuries, been Christian, and has the Christian Church, over the centuries, been Christian? Has it really practiced what is written in the books? Has it been moral in its concern for the welfare of the individual man, or has it been more concerned with the welfare of the Church as a massive organization? On this point Becker writes: [25]

25 Russell J. Becker, *op. cit.*

It need hardly be argued that the patience involved in spending 50 or 100 or 200 hours with a single individual plus the depth of permissiveness, acceptance and respect involved in the therapist's capacity to be open to the emotional complexities of another person's life provide a new definition of what "caring" for another person means, of what charity or true "love" means, of what creative personal relationships may be, of what the ethical demands of religion upon daily living are. . . . What we have in the evolving field of psychotherapy is a new conception of the ethic of love and a new understanding of the worth of persons that has grown up largely outside of organized religion.

Thus it is probably correct to say that clergymen and counselors are both *concerned* with the morality of man, but that different religions represent different codified systems of morality, whereas the counselor tends to operate on a basis of personal morality. Thus there is no clash of one absolute with another, one truth with another, a clash that surely must occur if the counselor feels and believes that *his* set of truths and moral values is the only *true* set of truths and moral values.

(4) Another question that involves religion and its role in counseling has to do with the extent to which religion stands for authority and the control of human behavior rather than the acceptance of human behavior. There would probably be general agreement that religion has been a major factor in the control of human behavior over the centuries, and probably most people would agree that some form of control has been necessary. If, however, we talk in terms of the development of a free and democratic society, and think of the counselor as one who operates in a free and democratic society, with the rights of the individual paramount in his mind, there will possibly be a clash between the individual and the church trying to impose its controls for what it sincerely believes is the good of the individual. Ostow [26] refers to the various devices by means of which behavior can be influenced, and the way in which organized religion has made use of these devices. One method is imitation, the lives of saints and religious heroes being described in religious literature for the express purpose of inviting imitation. Second is by the communication of affect, accomplished on an individual-to-individual basis, by congregations worshipping together and sharing the same feelings, by religious rituals, by sacred objects, by religious art. Religion also intervenes in the pursuit of instinctual gratification, and thus exercises control by promising rewards for good behavior and threatening

[26] Mortimer Ostow, "The Nature of Religious Controls," *The American Psychologist* 13:571–574 (October, 1958).

frustration and injury for bad behavior. The invoking of obedience is a primary concern of religion, and God and his surrogates are seen as parental figures who require and deserve obedience, while human beings are seen as refractory children. Religion also exploits human susceptibility to signs of vulnerability, and weakness, innocence, humility, and suffering are displayed constantly. Ostow refers too to the encouragement, by religion, of a controlled regression, whereby the individual becomes more compliant to religious authority and hence to religion's effort to control human behavior to the end of social stability.

Thus, as clergymen become more involved in counseling, this is a problem that they must face. If they basically represent an organization that is obviously trying to control human behavior, then they enter the counseling relationship with a handicap, just as does the teacher, the policeman, the judge. All of these may be splendid people, consciously concerned with the improvement of the human lot, but they cannot function completely as counselors because they have other obligations that clash with their basic obligation, as counselors, to the individual.

(5) A final issue of some concern to the problem of counseling and religion is the matter of faith and belief. A therapist can be thought of as a man of science, whereas a clergyman has been traditionally considered a man of faith. It might be, however, that in recent years each one has been affected somewhat by the other, with the clergyman beginning to become more of a man of science and the therapist beginning to become more of a man of faith—a movement that has probably been good for all concerned. It should not be unempirical to say that the counselor who does not have faith in the capacity of his client to find an answer to his problems is not going to have much success in helping the client to find the strengths that the counselor does not believe exist. The person with strength is the one who has faith in himself, and the individual should originally derive this solidarity from his parents. If he does not, the counselor in a school system is probably the next person who will have the job of trying to help him to achieve some confidence in himself; but the counselor himself *must believe* if he is ever to help the client to believe.

There is no question about the fact that religion has traditionally given the individual a faith, but it may be that this in too many cases was a faith in somebody else's doing something for him and looking after him. Although such a faith may have led to stability of a sort, it gave the individual a strength deriving from his belief in the strength of someone or something else. A responsible member of a democratic society must come to have faith in himself, and man's greatest rationalization throughout the ages has probably been the statement, "It is God's will." It has been, in a way, a comforting thought, but man would never have pulled himself out of the caves if he had accepted all of his misfortunes as God's will, never to be tampered with. Man became a forward-moving creature when he could really look at himself, blame himself for his own mistakes, and at the same time have confidence in his capacity to move ahead. Thus the counselor needs more faith—faith in the capacity of the individual client actually to learn, with his help, how to move ahead. The clergyman needs the same sort of faith—possibly less of the faith in someone else—and more faith in himself, not just as an arm of the church, but as a human being with human responsibilities toward his fellows that may even transcend his responsibilities toward his church.

On the other hand, all of this need not in any way detract from the therapeutic possibilities of faith, since faith in one's self often comes from faith in someone else. Throughout the ages, miracles have been testimony to the power of faith. It is not so much *what* one believes in, as it is that one deeply *believes* that something positive, or negative, will happen. Converts are sometimes good examples of the power of faith; a Jew who becomes a Catholic may find tremendous new strengths because of his faith in his new religion, while at the same time a Catholic who becomes a Methodist, and a Methodist who becomes a Jew will also find tremendous new strengths in their respective new religions. It is obviously not the religion, per se, that has the effect, but rather what the individual sees in it.

Another example of the power of faith is seen in various experiments, in which placebos containing inert substances have been given to some patients as having curative powers, while the same substance is given to other patients as something that has doubtful curative powers. The general procedure has been used in a variety of ways, and in most cases there is a significant difference in the improvement of those individuals who *have a belief in what they are taking*. The druggist could likely substitute placebos in half of his aspirin bottles, and it would be doubtful if those who benefit from aspirin would benefit any less. An excellent discussion of the power of faith is presented in a paper by Frank.[27]

These then, would appear to be some of the issues that face the

[27] Jerome D. Frank, "The Dynamics of the Psychotherapeutic Relationship," *Psychiatry* 22:17–39 (February, 1959).

counselor who is also involved in religion, either as a lay individual or as a theologian. Organized religion has already moved into the field of counseling, and discussions of issues such as those raised in this section are becoming commonplace in seminaries and schools of theology. Both counseling and religion, and thus, in the long run, man, should benefit from this rapprochement.

COUNSELING, SCIENCE AND DETERMINISM

Science, like religion, is a rather large word, and takes in a rather broad area. One may wonder whether man, as an existential being, has greater likelihood of growth under the autocracy of religion or under the autocracy of science—or, possibly, in a humanistic, existential society in which man is viewed as the center and the reason for being. Some might ask, of course, cannot humanism and existentialism exist in a religious or a scientific society, or in a society that is religious-scientific, if such a thing is possible? It would certainly seem that in somewhat modern Western times, the Greek society was one in which man reached a high point of being. His existential being was realized to a high degree, and he was seen as a reasoning man, living on this earth. In the many dark centuries that followed, however, man all but disappeared. He was viewed by the Christian church as a soul, with faith as the primary asset and reason as the primary sin. His purpose on earth was not to live, but to prepare for the hereafter. With the Renaissance, the light began to shine once again on reason, and science began the movement that is accelerating to this day. Increasingly, however, to science man became a thing, and as medicine graduated from the barber pole to the status of a profession it too saw man as a part of a thing—namely, a disease. The psychologist, striving for status, kept within the scientific fringe, and tended to see man as a problem. It is somewhat intriguing to note that the basic underlying theme of today's "new," "dynamic" "revolution in psychiatry" is the dawning realization that it is just possible that man is a total being after all—he is not a soul, or a thing, or a disease, or a problem.[28] He is a total existential being, and he should be considered as such.

It would appear, then, that science today tends to view man in a deterministic fashion, and that the humanism that is to be found in the existential and Client-centered view of man is not too visible in the determinism of modern science. Science tends to be somewhat skeptical about philosophy, and some of the initial reaction to Rogers

[28] See Karl A. Menninger, *The Vital Balance* (New York: The Viking Press, 1963).

was probably caused by his raising some very basic questions about the nature of man, questions that challenged some of the basic assumptions of the psychology of Freud and the religion of various denominations.

Psychiatrists and psychologists whose full-time job was a service relationship have not generally functioned as scientists,[29] but until the advent of Rogers, counseling and psychotherapy were generally accepted, professionally, as scientific pursuits. Rogers' careful elaboration, through the years, of Client-centered psychotherapy, however, has brought to the fore the question of the relationship of counseling to philosophy. For many of the more empirical psychologists, philosophy was, and is, a meaningless word, and I have heard Rogers described more than once somewhat scornfully as "nothing but a philosopher." The psychologist as a scientist is by no means all wrong, of course, in being somewhat suspicious of the philosopher, who may sometimes be too prone to accept on "faith." History presents a dismal picture of what happens when people do not insist on asking "why" or on wanting some evidence before they accept a doctrine as the truth, to be followed blindly. The scientists do not want the faith that makes one say, "I know that I can see a new body in the heavens, but my faith says it cannot be there, so it cannot be there." This is the sort of faith that has made religion the enemy of science.

Typical of the negative reaction to the philosophically oriented concept of the counselor are two letters written in reply to an article by Rogers called "Persons or Science? A Philosophical Question." [30] One of the letters states: [31]

> Rogers' article was painful in its implication for those who are now struggling for scientific method to clarify our present state of development. It could be more harmful to the graduate student who is looking for leadership in this field. How can such an integration as Rogers' which reifies science, glorifies mute feelings of ignorance by calling them personal subjective values, and abounds in infallible premises be looked upon as typical of the clinician's or psychologist's viewpoint. . . .

Another letter writer, commenting on the same article, says: [32]

---

[29] See Dugald S. Arbuckle, "Counseling: Philosophy or Science," *Personnel and Guidance Journal* 39:11–19 (September, 1960).
[30] Carl R. Rogers, "Persons or Science? A Philosophical Question," *The American Psychologist* 10:267–278 (July, 1955).
[31] Letter in "Comment," by George F. Castore, *The American Psychologist* 11:154–155 (March, 1956).
[32] Letter in "Comment," by Richard A. Lake, *The American Psychologist* 11:155 (March, 1956).

Comment on Rogers' article is irresistible, yet difficult and saddening. . . . Yet what graduate student could get by with such talk of "the essence of therapy," "the subjective and the objective person," "the scientific versus the experimental viewpoint," etc.? . . . The greatest disservice that Dr. Rogers does for psychotherapy seems to be his insistence on something mystical in the therapeutic process. There is nothing mysterious about the source of this mysticism. . . . There is another trace of mysticism in his seeming naïveté about learning. What happens in therapy, he says, is a type of learning that cannot be taught. . . .

In the article that evoked the above comments Rogers had pointed out some of the basic questions of the scientist as compared with those of the experientialist. The questions asked by the scientist might be as follows:

(1) How can you know that this account, or any account given at a previous or later time, is true? How do you know that it has any relationship to reality? If we are to rely on this inner and subjective experience as being the truth about human relationships or about ways of altering personality, then Yogi, Christian Science, dianoetics, and the delusions of a psychotic individual who believes himself to be Jesus Christ are all true, just as true as this account.

(2) Any experience that can be described at all can be described in operational terms. Hypotheses can be formulated and put to test, and the sheep of truth can thus be separated from the goats of error.

(3) Implicit in the description (by the experientialist) of the therapeutic experience seems to be the notion that there are elements in it that *cannot* be predicted—that there is some type of spontaneity or (excuse the term) free will operative here. Why not at least *aim* toward uncovering the causes of all *behavior?*

(4) Why must the therapist challenge the one tool and method that is responsible for almost all of the advances that we value— namely, the method of science?

In reaction to these thoughts of the scientist, Rogers has the therapist responding as follows:

(1) Science has always to do with the other, the object. It never has anything to do with the experiencing me.

(2) Because science has as its field the "other," the "object," everything it touches is turned into an object. This has never presented a problem in the physical sciences, but in the biological sciences it has caused certain difficulties. It is in the social sciences, however, that it becomes a genuinely serious issue. It means that the people studied by the social scientists are always objects. In therapy, both client and

therapist become objects for dissection, but not persons with whom one enters a living relationship.

(3) When science transforms people into objects, it has another effect. The end result of science is to lead toward manipulation. If we know how learning takes place, we use that knowledge to manipulate persons as objects. It is not too strong a statement to say that the growth of knowledge in the social sciences contains within itself a powerful tendency toward social control, toward control of the many by the few. An equally strong tendency is toward the weakening or destruction of the existential person. When all are regarded as objects, the subjective individual, the inner self, the person in the process of becoming, the unreflective consciousness of becoming, the whole inward side of living life, is weakened, devalued, or destroyed.

(4) Is not ethics a more basic consideration than science? In the physical sciences it took centuries for the ethical issue to become crucial. In the social sciences the ethical issues arise much more quickly because persons are involved. But in counseling the issue arises most quickly and most deeply. We should think long and hard before we give up the values that pertain to being a person, to experiencing, to living a relationship, to becoming, that pertain to one's self as a process, to one's self in the existential moment, to the inward subjective self that lives.

This article has been referred to at some length because it poses this problem of the counselor and the scientist as succinctly as any with which I am familiar, probably because its author is the one who has raised this problem as an issue more than any other contemporary counselor. In pondering how to solve this dilemma, Rogers concludes his article by saying "If I am open to my experience, and can permit all of the sensings of my intricate organism to be available to my awareness, then I am likely to use myself, my subjective experience, *and* my scientific knowledge, in ways which are realistically constructive."

In discussing the counselor's responsibility in rehabilitation, Patterson effectively describes what is all too often thought of as the scientific method in counseling. It is also deterministic.[33]

He *determines* the eligibility of clients as clients and the feasibility of their rehabilitation; he *appraises* the client's vocational potential and the probability of his success; he *evaluates* the suitability of various jobs; he *interviews* the client *toward realistic* (as defined by himself) goals; he

[33] C. H. Patterson, "The Counselor's Responsibility in Rehabilitation," *Journal of Rehabilitation* 24:7–11 (January-February, 1958).

develops a vocational rehabilitation plan with all its parts; he *carries out* the plan, implementing and administering its various aspects; he *makes referrals* to related services. One might ask: What is the client doing all this time? Too often he is literally doing nothing, except what he is told to do by the counselor.

The possible reason that the client is doing nothing is that he is viewed as an object, a piece of material, to be manipulated by the counselor who has the knowledge and the know-how not possessed by the client. Patterson wrote this as a protest against the all too prevalent concept of vocational counseling, but surely it describes frighteningly what happens when the client becomes lost as a person, as a human being, and is treated as one who is not to be accepted and understood as he is, but rather must be manipulated and modified until he becomes another faceless creature.

The function of science is to determine what is, and, as a result of this determination, to predict what might be. Such a scientific prognosis is based on evidence and facts; it is not concerned with values, with what ought to be. Generally this has not been a problem for the medical doctor, since man's physical body is not concerned with what ought to be either. A leg is smashed; there are certain proven techniques which have shown themselves to be superior over others in the mending of the broken leg. The leg does not ask, "Why should I mend?" or "What difference will it make if I do mend?" or "How did I come to get into this situation which resulted in a broken leg?" Thus as long as the medical doctor functioned as a surgeon, he could well be scientific. But as soon as he began to work with the owner of the leg, a human being who had a mind, his organic scientific knowledge began to fail him.

This circumstance probably posed no problem for the earlier medical doctor, who actually knew very little other than how to use his few skills and dispense his few medicines; however, if he was an intelligent individual, concerned with human values, then he probably functioned very much as a philosopher and a counselor. When Freud appeared on the scene with the first studied presentation of counseling and psychotherapy, it was presented as a science, although Freud [34] was probably thinking of the dangers of the "too scientific" approach when he said, "Cases which are thus destined at the start to scientific purposes and treated accordingly suffer in consequence;

[34] Sigmund Freud, "Recommendations for Physicians on the Psychoanalytic Method of Treatment," *Collected Papers, II* (London: Hogarth Press, 1925), pp. 326–327.

while the most successful cases are those in which one proceeds, as it were, aimlessly, and allows oneself to be overtaken by any surprises, always presenting to them an open mind, free from any expectations." [34] Freud was no doubt influenced by his medical background, and with his generally anti-religious point of view, it is little wonder that there was not much in the way of a philosophical approach to his psychotherapy. It should be noted, too, that then as now philosophy tended to be related to religion. While this is obviously true, it is not correct to assume, as some theologians do, that in order to be a philosopher one must be allied with a denominational religion. Some of the greatest minds in philosophy have been, and are, looked at with some suspicion by the more orthodox of their brethren, and the narrowness of philosophical breadth of some individuals may be correlated with their concept of religion as a set of dogmas, mostly telling man what not to do.

Thus, in a way, man moved into the study of the psychological and philosophical nature of man, with very little in the way of knowledge about the former, and a general bias or suspicion toward the latter. To some degree this condition still holds today, with the psychologist, as the newcomer in the field, taking on many of the characteristics of the medical profession, even while he strives with might and main to prove that he is different, as obviously he is.

The theologian has not generally been considered to be very scientific, being, rather, a man of faith. As he moves into the therapeutic arena, however, will he tend to become more scientific, and if he does, what will this attitude do to his faith? Although one might agree with Walters [35] that "existential anxiety is properly the object of priestly concern, while pathologic anxiety is the concern of the psychotherapist," I cannot accept the implication that existential anxiety is not the concern of the psychotherapist. This very example might be an excellent indication of the difference between the counselor and the psychotherapist as scientists and as philosophers. If the counselor is concerned only with the pathological, and this is often thought of as the logical concern of the medical doctor and the clinical psychologist, then he can probably remain as the empirical scientist. Once, however, he becomes concerned with the more "existential" aspects of anxiety (and how could one be a counselor without having this concern?), then he has entered the realm of philosophy. Certainly it is not man's acts that cause him stress and strain so much as it is the guilts, the anxieties,

[35] Orville S. Walters, "Metaphysics, Religion and Psychotherapy," *Journal of Counseling Psychology* 5:243–252 (Winter, 1958).

the fears, the frustrations that have come to be associated with these acts. An individual is not disturbed by the physical act of masturbation until he learns that it is bad for him to masturbate, or that something dreadful will happen to him if he does; one is not distressed about hating a miserable parent unless one has learned that one is supposed always to love one's parents; one is not concerned about killing one's fellows as long as he knows that they are his enemy and must be killed, and that he will be rewarded for the act. These are surely matters of values that bring in questions about who we are, what we are around for, what is right, and what is wrong. And these are questions for which it is difficult to pose clear-cut empirical answers. One might be scientific in his attempts to evaluate what happens as a result of his counseling, what might happen if he does this instead of that, what happens if a certain variable (difficult to isolate in the social sciences) is introduced, and so on; but how scientific can one be in actual relationship with the client? And this, after all, is what counseling is.

Certainly the organic aspects of counseling can be scientific. Neither the patient nor the medical doctor is in the realm of philosophy when both are involved in a brain lobotomy or an electro-shock, or in the injection of various drugs. Here one can be somewhat pragmatic, and on the basis of statistical evidence, say that he will proceed thus and so with this helpless patient, with no involvement on his part; and he knows the statistical odds that this, instead of that, will happen.

The traditional case study approach, revered by social workers, might also be considered to be somewhat scientific, since it tends to be an investigation of what is, without the personal involvement of the client, and without the personal involvement and intrusion of the values and ideas and thoughts and feelings of the counselor, other than those that are based on evidence. Again, however, when the social worker becomes a counselor, she is no longer working *on* a case, but *with* a human being, and again the question arises. How scientific can you be in the actual close personal relationship between client and counselor, or does the very "scientificness" of one's approach render you less effective?

Many of the techniques and methods of counseling might logically be described as scientific. Thus, diagnosis is an empirical means of assessment of an individual or his problems. The whole process of analysis and interpretation can really be defended only on the basis of a scientific validation of their use. Thus it would probably be correct to say that counseling, as it is allied with or descended from medicine or psychology, will tend to have a strongly scientific tinge; and certainly many counselors, in their descriptions of counseling, would refer to it as "the science of. . . ."

Probably all counselors would agree that if counseling is to have the status of a profession, then its practitioners cannot say that they operate on faith and intuition, or that they need no evidence of whether the client is better or worse off because of their ministrations. This is surely the road to quackery, and counseling already has more than its share of quacks. On the other hand, if one thinks of counseling as basically a human relationship between two individuals, rather than as things the counselor does with or to the client during the relationship, then he enters the realm of the more subjective, the realm of human feelings.

Empirical science is deterministic, and man usually appears as a rather hapless and helpless creature, fated to be buffeted around during a rather miserable existence by various forces—the id, the culture, and others—over which he has no direction and no control. Orwell [36] paints his society as an example of what might happen to man, but Skinner's version [37] is even worse, in that it is painted objectively as the inevitable fate of man. As a determinist, Skinner assumes that behavior is lawful and determined. As his hero says,[38]

> . . . democracy . . . isn't, and can't be, the best form of government, because it's based on a scientifically invalid conception of man. It fails to take account of the fact that in the long run *man is determined by the state.* A *laissez-faire* philosophy which trusts to the inherent goodness and wisdom of the common man is incompatible with the observed fact that men are made good or bad, and wise or foolish by the environment in which they grow.

This is the world of the empirical scientist, and in it the existential man, the living being, is nowhere to be seen. A counselor with such a concept would probably be acceptant of the statement by Michael and Meyerson [39] that "the phenomenon with which counselors deal, then, is behavior. . . ." They would probably share the apparent lack of concern of the same writers when they say: [40]

[36] George Orwell, *1984* (New York: Harcourt, Brace and Co., 1949).
[37] B. F. Skinner, *Walden Two* (New York: The Macmillian Co., 1948).
[38] *Ibid.*, p. 273
[39] Jack Michael and Lee Meyerson, "A Behavioral Approach to Counseling and Guidance" *Harvard Educational Review* 32:383–402 (Fall, 1962).
[40] *Ibid.*

> Parents, educators and guidance workers make no bones about their
> earnest intention to create and maintain the "good" behavior that is
> valued and approved of by the culture and to eliminate "bad" be-
> havior to the maximum degree of which they are capable.
> . . . For most of those to whom society entrusts the guidance of others
> influencing or inducing people to behave in ways that society says
> are "good" ways is an accepted goal, and the critical question is "How
> can we 'motivate' a person so that he does behave, 'wants' to behave,
> and 'enjoys' behaving in good ways?"

The behavioral scientist would probably subscribe to the above,
possibly with some variations, but in general he would tend to feel not
only that man lives in a lawful and determined world, but that man is
a bit of that lawful and determined world. Man is the product of his
culture, and any such ideas as freedom and choice are subjective and
sentimental myths. Man is "fated" to be what he is, and there is little
or nothing that he can do about it. Man becomes another creature, or
possibly not even a creature, but rather another thing, to be manipulated and directed by someone to do something for somebody. The
manner in which one becomes a manipulator instead of the manipulated is also determined. This is a sort of womb-to-tomb philosophy of
life, in which man has given up the risks of freedom, and instead has
accepted, as inevitable, the security of the autocrat. In a way, it accepts
what Fromm has described as the authoritarian ethic, which: [41]

> . . . denies man's capacity to know what is good or bad; the norm
> giver is always an authority transcending the individual. . . .
> Materially . . . authoritarian ethics answers the question of what is
> good or bad primarily in terms of the interests of the authority, not
> the interests of the subject.

It is this point of view of man that seems to predominate in much
of the current literature dealing with plans for the welfare of our
fellows. Thus when Hilliard [42] talks about "manpower" planning, one
has the uneasy feeling that man, the human being, is somehow being
minimized. "Manpower" is people, not machines, and any planning
about what to do with people carries with it the implication of the
renunciation of the idea of a free society, with its chaos and problems,
for a well planned society, in which man may exist, secure and cozy,
from birth to death.

[41] Erich Fromm, *Man for Himself* (New York: Rinehart & Winston, 1947), p. 10.
[42] John F. Hilliard, "Essentials of Manpower Planning in Economic Development,"
International Development Review 4:No. 1 (March, 1962).

Fromm describes our movement toward this deterministic concept of society in this way: [43]

> Our moral problem is man's indifference to himself. It lies in the fact that we have lost our sense of the uniqueness and significance of the individual, that we have made ourselves into instruments for purposes outside of ourselves, that we experience and treat ourselves as commodities, and that our own powers have become alienated from ourselves. We have become things, and our neighbors have become things. The result is that we feel powerless and despise ourselves for our own impotence. Since we do not trust our own power, we have no faith in man, no faith in ourselves or in what our own powers can create. We have no conscience in the humanistic sense, since we do not dare to trust our judgment. We are a herd believing that the road we follow must lead to a goal since we see everybody else on the same road. We are in the dark and keep up our courage because we hear everybody else whistle as we do.

It would, of course, be extremely naive to assume that one can live his individual life, in the company of other individuals, past, present, and future, without being affected by them. It is equally obvious that, to a great extent, we live in a determined world. But there is a vast difference between the individual who knows and feels and believes that he *is* the master of his fate, that in the long run he *can* choose, even though, because of circumstances, that choice might be infinitesimally small, and the individual who has not this conviction. Man always, even in the most oppressive of circumstances, possesses the small, thin wedge of freedom, and if we feel that education is a process or a means by which one can become what he is, and if we believe that learning is growing into greater depths of freedom and creativity, then the counselor must surely be one who does not accept the concept of the determinism of man. The counselor, we could hope, would be sympathetic to the protest of Scher when he says: [44]

> Life for most of us so-called normals is a constant struggle to scorch the feelings of richest life, to render ourselves unconscious, stamp out individuality, and all in the name of normality. Better a bit more abnormality than this living death we call normal living.

If the counselor is willing to accept the deterministic concept of the nature of man, and of course many are, it would seem that he

[43] Fromm, *op. cit.*, p. 248.
[44] Jordon M. Scher, "Vivacity, Pathology, and Existence," *Journal of Existential Psychiatry* 3:205–210 (Fall, 1962).

must be willing to accept his function as that of a manipulator of the individual for the pre-determined "good" of some current body or organization of people who are no longer individuals. It would also seem that he must, in some respects at least, be the enemy of the free man, since he is surely saying to man that he has no rights as an individual, that he has no integrity as a human personal entity, that his only purpose is, like the cows in the field, to serve the pre-determined state.

This, of course, may be considered a somewhat exaggerated point of view, but it is no exaggeration of my deep concern for the extent to which the counselor might become the servant of the scientific state, which, rather than helping the individual to grow to greater freedom as an individual, may manipulate and control him so that he becomes a numb and voiceless instrument. The attack on the freedom of the individual occurs, of course, in our current "free" world as well as in our "slave" world, and in that part of the world that is considered to be in somewhat of a limbo. Probably no better example in the United States could be found than in the fact that a citizen who makes use of a constitutional right such as the Fifth Amendment is considered, by some, to be "guilty" of un-Americanism, and this, of course, is a minor restriction compared to those that entrap the individual in some of the new "people's democracies." Americans might well wonder if some of the freedoms that they now possess, freedoms that were written in the books of the past, would be as easily written in the books of today's America. The people of the "free" new nations might well be concerned about the paucity of the guarantees of individual freedom that are being written into their books of the present.

One may wonder, however, if even the science of physics is as exact as it might appear to be, in that while it may be laws of nature that are being examined and studied, it is *man* who is involved in the examining. He sees what he sees, and what he sees depends on certain assumptions and suppositions. As May says: [45]

> Every scientific method rests upon philosophical presuppositions. These presuppositions . . . determine not only how much reality the observer with this particular method can see . . . they are indeed the spectacles through which he perceives, but also whether or not what is observed is pertinent to the real problem, and therefore whether the scientific work will endure. It is a gross, albeit common, error, to assume naively that one can observe facts best if he avoids all preoccupation with

[45] Rollo May, *Existence* (New York: Basic Books, 1961), p. 149.

philosophical assumptions. All he does, then, is mirror uncritically the particular parochial doctrines of his own limited culture. The result in our day is that science gets identified with isolating factors and observing them from an allegedly detached base—a particular method which arose out of the split between subject and object made in the seventeenth century in Western culture and then developed into its specialized compartmentalized form in the late nineteenth and twentieth centuries.

Much the same thought is expressed by Rogers: [46]

Science exists only in people. Each scientific project has its creative inception, its process, and its tentative conclusion, in a person or persons. Knowledge—even scientific knowledge—is that which is subjectively acceptable. Scientific knowledge can be communicated only to those who are subjectively ready to receive its communication. The utilization of science also occurs only through people who are in pursuit of values which have meaning for them.

And by Walters: [47]

The therapist usually conceives of himself, and is often represented as the detached, dispassionate scientist. A more realistic view would see him as an involved participant with an interest in the outcome, following a sectarian psychotherapeutic doctrine or combination of doctrines, the selection, and practice of which are tinctured by his own basic philosophy of life.

Einstein was also thinking of the human aspect of science when he wrote: [48]

For the scientific method can teach us nothing else beyond how facts are related to, and conditioned by, each other. . . . Yet it is equally clear that knowledge of what *is* does not open the door to what *should be*.

As was Burtt: [49]

[46] Carl R. Rogers, *On Becoming a Person* (Boston: Houghton Mifflin Company, 1961), p. 216.
[47] Orville S. Walters, "Metaphysics, Religion and Psychotherapy," *Journal of Counseling Psychology* 5:243–252 (Winter, 1958).
[48] Albert Einstein, *Out of My Later Years* (New York: Philosophical Library, 1950), pp. 21–22.
[49] E. A. Burtt, "The Value Presuppositions of Science," in Paul C. Obler and Herman A. Estrin (Eds), *The New Scientist: Essays on the Methods and Values of Modern Science* (New York: Anchor Books, 1962), p. 282.

In its most general historical meaning the word "science" simply denotes the search for some orderly pattern in the world around us; its aim is to conquer the contingency and chance that initially confront us wherever and as far as it can. But it is evident when we think about it that this aim, merely as such, is quite ambiguous and indeterminate. Many different kinds of order are discoverable; in fact, everything that one experiences is related with some measurable degree of regularity to an indefinite number of other things. Accordingly, what sort of order is discovered depends primarily on the sort that scientists aggressively look for, and what they look for depends in turn on the further ends which, consciously or unconsciously, they want their explanations to serve.

The question has also been raised whether predictions obtained in the past, based on units larger than the electron, occurred because one could predict the future behavior of an electron or because laws of statistics come into play when we deal with appreciable lumps of matter.[50]

DETERMINISM AND PHENOMENOLOGY

Phenomenology is somewhat different from determinism, but is nevertheless related to it in its concept of man and his behavior, and both might be considered to be part of the behavioral science concept of man. Phenomenological psychology is by no means new, and in a way it grew up with psychology. Descartes, in the early seventeenth century, was probably the first phenomenological psychologist, and his approach was simply to study the mind through the immediate experience as it appears at the conscious level. This was, of course, long before the unconscious became postulated as the major aspect of the mind, and the maker of human behavior. A century later, in Ireland, Berkeley was arguing much the same way—that is, that perception is reality, that what we perceive is real. Currently, the phenomenological approach is best described in a book by Combs and Snygg. They refer to the phenomenological approach to psychology as seeking: [51]

> . . . to understand the behavior of the individual from his *own* point of view. It attempts to observe people, not as they seem to outsiders, but as they seem to themselves. . . .

50 J. W. N. Sullivan, *The Limitations of Science* (New York: Mentor Books, 1961), p. 72.
51 Arthur W. Combs and Donald Snygg. *Individual Behavior* (revised) (New York: Harper & Row, Publishers, 1959), p. 17.

This concept of the perceptual or phenomenal field as the determiner of what one sees, what one does, and what one chooses need not be deterministic if one feels that this field is primarily created by, and can be changed by, individual man. Determinism must hold, however, if we feel that man must be the victim of his perceptual field when he says ". . . the perceptual field is usually organized direction nor control over it. Combs and Snygg [52] would appear to be deterministic when they say ". . . let each one of us look at his behavior as we actually see it at the moment we are behaving. At once we find lawfulness and determinism," and again,[53] ". . . The concept of complete determinism of behavior by the perceptual field is our basic postulate. . . . All behavior . . . is completely determined by, and pertinent to, the perceptual field of the behaving organism." On the other hand, Combs [54] does stress the primacy of the self over the field when he says ". . . the perceptual field is usually organized with reference to the behavior's own phenomenal self," and ". . . the phenomenal self is both product of the individual's experience and product of whatever new experience he is capable of."

Thus one can be phenomenological in the sense of accepting the concept that we operate within our perceptual fields, and our perception of reality as *we* see it, without being deterministic. On the other hand, if we see the phenomenal field as being the determiner of the phenomenal self, then choice and freedom are both illusions, and man must accept his determined fate.

EXISTENTIALISM

There is a more humanistic, a more individualistic concept, however, in which man is viewed as the creator of his culture. It exists for him, not he for it. This existential concept views man as *being;* life is now, and man is as he is. Determinism may say, "You cannot be what you are, you must not be what you are, you simply cannot *be,*" but the existentialist would say that human existence is *being,* and that man is the being who is there.

Existentialism, as a factor in counseling in the United States, is interesting in that it is primarily a European product, and it is philosophical rather than psychological in nature. It is also interesting to note that the current psychological involvement in existentialism

52 *Ibid.,* p. 17.
53 *Ibid.,* p. 20.
54 *Ibid.,* p. 146.

has been primarily brought about by practicing counselors and psychotherapists, rather than by psychological theoreticians. There are also, of course, many differences among the major figures of existentialism, such as Sartre, Heidegger, Kierkegaard, Jaspers, and Frankl, and the range of religion that they represent extends from atheist to theologian.

Here are a few of Sartre's thoughts on existentialism: [55]

> . . . by existentialism we mean a doctrine which makes human life possible, and, in addition, declares that every truth and every action implies a human setting and a human subjectivity.

And again: [56]

> Not only is man what he conceives himself to be, but he is also what he wills himself to be after this thrust toward existence. . . . Man is nothing else but what he makes of himself. Such is the first principle of existentialism.

And again: [57]

> There can be no other truth to take off from than this: I think, therefore I exist.

For Sartre, man is free, man *is* freedom. If we accept the concept that existence does precede essence, then there can be no determinism. Man can be what he will.

The existentialist is anti-deterministic in that he sees the person as transcending both himself and his culture. May describes existential thought in this way: [58]

> Existentialism means centering upon the *existing* person; it is the emphasis on the human being as he is *emerging, becoming.* . . . Traditionally in Western culture, existence has been set over against *essence*, the latter being the emphasis on immutable principles, truth, logical laws, etc. that are supposed to stand above any given existence.

Maslow is speaking about the existential self as he describes his authentic person as one who: [59]

[55] Jean-Paul Sartre, *Existentialism and Human Emotions* (New York: The Wisdom Library, 1957), p. 10.
[56] *Ibid.*, p. 15.
[57] *Ibid.*, p. 36.
[58] Rollo May, *Existential Psychology* (New York: Random House, Inc., 1961), p. 16.
[59] A. H. Maslow, in Rollo May, *op. cit.*, p. 55.

. . . not only transcends himself in various ways; he also transcends his culture. He resists enculturation. He becomes more detached from his culture and his society. He becomes a little more a member of his species and a little less a member of his local group.

Von Kamm describes a basic aspect of existentialism when he says: [60]

Existential psychology . . . insists on the free responsibility and the spontaneous creativity which remain the unique and fundamental characteristics of existence. It retains awareness of the limits of freedom revealed by deterministic psychologies, yet it transcends determinism by its recognition of man's radical freedom.

And again: [61]

The main characteristic of the human existant is that he exists, literally stands out in a world of meaning. Subject and world, self and world are correlatives . . . the counselee is best understood from his personally lived and experienced universe.

Lyons [62] comments that "existentially one always begins within human subjectivity; it is the given framework and source . . . ," and Howland [63] states that "To put it in existential terms, a part of being always consists of 'having been.' 'Having been' is a kind of immortality in that it can never be destroyed or taken away."

The self, the person-in-being as seen by the existentialist, is not one who is subject to empirical prediction and control. Ostow expresses this anti-deterministic concept when he says: [64]

If religion, then, has failed to obtain complete control over human behavior, if its effect is merely one of influence and modulation, it is not because of poor technique, but because of the ultimate independence of the human spirit and the essential autonomy of the instinctual apparatus.

[60] In a statement at an Arden House conference, January, 1963.
[61] Adrian Von Kamm, "Counseling from the Viewpoint of Existential Psychology," *Harvard Educational Review* 32:403–415 (Fall, 1962).
[62] Joseph Lyons, "The Problem of Existential Inquiry," *Journal of Existential Psychiatry* 4:142 (Fall, 1963).
[63] Elihu S. Howland, "Nostalgia," *Journal of Existential Psychiatry* 3:197–204 (Fall, 1962).
[64] Mortimer Ostow, "The Nature of Religious Controls," *The American Psychologist* 13:571–574 (October, 1958).

As does Frankl: [65]

A real person is not subject to rigid prediction. Existence can neither be reduced to a system or deduced from it.

Although one could hardly be both deterministic and existential, neither can be considered as absolute terms. Skinner might be considered to represent the deterministic end of a continuum, where man would appear to be a nothing, manipulated and controlled for the furtherance of the ends of some faceless and unknown "group," whereas Sartre would represent the other end of the continuum, which would see man as supreme, responsible for his own actions, answerable only to himself. Such a man lives in a world in which things and events have not been determined by him, but the human self is the determiner of the reaction to these events, and the human self will determine the manner and the mode in which man will live and grow and die.

The existential view of man could not accept the concept that the ends might justify the means, since the human person and his world of reality cannot be separate, and they are not tomorrow, but today. Thus the world of work for the child is a very real world of work. However, it is not something in the vague future; it is today. A "stay-in-school" campaign will seem a little pointless to a child, when, from his reality, nothing has changed, either in his view of the world or in its view of him.

Nor would the existentialist help to maintain, for the child, the myth of equality, at least in the sense that every young American child has the same chance. Even worse, of course, is the attendant myth that inequality and difference are synonymous with inferiority. Having a dark skin instead of a white skin, being a male instead of a female, having an IQ of 90 instead of 140, these may be very real outer restrictions, but the existentialist operates with what *is,* and thus, in a very real sense, helps to change what is. Excellence is within the reach of all, but excellence is an inner concept of self, and it is the excellence that is missing in many of our fellows because we have alienated them from us, and we have helped them to come to believe that they are small people. They have not transcended their culture, and their fight against it seems hopeless, because they have become enculturized and entrapped by it.

Choice, too, becomes an inner, relative matter. The child who

[65] V. E. Frankl, "On Logotherapy and Existential Analysis," *American Journal of Psychoanalysis* 18:28–37; No. 1 (1958).

can be helped to choose really freely to stay in school has immediately removed from himself some of the restrictions and impositions of that school, even though there has been no outer change of either curriculum or teachers. The very fact of choice is freedom, and this immediately changes the outer world around us. Man may live in a determined world, but he is not determined. Choice of a job, after all, in the sense of "I want to be able to choose any job I want" has always been an illusion. It is unfortunate that some American children come to view freedom and choice as "something I can do to someone," rather than as a continuing struggle by one to maintain his integrity and his responsibility. For many children, choice becomes more and more restricted, but the real restriction comes in the sense that they have allowed themselves to come to believe that they are determined victims of a determined world. Freedom and choice have nothing to do with outer restrictions. They are an inner matter, a matter of the self—of the spirit, if you will. The man who kills is usually less free than his victim; the man who hates is less free than the man who loves.

In education, the existential view is being expressed by Mathewson,[66] when he says ". . . in the form of education which emphasizes development of individual potential and adaptability, narrow forms of information acquirement may cease to remain at the center of the educational target," and by Murphy,[67] who comments that "the teacher must help the learner to believe in his own individuality and his capacity to learn." Vanderberg [68] also points out an existential view in commenting that education is the process of becoming oneself, that freedom is restricted when pupils are treated as objects, and that the authentic teacher thinks only in terms of the interactions of individuals who have achieved different degrees of becoming themselves.

EXISTENTIALISM AND CLIENT-CENTERED COUNSELING

It is unfortunate that counseling has come to have certain tags and handles, since these carry with them the implication that counseling is a technique or a method, quite divorced from the personality of the counselor. The term "Client-centered counseling" is not a description of a method of counseling, but it refers, literally, to what it says —it is a human relationship between two people, and it is centered

[66] Robert H. Mathewson, *Guidance Policy and Practice* (New York: Harper & Row, Publishers, 1962), p. 374.
[67] Gardner Murphy, *Freeing Intelligence Through Teaching* (New York: Harper & Row, Publishers, 1961), p. 47.
[68] D. Vanderberg, "Experimentalism in the Anesthetic Society: Existential Education," *Harvard Educational Review* 32:155–187 (Spring, 1962).

on one of the two people involved—the client. And the Client-centered concept of man, and of the counseling relationship, is very much an existential point of view. This, it might be pointed out, is not the traditional doctor-patient relationship of medicine, nor is it the student-teacher relationship of education. In the former, it is obvious that there is no patient choice, and in the latter, only lip service is paid to the concept that the student must be the central figure, and the deciding agent as far as any choice or decision is concerned.

Thus, philosophically, the existential version of the human relationship appears to be very similar to the therapeutically oriented version of the Client-centered counselor. Titus, for example, describes existentialism thus: [69]

> Existentialism is an emphasis on the uniqueness and primacy of existence in the sense of the inner, immediate experience of self-awareness. . . . The most meaningful point of reference for any person is his own immediate consciousness.

This would not appear to differ much from Rogers' description of the Client-centered counseling relationship: [70]

> I launch myself into the therapeutic relationship, having a hypothesis, or a faith, that my liking, my confidence, my understanding of the other person's inner world will lead to a significant process of becoming. . . . I enter the relationship . . . as a person. . . . I risk myself. . . . I let myself go . . . my reaction being based (but not consciously) on my total organismic sensitivity to this other person.

In a somewhat similar manner, May describes the existential approach to psychotherapy: [71]

> [I]t is not a system of therapy, but an attitude toward therapy, not a set of new techniques but a concern with the understanding of the structure of the human being and his experience that must underlie all techniques.

This appears to be what Client-centered therapist Gendlin describes as he writes: [72]

[69] Harold H. Titus, *Living Issues in Philosophy* (New York: American Book Co., 1959), p. 292 (4th Ed., 1964).
[70] Carl R. Rogers, "Learning to be Free," an unpublished paper.
[71] May, *op. cit.*, pp. 18–19.
[72] Eugene T. Gendlin, "Client-centered Developments and Work with Schizophrenics," *Journal of Counseling Psychology* 9:205–212 (Fall, 1962).

As I express my present feeling and my vague images of what may be happening between us now, a very personal quality enters into my expressions. I am giving words to my ongoing experiencing with him. There is a quality of personal risk and openness in my saying these things. . . . The client lives in a responsive context made up of my person and my openly expressive interaction with him. Yet, his side of the interaction might be quite tentative, implicit, until he wishes to make it explicit as his.

It would thus seem that at least the Client-centered counselor and the existential therapist are talking much the same language when they discuss man, the person-in-being, and the counseling relationship, the process of becoming. It should be noted too, that existentialism is primarily a product of European philosophers, rather than psychotherapists. The earlier existentialists, Kierkegaard (some would add Marx and Neitzche), Sartre, Heidegger, Marcel, Jaspers, Maritain, and Buber, were and are tremendous beings, and while they lived fully, and wrote extensively about man, they wrote from a philosophical and theistic or atheistic point of view. It may be, in a living and experiencing way, they knew more about man than they knew man. Their modern American counterpart might be Tillich, whereas May would appear to be an American therapist who has an existential approach to man. This might be one reason; the older non-therapist existentialist had a somewhat more pessimistic and deterministic viewpoint of man, and the more optimistic point of view of Client-centered therapist Rogers would appear to be shared more by therapist May than by theologian Tillich. Again, we note here that religion, at least in a formal and doctrinaire sense, appears to be more a part of the make-up of Tillich and Curran, somewhat less of May and van Kaam, and still less of Rogers and Shlien. On the other hand, both Rogers and Shlien, at least in the sense of their deep respect for the integrity of others, and in their sense of responsibility that they share living with others, are surely deeply "religious" persons.[73]

Thus it would seem that Client-centered therapy, as it views man, and the human counseling relationship of man with man, is very much existential. It is not as pessimistic as existential philosophy would appear at times to be. It is phenomenological in the sense that the phenomenological world of the individual is the world of reality for the individual, but it is not phenomenological in a deterministic sense. This forward looking, existential Client-centered concept of

[73] This is, of course, my own frame of reference, and the gentlemen named here may not agree with me.

man as a free, self-evolving, self-actualizing Being would seem to me to be a good base on which to develop the practice of counseling and psychotherapy.

The basic human problem is never the overt issue, but the individual concept of the degree to which that issue controls and dominates and determines his life. Deprivation becomes crucial and controlling only when it is of the *inside* as well as of the outside. In a way, the counselor would help the child who is having difficulties in school to make his school experience more real, not in the sense that it would become any more pleasant, but rather that it is there, and he is there, and he can make reality out of the unpleasant as well as the pleasant. One does not have to run; one runs only because one chooses to.

Nor does this counselor see himself as the provider of information, since most children who come to him are not suffering from lack of information, but rather from the personal inability to make any sense out of the vast quantity of information that is constantly being poured and shoved and stuffed into them. He would not be the sort of counselor described by he United States Department of Labor,[74] who would appear to be overwhelmingly a center of information, and I would question the effectiveness of information in actually helping a child who is already alienated from this group, one who has the outer characteristics of failure, and who has likely come to believe them, one who is hostile and afraid of self. This person, surely, needs the warmth of human closeness; he needs unconditional acceptance of him as he is; he needs to live close to security and freedom so that he can eventually come to know, and to believe, that they are within his grasp too.

Nor would he be the sort of counselor described by the recent Federal manpower employment legislation, in which the counselor both "counsels" and "selects." One of these actions would seem to contradict the other.

Counseling is not helping the client either to adjust to society or to fight it. It is helping him to come to see who he really is, and what he has and what he does not have; what he can do easily, what he can do with difficulty, and what he probably cannot do at all. This might, I suppose, be called self-actualization, and the person comes to see that the struggle for being is really the struggle to have people take him as he is, rather than accepting the culture's version of him. This obvi-

[74] *Counseling and Employment Services for Youth* (Washington, D. C.: Department of Labor, November, 1962)

ously is a process of living and experiencing; it is a far cry from the rather simple telling and directing, and since it involves a good deal of personal sharing, we can assume that the counselor himself must be one who sees himself as a free human being, one who has personally achieved a high level of self-actualization.

Thus the counselor, as a human being, is more important than the counseling, just as every child and adult is more important as a human being than the title that purports to describe him. Whatever the current status of the client might be, he still has strength, he still has the potential for freedom, and although many things on many fronts must be done to help him, the counselor is the one who, now, *should* be able to offer him what he needs most. This is a close sharing of a human relationship with one who has for him a high regard; one who can offer him unconditional acceptance, but one who has no guarantees, no answers; one who can help him to see freedom, but freedom with risk; one who can help him to come to see that freedom and self integrity are the same thing, that they are within the grasp of each of us, and that we are the ones to determine whether we wish to hold them tightly or let them fall.

PART TWO

THE NATURE
OF COUNSELING

Chapter Two

THE COUNSELING PROCESS

WHAT ONE DOES, the way one lives his life—this would surely appear to be the best indication of any individual's philosophy of life and living. The counselor is no different from any other human being in this respect, and in this chapter we will attempt to examine the rationale, the "why" of his counseling, as well as the "what" of the counseling process. It is assumed in this book that counseling and psychotherapy are synonymous terms, and this somewhat semantic issue will be dealt with later on. It may also be assumed that I can do no more than write from my own frame of reference, so that although other ideas and other thoughts and other systems will be examined, they are being examined through my own particular (some might even say peculiar) set of glasses! Thus, for want of better words, one might say that this book is written from a somewhat existential Client-centered frame of reference.

THE "WHY" OF COUNSELING

Far too many counselors do not know *what* they are doing, but an even larger number do not appear to have a very good understanding of *why* they are doing what they are doing, or what they think they are doing. Thus we have counselors who know what they are doing, but do not know why they are doing it; we have others who know why they should be doing something, but not how to do it. Then, though there are other counselors who know both the what and the why of their professional activities, these in turn are balanced by those who call themselves counselors, but know neither the what nor the why of their activities.

It would seem that the preliminary basic responsibility of any professional worker is to come to some understanding of the basic purpose of the professional activity that he plans to enter, since there would seem to be no point in going further with one's professional education if this is not understood and accepted. Professionally, however, one can hardly be satisfied with the individual who is able to give no better reason for his professional activities than "just because." Far too many counselors, supposedly professional workers, can give little in the way of valid and scientifically defensible reasons for their actions. Somewhat biting comments have been made by some authorities in the field of human behavior regarding the activities of counselors. Lecky,[1] for example; states:

> Thus the psychoanalytic pursuit of unconscious complexes with no stated goal except to destroy them, suggests the superstitious fervor of the witch burner, and psychiatry in general may be thought of as engaged in a moral crusade against the demon Neurosis.

When one pauses to wonder just what the objectives of counseling *are,* he is struck by the fact that his list of answers is usually smaller and more difficult to arrive at than when he wonders what his objectives *are not.* Such a circumstance is understandable, since a good deal of the professional education of the counselor has to do with unlearning rather than learning. Much of what he has learned as a citizen of his community will not make him effective as a counselor, and much of what he has learned professionally, whether he be a theologian, a medical doctor, or a teacher, will help him even less. White, for example, states that: [2]

> when a person acts in the capacity of therapist, his goal is not to dominate or persuade, but simply to restore a state of good health. . . . A therapist has nothing to sell and nothing to prescribe.

It is likely that the goals and objectives expressed by individuals for other people are reflective rather of the needs of the person who

[1] Prescott Lecky, *Self Consistency* (New York: Island Press, 1951), p. 186.
[2] Robert W. White, *The Abnormal Personality* (New York: The Ronald Press Company, 1948), p. 314.

expresses the goals than of the people for whom we supposedly have the goals. Often when parents talk about goals for their children, there is no question that the children and their needs have little to do with these goals. They are an expression of the needs of the parents, which may, of course, also be the needs of the children. When the teacher talks about objectives for her pupils, these again are the objectives of the teacher for someone else; often they make little sense to individual children, since they ignore the child completely.

The professional counselor, however, when thinking about goals must be thinking in terms of client satisfaction, not counselor satisfaction. The important question is not whether the counselor will feel better if the client decides to get a divorce, but rather whether this is what is best for the client. Similarly, the teacher may feel happy if the child decides not to run away from home, but the departure from home could be the better answer to the problems of the child. We might, therefore, seriously question the objectives of counseling if they are the objectives of the counselor rather than the objectives of the counseling experience as it will apply to a certain individual. Indeed, one may raise the rather intriguing question of whether or not the counselor should have any specific objectives for the client; whether, rather, he should hold to broad general objectives of counseling, which may become more specific as the counselor helps the client to become more realistically oriented in the search for his own goals.

There will be little agreement on the objectives of counseling as long as such objectives are those of the counselor, although evidence tends to indicate that there is more agreement on objectives among counselors who have a high level of professional preparation (such as indicated, say, by having a doctorate in the field and being a Fellow of the American Psychological Association, or a Diplomate of the American Board of Examiners in Professional Psychology) than there is among counselors who have little in the way of professional preparation. Even with professional counselors, however, one has to step carefully before making any blanket statements about the objectives of counseling. This has been brought out most effectively in an article by Walker and Peiffer.[3] They point out, most logically, that we can hardly think in terms of self-adjustment, since a psychotic patient might well have reached a stage of adjustment in purely private terms; nor can we accept client contentment, since we cannot defend the position that all schizophrenics are unhappy or that all sexual psychopaths are sad. Each person must speak from his own personal frame of refer-

[3] Donald E. Walker and Herbert C. Peiffer, Jr., "The Goals of Counseling," *Journal of Counseling Psychology* 4:204–209 (Fall, 1957).

ence, no matter how sensitive he may be to the other person's frame of reference. Each person's verbalizations will also tend to be at least somewhat indicative of his own particular professional background, and one of the difficulties of communication in counseling may be owing to the many different professional groups involved in it. Thus when we discuss the "why" of counseling, our differences may not be as great as they appear, and even when we talk about what we do, the discrepancies may not be as large as they would seem to be. The student of counseling is continually faced with the danger of superficially "accepting" some goal or objective of counseling, and only by examining himself in operation can he come close to determining whether or not this goal is even remotely related to his total person. Our basic goals of living, and our basic attitudes toward others, are revealed by what we do, not by what we say. Goals, too, are human, so we should talk in terms of the goals of the counselor, not of counseling. Thus, it is extremely difficult for one person—at least for me—to determine just what another person "is," and if one were to ask, "Is he a Client-centered counselor," the most honest answer might be, "Well, on the basis of some of the criteria I try to use on myself, he seems to be sort of far away from it, but then, I don't *know* if that is so or not. . . ."

Rogers, the original "Client-centered" counselor, or at least the original Rogerian, shows his intensive involvement with the "other" in all his writings. More than most counselors, he tends to speak through his clients, and his most recent book,[4] a compilation of articles written over a ten-year period, illustrates the extent to which he is centered on the client. When he says that the outcome of therapy is "a more broadly based structure of self, an inclusion of greater proportion of experience as a part of self, and a more comfortable and realistic adjustment to life," [5] he is describing a very personal operational objective, which he illustrates in his counseling.

The Client-centered counselor, in talking about objectives, would at least appear to stress more doing something *with* the client than *for* him; experiencing and living with him, rather than discussing and explaining to him, thus stressing the affective rather than the cognitive; a concern with the total existential being, today, rather than parts of him, yesterday; a high level of confidence in the self-actualizing ability of the individual; a non-deterministic view of man as the maker of his culture.

[4] Carl R. Rogers, *On Becoming a Person* (Boston: Houghton Mifflin Company, 1961).
[5] Carl R. Rogers, *Client-Centered Therapy* (Boston: Houghton Mifflin Company, 1951), p. 195.

When Boy and Pine describe the goal of Client-centered counseling, they are talking about *their* goal as Client-centered counselors: [6]

> . . . to help the student become more mature and more self-actuated, to help the student move forward in a positive and constructive way, to help the student grow toward socialization by utilizing his own resources and potential. . . . The counselee's perceptions change, and as the result of newly acquired insights there is a positive reorientation of personality and living for the counselee. The counselor's focus is more on the affective than on the cognitive components of behavior.

When they describe the goals of the clinical counselor, however, they are on less certain, less personal ground. We might say that they are being less affective, but more cognitive, in the sense that they are using descriptions of the counseling activities of others who have been called, by some, "clinical counselors": [7]

> . . . to help the counselee "feel better," i.e., to help the counselee accept himself, to diminish the disparity between real self and ideal self; and "to help persons *think* more clearly in solving their own personal problems." The counselor must be concerned with feelings and affect as prerequisite to clear thinking. The objective is to help the counselee arrive at the point where he understands himself not only affectively but also rationally or intelligently. At this point he needs external information to understand himself in terms of other persons around him. Man is essentially striving to become a rational, problem-solving organism.

Byrne discusses goals in an existential sense, with possibly one notable exception: [8]

> The counselor's goal, firmly based on the human worth of the individual, regardless of education, intelligence, color, or background, is to use his technical skills (a) to help each counselee attain and maintain an awareness of self so that he can be responsible for himself, (b) to help each counselee confront threats to his being, and thus to open further the way for the counselee to increase his concern for others' well being, (c) to help each counselee to bring into full operation his unique potential in compatibility with his own life style and within the ethical limits of society.

[6] Angelo V. Boy and Gerald J. Pine, *Client-Centered Counseling in the Secondary School* (Boston: Houghton Mifflin Company, 1963), p. 43.
[7] *Ibid.*
[8] Richard Hill Byrne, *The School Counselor* (Boston: Houghton Mifflin Company, 1963), pp. 19–20.

The somewhat clashing aspect of this description is Byrne's reference to the counselor's using his "technical skills." Existentially, it is rather difficult to think of a close and intimate human involvement, such as that between counselor and client, in which the counselor *uses* technical skills. The counselor gives of himself, and part of that self may be a technical skill.

Hora also talks in an existential sense, with the stress on self realization: [9]

> . . . health is being what one really is . . . the psychotherapeutic process aims at bringing about this authenticity in a human being. . . . It consists of a realization of the attainment of the open mind. . . . The open mind . . . is attained by the realization of the closed mind.

Others also indicate their own personal concept of man and his nature, as viewed from their particular frames of reference, when they write about the goals and objectives of counseling. Tyler,[10] for example, feels that ". . . the psychological purpose of counseling is to facilitate development," while Shoben [11] thinks of values as he writes, "At any rate, perhaps the crucial learning that occurs in psychotherapy is the acquisition of a functional, critically held, and personally relevant system of human values."

Thorne [12] feels that, from the viewpoint of the counselor, the main objective of personality counseling is to protect and secure mental health by preventing or modifying pathogenic etiologic factors productive of maladjustment or mental disorder. The prime obligation of the counselor, he feels, is to help people to live happier and healthier lives by psychological methods of healing and re-education.

Sullivan states his position as follows: [13]

> The interviewer must discover who the client is. . . . And, on the basis of who the person is, the interviewer must learn what this person conceives of in his living as problematic, and what he feels to be difficult. . . . [That] the person will leave with some measure of increased clarity about himself and his living with other people is an essential goal of the psychiatric interview.

[9] Thomas Hora, "Psychotherapy: Healing or Growth," *Annals of Psychotherapy* 4:9; Monograph Number 5 (1963).

[10] Leona Tyler, *The Work of the Counselor* (New York: Appleton-Century-Crofts, 1961), p. 17.

[11] Edward J. Shoben, "The Therapeutic Object: Men or Machines," *Journal of Counseling Psychology*, 10:264–268 (Fall, 1963).

[12] F. C. Thorne, "Principles of Personality Counseling," *Journal of Clinical Psychology*, Brandon, Vt.: 1950, p. 89.

[13] Harry S. Sullivan, *The Psychiatric Interview* (New York: Norton, 1954), p. 18.

Williamson describes the objectives of counseling by stating that "the counselor assists the student to choose goals which will yield maximum satisfaction within the limits of those compromises necessitated by uncontrolled and uncontrollable factors in the individuals and in society itself." [14] He also feels that the counselor "should be prepared to assist the student to solve, choose, master, learn and deal with situations and problems of a wide variety." [15]

Hadley feels that "the most essential goal [of psychological counseling] is to aid the individual in his efforts to achieve an effective relationship with his environment," [16] while Alexander maintains that the aim of psychoanalysis "is to effect permanent changes in the personality by increasing the ego's integrative power . . . to change the ego by exposing it to conflictful repressed material." [17]

The Committee on Definition of Division 17 of the American Psychological Association describes the objectives of counseling by stating that the counseling psychologist contributes to the following: [18]

> (a) the client's realistic acceptance of his own capacities, motivations, and self-attitudes, (b) the client's achievement of a reasonable harmony with his social, economic and vocational environment, and (c) society's acceptance of individual differences and their implications for community, employment, and marriage relations.

Although these authorities may use different terms such as counseling, therapy, and psychiatry, and although they may use different methods of description, they are all likely describing the same basic process, and their differences reflect a personal difference rather than the differences, say, between those who might be called counselors or psychologists or psychiatrists.

There are human and personal differences as counselors and therapists talk about their objectives of counseling, and there are the same differences when they discuss those things that *should not* be considered as goals or objectives. These differences, however, tend to be reduced when the primary professional function of the individual is counseling or psychotherapy. If, for example, we talk with school

---

[14] E. C. Williamson, *Counseling Adolescents* (New York: McGraw-Hill, 1950), p. 221.
[15] *Ibid.*, p. 219.
[16] John M. Hadley, *Clinical and Counseling Psychology* (New York: Alfred A. Knopf, 1958), p. 26.
[17] F. Alexander, *Fundamentals of Psychoanalysis* (New York: Norton, 1948), pp. 275–276.
[18] Reported by C. Gilbert Wrenn, "Status and Role of the School Counselor," *Personnel and Guidance Journal* 36:175–183 (November, 1957).

counselors rather than school teachers, counseling psychologists rather than clinical psychologists, psychiatrists rather than medical doctors, existential therapists rather than existential philosophers, the level of agreement rises markedly. I can probably safely say that a number of counselors share with me the feeling that the following might be considered some of the "should not's" among counselor objectives:

(1) Considering the multi-disciplined background of counseling, it is not surprising that many counselors still talk of the "solution of the client's problems" as one of their objectives. After all, teachers have solved problems for children, medical doctors have told patients what their trouble was, and what they, the doctors, would do to alleviate that problem, and psychologists have probed the psyche to help us to determine how the conscious might better guide the unconscious! Humphries, Traxler, and North make what would still be, for many school counselors, a perfectly acceptable statement when they say that ". . . in counseling, the immediate goal of the counselor and counselee is to arrive at the most satisfying solution as quickly as possible." [19] Still, many counselors would also feel that most individuals become clients because they have not learned to solve their own problems; while assistance in the solution of a problem may afford temporary relief, it does not help the individual to do something about changing the causes of his problems. Thus the assistance that might be given to an individual toward learning how to solve his own problems would seem to be a more valid objective than the actual solution of a specific problem. In most cases, of course, the personal problems of a human being cannot be *solved* by another person, even if the latter is aware of the real problem. Since the client himself is quite frequently unaware of his basic problem, it is unlikely that the counselor would have this awareness, although this in itself would not usually mean too much. It would be unlikely that any professional counselor would feel that he could solve for the client problems which might be expressed by such statements as, "I feel so lonely and worthless, I don't know what to do, and you've just got to tell me what to do to get rid of this awful feeling . . . ," or "I just hate him . . . I hate his guts, and I know I shouldn't feel this way because he is my father; but I do, and I don't know what to do about it . . . ," or, "sure it's time that I burst loose—I'm sick and tired of being tied down by my wife, but I need your advice on just what I can do about it . . .," or, "I shouldn't have to compete and excel and be better than my husband, but it

[19] J. A. Humphries, A. E. Traxler, and R. D. North, *Guidance Services* (Chicago: Science Research Associates, 1960), p. 345.

seems that I just have to, and I wonder why . . . ," or, "My sister's whining and crying is driving me crazy, and I can't see how I can stay in that house until I graduate, but what can I do . . . ?"

These are a few statements made over the space of a short time to one counselor by several of his clients. They are not unusual, certainly, but would any reader of these words feel that he could solve even the immediate problems of these clients, as they have expressed them?

(2) We may also question the idea that a primary goal in counseling is to make the client happy and satisfied, although this depends on how one views happiness and satisfaction. A human being may be helped, through counseling, to take a risk and make a choice that may result in pain and failure; another may decline a well paying position because he now realizes that, although he could have easily satisfied his employer, he would not have satisfied himself. Thus while counseling may, in the long run, help the client to develop in himself a deep and personal satisfaction with self, any sort of overt and immediate happiness and satisfaction is a by-product, rather than a primary objective. Indeed, as a result of counseling the client may become less smug, less self-centered, and more concerned with the world around him. He may be helped to move toward such a stage of security that he does not have to be happy all the time to feel that all is well. He may become secure and solid enough so that he can accept a certain degree of unhappiness and sorrow and despair as a normal part of living, rather than something to be avoided at all costs. It might even be safe to say that the one who pursues happiness—his own happiness, that is, as a major objective of his life—is not revealing a high degree of security and stability.

(3) Making society happy and satisfied with the client is an even more unacceptable goal. Indeed, it could hardly be called an objective of either counseling or mental health, although it is true that increasingly in our culture adjustment seems to be measured by the extent to which an individual gets along with the group, is acceptable to the group, and is eventually absorbed by the group. While adjustment may have to be related to the culture, since the individual does not live alone, it might be that real security is something that is a good deal deeper, more internalized, and thus independent of the whims and the likes or dislikes of the passing crowd. The secure individual will not be independent just to be independent. He will not stand up, alone, just because standing up alone gives him a special thrill and a feeling of independence. If it must be, however, that in order to be true to

himself he must stand up and be counted, he will do so; and in such a case, whether he stands alone or has the entire group with him will be of little consequence.

A goal of counseling might be to help the individual attain a stage of development at which he can look honestly at himself, and eventually a point where he can derive some element of satisfaction in what he sees. He might, indeed, be able to say to himself, deeply, and with meaning, "I can certainly be a lot better than I am, but all in all, I am not too bad. I can afford to hold my head high, even though others may think I am nothing." This is the sort of person who will be less dependent on the group. He will draw his strengths from his inner self. This is the man who may make society very unhappy with him. He is no organization man, and he may utter truths that others would rather ignore. He will accept the fact that he has to live within the mores of his society, but he will not feel that his very life depends on the adulation and approval of that society. The goals of counseling, at least as I see them, do not include the concept that the counselor must somehow help the client to become a passive, acceptant, agreeable fellow who resembles a vegetable much more than an independent human being.

If, on the other hand, one accepts the concept of a completely determined state of being, then it would seem that we have no choice, and each man must become a simple pawn, the victim of his culture, to do as it demands. The counselor in such a world would also, of course, be the inanimate voice of the state. Any concept of the existential being, of the self-actualization of the individual, of the inner integrity of the person, of the potential for human growth—all of these would be naive illusions. While we may hope that this would not be the view of the counselor, there is no doubt that it is the view of many individuals. A statement, for example, that smacks remarkably of *1984* [20] and *Walden Two*,[21] or the writings in journals like *Pravda,* is seen in a booklet written for school counselors by the Orientation Group, USAF, Wright-Patterson Air Force Base, Ohio, entitled *The Struggle for Men's Minds.* There appears in the introduction a quotation from Samuel Johnson. It reads as follows:

> Every society has a right to preserve public peace and order, and therefore has a good right to prohibit the propagation of opinions which have a dangerous tendency. . . . Every man has a physical right to think as he pleases; for it cannot be discovered how he thinks. He has

[20] George Orwell, *1984* (New York: Harcourt, Brace & World, Inc., 1949).
[21] B. F. Skinner, *Walden Two* (New York: The Macmillan Co., 1948).

> not a moral right, for he ought to inform himself, and think justly. But, Sir, no member of society has a right to teach any doctrine contrary to what the society holds to be true.

This is not a statement that one would expect to find in a document published by a service that is dedicated to defend the freedom and integrity of every individual American.

(4) Another common but questionable idea is that an objective of counseling should be to persuade the client to change certain decisions and choices in favor of those that are "right." The professional counselor approaches the client, not with a bag of answers, but rather with an open and understanding mind that respects the integrity of his client to the extent of believing that he has the right to make his own decisions and choices; and whether or not these would be the decisions and choices of the counselor is of no importance. The professional counselor cannot have preconceived notions and ideas regarding choices and decisions to be made by the client. Many teachers, for example, find it extremely difficult to accept the idea that a student has the right to say nasty things about a faculty member to a counselor, if the student feels secure enough, or harried enough, to make such a statement. The preconceived notion here is that all children are supposed to be respectful toward adults, no matter how miserable these adults may be, just as all nurses are supposed to respect all medical doctors, all students to respect all teachers, all privates all officers, and so on. But respect is obviously an attitude that one person develops toward another person because of his feelings toward that person; and people cannot be "told" to feel a certain way. Thus the counselor does not plan and decide for the client, since he honestly does not know what is best for him. His function is to help the client to decide what is best for *him*, not for the counselor, or society, or anyone else, although there will very often be a close relationship among all of these.

It is difficult to talk about the specifics of goals or objectives of counselors who are involved in the counseling process, since the more specific one becomes, the more personal he is. There would seem, however, to be several general points on which counselors and therapists tend to agree when talking about objectives:

(1) Any "objective" is affected by the humanistic feeling that man is, basically, a capable, self-determining creature. This is not determined by any particular title that the counselor may give to his counseling, and it applies equally well to those who may call themselves Adlerians or Freudians or Rogerians, or clinical counselors, or

eclectic counselors, or Client-centered counselors, or rational counselors. The methods or procedures of the individual counselor may
differ, but their views of man tend to be somewhat alike. They are
optimistic, and although some might scoff, they would appear to
have some degree of faith in the fellow man. Certainly they trust him
far more than do most of his fellows.

(2) Most counselors would probably feel that another somewhat
general objective is that of working with the client to help him to
move toward a greater level of self-acceptance and self-understanding.
He learns, one might say, to be. An individual cannot change himself
if he refuses to recognize and accept himself as he is. Such a person
spends his life in a futile attempt to convince himself that he is what
he is not. Understanding, for the counselor, is a good deal more than
just an intellectual statement. True understanding implies self-acceptance, and this understanding will likely come through a re-living, an
experiencing, a feeling, rather than through an intellectual step-by-step
process.

Much of one's behavior, for example, such as aggressiveness,
hostility, promiscuous sexuality, may be part of a vain attempt to
convince oneself of one's maleness, an attempt to flee from the latent
homosexual tendencies that the individual has learned. The sneering
and contemptuous remarks that may be directed at higher education
generally, at a college degree, or toward a particular university may
indicate the individual's struggle to avoid the acceptance of his own
unimpressive intellectual competence. As children grow, they soon
learn that they should not be what they are, they should not think
what they think. The growing adolescent girl will find it difficult to
accept calmly and securely her six feet of height; in another culture,
it might not be a problem, but in America it is. A child may soon learn,
from his parents and from his teachers, that lack of intellectual competence is not good; since he can do nothing directly about it, he will
almost certainly, if he is to survive, find ways to compensate. He may
learn too, that he cannot be "poor," and that he must have the ambition to be better than his parents. Sometimes changes are possible,
but since the individual is not changing because he wants to, the
psychological and physical price that he has to pay is too high. More
often than not, however, an actual direct change is not possible, and
the individual is placed in the impossible position of having to be
what he cannot be. It is unfortunate that the school does not do more
to help the child to accept what he is, and work with what he has,
rather than pretend that he can do what he cannot, or that he has

what he has not. Such a pretense tends to drive him even deeper into the rut of unacceptance, and to set the pattern for years of frustrated striving and avoidance of his real self.

A move toward greater self-acceptance also means that the individual tends to decrease the discrepancy between his real self and his ideal self. Seeing himself as he really is, he is more likely to think in terms of realistic goals rather than fantastic fantasies. Yet some people do become adept at satisfying the cultural demand without any real personal change. A good example is the way in which some school people get around the need for a higher degree. They do not want to become more educated; in some cases they are not capable intellectually of doing any legitimate graduate work. But since they must have a degree, they in effect buy one.

Generally, however, a person who has moved to a greater stability will not try to be a college professor if he is of low intellectual capacity; with a small physique he will not strive vainly to be a football hero; with a lack of understanding of music, and no real interest in it, he will cease trying to pretend that he is lover of the opera and all things cultural; with a modest income, he will not try to convince himself that somehow his fairy godmother will appear and help him to maintain the standard of living that he feels he must pretend he can afford. He will, in effect, come fairly close to accepting himself as he is. In this frenzied culture most children will need assistance if they are to develop into this very stable sort of fellow.

(3) A somewhat related goal has to do with the development of a greater level of honesty, particularly honesty toward self, in the client. An essential quality of the counselor is his congruence and his honesty, both toward the client and toward himself. In a human relationship with such an individual, the client may come to have less need to pretend that he is what he is not. The counselor does not buoy the client up with false support, and indeed, if he tries, the client is usually quite aware that such support is false. What man who has lost a hand believes that "things will be just as they were before"? what child who has been forced to repeat a grade believes that "this will really be much better than it was last year"? what girl who has been jilted by her one and only love believes that "you'll soon get over this and forget that it ever happened"? what child who has to go back and live with a brutal parent believes that "things will be much better now"? People have a habit of giving support that is not really honest, although they do not do so deliberately with malice in mind.

On the whole, we live in a culture where we do not call a spade a spade, particularly if the spade happens to be an unpleasant one. We like to pretend that what should be is. Although everyone must live to some degree in the realm of fantasy, such a practice can get to a point where it begins to make living somewhat difficult. It is nice— and it may sometimes be good—to feel that if we believe long enough, what we believe will come true. But we are on psychologically danger- ous ground if we assume that we can wish things away, since this very attitude usually indicates that we are carefully avoiding the real basis for our problems. The counselor should not help the Jewish student to believe that it is just as easy for him to get into an American college as it would be if he were a Catholic or a Protestant; it is not. The counselor should not increase the unreality of the Negro student's dreaming by giving him the idea that it is just as easy for a Negro to get a job as it is for a white student; it is not. Acceptance of the reality —and including here an acceptance of the reality of all of the factors involved (a Jewish student may not get into a certain college simply because his grades are too low; a Negro may not get a job because he does not have the required education and skill)—is not passivity and hopelessness, or bitterness, but it is the first step toward doing some- thing about reality.

It is important to note, too, that the counselor *can* be honest be- cause of his own high level of self-actualization, because of his own level of being. He feels no personal pressure to take sides, to agree or dis- agree, to tell the client what is right and what is wrong, to encourage or discourage. He can be easily acceptant of the fact that in most human differences what is right for one may be wrong for another. He is aware that the husband who talks about his wife's negative qualities and his plans for a divorce *may* be right about her and about his plans; he *may* be. The student who talks about his miserable teachers and parents *may* also be right on all counts. But the counselor is not the judge, he is not the chooser of sides; by remaining impartial he is more likely to be able to help the client to achieve a realistic outlook on his life and on the lives of others.

(4) Objectives should be based on client need, not counselor need. Although any professional worker, including a counselor, should like what he is doing, an even more basic question for those people whose work is with other human beings has to do with the effect of what he does on the recipient of his efforts. Counseling cannot be justified on the basis of satisfactions that accrue to the counselor; it can only be justified on the basis of its effect on the client. More often than not, when the counselor feels, "That was a very good session," it doubtless

was a good session; but ultimately the only true measure of the effectiveness of the session is found in what happens to the client. Since every person exhibits himself in what he does and what he says, the counselor must be sure that he is not functioning in a certain manner simply to satisfy some of his own frustrations and unmet needs, rather than to benefit the client. Too frequently the defense of a supposed method or technique is a defense of the self. The rigid type of counselor, who cannot accept the idea that there are "other ways," unconsciously indicates that what he does is very much for his own satisfaction rather than that of the client. There is a marked resemblance between the father who says "I don't want to beat you, but I'm doing it for your own good," the teacher who says, "The only way to gain the respect of the child is to bear down on him so that he'll know who's boss," and the counselor who says, "This client-centered stuff is a lot of nonsense. I've tried it and it never works for me." The father, the teacher, and the counselor are all giving a display of self, rather than showing their professional and learned skills and understandings. The father who beats his child, the teacher who happily bears down, the counselor who dismisses any contradictory point of view —their actions must be taken to bolster self. If the results are positive for the client, it is a fortunate accident rather than the result of any professional action.

Thus there is a very real point to the argument that counselor preparation should include experience in counseling under supervision, and indeed personal counseling of the student counselor himself, so that he may become more aware of the extent to which he is becoming a counselor to satisfy his own needs regardless of the effects on the client. When the counselor can benefit the client as well as satisfy his own needs, all is well, but certainly every counselor should have an awareness of the extent to which he is possibly harming the client in his attempts to satisfy his own needs. The low level of professional competence required of school counselors at the present time almost surely means that many school counselors are working almost entirely for self-satisfaction, with very little in the way of professional evidence to back up their actions and their deeds. "I like my work" is not always a valid criterion to use in measuring one's effectiveness.

THE "WHAT" OF COUNSELING

The "what" of counseling is because of the "why," but in some ways a verbal or written definition of counseling is somewhat pointless, since it is most unlikely that it will mean to the reader what it meant to the writer, even if the writer was consciously aware of its meaning. Counseling is a verb, it is action, it is the process of human involvement, probably the most complicated of all processes. When one says, "The client is in need of counseling," this is by no means as clear a statement as when the medical doctor says, "The patient needs to take two of these pills three times a day," or when the mechanic says, "What your car needs is a new battery." A definition, however, does tend to give some indication of what a person *thinks* he *feels,* although some would say it is more likely to be what he *feels* he *thinks.* Definitions of functioning counselors and therapists tend to be more process oriented, in that they reflect what the counselor actually does, usually in a feeling and personal sense, whereas the theorist will be more likely to write about what he thinks others do, or what he thinks they should do. He writes in a more cognitive than affective sense.

We must, then, take with some grains of salt the extent to which a definition of counseling really reveals the internalized version of one human being's concept of his relationship with another. We might assume, however, that the practitioner would be somewhat closer to his own personal mode of operation than is the theorist, who tends to talk more about others than about self. The human, learning aspect of counseling has long been stressed by both practitioners and theorists. Some years ago, for example, Jung stated: [22]

> What was formerly a method of medical treatment now becomes a method of self education, and therewith the horizon of modern psychology is immeasurably widened. The medical diploma is no longer the crucial thing, but human quality instead.

Combs thinks of counseling as a function of learning, but he stresses even more the fact that it is people who learn in counseling. His skepticism about the value of learning theory in the process of counseling is indicated when he says that ". . . *almost any* personality theory is a more effective guide to practice than the best our traditional learning theories have so far produced." [23]

Fromm stresses his version of the experiencing, human involve-

[22] C. G. Jung, *Modern Man in Search of a Soul* (New York: Harcourt, Brace & World, Inc., 1933), p. 53.
[23] Arthur W. Combs, "Counseling as a Learning Process," *Journal of Counseling Psychology* 1:31–36 (February, 1954).

ment aspect of counseling when he makes the following comment: [24]

> As long as the patient remains in the attitude of the detached self-observer, he is not in touch with his unconscious, except by *thinking* about it; he does not experience the wider, deeper reality within himself. Discovering one's unconscious is, precisely, *not* only an intellectual act, but also an affective experience, which can hardly be put into words, if at all. . . . [T]he act of discovery is not an act of thinking but of *being aware*, and, still better, perhaps, simply of *seeing*.

Buchheimer and Balogh, on the other hand, tend to be somewhat wary of the unconscious, and see it as a "therapeutic" area where the counselor dare not tread. They do, however, feel that "change" is a legitimate aspect of the counseling process.[25]

> . . . through the process of the counseling conversation the individual will revise his distortions and thereby alter his behavior. The emphasis is on the present, and on verbal material that is within the individual's immediate awareness or that he can easily be made aware of.

Tyler somehow seems to feel that "change" is in the therapeutic area that is forbidden to the counselor, and her concept of counseling gives the rather odd impression that the client should do something and take some action, but at the same time, change is not the business of the counselor.[26]

> Let us use *counseling* to refer to a helping process the aim of which is not to change the person but to enable him to utilize the resources he now has for coping with life. The outcome we would then expect from counseling is that the client *do* something, take some constructive action on his own behalf.

Byrne accepts the counselor as one who influences the behavior of an individual in the direction of growth and change.[27]

> Counseling is (1) a service of assistance by a person professionally prepared to counsel (2) in which the intention is to influence the behavior of another person who seeks help in matters of plans and decisions, and in matters of satisfying interpersonal relationships, (3) by inducing

[24] Erich Fromm, *Beyond the Chains of Illusion* (New York: Pocket Books, Inc., 1962), p. 101.
[25] Arnold Buchheimer and Sara Carter Balogh, *The Counseling Relationship* (Chicago: Science Research Associates, 1961), p. x.
[26] Tyler, *op. cit.*, p. 12.
[27] Byrne, *op. cit.*, p. 61.

growth or change in that person (4) through a unique relationship and verbal practices that are based on scientifically discovered knowledges of human behavior in general, and on the nature of behavior change through counseling in particular.

The above definition sounds somewhat deterministic, and it would almost appear to put "behaviors" ahead of man. It differs somewhat, however, from the didactic picture of counseling that is given by Wrenn when he describes the functions of the counselor as contributing to student self-understanding and self-acceptance; being sensitive to cultural changes that affect student self-understanding; helping students to make informed educational and vocational choices; developing group learning experiences for students; increasing student self-reliance; counseling girls realistically; accepting and encouraging diversity in talents.[28] One could hardly disagree with this rather cold listing, but it is, possibly, as meaningless as would be a list of how-to-be-a-good-mother statements to a pregnant girl.

Cottle and Downie refer to the relationship as being the most important element in counseling, and yet at the same time, they make this relationship a created artificial sort of thing. They refer, for example, to ". . . the attempt by the counselor to make the client comfortable and somewhat relaxed. . . ."[29] Along with some other counselors, I would tend to feel that the counselor who has to "attempt" to make the client relaxed still has some distance to go on the road leading toward his own self-actualization.

Different definitions also give some indication of the extent to which one views counseling as something done by one person who knows more, who is stronger, who is more secure, to or for another person. These are counselor-centered definitions. For example: [30]

Counseling is essentially a process in which the counselor assists the counselee to make interpretations of facts relating to a choice, plan or adjustment which he needs to make.

and: [31]

28 C. Gilbert Wrenn, *The Counselor in a Changing World* (Washington, D.C.: American Personnel and Guidance Association, 1962), pp. 127–132.
29 Wm. C. Cottle and N. M. Downie, *Procedures and Preparation for Counseling* (New York: Prentice-Hall, Inc., 1960), p. 61.
30 Glenn F. Smith, *Counseling in the Secondary School* (New York: The Macmillan Co., 1955), p. 156.
31 E. G. Williamson and J. D. Foley, *Counseling and Discipline* (New York: McGraw-Hill Book Co., Inc., 1949), p. 192.

Counseling has been defined as a face-to-face situation in which, by reason of training, skill or confidence vested in him by the other, one person helps the second person to face, perceive, clarify, solve, and resolve adjustment problems.

and: [32]

A situation of primarily *vocal* communication in a two-group, more or less *voluntarily integrated,* on a progressively unfolding *expert-client* basis for the purpose of elucidating *characteristic patterns of living* of the subject person, the patient or client.

While the relationship described in these definitions is a professional one, there seems to be no question as to the superior role of the counselor, and the inferior role of the client. Even though the client may talk most of the time, and appear to dominate the counseling sessions, the counselor's attitude, as expressed in these definitions, is a sort of "I am the one who is in control, and thus I am the one who knows what is best for you." This is not an uncommon attitude. It is the attitude, possibly, of the majority of parents and teachers, and probably of school counselors as well. But does not the counselor with this attitude then reinforce and continue and perpetuate a relationship that, more often than not, is the basic problem of the client—namely, dependence on someone else to do something for him, to get him out of a hole? The client may, of course, greatly appreciate this attitude, but in the long run it surely gives no more help than does the reassurance of the medical doctor to the patient with a terminal disease.

A Client-centered counselor, on the other hand, does not think of himself as the authority who has the answers and the skills that will help this other person, the client, to greater maturity. It is of much importance, too, to emphasize that this is the way the Client-centered counselor *feels,* personally, deeply, about himself as a counselor. Many student counselors who are attempting to function as Client-centered counselors conscientiously try to function as nonauthoritative counselors, but because they do not really believe it, their efforts are often not successful. Often too, alas, it is Client-centered counseling that then takes the beating! "It's no good because it didn't work for me. . . ." To say that one has to believe in what he is doing is perhaps an outworn cliché, but the counselor who tries to put into effect a human

[32] Harry S. Sullivan, *The Psychiatric Interview* (New York: W. W. Norton & Company, Inc., 1954), p. 4.

relationship that he neither believes nor accepts is surely doomed to failure. One of the common failings of people, too, is that we blame the "something" rather than the "me."

Definitions that have more of a tendency to stress the quality of the participants are illustrated below. This does not mean that the participants are the same in intelligence, in stability, and in knowledge. It simply means that the counselor views himself as a participant in a human relationship with another person. His relation status as compared with that of the other person is not the point.[33]

> An emotional exchange (process) in an interpersonal relationship which accelerates the growth of one or both participants.

Also,[34]

> Counseling is a personal and dynamic relationship between two people who approach a mutually defined problem with mutual consideration for each other to the end that the younger, or less mature, or more troubled of the two is aided to a self-determined resolution of his problems.

In the above case, however, we might say that the client, very often being under stress and tension, would not be expected to have as much consideration for the counselor as the counselor has for the client. In fact, it might well be that the client would approach the counselor with hatred and hostility, but he would receive from the counselor love and understanding.

Most definitions, of course, do not indicate, in the definition itself, the relative dominance of the counselor and the client in the counseling process. Thus Rogers' own definition of counseling simply describes it as: [35]

> . . . the process by which the structure of the self is relaxed in the safety of the relationship with the therapist, and previously denied experiences are perceived and then integrated into an altered self.

Other similar definitions in which the relationship of the client and the counselor is not stressed are:

[33] Carl A. Whitaker and Thomas P. Malone, *The Roots of Psychotherapy* (New York: McGraw-Hill Book Co., Inc., 1953), p. 233.
[34] C. Gilbert Wrenn, *Student Personnel Work in College* (New York: The Ronald Press Company, 1951), p. 59.
[35] Carl R. Rogers, "Client-centered Psychotherapy," *Scientific American* 187:70 (November, 1952).

. . . a warm, permissive, safe, understanding, but limited social **relation**-ship within which therapist and patient discuss the affective **behavior** of the latter, including his ways of dealing with his emotionally toned needs and the situations that gives rise to them.[36]

. . . a process by which help is given, referred to as counseling. Here the client and counselor interact . . . and the function of the inter-action is to help the client change his behavior so that he may obtain a satisfactory resolution of his needs.[37]

Therapy seems to be constituted in the process of the client's reorganiz-ing of the meaning of events in his life, and in the process of the client's learning new attitudes, new ways of feeling, toward himself and his environment.[38]

It must be stressed, of course, that a verbal definition has mean-ing only to the extent that the person practices what he says. Thus the student in the field of counseling may have a difficult time in moving away from his years of formal education, which frequently have taught him that what is important is what he knows, rather than what he does with what he knows. Examinations usually test the former rather than the latter. The definitions that are quoted in these pages, for example, are not quoted so that the student can memorize them, but so that the student may have a general picture of how a number of authorities in the field of counseling verbalize their concept of counseling. Every counselor must come to see the discrepancy between his *stated* defini-tion of counseling, and his *practiced* definition of counseling; and the real definition, of course, is the latter.

Many capable counselors and therapists have never actually worked out their own personal definitions of counseling, and often this does not matter much. If one never gives a close look at the actual meaning of what he is practicing, however, there is a likelihood that he may not be doing what he says he is doing, or that what he thinks he is doing is not so effective as he assumes it to be. The therapist who says, "And then the patient went into therapy," might be somewhat flustered if someone were to push him as to just exactly what this means. The way the question would usually come, by the way, would be, "What did you *do* then to the patient?" since people assume, gen-

---

[36] Edward J. Shoben, "Some Observations on Psychotherapy and the Learning Process," in O. Hobart Mowrer (Ed.), *Psychotherapy: Theory and Research* (New York: The Ronald Press Company, 1953), p. 127.

[37] Harold B. Pepinsky and Pauline N. Pepinsky, *Counseling: Theory and Practice* (New York: The Ronald Press Company, 1954), p. 3.

[38] Edward S. Bordin, *Psychological Counseling* (New York: Appleton-Century-Crofts, 1955), p. 15.

erally correctly, that anyone who is a doctor does something to someone.

As the student counselor works out his own functioning definition of counseling, he will need a good deal of personal security in order to look at himself squarely, and accept what he sees. Many student counselors will be in need of therapeutic help before they are able to look at the self picture, let alone to accept it. This process must occur somewhere in the education of the counselor, if he is to go forth as a professional therapist with a personally formulated definition of just what he is doing as a counselor, rather than simply reciting by rote some memorized definition that has no reality whatsoever. In looking at this problem, moreover, the student counselor should not limit himself just to what he does in the counseling relationship, but should look beyond this at what he does in all of his human relationships.

A definition of counseling that I have attempted to work toward is one of a human relationship—a warm relationship in which the counselor, fully and completely, without any ifs or buts, accepts the client as a worthy person. In this relationship of complete acceptance, the client can grow and develop, and come to use the strengths and capacities that are his, and to make decisions and choices that will be satisfactory to him, and thus to his fellows. Such decisions will be rational and logical in that they will bear some relationship to the assets and the liabilities that are possessed by the individual.

One could take for granted that it would follow that in this relationship there would be an absence of feelings of criticism, of judgment, of evaluation, of distaste. The client is a person, and no matter who he is, or what he has done, or what he is like, he is a person who is worthy of the counselor's acceptance and respect. There is a very good chance, too, that he is as he is because the experience of acceptance is one that he has never had in his lifetime.

This attitude is something that comes hard to most student counselors, particularly to those who have been in positions of authority, such as teachers and clergymen and medical doctors. The idea of acceptance without evaluation and criticism is easy to say and to write, but very difficult to practice. Actually, however, it is hard to see how one can be an acceptant critic or an acceptant evaluator. One surely contradicts the other. It is almost like saying that one can be a democratic autocrat. There seems to be a negative correlation between love, or warmth, and criticism, since the latter implies rejection—if not of me, then of something I have done. Although theoretically a person may be able to disassociate himself from what he has done, not many individuals can put themselves in this position. This fact can easily be demonstrated by having a student act as a sharp but honest critic of the attitudes and ideas and work of some of his fellow classmates, and then afterwards have them "let their hair down" in a session on just what feelings developed during this "honest" criticism. It is very seldom that I have found any student who reported that his feelings of warmth, security, and closeness to the student instructor increased.

Probably one of the basic reasons for the number of unhappy marriages is that too many partners think that taking a marriage vow does not mean that the individual is to be accepted, for better or for worse, as he is, but rather that this is the first day of a job of reconstruction to be carried out on the poor unsuspecting partner. When both partners are thinking in this manner, trouble lies ahead. People who are "out to change you" get frustrated enough when the other person will not change, but they become doubly frustrated when they find that the other person is busily engaged in trying to change them.

There is some evidence that counselors, as a group, are acceptant individuals. They are the ones who are most often accused of being "soft" toward various anti-social individuals. The hue and cry of softness has been raised in schools and colleges for many years by the more academic-minded staff members toward the members of the staff oriented toward mental hygiene. The recent increasing incidence of juvenile delinquency has led counselors, social workers, and psychologists in many cities to be accused of softness towards those who are getting in trouble with the law.

This would surely mean, too, that if individuals coming into counseling as a profession possess a very rigid system of values, their success as counselors, unless they undergo counseling themselves, is to be doubted. If a person really feels deeply that homosexuality is disgusting or degrading, or that a divorce can never be countenanced under any circumstances, or that a girl who has had an abortion has committed an unpardonable sin, or that one who has given up his religion is guilty of betrayal, how can such a person function as a counselor? It is not a question of whether these are or are not good or bad acts. This simply is not the question, and it never becomes a question for the counselor. He is a person who accepts the reality of the person as he is, and the question of good or bad does not come into the situation at all. To a lesser degree, it might be somewhat like the case of the army surgeon, who cares for the wounded and does the best he can for all of his patients, regardless of whether they are his own men or the enemy. In World War II there were instances when

Jewish doctors worked themselves to exhaustion to save the lives of German Nazis who believed that every Jew should be exterminated. One gave his hatred, the other gave in return his love and acceptance. This is the sort of relationship in which the counselor, *as a person,* must be capable of being involved. Unless counselor education is primarily concerned with self-understanding on the part of the student counselor, it is likely that many counselors will be quite incapable of counseling, at least as it is viewed in this book, even though they may possess a doctorate in the area.

Counseling, then, is a process which takes place because of the relationship between two people. It is in the uniqueness of this relationship that the individual called the client begins to see things that he never saw before, begins to realize strengths that he never knew he had, so that he can see and accept the unpleasant, and begins gradually to see a new and a brighter world. The magic that causes this is indeed magic, but it is not supernatural. It is not to be found in a set of secret formulae and techniques, but rather in the rare experience the client has in finding someone secure and.capable enough to accept him completely and without question as he is, and thus to help him to learn, because now he has reason to learn new and better things.

Very often the student counselor sees as his first task the discovery of the best techniques and methods of counseling. It is likely that he first sees these as being divorced from self, and that only later will he discover that a "method" in a human relationship is the means by which one expresses oneself toward another person. A true methodology can be no more than an expression of self, and, as such, cannot be "learned" as a method or technique. To the student's eager question, "What do I have to learn to become a good counselor?" there is often no answer, or at least no quick and easy answer. A certain manner of proceeding that might be effective in establishing a good relationship between Dr. Brown and Don Del might be quite ineffective in establishing a good relationship between Dr. Din and Don Del, because this manner of proceeding is not really Dr. Din's, but simply something that he has borrowed. It might, for that matter, be equally ineffective between Dr. Brown and Martha Pen, because Martha Pen is quite a different person from Don Del, and she does not see Dr. Brown as he is seen by Don Del. Thus while we might say that all professional counselors have a somewhat similar broad basis of operation, they would use many different methods and techniques, none of them being effective with all counselors and all clients. This would also mean that one's client-centeredness does not necessarily depend on one's methodology tag, or one's orientation—Rogerian, Adlerian, psychoanalytic, or what have you—although it is true that counselors of different orientations do use different methodologies, thus reflecting their personal differences.

In a study by Fiedler, for example, it was found that although therapists did use different methods and techniques, there were common elements in their relationships with clients, such as the ability to understand the client's feelings and meanings, a sensitivity to the client's attitudes, and a warm interest without an emotional over-involvement.[39]

Heine found a somewhat similar result when he studied the attitudes of individuals who had experienced counseling with therapists of various orientations.[40] Although the therapists were classified as non-directive, Adlerian, and psychoanalytic, the clients had similar feelings as to the reasons for the changes that had taken place in themselves. Typical reasons given were the trust they felt in the therapist, the fact that they felt they were understood by the therapist, their feeling of independence in making their own choices and decisions. Thus one might say that while these therapists were classified as being of three different methodologies, there was a client-centeredness that was common to them all and to which the clients responded in a positive manner.

Too many school counselors will say that they are using methods that the books say are good, or bad, but that these methods are good enough for them, that they are comfortable in using them, and that therefore the methods are quite all right. This, of course, is not enough. The counselor must, ideally, be comfortable with, and believe in, whatever method or technique he may be using, but he must also find out what is happening as a result of his actions. If his clients are becoming more dependent or more fearful or more insecure, then he can hardly excuse himself on the basis of his own neurotic comfort.

The great discrepancy between methodologies and the concepts that they reflect is shown by the difficulty some counselors have in intellectually accepting the idea that certain procedures, used by certain counselors, really can be beneficial for individuals under stress and strain. I meet such an attitude not infrequently when a coun-

[39] Fred Fiedler, "Quantitative Studies on the Role of Therapists' Feelings toward their Patients," in O. Hobart Mowrer (Ed.), *Psychotherapy: Theory and Research* (New York: The Ronald Press Company, 1953).
[40] R. W. Heine, *A Comparison of Patients' Reports on Psychotherapeutic Experience with Psychoanalytic, Non-Directive, and Adlerian Therapists* (unpublished doctoral dissertation, University of Chicago, 1950).

selor says, in effect, "But how can a person grow and improve if you don't give him some direction and advice? This is what he wants, this is what he needs, and this is what he should get. If all you do is reflect feeling, he'll never get anywhere." To this about all one can say is, "Well . . . ," or "You mean that it just doesn't seem possible that this could really result in client growth. . . ." All of this does point up the danger of becoming too attached to certain ways of doing things, even if one has evidence that they work well for him. Needless to say, all would question the professional wisdom of becoming attached to procedures for which one had no evidence as to outcome.

On the other hand, every counselor probably feels this attachment to some degree. I can well remember listening to a tape of a certain professional counselor in action—one who is well known and apparently successful with some clients—and being quite unable, intellectually and emotionally, to see how this counselor's approach could possibly do any good for the client involved. Doubtless the reaction was a personal one to the personality of the counselor, and yet this counselor does have clients who apparently improve as a result of their counseling relationship with him. There are obviously many, many roads that lead to Rome, Heaven, or wherever it is that one wishes to go!

The concept that the counselor is a professional person who does not so much use a technique, but rather in the counseling relationship gives of himself, is one that is not always accepted or understood—not only among student counselors, but among experienced professional counselors as well. It is interesting, for example, to note Rogers trying to explain it to a group of colleagues at a professional meeting of therapists:

> Though I think there is much to be said intellectually for an intelligent eclecticism, yet I would have to say, Henry, that you couldn't start with some, quote, "techniques," that I used today, if, in the back of your mind—if the feeling that it is your judgment that you are trusting as to when to change this approach—ah—because—a very basic part of my approach—of me, in this situation, was (unintelligible) for today, even when I had momentary feelings of—oh, my goodness, such trivial stuff —and so on—I was willing for it to be her situation, and, and, to follow. In other words, you can't—ah—you can't—ah—if I'm only going to trust her potential for movement up to the point where I decide I'd better do something else about how to have her move—then that represents a different quality than really trusting her potential.[41]

41 From the tape, *Loretta* (The American Academy of Psychotherapists).

The great battle, joined in 1942 with the publication of Rogers' epochal book, between the forces of the "non-directive" and the forces of the "directive," has been to a great extent resolved.[42] Tempers still flare, however, and we still see articles that are not so much a studied presentation of evidence as a personal sort of thing in which one side is saying, "My Daddy is better than your Daddy." In some ways the battle that raged between the directive and the non-directive advocates was somewhat like the battle that still goes on, unfortunately, between the M.D. therapist and the Ph.D. or D.Ed. therapist.

The concept of counseling as a human relationship is in keeping with an existential, humanistic concept of man. Bugental comments that ". . . the defining concept of man basic to the new humanistic movement in psychology is that *man is the process that supersedes the sum of his part functions.*"[43] He is also critical of the psychologist's aping the more method-centered medical practitioner:[44]

> . . . we cannot follow a pattern of esoterically diagnosing our patient's difficulties and writing prescriptions in Latin and an illegible scrawl, which the patient dutifully carries to a pharmacist for compounding, and then takes with complete ignorance of the preparation or its intended effects.

Evraiff's Client-centered definition of counseling fits this humanistic concept of man. He views counseling as an ongoing process in which a student is free to explore his feelings and what he perceives to be his problems, in which the counselor provides an accepting, understanding, nonjudgmental climate, and in which a relationship is created whereby the student may become increasingly self-directive and capable of dealing with the world around him.[45]

While Cottle goes back some thirty years to discuss "methods" and "techniques" of counseling,[46] Client-centered counselors, both in their counseling and in their writing and talking about their counseling, at least perceive themselves as individuals who do not, in the counseling process, deliberately invoke the use of a technique or a method to

---

[42] Carl R. Rogers, *Counseling and Psychotherapy* (Boston: Houghton Mifflin Company, 1942).
[43] J. F. T. Bugental, "Humanistic Psychology: A New Break-Through," *The American Psychologist* 18:563–567 (September, 1963).
[44] *Ibid.*
[45] William Evraiff, *Helping Counselors Grow Professionally* (New York: Prentice-Hall, Inc., 1963), p. 10.
[46] Cottle and Downey, *op. cit.*, p. 89.

solve a certain personal problem. This is because they see the counseling process as a human relationship, and they feel that one cannot become involved in a real human relationship if one is playing a role, using the bedside manner which seems to be most appropriate for the occasion. Such comments as the following, for example, are not likely to be found in the writings of Client-centered counselors:

> Enthusiasm for their own ideas and successes cause many child therapists to think that their technique is best and should replace all others. Relating the use of a certain technique to the characteristics of the cases in which it is effective is neglected in most presentations. . . . When we know *which technique is best suited for which particular disturbance,* we will be able to make optimum use of the constructive ideas on child therapy produced under the influence of psychoanalysis.[47]

> I refer here to a new and fundamental trend—namely, the use of psychotherapy as an etiologically oriented method of treatment which requires specific knowledge and training. The fact that this knowledge is, to a large degree, derived from psychoanalysis has occasioned heated disagreement among psychoanalysts regarding the relationship of psychoanalytic theory to other forms of therapy.[48]

Marzolf also at times seems to give what might be called a "method point of view." [49] For example, in referring to psychoanalysis, he writes, ". . . while the analyst, seated outside his range of vision, takes notes and makes whatever comments the method requires." This is a tenuous point, and yet it would seem that this sort of comment at least implies that the counselor is a person who has certain methods to which he is committed, or that, if he is eclectic, he is not committed to any method or technique, but uses a great variety of them.

One might say that surely the procedures that are used by the Client-centered counselor, the ones that are being described in this chapter, must, if they are different, constitute a method. The basic difference would probably be that the Client-centered counselor does not see these procedures as constituting a method that he uses in a counseling session, but rather as descriptions that reflect his own deep personal feelings. They are therefore related to him as a person, rather than being methods that are used in unique and particular situations.

[47] Edith Buxbaum, "Techniques of Child Therapy," in Eissler, Freud, *et al* (Eds.), *The Psychoanalytic Study of the Child* (New York: International Universities Press, Inc., 1954), p. 297.

[48] Franz Alexander, *Psychoanalysis and Psychotherapy* (New York: W. W. Norton & Company, Inc., 1956), p. 150.

[49] Stanley S. Marzolf, *Psychological Diagnosis and Counseling in Schools* (New York: Henry Holt & Co., Inc., 1956), p. 331.

It is also true, unfortunately, that some counselors have literally taken on "Client-centered" as a method or technique; and though they operate at a very superficial level, they call themselves "Client-centered." They are actually trying to be what they are not. Or at least they are becoming involved in a procedure which, to be effective, must be close to the person of the counselor, and in their case this is not so. This is possibly why, too, some of the critics of Client-centered counseling look at it with some scorn, thinking of it as a light sort of thing which can be used by anyone without any particular preparation, whereas the *real* psychotherapist is one who uses much more complicated procedures which obviously need a high degree of preparation. The trouble here is that the counselors they are looking at are not Client-centered counselors; they are just poor counselors. If, however, the critic will take the time to go beyond this level, and even review only the research, he will surely come to accept the fact that Client-centered counseling has done much good for large numbers of seriously disturbed individuals. His criticism may then be of a much more studied and professional kind, the kind that may result in growth both for Client-centered counseling and for the critic.

Thus the varying definitions, if they are personal rather than memorized, reflect various philosophical concepts of man and his nature. Those definitions which stress the human relationship, the process, the client as the central focus, would appear to be more existential and humanistic, while those which stress method, diagnosis, the counselor as the central focus, appear to have a more deterministic vision of man. The reader may find that the discussion of the counselor, in following chapters, provides a better description of the "why" and the "what" of counseling than have the preceding pages!

THE RESULTS OF COUNSELING

The "why" of counseling is concerned with the objectives and goals, and the "what" gives some indication of the actual process. A most pragmatic third question, however, has to do with the results, if any, of counseling. The critic poses a most reasonable question when he says, "What's the sense of all this anyway? Does it do any good? Do you really have any evidence that it makes any difference?" The counselor should be acceptant of such questions, and it is part of his professional responsibility to seek answers to these questions as they apply to his counseling.

When the counselor starts to seek these answers, however,

particularly if he is a hard-nosed, empirical sort of fellow, he at once becomes enmeshed in a whole series of difficulties and problems. Tyler [50] points out that two immediate issues are the question of whether the criterion of counseling success should be satisfaction or adjustment and the problem that has to do with the use of a control group with which the counseled group can be compared.

Dressel concludes that: [51]

1. Much research involves so many special restrictions that one dare not generalize from it.
2. Seemingly related researches commonly turn out to differ in fundamental ways. . . .
3. Much research appears to have been done to satisfy the curiosity of the moment without regard to whether it has any real implications for practice. . . .

Boy and Pine comment that: [52]

Measuring the outcomes of counseling is basically a matter of measuring human behavior and personality, for if counseling has been successful, then positive behavioral changes have taken place. But objectively measuring behavioral changes is extremely complex and involves first selecting objective evaluative criteria.

There is no question that determining, with some degree of scientific exactness, the specific outcomes of the counseling of *a* counselor with *a* client is fraught with much difficulty. If we hold to the concept that each human being is unique, obviously the complexity of the human relationship varies with each counselor and each client, and the existentialist would feel that the total examination of man, piece by piece, is impossible. The behaviorist would not agree with this, and Eysenck [53] would appear to be fairly well satisfied that counseling and psychotherapy have no effect whatsoever on human behavior.

In many of the current journals, the research being reported has taken place in an educational milieu, and the criteria that are used are

[50] Tyler, *op. cit.*, pp. 261–264.
[51] Paul L. Dressel, "Implications of Recent Research for Counseling," *Journal of Counseling Psychology* 1:100–105 (Summer, 1954).
[52] Angelo Boy and Gerald P. Pine, *Client-Centered Counseling in the Secondary School* (Boston: Houghton Mifflin Company, 1963), p. 234.
[53] H. J. Eysenck (Ed.), *Handbook of Abnormal Psychology* (New York: Basic Books, 1960), pp. 697–725.

usually the achievement of the individual in this educational setting, or some modification in his attitudes, concepts and general behavior. For example, Spielberger, Weitz and Denny [54] report, as a result of a study, that anxious college freshmen who regularly attended group counseling sessions showed more improvement in their academic performance than students who were not counseled or did not regularly attend counseling. Ivey [55] reports that "there is some indication in this study that students who receive more intensive and long-term counseling are more likely to improve their marks than those who receive short-term counseling." Baymur and Patterson,[56] referring to an underachieving high school population, state that "a comparison of the two counseled groups with the two noncounseled groups indicated that they differed significantly in Q-sort adjustment score change . . . and in increase in grade point average."

Similar positive growth of a group of high school children with behavior problems, who had experienced counseling, as compared with the lack of growth of those who had not, was indicated in a study reported by Arbuckle and Boy.[57]

In somewhat different words, Broedal, Ohlsen, Proff and Southard [58] reported the same thing with a population of gifted underachieving high school students.

On the other hand, Searles [59] reports as a result of his study that three-interview counseling does not appear to have any significant effect on the first semester academic achievement of superior freshmen in a small liberal arts college, while Goodstein and Crites [60] state that

[54] Charles D. Spielberger, Henry Weitz, and J. Peter Denny, "Group Counseling and the Academic Performance of Anxious College Freshmen," *Journal of Counseling Psychology* 9:195–204 (Fall, 1962).
[55] Allen E. Ivey, "The Academic Performance of Students Counseled at a University Counseling Service," *Journal of Counseling Psychology* 9:347–352 (Winter, 1962).
[56] Feriha B. Baymur and C. H. Patterson, "A Comparison of Three Methods of Assisting Underachieving High School Students," *Journal of Counseling Psychology* 7:83–90 (Summer, 1960).
[57] Dugald S. Arbuckle and Angelo Boy, "An Experimental Study of the Effectiveness of Client-centered Therapy in Counseling Students with Behavior Problems," *Journal of Counseling Psychology* 8:136–139 (Summer, 1961).
[58] John Broedal, Merle Ohlsen, Fred Proff, and Charles Southard, "The Effects of Group Counseling on Gifted Underachieving Adolescents," *Journal of Counseling Psychology* 7:163–170 (Fall, 1960).
[59] Aysel Searles, Jr., "The Effectiveness of Limited Counseling in Improving the Academic Achievement of Superior College Freshmen," *Personnel and Guidance Journal* 40:630–633 (March, 1962).
[60] Leonard D. Goodstein and John O. Crites, "Brief Counseling with Poor College Risks," *Journal of Counseling Psychology* 8:318–321 (Winter, 1961).

there was no evidence, from their study, that vocational educational counseling, as it is usually conducted, leads to greater academic achievement by low ability college students.

One might safely assume that a change in academic achievement is the result of some behavioral change or modification in the individual, and this, of course, might occur because of some modification of the environmental milieu. Braaten,[61] for example, concludes that in "successful" Client-centered therapy there is a highly significant movement in the verbal communications of the client from nonself to self. In another study, Williams [62] concludes that educational-vocational counseling restores a normal level of adjustment and degree of congruence among the client's perceptions of himself, his ideal self, and other persons. After a long-range "eight years after" follow-up study, Merenda and Rothney [63] appeared satisfied that intensive counseling with high school students resulted in more favorable attitudes and behaviors. The conclusion of a study reported by Sorenson [64] is that a few counselor-initiated interviews do not produce sufficient change in the classroom behavior of low ability high school students to result in grade improvement. Gonyea [65] reports that vocational counseling with college students does not appear to be a factor in significant change in the appropriateness of vocational choice.

These studies, which are probably fairly representative of the research being conducted on the effectiveness of counseling, are all, to a greater or lesser degree, vulnerable. Since the object of investigation is the human being, they operate with a multiplicity of unknowns, and every study is subject to a series of "ifs" and "buts." This in no way detracts from their value, but all results should be taken as highly tentative, subject to possible drastic change at any time.

There is also disagreement among counselors as to the validity of client satisfaction as a criterion of counseling effectiveness. Patterson,[66] for example, feels that studies of client satisfaction are of little value,

[61] Leif J. Braaten, "Non-Self to Self in Client-Centered Psychotherapy," *Journal of Counseling Psychology* 8:20–24 (Spring, 1961).

[62] John E. Williams, "Changes in Self and Other Perceptions," *Journal of Counseling Psychology* 9:18–30 (Spring, 1962).

[63] Peter F. Merenda and John W. M. Rothney, "Evaluating the Effects of Counseling —Eight Years After," *Journal of Counseling Psychology* 5:163–168 (Fall, 1958).

[64] Mourits A. Sorensen, "Counseling Marginal Students on Classroom Behavior," *Personnel and Guidance Journal* 40:811–812 (May, 1962).

[65] George G. Gonyea, "Appropriateness of Vocational Choices of College Students," *Journal of Counseling Psychology* 10:269–275 (Fall, 1963).

[66] C. H. Patterson, "Client Expectations and Social Conditioning," *Personnel and Guidance Journal* 37:136–138 (October, 1958).

whereas Goodstein and Grigg [67] conclude that client satisfaction is an important factor in any over-all evaluation of the counseling process. Wright [68] tends to support Patterson, and he concludes from his study that a client need not feel completely satisfied with, or highly positive about, counseling in order to benefit from the experience.

From an existential and a Client-centered point of view, client feelings about the counseling experience would be most crucial, since in the long run it is the client who must determine, in his own version, whether he is any better or any worse off as a result of counseling. Pieces of paper and other individuals may say that I am better, but if I feel that I am worse, then operational reality for me is that the sky is darker, not brighter. The following client statements would seem to be one of the most genuine ways of answering the question what is happening as a result of counseling.

An adult male client, for example, says:

"I think I learned, for one thing—I learned to trust someone with information. It gives me a good feeling to trust, and to allow myself to experience the feelings that go along with the verbalization. It's one thing to be able to speak in a detached and specific manner about some specific subject—some particular problem. But it's another thing entirely to be able to allow yourself the luxury of indulging in all the same feelings that should go along, that are natural concomitants of this particular problem, or whatever it is."

Another adult male client:

"And it was quite clear, Dr. San, that I couldn't accept myself as I was, so I had to construct someone that I could like and accept. I introjected how others felt about me, and God knows how much of this is left. All I know is—and it's kind of amazing—I remember clearly the feeling—I don't know why I couldn't tell you—but it—was a kind of good-bye. I realize that one of my characters, one of my favorite characters, was leaving—and I felt sad and resentful."

A number of junior high school boys and girls comment in this way about the effects of counseling:

"It's made me confident—sort of better able to do things."

"It's made me less afraid—I don't fear new people or new things."

"It has enabled me to face the issue of being dominated."

[67] Leonard D. Goodstein and Austin E. Grigg, "Client Satisfaction, Counselors, and the Counseling Process," *Personnel and Guidance Journal* 38:19–24 (September, 1959).

[68] E. Wayne Wright, "A Comparison of Individual and Multiple Counseling for Test Interpretation Interviews," *Journal of Counseling Psychology* 10:126–135 (Summer, 1963).

"It made me realize that I'm not sick."

"It enabled me to stop fighting things in my life which were, really, now that I look at them, pretty unimportant."

"It enabled me to realize that my progress depends more on me than on the teacher."

"It has helped me to become more clear about my future."

"It has made me realize that I don't have to always be in a state of anger—always suspicious of people."

"It has helped me be less nervous and tense when I'm in school."

"It has helped me to improve my school work because—well—I'm not fighting school anymore."

When asked "How do you feel about the effects of counseling," a number of clients replied in the following manner.

A female said:

"How Do I Feel? Through the help given me in these sessions of therapy, I have been able to get on an even keel again. The permissive atmosphere which was established allowed for an outpouring of feelings and emotions from the past and present such as I had never experienced before. This left me free to concentrate on regaining control of myself, and I learned how to help myself over any bad spots which come along. I don't know what the future will bring, but in the past three weeks I have succeeded in throwing off a life which I had grown to hate but had allowed to become a habit which could not be shaken. I know I have many more problems to face and temptations to resist, but somehow I feel I have gained the strength to face life squarely and accept what it has to offer.

"All this I was not able to do with medical and spiritual help, so I feel Client-centered counseling was most successful in my particular case. I also feel I can return again if necessary. It's wonderful to feel like a human being again and to be able to face people again."

A male client said:

"How Do I Feel? Although I do not feel that we have fully worked through the problems at the present time, several positive things have happened. The anxiety about my school work has been reduced to the point where I could at least do some studying—although it has been neither adequate nor very efficient. Secondly, the recurring thoughts have receded to the point where I have them only occasionally and for not very long and where I can inhibit them. This has resulted in a very great drop in my anxiety, because, although intellectually I know that this is sheer nonsense, emotionally I have been very afraid of becoming mentally ill, and of losing control of my thought processes. Just a few meetings were enough to reduce this fear very markedly. With that, my irritability at home decreased."

A female client said, simply:

"Did I gain anything yet—honestly—No—just more analyzing myself and more confusion."

Another, feeling more growth, said:

"I have gained a greater understanding of myself, and, indirectly, others. I think I know myself better—can understand my reactions to situations in a better light. I surely feel more at ease—at peace even."

Comments of other clients were:

"As a client now, I see myself as a person who has a much greater understanding of himself . . . why he has the need to behave in a particular fashion; however, there still is this need in some areas which, though understood, has not been fully accepted as to its origin; appearingly the acceptance of the why, at the moment, is too threatening to me. Intellectual understanding is one thing, acceptance of this understanding on the emotional level is something else. I feel now that, though I still have feelings of inadequacy, I have become free in part from much of the painful life that has little or no purpose and thus lacks the solid satisfaction that endures . . . the needs which are insatiable and lending to a circular form of existence can only supply one with a moment or two of satisfaction which then dies in the wake of the insatiable need itself; satisfaction that endures is derived from living which implies growth, not existing. At the moment I have great hopes or better said, 'Great Expectations' which have been formed by a realistic understanding and partial acceptance of me; the 'Great Expectations,' however, in my case, are somewhat different from Pip's in that mine are associated with a greater understanding and acceptance of myself, and thus the freedom to grow in the direction of man's potential goodness . . . to approximate as closely as possible my potential, which is living."

and:

"I really don't know. I do know that I am trying to accept myself and others. I still have many fears and superstitions. My problems on sex and religion are being solved."

and:

"So many things it is hard to boil them down. I find courage to disagree openly with my mother and sister and argue. This carried over to other people in work. In other words, I "stuck up for myself." I learned to question things instead of knowing a little and imagining the rest. I felt a certain power—over myself—and understood that events depend to a certain extent on what choices I made. The greatest realization I have is that I am an individual, not a puppet. A terrifying paralyzing fear of nothing, everything or any change at all is going. I feel free to feel, think, and do what I think best. I do say that when a person starts in any such treatment, he or she realizes that even after it is over, it is just beginning. The responsibility I feel is still enormous. It is no longer so important to be "approved" and try to get along with everyone. It is impossible! I am still fighting contrary impulses."

The individual counselor, with a sense of professional responsibility, might be expected to keep up with the research literature, and to be periodically involved in research projects that have to do with the effectiveness of the counseling of himself and his colleagues. For most counselors, however, the major measure of their success in counseling will be each individual client—how he feels, how he thinks, and how he acts. The counselor should be sensitive to the client during the counseling process, and equally sensitive to the feelings and the behaviors of the client as a result of the counseling experience.

the feeling of the counselor

Chapter Three

THE COUNSELOR:
PERSONALITY AND JOB

MANY AND VARIED are the lists of virtues that should be possessed by that, apparently, paragon of virtue known as the counselor. If, indeed, there were some human creature who possessed all of these characteristics to a high degree, a client would probably find the development of a warm relationship with him a difficult thing, since he would be so far removed from the world in which the client lived. Some years ago, Pepinsky and Pepinsky stated, with some justification, that if the counselor were to possess all the characteristics that supposedly should be his, then he would be better equipped for divine than for vocational guidance! [1] And yet, in a more serious vein, could one say that Gould is wrong when he writes, "a teacher (or a counselor) is a person with a sense of immortality, for to leave a vestige of oneself in the development of another is a touch of immortality. Through this we find an impelling and sufficient reason for living. Through this we live far beyond our span of years." [2]

It might even be that Ruskin, in discussing great men, was talking about the counselor as he could be, when he said ". . . the first great test of a truly great man is his humility. I do not mean, by humility, doubt of his own power, or hesitation in speaking his own opinions;

[1] Harold B. Pepinsky and Pauline N. Pepinsky, *Counseling: Theory and Practice* (New York: The Ronald Press Company, 1954), pp. 139–140.
[2] As quoted by C. Gilbert Wrenn in "Status and Role of the School Counselor," *The Personnel and Guidance Journal* 36:182 (November, 1957).

but a right understanding of the relation between what *he* can do and say, and the rest of the world's sayings and doings." [3]

It should be noted, too, that when I am discussing the counselor, I am obviously talking about the counselor as I see him, involved in counseling as I see it. Actually, these perceptions do not appear to differ too much from those appearing in policy statements that were adopted at the annual convention at San Francisco, in March, 1964, by the American Personnel and Guidance Association, the American School Counselors Association, and the Association for Counselor Education and Supervision. The adopted policy statement of the American School Counselors Association, for example, states that:

> *School Counselor* is a term used in this policy statement to designate a counselor working in a secondary school setting, concerned with and accepting a responsibility for assisting all pupils, and having as his major concern the developmental needs and problems of youth. Counseling is perceived as involving a dynamic relationship between counselor and counselee, and thus the school counselor accepts the responsibility of involving himself in the lives of pupils with clear and humble knowledge of the implications.

Since such stated definitions of counseling differ little from what I would refer to as either counseling or psychotherapy, it seems logical to refer to studies that may use the word "therapist" or "psychotherapy," even though some counselors and some counselor educators recoil in horror whenever these terms are mentioned. I will even possibly refer to studies involving psychiatrists, since quite frequently, in modern schools, we find school counselors and psychiatrists working quite closely together with the same clientele. This clientele, while it consists of "normal" individuals in the sense that most of them do not suffer any abnormal personality disorientation, does, nevertheless, have problems and questions and difficulties and anxieties and concerns that cannot be alleviated by other personnel in the school. It is the counselor who provides the needed service, and it is about this person that we speak in this chapter.

THE PERSONALITY OF THE COUNSELOR

In discussing characteristics of counselors one must be cautious of the validity of tags and labels. Most reports, for example, will say that counselors should be "kind"; yet kindness may be a symptom of

[3] A. H. R. Ball (Ed.), *Ruskin as Literary Critic* (Cambridge: The University Press, 1928), pp. 248–249.

neurotic behavior, and there may be some question as to how effective a neurotic individual can be as a counselor. In most cases, when we talk generally about the characteristics of counselors, we are thinking about them as we see them rationally. But we should not forget that many clients are not looking at things in a particularly rational manner; if they were, it is unlikely that they would be in need of counseling.

Different clients, too, may react to a similar characteristic in different ways. Thus a client with extreme paranoid tendencies may view an honest gesture of kindness as very threatening, while another client would feel warmly grateful because of it. Probably the most pragmatic question is not so much what counselors think of as "good" characteristics, but, rather, what is the evidence to indicate that there are or are not certain counselor characteristics that seem to produce positive results in the development and the growth of the client.

Some years ago the National Vocational Guidance Association issued a publication on Counselor Preparation that referred to the general characteristics of counselors as being: a deep interest in people, patience, sensitivity to the attitudes and reactions of others, emotional stability and objectivity, a capacity for being trusted by others, and respect for the facts.[4]

Hamrin and Paulson reported a study in which counselors themselves listed the traits necessary for counseling, in order of frequency, as understanding, sympathetic attitude, friendliness, sense of humor, stability, patience, objectivity, sincerity, tact, fairness, tolerance, neatness, calmness, broadmindedness, kindliness, pleasantness, social intelligence, and poise.[5] This study would have been more interesting if there could have been some indication of the extent to which clients felt that these counselors possessed the traits that they themselves said were essential for good counseling.

Rogers [6] has stated that the counselor should (1) be sensitive to human relationships; (2) have an objective attitude and an emotionally detached attitude—in short, a capacity for sympathy that is not overdone; (3) have respect for the individual and an ability and willingness to accept the child as he is, giving him freedom to work out his own solutions; (4) understand himself, and his emotional limitations and shortcomings; (5) know human behavior.

An earlier summation of the evidence and research on the ques-

[4] National Vocational Guidance Association, *Counselor Preparation* (Washington, D.C., 1949).

[5] S. A. Hamrin and B. B. Paulson, *Counseling Adolescents* (Chicago: Science Research Associates, 1950).

[6] Carl R. Rogers, *Counseling and Psychotherapy* (Boston: Houghton Mifflin Company, 1942).

tion of who counselors are and what they should be is to be found in the classic volume by Jones,[7] and a summation by Cottle.[8]

Weitz[9] has pointed out three traits that he considers essential for counseling effectiveness: security, a sense of self-acceptance; sensitivity, the capacity of generalizing one's own feelings of self-acceptance to the acceptance of other people; and objectivity, the capacity to distinguish between objective and symbolic behavior, and yet understand the intimate relationship between the two.

In the last few years, what would at least appear to be an interesting change has occurred in the various "should be" articles that are written about counselors. Older articles by counselors and counselor educators, such as some of those just mentioned, tended to refer to broad and general characteristics of what might be generally described as "good" people. Those referring to more specific aspects of human behavior tended to be written by psychologists, or persons such as Rogers, known as therapists. Today, however, this stress on the more psychological aspects of the human being of the counselor is to be found in almost all of the literature. Emphasis is placed on the counselor's ability to look at, and to understand and accept *his* self, as well as the self of the other person.

For example, a few years ago Hobbs was less representative than now, when he stated that: [10]

> The life style of the counselor is perhaps as important as his competencies, and whereas one would expect a multiplicity of life styles among counselors, there are two ingredients which I would hope our training programs would uniformly foster. One of these we might call a sense of time or dimensionality; the other is creativity, and the two may turn out to be different faces of the same coin.

So was Wyatt, when he was warning about the temptations encountered by the therapist: [11]

> (a) The gratification of his instinctual needs in the disguise of therapeutic activity which is likely to follow along the repetition of certain

[7] A. J. Jones, *Principles of Guidance* (New York: McGraw-Hill Book Co., Inc., 1951), pp. 542–583.
[8] William C. Cottle, "Personal Characteristics of Counselors: I," *The Personnel and Guidance Journal* 31:445–450 (April, 1953).
[9] Henry Weitz, "Counseling as a Function of the Counselor's Personality," *Personnel and Guidance Journal* 35:276–280 (January, 1957).
[10] Nicholas Hobbs, "The Compleat Counselor," *Personnel and Guidance Journal* 36:594–602 (May, 1958).
[11] Frederick Wyatt, "The Self-Experience of the Psychotherapist," *Journal of Consulting Psychology* 12:83–87 (February, 1948).

subjective patterns of his own development; (b) indulgence in the nar-
cissism which the therapeutic situation amply occasions.

More representative, today, are Stone and Shertzer, when they say: [12]

> The true professional knows not only who he should be but also what
> he is. . . . All too many counselors invest their energy in arguing what
> they should be without stopping to look at what they are both per-
> sonally and professionally. . . . The counselor who waits upon an
> externally supplied solution to his questions "Who am I?" and "What
> do I do?" does a disservice to himself and to the profession.

And Appell, when he comments: [13]

> The most significant resource a counselor brings to a helping relation-
> ship is himself. It is difficult to understand how a counselor unaware of
> his own emotional needs, of his expectations of himself as well as
> others, of his rights and privileges in relationships, can be sensitive
> enough to such factors in his counselee. More than that, it would seem
> that he needs to experience himself as a person of worth and of
> individuality before he can afford another such privileges. Indeed, in a
> most profound sense, the greater his congruence, the freer he can be
> in assisting others to actualize themselves.

School counselors Boy and Pine [14] describe the counselor's personal problems as discovering his professional identity, freeing himself
of himself, developing a humanistic attitude, being professionally
secure, counselor anxieties, transference and counter-transference. They
comment that "the school counselor must be sensitive to his own
desires to 'wrap up a case' and to how much such an attitude can influence him to prod the client instead of allowing him to proceed
at his own rate in solving a problem." [15]

Even Williamson,[16] while talking in a rather odd way about the
counselor as technique, indicates that the counselor's philosophy of
human development should show through his behavior, that his efforts
at relating effectively with the student must issue from his own accept-

[12] Shelley C. Stone and Bruce Shertzer, "The Militant Counselor," *Personnel and
Guidance Journal* 42:342–347 (December, 1963).
[13] Morey L. Appell, "Self-Understanding for the Guidance Counselor," *Personnel
and Guidance Journal* 42:143–148 (October, 1963).
[14] Angelo V. Boy and Gerald J. Pine, *Client-Centered Counseling in the Secondary
School* (Boston: Houghton Mifflin Company, 1963), pp. 188–202.
[15] *Ibid.*
[16] E. G. Williamson, "The Counselor as Technique," *Personnel and Guidance
Journal* 41:108–111 (October, 1962).

ance of himself as he is, and that his behavior should be such as to be identified as the carrying on of his own "independent intellectual life," both in his own technical field and in the broad literature of human cultures.

Wrenn's reference to counselor personality, in one of his "recommendations," also stresses counselor self-understanding: [17]

> That counselors understand that they tend to be security-oriented, in part because they relate themselves more easily to the past than to the future, in part because they safeguard their *influential relationship* with students in the direction of "safe" decisions. But safety for the present may mean disaster for the future. Counselors need to balance undue caution with a risk-taking orientation which will encourage students to look to the future and to dare to be intellectual and vocational pioneers.

Nor are such statements limited to individuals. In a joint report by the New York State Counselors Association and the New York State Association of Deans and Guidance Personnel, essential personal competencies of the counselor are described as: [18]

> . . . a knowledge of self: needs, values, strengths, and weaknesses.
> . . . an understanding and acceptance of individual differences: intellectual, personal, physical, cultural, and socio-economic.
> . . . the capacity to relate to and work with others.
> . . . skill in communicating with others.
> . . . the ability to recognize a need for continual personal and professional development.

The report of the Committee on Professional Preparation and Standards of the American Personnel and Guidance Association was accepted at the annual convention in San Francisco in March, 1964. It described as basic qualities of the effective counselor a belief in each individual, a commitment to individual human values, alertness to the world, open-mindedness, understanding of self, and professional commitment. A statement of policy for secondary school counselors was accepted by the American School Counselors Association at the same convention. It described the counselor as follows:

[17] C. Gilbert Wrenn, *The Counselor in a Changing World* (Washington, D.C.: American Personnel and Guidance Association, 1962), p. 109.
[18] *An Exploration of the Role and Preparation of the Counselor in the Secondary School.* A Report of the Professional Advancement Committee of the New York State Counselors Association and the Professional Development and Research Committee of the New York State Association of Deans and Guidance Personnel, 1963.

The counselor is dedicated to the idea that most pupils will enhance and enrich their personal development and self-fulfillment by means of making more intelligent decisions if given the opportunity to experience an accepting, non-evaluating relationship in which one is helped to better understand himself, the environment he perceives, and the relationship between these. Counseling is essentially such a relationship. The school counselor views himself as the person on the school staff with the professional competencies, behavioral science understandings, philosophical orientation, and position within the school necessary to provide such help to pupils.

These then, are thoughts and ideas, by individuals and organizations, as to who the counselor should be, and they are important in that they will play a major role in the development of the counselor of tomorrow. Is this the way, however, that the counselor is today? Let us look at some of the evidence that describes the counselor as he is today. There is, obviously, no such thing as a "counselor"—he comes in many sizes and shapes. There are, however, certain similarities among professional counselors, and there are certain differences that may be caused by their orientation, their background, where they were educated, and the sort of education they experienced. Arbuckle [19] made a study of certain differences between student counselors who were chosen by their fellows as potential counselors and those who were rejected by their fellows. Those who were chosen by their fellows as individuals they would like to have as counselors showed a higher degree of confidence (as measured by the Heston Personality Inventory) than those who chose them. They were more normal in that they scored lower on the Hypochondriasis, Depression, Paranoia, Hysteria, Schizophrenia, Social I.E., and Psychasthenia scales (as measured by the Minnesota Multiphasic Personality Inventory). They showed a higher degree of interest in such areas as social service, persuasive, literary, and scientific activities (as measured by the Kuder Preference Record). On the other hand, those students who were rejected by their fellows as potential counselors indicated less in the way of home satisfaction than those who chose them. They were more abnormal in that they scored higher on the Hypochondriasis, Paranoia, Hysteria, Schizophrenia, Psychopathic Deviate, and Hypomania scales. There were no significant differences in interest areas.

Several years later, in a somewhat similar study, forty participants in an NDEA Guidance Institute judged each other as potential counselors. The nine "most chosen" participants were compared on a

[19] Dugald S. Arbuckle, "Client Perception of Counselor Personality," *Journal of Counseling Psychology* 3:93–96 (Summer, 1956).

number of variables with the nine "least chosen." Most chosen participants had a higher academic performance, somewhat more appropriate Strong scores, and less dogmatism as indicated on the Rokeach scale.[20]

In another study using an NDEA Institute population, the criterion for "good" or "bad" counselor was supplied by the staff ranking the student counselors in the order in which they would hire them as counselors. Using this criterion, the perceptual organization of effective counselors was significantly different from that of less effective counselors. The more effective counselors tended to perceive from an internal rather than external frame of reference; they perceived in terms of people rather than things; they perceived people as able rather than unable, dependable rather than undependable, friendly rather than unfriendly, worthy rather than unworthy, identified rather than unidentified; they perceived their self as enough rather than not enough, revealing rather than not revealing; they perceived their purpose as freeing rather than controlling, altruistic rather than narcissistic, in larger rather than smaller meanings.[21]

Using an audio scale, O'Hern and Arbuckle [22] found that student counselors in seven summer NDEA Guidance Institutes who were considered to be most sensitive as counselors were significantly younger, they had attained a lower educational degree, and they had been employed fewer years than those who were considered to be least sensitive. These results raise some questions about certain assumptions having to do with counselor effectiveness! In an earlier study by Abeles,[23] somewhat related results were found when it was determined that the differences between student counselors rated by supervisors as more or less promising were in values and interests rather than in ability and general adjustment.

Truax, Carkhuff and Douds [24] appear to be satisfied that enough evidence has been produced to indicate that the three therapist charac-

20 Buford Stefflre, Paul King, and Fred Leafgren, "Characteristics of Counselors Judged Effective by Their Peers," *Journal of Counseling Psychology* 9:335–340 (Winter, 1962).

21 Arthur W. Combs and Daniel W. Soper, "The Perceptual Organization of Effective Counselors," *Journal of Counseling Psychology* 10:222–226 (Fall, 1963).

22 Jane S. O'Hern and Dugald S. Arbuckle, "Sensitivity: A Measurable Concept?" *Personnel and Guidance Journal* 42:572–576 (February, 1964).

23 N. Abeles, *A Study of the Characteristics of Counselor Trainees* (doctoral dissertation, University of Texas, 1958).

24 Charles B. Truax, Robert R. Carkhuff, and John Douds, "Toward an Integration of the Didactic and Experiential Approaches to Training in Counseling and Psychotherapy," *Journal of Counseling Psychology* 11:240–247 (Fall, 1964).

teristics that determine the depth of self-exploration on the part of the client are therapist empathic understanding, therapist non-possessive warmth, and therapist self-congruence or transparency.

Comrey described some of the differences among samplings of American Psychological Association members with different professional interest areas.[25] Those with interests in counseling and guidance thought that more psychologists lived up to their standards of what a psychologist should be than not; they judged religion to be more of a positive force in their lives than the others; they liked group projects; they liked administrative work in psychology; they liked psychotherapy; they liked teaching; they wanted to spend more time with their families; they wanted to do something for society; they wanted to help people who needed help; they were less productive in research articles than other groups; they had spent less of their time in positions where they had to do research; they believed that most institutions placed too much emphasis on research; they believed that less emphasis should be placed on research in training clinical psychologists; they were less interested in doing research; they attended either few or many professional meetings; they neither liked nor disliked competitive situations; they devoted either few or many weeks to vacation from professional work; they were less interested in sex; they liked a job where forty hours per week were devoted to teaching and preparation; they liked a well-paid teaching position in a small college.

On the other hand, predominant among those with interests in psychotherapy were some of the following attitudes: they allowed the expressed interests of graduate students to determine the content of a graduate course; they liked the idea of doing counseling and guidance; they wanted to help people who needed help; they had less resentment than others of a colleague who was a homosexual or an adulterer; they spent neither very little nor an excessive number of evening hours on professional work; they neither strongly liked nor disliked competitive situations; they expected to reach a higher income; they found it less unpleasant than many to be alone; they believed that life in our society is too competitive; they found mathematics distasteful; they were most interested in having quite a lot of money; research was not their forte.

In an interesting article on neurotic interactions between counselors and clients, Lawton [26] refers to some of the therapist's insecurities

[25] Andrew L. Comrey, "Publication Rate and Interests in Certain Psychologists," *The American Psychologist* 11:314–322 (July, 1956).
[26] George Lawton, "Symposium on Neurotic Interaction in Marriage Counseling," *Journal of Counseling Psychology* 5:28–33 (Spring, 1958).

as being expressed in the following ways. The therapist tends to dominate the patient because of his fear that he will lose control of the relationship; he competes with other significant authority figures in the life of the patient; he showers the patient with excessive love and attention, going to extreme lengths to prevent marriage failure (his attitude seems to be, "This marriage must succeed"); he functions as the child of the patient, misses him when he is away and welcomes him back with a sigh of relief and pleasure; he indicates a sort of Pygmalion complex, in the sense that he needs to make the patient like the therapist; he resents the patient's demands; fearing the patient's hostility, he tries to appease him; he is unable to stand the patient's tension and anxiety. On this latter point, Lawton points out, this sort of anxiety is likely to result in glittering pseudo-optimism: "Don't worry; everything will be all right!"

In the same paper Lawton points to the seductive role of the more immature therapists. Verbal wooing may take the form of calling the patient by his first name too soon or without ascertaining the patient's wishes; of using affectionate or meaningful intonation of words; engaging in long, cozy telephone conversations; talking, explaining, interpreting excessively; asking for deep material too soon or too obviously. Non-verbal seduction of the patient may take such means as visiting the patient's home at the request of the patient whenever the latter undergoes an emotional emergency connected with transference; giving affectionate or meaningful glances; putting an affectionate hand on the patient's shoulder or giving a parental pat; allowing the patient to telephone regularly after hours or to see the therapist at times not ordinarily office hours; charging the patient a fee which the patient feels is lower than called for in a particular situation and letting the patient know that this is done because the therapist likes him; regularly overrunning the usual and conventional time limits for sessions.

In another paper from the same symposium, Harper [27] lists still other neurotic interactions among counselors as being the pose of objectivity, the overemphasis on likeability, and the effort on the part of the counselor to show that he is a good fellow, just like everyone else.

A study of Fiedler indicated that there was less in the way of differences among expert counselors of supposed different orientations than there was among inexperienced counselors of supposedly similar

[27] Robert A. Harper, "Symposium on Neurotic Interaction in Marriage Counseling," *Journal of Counseling Psychology* 5:33–38 (Spring, 1958).

orientations.[28] The expert counselors were close together in their ability to understand the client's meanings and feelings; their sensitivity to the client's attitudes; their warm interest in the client without emotional involvement.

On the other hand, there would seem to be no doubt that counselors do use different techniques and methods. Strupp, for example, made a study of Rogerian and psychoanalytically oriented psychotherapists, and while the differences tended to diminish among the more experienced as compared with the less experienced, there were, nevertheless, significant differences.[29] For example, with the Rogerian psychotherapists, 75.5 percent of the responses were of a restating, clarifying, reflecting type, whereas only 14.2 percent of the psychoanalytically oriented psychotherapists used this type of response; 9.8 percent of the responses of Rogerians were of an exploring nature, asking for clarification, or expressing feeling, while 35.6 percent of the responses of non-Rogerians were of this type.

In a later study, Strupp gave evidence of differences in the attitudes of psychoanalytic and Client-centered counselors, as indicated by their reactions to the showing of a sound film of a first interview.[30] The Client-centered counselors judged the prognosis with therapy to be more favorable than the members of the psychoanalytic group; a larger proportion of the Rogerian counselors than of the others professed a positive attitude toward the client; Rogerians either declined to specify attitudes and behaviors that the therapist should encourage in therapy with his patient or stressed the expression of feelings, while the others stressed such things as a sense of responsibility, increased socialization, and relating feelings and symptoms to interpersonal situations. Conversely, psychoanalytic therapists were more likely to discourage attitudes and behaviors such as intellectualization, obsessive ruminations, self-pity, self-depreciation, helplessness, refusal to accept responsibility, demanding attitudes, and acting out; Rogerians tended to say they would discourage nothing or leave it to the patient. No member of the Rogerian group advocated strictness by the therapist,

[28] Fred Fiedler, "Quantitative Studies on the Role of Therapists' Feelings Toward Their Patients," in O. Hobart Mowrer (Ed.), *Psychotherapy: Theory and Research* (New York: The Ronald Press Company, 1953), p. 296.
[29] Hans H. Strupp, "An Objective Comparison of Rogerian and Psychoanalytic Techniques," *Journal of Consulting Psychology* 9:1–7 (February, 1955).
[30] Hans H. Strupp, "An Objective Comparison of Rogerian and Psychoanalytic Therapists in an Initial Interview," *Journal of Consulting Psychology* 22:265–274 (August, 1958).

as contrasted with more than one third of the members of the psycho-analytic group, who considered strictness therapeutically desirable. Rogerians commented on the patient's feelings and attitudes, but in contrast to the others, paid less attention to such clues as gestures, bodily movements, manner of speaking, the patient's past and present interpersonal relations with his mother, wife, brother, or father. In terms of the handling of the transference problem Rogerians recommended understanding, clarification, and reflection; analytically oriented therapists preferred an interpretive approach. Rogerians were more definite in their assertion that they would have conducted the interview in a different manner. They dissociated themselves from the therapist's approach, tending to evaluate his performance as inadequate; the analytic therapists considered his performance reasonably adequate. Over 75 percent of the Rogerians said that they would have spent somewhat less or considerably less time in obtaining data on the patient's life history than did the film therapist; almost one half of the analytic group said that they would have devoted somewhat more or considerably more time. The majority of the Rogerian therapists described their attitude toward the therapist in the film as negative, whereas most analytically oriented therapists professed a positive or neutral attitude.

Another interesting picture of counseling methodology was obtained in a study by Arbuckle and Wicas [31] that tended, among other things, to indicate that there was as much disagreement among counselors who received their training for the doctorate in the same institution as there was among those who received their doctorates in different institutions. Thus, among the members of the jury that was used in the study, the four experts who had the greatest number of Client-centered responses had received their doctorates at, respectively, the University of Chicago, Columbia University, the University of Minnesota and Harvard University. There was no significant difference in the degree of "Client-centeredness" of the responses of four members of the jury who received their training at Columbia, as compared with the four members who received theirs at Chicago.

The possession of a medical degree has historically come to be generally accepted as a requirement for competence in the matter of therapy of any kind, including psychotherapy and counseling. There is little or no actual relationship between the possession of such a

[31] Dugald S. Arbuckle and Edward Wicas, "The Development of an Instrument for the Measurement of Counseling Perceptions," *Journal of Counseling Psychology* 4:304–312 (Winter, 1957).

degree and competence in psychotherapy, and medical doctors are the first to agree that their background gives them little in the way of understanding or skill when dealing with matters that are of the psychological. Many psychiatrists would agree with Colby, who tends to feel that his medical background was a hindrance rather than a help in his development into a capable psychotherapist.[32]

> Outstanding among educationally induced handicaps are detachment and dehumanization achieved in medical school. One tends to become interested almost entirely in diseases per se rather than in the people who have diseases. A once-active imagination may become stunted in the name of false scientific objectivity. The traditional medical single cause-and-effect concept of disease narrows the observation and sympathetic understanding of inter-human processes. . . . In the matters of treatment also, medical attention directs the axis of the student's interest toward mechanisms that can be seen and touched.

Freud, as the first outstanding "psychotherapist," stressed the fact that the possession of a medical degree had little or nothing to do with effectiveness as a psychotherapist. Freud's medical colleagues, however, paid no attention to this feeling, and medicine took over the responsibility for the study of human personality, conscious and unconscious. The effects of this will be noted in the next section, but let it suffice to say that we are currently caught in the confusion of talking about "mental health," and "mental illness," when we are discussing problems and tensions and disturbances that are primarily the result of the psychological process of learning rather than the physiological process of being born.

Mowrer has this to say on the subject: [33]

> We psychologists do not, I believe, object *in principle* to the type of authority which psychiatrists wish to exercise, or to our being subject to other medical controls, if they were truly functional. But authority and power ought to go with demonstrated competence, which medicine clearly has in the physical realm but, equally clearly, does not have in "psychiatry." Despite some pretentious affirmations to the contrary, the fact is that psychoanalysis, on which modern "dynamic" psychiatry is largely based, is in a state of virtual collapse and imminent demise. And the tranquilizers and other forms of so-called chemotherapy are admittedly only ameliorative, not basically curative. So now, to the extent that we have accepted the "illness" postulate and thus been lulled under

[32] Kenneth M. Colby, *A Primer for Psychotherapists* (New York: The Ronald Press Company, 1951), pp. 20–21.
[33] O. Hobart Mowrer, " 'Sin,' the Lesser of Two Evils," *The American Psychologist* 15:301–304 (May, 1960).

the penumbra of medicine, we are in the ungraceful maneuver of "getting out."

Since the possession of a medical degree is assumed by some to be an absolute prerequisite to the practice of psychotherapy, a book that takes a look at the applicants to medical schools is of much interest.[34] Kelly, discussing the results of an intensive testing and evaluation of one graduating class from one medical school, makes the following comments: [35]

> Essentially, our medical students are persons who, if they were not becoming physicians, would be planning to become manufacturers, big businessmen, production managers, engineers; they are not the kind of people who would become teachers, ministers, social workers, i.e., professional persons interested in doing something for the good of mankind. As a group, the medical students reveal remarkably little interest in the welfare of human beings. . . . All of the evidence available to us leads to the conclusion that the *typical* young physician has little interest in cultural aspects of the society in which he lives, has very little sensitivity to or feeling for the needs of the community, and is generally not inclined to participate in community activities unless these contribute to his income. I am not saying this is true of all physicians; I am saying this is true of the model young man going into one medical school.

It is also pointed out that whereas a decade or so ago medical students tended to be A or B students, in recent years they have been drawn primarily from the ranks of the B students in the colleges.[36]

In this same report, too, Handler, discussing the results of psychiatric interviews with three classes of freshmen medical students, comments as follows.[37]

> Our impression was that the majority of the students we saw were quite conformist, emotionally constricted young men and women, given to internalizing their hostility either with depressive or compulsive traits for the most part, or sometimes with somatic manifestations. We felt that there was a high premium put on this in pre-medical competition, and, provided that it was not too extreme, we thought of this matter of conformity and constriction as actually one of the criteria of success both in premedical work and in getting through medical school.

[34] Helen Hofer Gee and John T. Cowles (Eds.), *The Appraisal of Applicants to Medical Schools* (Evanston: Association of American Medical Colleges, 1957).
[35] *Ibid.*, pp. 195–196.
[36] *Ibid.*, p. 13.
[37] *Ibid.*, p. 68.

On the basis of a more comprehensive study of data obtained from nearly 2,500 first-year medical students in twenty-eight medical schools, Gee describes the "average" entering medical student as a man who values the pursuit of scientific truth above all.[38] He values prestige and power next to theoretical values, but holds these values no higher than does the average college student. He is considerably less interested in economic and material gain than is the average college student, and somewhat more interested in the cultural aspects of community life. He is strongly motivated by needs to achieve and to work hard and persistently toward achievement of his goals. He is not prone to be motivated through altruistic love of his fellow man, it is true, but he is likely to want to understand why that fellow man behaves as he does, and is likely to be motivated by a desire to help him when he is in trouble and to treat him with sympathy and kindness. His interests cannot be characterized as being very much like those of social workers; they are more like those of physicians, osteopaths, and public administrators. But he is more likely to have the interests of a teacher or social worker or of an author-journalist than he is to have the interests of a businessman or farmer.

These various statements may be somewhat contradictory, but they are probably representative. They tend to raise at least some doubt as to the validity of the concept that the possession of a medical degree is a prerequisite for the practice of psychotherapy.

There is also evidence of a difference between psychiatric and psychological opinion regarding personality disturbances. Glosser [39] contacted 90 psychiatrists and 60 psychologists, and had a 56 percent return from the psychiatrists and a 61 percent return from the psychologists. Glosser's questionnaire consisted of 100 statements of opinion regarding psychological disturbances. On 81 percent of the items there was a virtual unanimity of opinion. On 63 of the 100 items, however, a higher percentage of psychologists than psychiatrists selected the "?" response indicating some doubt or skepticism of the validity of either a "yes" or "no" response. The psychiatrists leaned more strongly toward psychogenic than physiogenic concepts, generally opposing physiological, biological, and biochemical accounts of mental and personality disturbances. They expressed a favorable attitude toward the psychodynamics of Freudian and psychoanalytic theory. The psychologists were somewhat more inclined to accept the existence of underlying physiological disturbances in mental disorders. They were

[38] In a personal communication from Dr. Gee to the author.
[39] Harry J. Glosser, "Psychiatric Versus Psychological Opinion Regarding Personality Disturbances," *The American Psychologist* 13:477–481 (August, 1958).

more inclined to oppose certain Freudian and psychodynamic concepts. They were somewhat more inclined to accept hereditary influences in the susceptibility of the individual to certain mental and personality disorders, and more strongly opposed to the view that therapy cannot exist without direction. On this latter item, the reaction to the statement, "Therapy cannot exist without direction; therefore, the nondirective method is not really therapy," for the psychiatrists was 32 percent "yes," and 44 percent "no," whereas the reaction of the psychologists was 8.3 percent "yes," and 70 percent "no." This is probably surprising to many psychiatrists and psychologists!

If one is to be able to enter into a helping relationship with another individual, Rogers postulates a few of the questions that he may ask himself. These questions give an excellent picture of Rogers' concept of the personality of the counselor: [40]

1. Can I *be* in some way which will be perceived by the other person as trustworthy, as dependable or consistent in some deep sense . . . ?
2. Can I be expressive enough as a person that what I am will be communicated unambiguously . . . ?
3. Can I let myself experience positive attitudes toward this other person—attitudes of warmth, caring, liking, interest, respect . . . ?
4. Can I be strong enough as a person to be separate from the other? Can I be a sturdy respecter of my own feelings, my own needs, as well as his? Can I own and, if need be, express my own feelings as something belonging to me and separate from his feelings? Am I strong enough in my own separateness that I will not be downcast by his depression, frightened by his fear, nor engulfed by his dependency?
5. Am I secure enough within myself to permit his separateness? Can I permit him to be what he is—honest or deceitful, infantile or adult, despairing or overconfident? Can I give him the freedom to be . . . ?
6. Can I let myself enter fully into the world of his feelings and personal meanings and see these as he does? Can I step into his private world so completely that I lose all desire to evaluate or judge it . . . ?
7. Can I receive him as he is? Can I communicate this attitude? Or can I receive him only conditionally, accepting some aspects of his feelings and silently or openly disapproving of other aspects . . . ?
8. Can I act with sufficient sensitivity in the relationship that my behavior will not be perceived as a threat . . . ?
9. Can I free him from the threat of external evaluation . . . ?
10. Can I meet this other individual who is in the process of *becoming*, or will I be bound by his past and by my past . . . ?

[40] Carl R. Rogers, "The Characteristics of a Helping Relationship," *Personnel and Guidance Journal* 37:6–16 (September, 1958).

Two counselors, wondering about why they happen to be counselors, are, in a way, answering for themselves some of these questions. One of them says:

"The essence of democratic life is a person's individuality. In our society the individual can easily become the victim of the group. The individual finds it difficult to be himself, to be the master of his fate, because of the pressures of conformity that the group imposes upon him. The individual can become swallowed by the group. A person's individuality is consumed because of the neurotic need of the group for conformity. The individuality of the free thinker is the cornerstone of our democratic life. In a totalitarian state there is no room for individuality. In a democratic state the individual must be preserved. It is from the free thinking of an individual that a democracy thrives. I guess I'm a counselor because of a caring for the individual and the things that his free spirit can contribute to mankind. I desire to see the individual function freely so that whatever he contributes to civilization will be a maximal contribution, an unrestricted contribution. Enlightened ideas that improve civilization come from men who are free enough to think and to create. I am a counselor because I think I can help men to be free. I am a counselor because I believe in democracy, and without the free-thinking individual who is master of himself there is no democracy. I feel that as a counselor I can help man to be free, and thus preserve democracy."

The other counselor, half a continent away, comments:

"I see my function as a counselor as providing a growth-producing and non-threatening environment for the client. I see my function as establishing a relationship in which I can communicate understanding and acceptance. I am committed to the idea that nothing is more important to the individual than self-understanding. I can imagine no more worthwhile goals than to help my client and myself to achieve self-understanding."

In the long run, however, despite the evidence and the empirical studies, the concepts that counselors may have of their self and their function, it is the concept that the client has that will determine the effectiveness of the counseling relationship. Here is the way a number of self-referred junior high school boys and girls feel about the counselor they have experienced:

"He's me . . . in some strange and mysterious way he's felt exactly the way I've felt about things."

"That's not complicated—he's simply someone to whom I can

talk easily and honestly. He's someone I don't have to put on a front with."

"He's someone who *really* cares about me and what happens to me."

"He's a person who has the time to help me in dealing with my parents."

"He's not easily shocked—no matter what I tell him."

"I suppose—well—he's someone I can trust. He isn't always judging me—he's letting me judge myself."

"He's someone to whom I can turn when things pile up . . . someone who helps me deal with this business of living."

"He's someone who doesn't get mad when I tell him about my foolish plans for the future."

"He's someone who doesn't get bugged when he hears about kids and what they're like."

"He's someone who makes school tolerable . . . if I couldn't get together with him I'd have quit school a long time ago."

"I'm making my own decisions for the first time . . . whatever he did helped me to do this."

Not all student clients, however, see the school counselor in such a positive light. Here are a few comments from students who have experienced counseling:

"I wouldn't go to the counselor because he is so dense."

"Counselors have no wisdom. . . ."

"He is just like my father. . . ."

"He stands up for the teachers and protects them. . . ."

"Counselors tell the teachers what we say. . . ."

"They just sit around and get paid for nothing. . . ."

"I don't want to bother him . . . he probably has problems of his own. . . ."

In a way, then, what much of this seems to say is that the counselor is a free man in a society that may or may not be free. As a free person, he is the one who determines his fate as a responsible citizen; as a counselor, he is the one who helps the other to become; he is the one through whom the other may get the first faint sense of freedom, and thus move, in his own way, toward freedom. He has moved well along the road in his own struggle for self-actualization; he is honest; he is easy. In the school he helps the child to be what he can be, so that he can never be chained, so that his total self can never be lost, so that the freedom of his person is never dependent on the whims and the vagaries of the society that surrounds him.

THE JOB OF THE COUNSELOR

In the past few years more attention has been paid to the question of the job and the education of the counselor than in several decades preceding. Three of the major reasons for this attention are the publication in 1962 of Wrenn's book, *The Counselor in a Changing World;* the passage of the National Defense Education Act in 1958, and its continued extension; and the work on the various policy statements on the functions and education of the counselor, accepted at the annual convention in March, 1964, by the American Personnel and Guidance Association, the American School Counselors Association, and the Association for Counselor Education and Supervision.

The stress in the NDEA Counseling and Guidance Institutes has moved steadily from the short-term summer session institutes to the full-year institutes, including several at the post-master's level. Thus the number of short-term summer institutes was 34 in 1965, as compared with 83 in 1960. The number of full-year institutes was 24 in 1965–1966, compared with 7 in 1959–1960. The fact that, for several years, each year 500 to 700 individuals have been receiving an academic year of full-time counselor education, at the master's and the post-master's level, is obviously bound to have a major impact on both the concepts of the functions of the counselor and the education of the counselor. Prior to the passage of the NDEA, the great majority of school counselors were products of a part-time education, and it is probably safe to say, right now, that the majority of the current school counselors who have had at least one year of full-time graduate study are products of an NDEA Counseling and Guidance Institute. Few will question the benefit of a full-time graduate education, with minimal financial worries, as compared to a part-time education, with a maximum of financial and other concerns.

There is still, however, as will be noted, a discrepancy between what counselors do, and what is generally accepted as their more professional function. It should be noted, too, that while there is some professional disagreement on various questions about counselor function, there is a very high level of agreement on what the counselor should *not* consider to be his function.

Much of what some counselors are doing they do simply because their professional education, and their professional sense of responsibility, is at such a low level that they do not understand, and are not concerned about, what they should do. Thus they function in the general role of lackeys or sweep-up boys who do all of the odds and ends about which neither the administrators, the teachers nor the janitors wish to be concerned. Some of the blame for this sort of situation probably lies at the door of the state department of education and, more specifically, at the door of the supervisor or director of guidance for the state. It is up to the state not only to continue to increase their professional certification requirements, but, even more important, to enforce the requirements already on the books. I hear quite frequently, from fairly authentic sources, of individuals who are employed as counselors for the most unprofessional of reasons, in various states. State departments may have good reasons why they cannot immediately take action about such situations, but they could at least indicate their awareness of the situation, and in some way try to make it clear to school committees and other citizens that their children are being cheated by having, in a critical position, individuals who have no professional preparation for their jobs. The professional organizations, too, might share some of the blame for this situation, since they could frequently give more support to state departments by looking at the quality of the apples in their own barrels. If, in any state, the primary requirement for achieving a top educational job in the state department of education is that one be a professional politician, then we can assume that the quality of leadership in the field of guidance and counseling in that state is going to be feeble.

Then, too, there are still too many schools where principals and superintendents are still living in the past century, and are woefully inadequate in the provision of any leadership in the development of a modern school program, including the provision of counseling and other pupil personnel services. Some school administrators lack the courage to do anything other than attempt to maintain the status quo, and counseling services will find little support from them. It is reasonable to assume that the school should provide the educational leadership in any community; in some communities, if this is not forthcoming from the school, there is no other source. Lay leadership may sometimes retard education rather than improve it.

In such school systems there is little likelihood of the presence of a professional school counselor, and if one does happen to be in such a system, he will obviously work under serious handicaps. Nevertheless, changes are possible, as long as the counselor is discrete, and not too much the bull in the china shop—and, of course, as long as he does not allow the system to wear him down and gradually erode his professional integrity. I have seen effective counselors doing a splendid job in a miserable school.

That some counselors perform nonprofessional tasks is not always, however, due to ignorance, feeble state departments, or inadequate school administrators. Some such counselors have had a fair degree of professional preparation. Probably every counselor-educator knows of former students who have gone through his program and have, for some reason, apparently got nothing from the program, who operate now as if they had never had any professional preparation whatsoever. The fault here lies on the doorstep of the counselor preparation institution, which might of course have good reasons for saying that it cannot, after all, guarantee the professional competence of all of its graduates. Nevertheless, every time a graduate of a counselor education program shows on the job that he is functioning in an unprofessional manner, the institution must look at its program, and at its admissions policies, and feel that somehow, somewhere, it has not done the job that it should be doing.

Such counselors, then, whether they perform their questionable acts because of ignorance or because of their own weaknesses, are a menace to the profession of guidance and counseling, and there is still an unfortunately large number of such individuals in schools and colleges. Without protest, they do all sorts of things, such as functioning as a policeman (check the corridors, check the lunch room, check the detention hall); or a disciplinarian (actually punish children for fancied or real misdemeanors, report deviate behavior to the principal); or a prosecuting attorney (try to get a child to admit that he has committed some offense, or get him into a verbal trap); or a spy (try to get information from various sources, which is reported faithfully to the principal); or a bigot (give all of his attention to the "better" children in the community, but none to those whose parents do not count for much). They also, in the supposed guise of counseling, give a display of their own ignorance—or more likely, their own neurotic needs—when, supposedly for the good of the child but almost certainly for their own ego satisfaction, they criticize children, they talk endlessly to them about how they should live their lives and what their behavior should be; they scold and they moralize; they talk and they talk and they talk; and they never listen, and they never understand, since they can hear nothing because of the noise of their own voices.

This, however, is the dismal side of the picture. Although one such person among the ranks of counselors can be considered as one too many, every counselor must be careful to distinguish the counselor whose job concept is an unprofessional one from the counselor whose job concept is different but by no means unprofessional. Probably the basic professional argument centers around the question of the extent to which the "counselor" is a guidance *counselor* with the stress on the emotions and feelings; with emphasis on helping the irrational individual get to the point where he can use information rather than providing him with information; with stress on the counselor's working a good deal with a minority of the children, but also working a good deal with all of the teachers so that his preventive function is put into effect in his work with teachers, and his work with children is primarily remedial.

There is also what might be called a sub-debate among counselors on the extent to which counseling is psychotherapy, and hence the extent to which the counselor should think of himself as requiring professional preparation so that he can function as a psychotherapist with most disturbed individuals who are not in need of institutionalization. Some counselors would feel that the distinction between those clients who may be referred to a psychiatrist and those who should not is a rather meaningless one, since what is really meant when one refers to psychiatry is psychotherapy; and the term psychiatrist is not a job description, but rather the name of a particular kind of psychotherapist who has had a particular kind of training which probably makes him more effective with some disturbed people, less effective than other kinds of psychotherapists with other kinds of disturbed people. These individuals would feel that the professional counselor should think of his ultimate training as fitting him to work effectively with most noninstitutionalized individuals. When a client is sent to an institution, it is not so much that he needs the services of a psychiatrist, as that he needs the services of a number of specialized workers—psychiatrists, psychologists, counselors, nurses, and others—and that he can get these total combined services only in an institution. Recent evidence shows, however, that even more important than certain services is the complete and unequivocal acceptance of the individual by all staff members in the institution. The evidence also tends to indicate that one of the reasons why some individuals must spend their years in an institution is that they are not accepted by the staff as worthy individuals; rather, they are looked upon as the schizoid, or the manic depressive, or some other name of a disturbance, but not as a person. Even the rational and secure individual does not respond well when, in going to a medical doctor for the treatment of some physical ailment, he is looked upon as a "case." The disturbed individual is much less capable of reacting in a positive manner when he is looked upon as a problem.

It is interesting to compare some of the more recent "should be" concepts about job function with those of only a few years ago. Tooker, for example, in 1957, listed the following job functions of the counselor: [41]

1. First of all, he is an educator. . . .
2. He has direct responsibility for individual counseling of students assigned to him. . . .
3. He often has responsibility for group methods in guidance. . . .
4. He is expected to establish relationships with great numbers of individuals, so that students will come to identify him as a person to whom they can turn for advice and help within the school setting. . . .
5. He is expected to be familiar enough with standardized tests of intelligence, achievement, aptitude, interest and personality so that he can utilize test results in the process of counseling. . . .
6. He is often given considerable responsibility in arranging transfers of students for both academic and personal reasons. . . .
7. He is called upon to help in such important projects as building and maintaining cumulative record systems. . . .
8. He is often expected to conduct follow-up studies of graduates and drop-outs. . . .
9. It is not unusual for him to be asked to function as a resource person in such educational projects as the setting up of systems of reporting to parents. . . .
10. He is usually expected to know current college admission procedures and to serve as adviser to both parents and students in this area.
11. He is expected to participate in school activities and to assume his share of extracurricular activities. . . .
12. He is expected to maintain a knowledge of and working relationships with local business and industry so that he may be in a better position to counsel students in the area of local vocational offerings. . . .
13. He is often expected to help in the sponsoring of guidance-related activities such as college nights, career days, and guidance committees. . . .
14. He is frequently called upon to provide leadership in broad areas where guidance aspects may seem remote. . . .

There is more than a subtle difference in the 1964 policy statement accepted by the American School Counselors Association at its

[41] Ellis D. Tooker, "Counselor Role: Counselor Training," *Personnel and Guidance Journal* 36:263–267 (December, 1957).

annual convention. It stresses the fact that the majority of the school counselor's time must be devoted to individual or small-group counseling, and describes his major professional responsibilities as the following:

1. Assist each pupil to meet the need to understand himself in relation to the social and psychological world in which he lives. This implies helping each pupil to understand his aptitudes, interests, attitudes, abilities, opportunities for self-fulfillment, and the interrelationships among these.
2. Assist each pupil to meet the need of accepting (defined as being able to behave consistent with) his aptitudes, interests, attitudes, abilities and opportunities for self-fulfillment.
3. Assist each pupil to meet the need to develop personal decision-making competency. Included is the responsibility of assuring that the pupil's opportunities for self-understanding and self-fulfillment are not restricted by the group consideration and processes inherent in schools.
4. Assist all members of the individual staff to understand the importance of the individual pupil and to provide information, material and consultative assistance aimed at supporting their efforts to understand pupils.
5. Determine the influence of the school program on pupil educational and psycho-social development, and to convey such information to other staff members.
6. Inform other staff members of significant changes in the school and nonschool environments which have implications for instruction, the psycho-social well-being of pupils, and to participate in related program development.
7. Assist parents to understand the developmental progress of their child, his needs, and environmental opportunities, for purposes of increasing their ability to contribute to their child's development.
8. Interpret to the community the importance of consideration for the individual and the contribution of the school counseling program to that end.
9. Promote in the community nonschool opportunities necessary for pupil development.
10. Use and/or promote community resources designed to meet unusual or extreme needs of pupils which are beyond the responsibilty of the school.

A decade ago, Pierson [42] commented that the school counselor was primarily an educator whose clients were students, parents and teachers. Mathewson,[43] too, felt that the counselor should spend less time

[42] George A. Pierson, "Aesop and the School Counselor," *Personnel and Guidance Journal* 32:326–329 (February, 1954).
[43] Robert H. Mathewson, "The General Guidance Counselor," *Personnel and Guidance Journal* 32:544–547 (May, 1954).

with poorly adjusted students and more time with teachers and parents.

The report accepted by the American Personnel and Guidance Association at its annual convention in 1964 described the role of counselors as follows:

1. The major responsibility of the counselor is to assist an individual through the counseling relationship to utilize his own resources and his environmental opportunities in the process of self-understanding, planning, decision-making and coping with problems relative to his developmental needs and to his vocational and educational activities.

2. The counselor also engages in related activities. For example, he makes effective use of the services of other professional personnel through referrals and consultation. He works with other persons in his employment environment in a manner which facilitates the achievement of desirable objectives for the benefit of the counselee. He may perform additional services for which he has the necessary preparation and the nature of which is such that they are logically his professional responsibility within the setting in which he works. However, he should not be expected to perform tasks which are inconsistent with his professional role as a counselor, or which are inappropriate for the social institution for which he works.

3. In all of his professional activities, the counselor maintains a high level of ethical practice in accordance with the Code of Ethics of the American Personnel and Guidance Association.

4. The counselor expects that in the employment setting in which he works conditions will be maintained which will enable him to work in a professional manner. These conditions include freedom to exercise his skills on a professional level, time to perform the counseling function, and adequate facilities.

In 1957, Wrenn felt that any discussion of counselor role should be based on the following assumptions: [44]

1. The school counselor is an educator with special professional training at the M.A. level and beyond.

2. The school counselor is a generalist in a number of school functions and may be a specialist in at least one type of service. The nature of this specialization may vary with each counselor's unique personal qualification and with the specific emphasis on his professional education.

3. The school counselor's clients include teachers, parents, and administrators as well as students.

4. The school counselor's skills should include not only those necessary

[44] C. Gilbert Wrenn, "Status and Role of the School Counselor," *Personnel and Guidance Journal* 36:175–183 (November, 1957).

for the individual counseling relationship but those essential to working effectively with groups.

5. The school counselor is concerned primarily with the normal growth needs of students, more with personality development than with problem crises.

6. The school counselor, because of the expectations of student, teacher, administrator, must have a fairly high level of psychological sophistication in his professional education and in-service development. . . .

Five years later, one of his four recommendations dealing with the counselor was as follows: [45]

> That the professional job description of a counselor specify that he perform four major functions: (a) counsel with students; (b) consult with teachers, administrators, and parents as they in turn deal with students; (c) study the changing facts about the student population and interpret what is found to school committees and administrators; (d) coordinate counseling resources in school and between school and community. From two-thirds to three-fourths of the counselor's time, in either elementary or high school, should be committed to the first two of these functions. Activities that do not fall into one of these four areas neither should be expected nor encouraged as part of the counselor's regular working schedule.

It may be noted, in these later statements, that the counselor is considered to be neither an "educator" nor a "teacher." He has his own particular professional function, counseling, which he performs in an educational environment, usually a school, and he is thus known as a school counselor. It may also be noted that while he may work with "most" children, he also works with children who may have problems, primarily of a developmental nature. It is at last being recommended by the major state and national professional organizations that the counselor's major function be recognized as counseling!

Even today, however, there are probably still thousands of school counselors whose actual functions clash sharply with those which are recommended as professional responsibilities. In a study conducted almost forty years ago, Edgerton [46] found that counselors felt that their functions consisted of (a) interviewing students; (b) teaching classes in occupations; (c) finding jobs for students and following them up; (d) administering tests; (e) doing research in the study of occupations.

[45] C. Gilbert Wrenn, *The Counselor in a Changing World* (Washington, D.C.: American Personnel and Guidance Association, 1962), p. 137.

[46] A. H. Edgerton, *Vocational Guidance and Counseling* (New York: The Macmillan Co., 1926).

At that time, as would be expected, the counselor's concept of his role was almost entirely vocational. Some years later, Cox [47] undertook an investigation of a group of counselors in secondary schools throughout the country. She found that their functions, in order of frequency, were: (1) work with parents; (2) educational-vocational-emotional guidance of pupils; (3) supervision of tests, both giving tests and interpreting test results; (4) cooperation with law enforcement agencies; (5) consultation with employers; (6) discipline; (7) placement; (8) coordinating the guidance program of the school; (9) home-room supervision; (10) cooperation with community guidance agencies; (11) teaching; (12) chaperoning parties and social needs; (13) follow-up of pupils who had left school.

This study tended to point up the increasing and conflicting functions that were supposedly performed by the counselor. About the same time, Wright,[48] in a report of an analysis by Minneapolis counselors of their function, indicated that the secondary school counselors felt that their job consisted of (1) checking credits for graduation and college entrance; (2) advising those students entering and those in military service; (3) interviewing and counseling failing students; (4) handling employment; (5) arranging group conferences; (6) writing letters of reference for pupils who were in school or who had left school; (7) conferring with students planning to withdraw from school; (8) doing clerical work; (9) conferring with teachers about pupils' problems.

Another study of high schools in the state of Washington indicated that counselors were expected to orient eighth graders; provide occupational information about colleges; provide a testing program for the four years, and assume the responsibility for recording the data; provide for social development; make adequate provision for exceptional students; arrange adequate occupational placement; do follow-up studies; evaluate the program for future improvement; and organize their time so as to be able to do individual counseling.[49]

The concept that the children themselves have of the counselor's function depends, of course, more than anything else on the individual counselor they may have, or have had. When children talk about the counselor's function, they have very frequently had little or no orienta-

[47] Rachel D. Cox, *Counselors and Their Work* (Harrisburg: Archives Press, 1945).
[48] Barbara H. Wright, "Minneapolis School Counselors Analyze Their Jobs," *Occupations* 24:214–219 (January, 1946).
[49] Werner C. Dieckmann, "What Kind of Guidance and Counseling Programs in the Small School," *The Bulletin of the National Association of Secondary School Principals* 37:233–235 (November, 1952).

tion, by either the counselor or any other school administrator, as to just who the counselor is and what he is supposed to do. A study by Grant,[50] for example, showed that in a number of schools in the state of New York, while 56 percent of the counselors felt that they should handle personal-emotional counseling, only 27 percent of the administrators, 33 percent of the teachers, and 4 percent of the students thought that they should work in this area. On the other hand, there was fairly high agreement in the area of vocational counseling, where 80 percent of the counselors, 80 percent of the administrators, 70 percent of the teachers and 50 percent of the students considered this to be the counselor's function; and in the area of educational counseling, where 88 percent of the counselors, 67 percent of the administrators, 76 percent of the teachers, and 62 percent of the students agreed on this as the counselor's job. While one might agree that no one of these groups seemed altogether sure of the counselor's function, it is noticeable that the students who are to experience the counseling are ones who feel that the counselor should be the least involved in the three areas that are surely part of his job.

In a study of the attitudes of a sampling of 8,000 high school students in Phoenix Union High Schools, however, counselors fared somewhat better in the minds of the students.[51] In general, the feeling of the students was positive toward the help they had received from counselors in all counseling-objective-problem areas. The students preferred counselors over parents, teachers, deans, and friends of their own age when the problems were concerned with discovering and making progress toward realistically chosen goals related both to school and to after-school activities. In other problem areas, parents and counselors were about equally favored by students. Both were preferred to teachers, deans, or friends of their own age. Even with problems related to making progress in school, counselors ranked higher than teachers. In all of the six problem areas described, deans received a lower number of votes than did any of the other adult groups—parents, teachers or counselors. It would thus seem that students steer away from those whom they regard as having a disciplinary function.

When Hitchcock[52] sampled 1,282 counselors in 1,255 schools

[50] Claude W. Grant, "The Counselor's Role," *Personnel and Guidance Journal* 33:74–77 (October, 1954).
[51] Ralph E. Jenson, "Student Feelings About Counseling Help," *Personnel and Guidance Journal* 33:498–503 (May, 1955).
[52] Wiliam L. Hitchcock, "Councilors Feel They Should," *Personnel and Guidance Journal* 32:72–74 (October, 1953).

throughout the United States, some of his findings were quite astonishing. For example:

> Of the counselors who were assisting pupils failing in their school work, 41 percent did not feel that this was their job.

> Of the counselors who were assisting pupils with their course planning, 40 percent did not feel that this was their job.

> Of the counselors who were assisting pupils with their occupational plans, 40 percent did not feel that this was their job.

> Of the counselors who assisted teachers with pupils' problems, 37 percent did not feel that this was their job.

> Of the counselors who interpreted test results to teachers, 33 percent did not feel that this was their job.

> Of the counselors who referred cases to other counselors, 33 percent did not feel that this was their job.

> Of the counselors who sat in on case conferences with other counselors, 29 percent did not feel that this was their job.

> Of the counselors who served on curriculum planning committees, 29 percent did not feel that this was their job.

> Of the counselors who were counseling parents of failing pupils, 34 percent did not feel that this was their job.

A few years later, when Warren [53] questioned 440 guidance directors and counselors in Massachusetts, he had a return of 203 questionnaires. He learned that the tasks that were considered as major job functions by the greatest number of respondants were academic counseling (62 percent of the directors, 69 percent of the counselors); testing (63 percent of the directors, 50 percent of the counselors); vocational counseling (49 percent of the directors, 39 percent of the counselors); personal-emotional counseling (31 percent of the directors, 17 percent of the counselors); and parental conferences (21 percent of the directors, 22 percent of the counselors). On the other hand, 31 percent of the directors, but only 14 percent of the counselors felt that placement was a major function; 23 percent of the directors, but only 2 percent of the counselors named administration as a major function; 24 percent of the counselors, but only 14 percent of the directors agreed on maintaining educational and occupational information as a major function; and 25 percent of the counselors, but only 4 percent of the directors on up-keep of records.

[53] Richard A. Warren, *A Study to Determine the Functions of Guidance Directors and Counselors at the Secondary Level in Massachusetts Public Schools* (master's thesis, Boston University, 1958).

In the Warren study a discrepancy was revealed between what the directors and counselors were doing and what they felt they should be doing. Only 26 percent of the directors were doing what they felt they should be doing, whereas 47 percent of the counselors were doing what they felt they should be doing. The five functions considered to be most necessary by the directors were, in order of preference: academic counseling (55 percent); testing (50 percent); vocational counseling (48 percent); placement (32 percent); and personal-emotional counseling (31 percent). The five considered to be most necessary by the counselors, in order of preference, were: academic counseling (60 percent); testing (52 percent); personal-emotional counseling (45 percent); vocational counseling (40 percent); and interviews with parents (24 percent). The major reasons given by the directors for this discrepancy were lack of time, lack of assistance, and too much clerical work; the major reasons given by the counselors were lack of time, too much clerical work, and teaching.

Shertzer and Stone [54] have stressed the importance of counselors' articulating their own identity, and of communicating their role to the public. Boy and Pine have indicated the functions that are outside the role of the school counselor. Their list of "does nots" is as follows: [55]

1. He does not have administrative duties such as, for example, providing parents with academic reports, issuing failure reports to parents, arranging for bus transportation. . . .
2. He does not have instructional, tutorial, proctorial, or supervisory duties. . . .
3. He does not discipline students.
4. He has no clerical tasks which prevent him from devoting his full effort to professional activities. . . .
5. He has nothing to do with the scheduling of classes or the arrangement of academic programs.
6. He does not check attendance or serve as a truant officer.

There have been, then, and there still are, conflicting concepts of functions, particularly at the operational level in the school.[56] Nor, of course, is this surprising. In many states, the state department of education apparently equates professionalism in terms of several semes-

54 Bruce Shertzer and Shelley C. Stone, "The School Counselor and His Publics: A Problem in Role Definition," *Personnel and Guidance Journal* 41:687–692 (April, 1963).
55 Boy and Pine, *op. cit.*, pp. 72–73.
56 See Dugald S. Arbuckle, "The Conflicting Functions of the School Counselor," *Counselor Education and Supervision* 1:54–59 (Winter, 1961).

ter hours of doubtful study in questionable institutions from instructors whose lack of understanding is clearly surpassed by their courage in teaching something about which they know nothing. Many state departments of education appear to believe that the counselor is really a teacher, and that certification carries with it the requirement of teaching experience—the assumption is that teaching experience somehow makes one a better school counselor. This is a highly debatable assumption, and evidence tends at least to point to the possibility that teaching gives one so many bad counseling habits that a major function of counselor education is to help former teachers to unlearn most of what they learned as teachers! No one will argue with the statement that the counselor should be aware of the day-to-day problems of teachers, and should be understanding of them; that he should understand the working of the school and its relations with parents and with the community; that he should be able to work with teachers, administrators and other professional workers in the school; that he should be able to work effectively with children. The question is: does several years of unsupervised teaching give any evidence of the competence of the individual in these areas? Would not an educational program of counselor education that would include carefully supervised experiences in these areas be a more valid measure of the effectiveness of the potential school counselor? This latter statement assumes, of course, that teaching and counseling are different functions.

In the long run, the professional competence of any worker is not determined at a political level, but by the professional workers in the particular professional discipline. We can hardly talk about the professional school counselor as long as we have fifty state versions of who he is, the only level of agreement being the generally low status of the counselor. At the same time hundreds of universities and colleges are all shouting their versions of counselor education, and it is truly phenomenal how so many institutions, with the advent of NDEA, suddenly discovered that they had counselor education programs. Actually, how many institutions, with the staff and facilities they now have, can be described as having a first rate counselor education program—ten, twenty, or the several hundreds who indicate to the U.S. Office of Education that they have a counselor education program? The American Personnel and Guidance Association is quite cognizant of this problem and at long last has started a massive project in the direction of determining just what constitutes an acceptable counselor education program. This may hurt some places and some people, but as long as the school counselor can be considered to be adequately educated by having picked up a few part-time courses from any one of hundreds of colleges and universities, then it is surely ludicrous to talk in terms of the professional status and the professional competence of the school counselor.

The professional stamp of approval must be on counselor education programs just as it is on counselors. This approval of counselors should come from the institution rather than from the state department of education or, rather, the approval of the state department should come through the institution. Once a counselor education program has been approved by the professional organization as first rate, a graduate of that program should meet state certification requirements anywhere in the country. There should be no need to have state department detectives checking to see if he has had this course, this course and this course—never, of course, asking where and from whom he took the courses! This also means that institutions will have to be named, identified, and periodically checked to determine the calibre of their programs. One does not become a medical doctor, a dentist, a lawyer, or an architect by attending a few classes at almost any institution in the United States. There are certain institutions that have professionally acceptable medical schools and law schools and schools of engineering, and so there must soon be certain institutions which will be identified as having professionally acceptable programs of counselor education. The American Personnel and Guidance Association, with its representatives of those who are school counselors, those who educate school counselors, and those who are involved at the state department level, is now actively involved in this task.

Once the school counselor becomes a graduate of one of the relatively few professionally acceptable counselor education programs, then we may see a rapid reduction in both the "part-timeness" of his education and the "part-timeness" of his function. There may even, for a time, be a reduction in the number of people who are entitled to the name "school counselor." This is not all bad, since the major problem in school counseling today is not lack of quantity, but lack of quality. Ideally we must try to increase the number of qualified school counselors, but it is better to have fewer qualified counselors than to have more unqualified counselors, and thus live under the illusion that numbers of bodies will satisfy our problem. This illusion appears to be somewhat acceptable in the field of education.

It would seem reasonable to say that there are three major professional groups in the modern American school—the teachers, the administrators and the specialized service personnel. It is interesting to note that of all these groups, it is only the school counselor who is willing to accept the part-time, dual-role status. Other professional workers may spend only part of their time in the service of the school, but they are not part-time doctors, or part-time nurses, or part-time psychologists, or part-time psychiatrists. They are medical doctors, or nurses, or psychologists, or psychiatrists. Like pregnancy, "they are or they ain't," and there is no in-between status. We have no doctor-teacher, or nurse-principal, or psychologist-janitor, but we have thousands of teacher-counselors, or even more absurd, principal-counselors, and even, horror added upon horror, superintendent-counselors. Even worse, this schizophrenic fellow doesn't seem to mind this dual or triple status, and goes blithely walking off in several directions at the same time, quite unaware that one set of feet is falling over the other.

There are many tasks that must be carried out to continue the necessary functions of the school, and while all of these tasks may be defended as being needed to achieve the broad and immediate goals of the school, they are tasks that cannot be done by one person's even assuming that he had the time. This is so because of his inadequate knowledge and education, because of his lack of skills, because of his personality structure, and because certain functions clash with other functions. Thus, a perfectly good mathematics teacher might be a very poor English teacher because he doesn't know English, and isn't interested in it; a perfectly good English teacher may be a poor physical education teacher because he lacks the physical coordination necessary for this task; a principal may be effective because he is the sort of person who likes organizing and administering and directing and controlling. All of these people *may* become good school counselors if they have, or if they develop, an understanding of people and human behavior, if they are deeply but not too neurotically interested in working with individuals as individuals, and if they master the knowledges and the skills that are part of the repertoire of the school counselor. They *may*, it should be noted, become effective school counselors, but they cannot do so while they still retain their previous occupational functions, since effectiveness as a teacher or a principal may often be equated with ineffectiveness as a counselor. The particular problems of the teacher as a counselor will be covered in more detail in a later chapter.

Chapter Four

THE COUNSELOR: EDUCATION AND PROFESSIONAL RELATIONSHIPS

It is reasonable to assume that the professional education of the counselor should be closely related to the professional functions of his position as a counselor. Much has happened in the past few years to clarify both the occupation of the counselor and the professional preparation for that occupation. Let us look now at his professional education.

THE EDUCATION OF THE COUNSELOR

As indicated in the previous chapter, three recent events have had a tremendous effect on the concepts regarding the most effective education of the school counselor—namely, the publication of the Wrenn report in 1962, the implementation of the National Defense Education Act of 1958, and the work that resulted in the acceptance of policy statements dealing with the functions and the education of the school counselors by three major national organizations in March, 1964. An article I wrote on this subject in 1958 [1] now seems totally out of date, and quoting what various authorities felt prior to this time now seems to have little, other than historical, significance.

The implementation of Title VB of the National Defense Edu-

[1] Dugald S. Arbuckle, "The Education of the School Counselor," *Journal of Counseling Psychology* 5:58–62 (Spring, 1958).

cation Act soon made it painfully clear that very few institutions had actually developed effective programs for counselor education. The number of institutions applying for contracts to conduct guidance and counseling institutes dropped off drastically when the U.S. Office of Education instituted a policy of requesting each institution that applied for a contract to present also an "Inventory of Institutional Resources." A perusal of these inventories made it clear that there were surprisingly few institutions that had more than one full-time staff member totally employed in the education of the school counselor. The answers to questionnaires sent out by the U.S. Office of Education [2] indicate an interesting institutional interpretation of the request for courses offering "specific preparation for guidance and student personnel." Some of the courses mentioned by various institutions were, for example, "Correctional Arithmetic," "Parent Counseling in Speech," "Research in Education," "Theories of Language," "Intercultural Relations," "Modern American Family," "Introduction to Social Work," "Labor Problems," "Contemporary Problems in Education," and so on. Practically every course that one could think of in the area of education, psychology, measurement, sociology and social service work was mentioned, and almost as many from almost every other area that might come under the heading of social sciences. Thus, institutionally, there was little agreement as to just what constituted the education of the counselor, although it is probably true that those institutions which might be regarded as the best known in the preparation of counselors had some similarity of experiences for their students.

It should be kept in mind, too, that an actual program for the professional education of the counselor is a rather new development, and the National Defense Education Act has been one of the major spurs in that development. The "counselor educator" is one of a new breed, and most of the oldsters involved in the education of counselors were not themselves educated for this purpose. As an increasing proportion of Title VB funds began to be diverted to academic year institutes, it became even more obvious that there simply were not many institutions in the country that could actually offer a full-year program at the master's level. Even fewer could offer a good program at the post-master's level. It should be noted, too, that decisions as to the worth of various plans of operation were not made by officials of

[2] *Preparation Programs and Course Offerings in School and College Personnel Work, 1959–60.* Washington: U.S. Department of Health, Education, and Welfare, Office of Education.

the U.S. Office, but rather by counselor educators who were brought in as consultants. They were the ones who determined that some of the programs presented by their colleagues were not worth very much, while others were top-drawer. Despite all the pros and cons, and with possibly some exceptions, as well as, possibly, the acceptance of some political involvement, the hard fact is that those institutions which received contracts for NDEA Counseling and Guidance Institutes had better programs in counselor education than institutions that did not receive contracts. As I write these words, I find it difficult to get up to the number forty when I try to count the institutions that would appear to provide excellent programs of counselor education.

The National Defense Education Act, Title VB, also spurred the American Personnel and Guidance Association to greater action in providing some indication of just what did constitute an effective program of counselor education. With the U.S. Office of Education, and the American people, ready to provide tens of millions of dollars for the more effective education of school counselors, it was rather embarrassing to discover that the professional organizations representing counselors and counselor educators apparently did not know just what constituted an effective program of counselor education. It is to their credit, however, that the officers and members of these organizations, despite their red faces, did press for action. And the acceptance of various policy statements at the March, 1964, annual convention did represent a real achievement. The three major organizations that were involved in these policy statements were the American Personnel and Guidance Association, the "parent" body, and two of its divisions, the American School Counselors Association and the Association for Counselor Education and Supervision. The basic parts of the American Personnel and Guidance Association policy statement, dealing with the education of the school counselor, are presented in Appendix 1. Those of the Association for Counselor Education and Supervision may be found in Appendix 2, and those of the American School Counselors Association are listed in Appendix 3.

In many ways, these policy statements are elaborations of the seven basic recommendations regarding counselor education presented in the Wrenn report in 1962: [3]

> 1. That state certifying agencies for counselors and graduate faculties in counselor education specify that, in addition to essential pro-

[3] C. Gilbert Wrenn, *The Counselor in a Changing World* (Washington, D.C.: American Personnel and Guidance Association, 1962), p. 161.

fessional courses and experiences, two other major cores be required in the counselor education curriculum; one major core is in the field of psychology, another in the social and other behavioral sciences, the two combined to represent a minimum of from one-third to one-half of the course work required for certification.

2. That the minimal two-year graduate program in counselor education include: (a) two major cores in psychology and the social sciences as described in Recommendation 1; (b) adequate orientation in educational philosophy and school curriculum patterns; (c) applied or professional courses as described in the text to the extent of *not more* than one-fourth of the total graduate programs; (d) supervised experience in both counseling and planned group leadership to the extent of *not less* than one-fourth of the total graduate programs; (e) an introduction to the understanding and utilization of changing research concepts; (f) an introduction to the problems of ethical relationships and legal responsibilities in counseling.

3. That the graduate courses in counselor education be taught by faculty qualified in the respective areas involved, *i.e.*, psychology courses by psychologists; counseling theory and technique courses by faculty who are both qualified in psychology and experienced in counseling; social science courses by social scientists; occupational information, psychological measurement, and research courses by qualified scholars in the areas involved.

4. That supervised counseling experience be required in every pattern of counselor certification; that certification be granted only upon the satisfactory completion of this experience and the recommendation of the graduate faculty involved.

The policy statements also stressed the selection and endorsement of counselors. Appendix 4 contains the statements presented by the American Personnel and Guidance Association, and by the Association for Counselor Education and Supervision.

Thus we now have a rather exhaustive indication of how the counselor should be educated, but the actual process of that education is complicated and difficult.[4] One of the human problems that arises is caused by the fact that the counselor educator often sees himself, as well he should, as primarily a counselor. He is, in effect, a counselor who has become a teacher, and he is well aware, with all other teachers, counselors, psychologists, and therapists, of the oft-reported statement that "learning is a process by which behavior is modified." Too frequently, it would seem, we place much stress on the *product* (which is

[4] See Dugald S. Arbuckle, "The Learning of Counseling: .Process, not Product," *Journal of Counseling Psychology* 10:163–168 (Summer, 1963).

not learning), and little stress on the *process* (which is learning). The teacher is traditionally one who is primarily involved with ideas and product, whereas the counselor is primarily involved with people and change and process. This may be why less understanding about learning seems to have come out of centuries of formal education than has come from a relatively few years of the practice of psychotherapy.

If you ask a teacher what he does, a fairly typical immediate reply will be, "I teach algebra." He is, in other words, at worst a teacher of algebra, and at best, a student of algebra, but very rarely would he feel that he is one who is involved in a learning process with another human, using algebra as a tool. It might be fair to say that the learning that occurs as a result of the algebra teacher's efforts is incidental and, generally, unknown. What is usually measured and considered as "learning" is the student's retention of algebraic knowledge. The teacher has as the end product in mind the understanding of algebra, and it is this that is important.

This may also be a logical reason why one can take a course in psychology of learning, get an "A," supposedly "learn" about the psychology of learning, and yet, actually *learn* nothing, in that he continues to do all the things that he "learned" he shouldn't do! There has been an increase in knowledge about change, but no change.

If you ask a counselor what he does, his reply will very likely at least include something to the effect, "I help a person to. . . ." He is concerned with helping *people,* and this, in turn, would appear to put him closer to process than the teacher. Most often, he has only a general idea about the product, since what happens as a result of the learning process in counseling depends on the client more than it does on the counselor.

The counselor may be the expert in the sense that he helps the client to become involved in a unique relationship with another human being, but it is the client who must determine where *he* wants to go and what *he* wants to do. Thus the client may be helped to come to feel that authority is not so threatening after all, but he must determine whether he wants to work under the same boss, seeing him in a different way, or change jobs, so that he works under a possibly different kind of authority.

The client may be helped to accept her hatred of her mother, and she may also need help to determine what she is going to do with this new "I have hated my mother" self rather than the old "I have always loved my mother" person. The counselor is the process expert, and although he helps in the determination, he is not the determiner of the product. Very often both he and the client are unaware of what the ultimate product might be.

It may also be noted that the counselor very often has to help the client in an unlearning process, or at least help him to do something about some of his "learnings" that are now causing him much stress and pain. It is very rarely that these learnings are part of his formal school curricular experience—except, of course, in those situations where the individual is being pressed to retain more knowledge than he is capable of retaining. It may be, too, that he is pressed to retain knowledge in which he has no interest and about which he has no concern. In most cases, however, the learnings that have caused trouble are those he has experienced in a variety of situations that are incidental in that they are not what the individual was supposed to learn. A child's learning from a teacher may be a hatred of authority or an excitement about discovery; a girl may learn from her mother to enjoy the company of boys or she may learn to fear them; from his church a child may learn an appreciation of different ways of living, or he may learn fear of death. There may be a relationship between the degree of negative learning and the extent to which the "other person" (the teacher, the counselor, the clergyman, the parent) is concerned with content and product rather than with person and process.

The astounding acceleration in man's increase in knowledge has not been accompanied by an equal increase of his ability to use this knowledge for the benefit of himself and his neighbors. As the gap increases, the possibility of man's destruction of himself would also seem to increase. With some notable exceptions throughout the centuries, formal education has, on the whole, paid much more attention to *what* is being "learned" than to *who* is involved in the "learning," with the possible result that educators know more about the content to be assimilated and retained than they do about the actual process of learning, and the actual outcomes and changes that occur as a result of this learning.

It is interesting to note that much that would seem to me, at least, to be very pertinent in this question of learning comes from sources other than education or psychology. For example, we may note Eliot commenting, in answer to the question, "To what does it lead, when you help a boy?": [5]

> To finding out
> What you really are. What you really feel.
> What you really are among other people.

[5] T. S. Eliot, *The Cocktail Party*, Act 1, Scene i.

Gibran's Prophet, speaking about teaching, says: [6]

> No man can reveal to you aught but that which already lies asleep in
> the dawning of your own knowledge. . . .
> . . . For the wisdom of one man lends not its wings to another
> man. . . .

Cicero also had some feelings on this question when he said, "The
authority of the teacher is generally prejudicial to those who desire
to learn." [7]

Somerset Maugham, on being asked what advice he gave young
people, said: [8]

> Really, you know, there's only one thing to do, and that's follow your
> own nose and make your own mistakes. By following one's nose one
> can't go too far astray.

Pasternak was speaking about learning when he said: [9]

> When I hear people speak of reshaping life it makes me lose my self
> control and I fall into despair. Reshaping life!

> People who can say that have never understood a thing about life—
> they have never felt its breath, its heartbeat, however much they may
> have seen or done. They look on it as a lump of raw material that
> needs to be processed by them, to be ennobled by their touch. But life
> is never a material, a substance to be molded. . . . Life is constantly
> renewing and remaking and changing and transfiguring itself. . . .

It may be that the educator has become so involved in teaching
something, that he has lost sight of the *somebody* who is learning. The
poet and the author may be able to talk about learning because they
are sensitive to people, but they do not have to become actually involved in a learning relationship with another human being.

The counselor possibly does well, in a "learning" sense, when he
is involved in a therapeutic relationship with a client, but what

[6] Reprinted from *The Prophet*, by Kahlil Gibran, with the permission of the pub-
lisher, Alfred A. Knopf, Inc. Copyright 1923 by Kahlil Gibran: renewal copyright
1951 by Administrators C.T.A. of Kahlil Gibran Estate, and Mary G. Gibran.
[7] Cicero, *De Fisibus* 11,1, quoted by Montaigne in *Essays*, Chapter 26, Vol. 1, Emil
Julius Trechmann, Trans. "Of the Education of Boys," letter addressed to Diane
de Faix, Comtesse de Gurson (Oxford: Oxford University Press, 1935).
[8] Joel Lieber, "Somerset Maugham Talks About Life," *This Week Magazine* (January, 1961).
[9] Quoted by H. Salisbury in "The Triumph of Boris Pasternak," *Saturday Review*
(November 8, 1958), p. 22.

happens when the counselor becomes a "teacher" of student counselors? What happens to what he has learned about learning when he becomes involved in a counseling practicum with student counselors? How does one criticize a student counselor in a "positive" way so that his learning will be positive? Should the human involvement of the counselor with a student counselor be any different than it would be with a client? Is hostility from a student counselor different from hostility from a client? Is fearfulness? Is a feeling of personal inadequacy? Is rigidity? It is difficult for me to see how we can say that we will react to expressions of feeling in one way when we are with a client, but in a different way when we are with a student counselor.

Here, for example, is an excerpt from a tape of a tape-critique between a counselor and a group of student counselors in a counseling practicum:

> C: If I criticized you on tape, Mary, would you feel mad at me. . . .
>
> Mary: (emphatically) No, Sir! (long pause)
>
> C: Uh-hu . . . how would you . . . uh . . . feel. . . .
>
> Mary: This is an opportunity to see (pause) . . . where I was not coming up stan (pause) . . . standard (voice shaky).
>
> C: Uh-hu . . . this was one thing more. . . .
>
> Mary: Because you're (pause) . . . you're (pause). . . .
>
> Don: I have the feeling of being supportive. . . .
>
> Mary: Huh . . . ?
>
> Don: I think, Mary, that what you're saying (word unintelligible).
>
> C: Uh . . . Don . . . is that what Mary is saying, or is it. . . .
>
> Don: (Interrupting) Well, it's what I'm saying. I'm being supportive. This is what I felt about it.
>
> Mary: Your feeling?
>
> Don: Well, I'm not sure this is true. . . . I'm asking for clarification in a way.
>
> C: You sort of feel, Don, that I'm pushing Mary too much. . . .
>
> Don: Ah . . . probably . . . in part. . . .
>
> C: Uh . . . hu. . . .
>
> Don: You didn't do this with the rest of us . . . and I'm

feeling right at this point that I need to support you, Mary. This is why I said that.

Mary: (Loud laugh).

Sarah: (Quite strongly). She didn't need your support.

Don: I felt that she needed it.

Sarah: (Even stronger). She didn't need your support.

Don: So I negated her, but (laughs) . . . this has been obvious to me. Maybe I've been the only one.

Mary: (Unintelligible) . . . that I might withdraw into a shell.

Don: That this could be real threatening to you. I don't know whether you'd withdraw or not.

Ann: Certainly Mary could tell us how she feels herself, you know. . . .

Mary: I haven't thought it out . . . (softly) . . . unintelligible). . . . I took this as a learning situation.

This is rather typical of the sort of situation that I may find myself in as an "instructor" in a counseling practicum, and I would imagine that this is true of most counselors who are also involved in the education of counselors. I would imagine, too, that most counselor educators would share my concern as to whether we have really changed anything other than our name when we moved from being counselor trainers to become counselor educators!

I have been greatly impressed over the years by the extreme reluctance and almost inability of graduate students to overcome years of disciplining in the matter of satisfying the instructor, and to arrive at a point where there is a high level of honesty in their expressions both about the instructor and his ideas and about themselves and their ideas. Even when formal evaluation is removed from a course, and the students know that their grades depend solely on what they want to give themselves, they find it difficult to believe that they are working to satisfy only themselves, not the instructor. The extent to which this is so varies greatly with different student counselors, of course, and Kemp describes the situation well when he says: [10]

> The more closed-minded, the greater the possibility that the counselor-in-training will stimulate change in accordance with the expectancies of the situation. This change is likely to be phenotypical, "party-line" change rather than integrated concepts and new directions for action.

[10] C. G. Kemp, "Influence of Dogmatism on the Training of Counselors," *Journal of Counseling Psychology* 9:155–157 (Summer, 1962).

As I try to identify some of the thoughts and feelings about the problems of the counselor as an "instructor," three points seem to stand out: [11]

Even a modestly insightful counselor must surely very soon come to question the apparent contradictions between his behavior toward that fellow human being known as a client and his behavior toward the other person known as a student counselor. Research would tend to indicate, and most counselors, overtly, at least, would appear to agree, that client growth and movement is facilitated when the counselor indicates self-congruence, genuineness and honesty; when he feels an unconditional positive regard toward the client; when he is capable of establishing a high level of empathic understanding. Here, it would seem, the counselor as a supervisor finds his first quandary. Can he function as a counselor when he is a supervisor? Is he the same person when he is either a counselor or a supervisor? Must he, basically, being the same human being, be the same person, or can he be the same person, but function in a different way because of the different function and responsibility he may have? There is much debate on these questions.

The problem of self-congruence, honesty and genuineness should not prove to be too much of a problem, since this is something that is an entirely personal business, within the control of the counselor or supervisor, although the extent to which his idea of genuineness and honesty will be viewed as genuineness and honesty by another will, of course, vary. Nevertheless, I would think of this as a personal problem; this is my struggle, and the basic question is the degree to which I am honest with *me*. Whether others view honesty as I do is, on this particular issue, of secondary importance. Empathic understanding, however, is something else again, and the door that must be opened *is* opened by both student counselor and supervisor, not just by one of them. This, in turn, is obviously related to the extent to which the supervisor feels toward the student counselor a high level of positive regard, and, even more important, the extent to which the student feels that this is the way the supervisor feels toward him. It is at this point, I would think, that the supervisor begins to be somewhat entrapped in the world of illusion; it is real to him, but illusion to the other people.

The counselor can, with self-congruence, with honesty, and with genuineness, say to the client, "The extent to which I am a threat to

11 See Dugald S. Arbuckle, "Supervision: Learning, Not Counseling," *Journal of Counseling Psychology* (in a forthcoming issue).

you can be determined by you, because in no overt, action-taking manner do I see me posing a threat to you. I will not do anything to you that may be hurtful or damaging." Can any supervisor, with honesty, say the same to the student counselor?

Peters and Hansen [12] comment that "The practicum provides learning situations which can facilitate the optimal growth of the person by freeing his potentialities to be himself." Indeed it does, but unlike a counseling relationship, it has limitations, and these limitations sometimes do not appear to be recognized by some supervisors.

Patterson [13] would appear to be somewhat contradictory when he says, "Supervision, like counseling, must provide a non-threatening, accepting and understanding atmosphere," and then, on the same page, comments, "The supervisor does evaluate, must evaluate, and should evaluate." In attempting to combine these two impossibles, the supervisor may become even more enmeshed in his illusion. Patterson [14] correctly comments that the use of grades S and U may reduce the threat of grading, but my own experience would not bear out his comment that "after discussions I have found that the threat of grading is not a problem or an inhibiting factor. . . ."

Some counselors feel that another aspect of the relationship which tends to reduce the evaluative element, and therefore the threat, is when the supervisor's reaction is an honest expression of a personal feeling rather than a judgment. In commenting on an article, for example, Rogers says: [15]

> It is stated that the supervisor has said, in effect "You are defensive as indicated by the use of your words." To me a more accurate summary of the supervisor's expression is, "My feeling about this is that you are using words to cover up, to hide behind." This may seem like a small difference, but the difference between a *judgment* rendered by a person in authority, and a *personal feeling* which is contributed to the inter-action as a part of the existing personal reality is, I believe, very great indeed.

I would hope, with Rogers, that the level of self-actualization of all supervisors would be such that their expressions generally would be those of personal feelings, rather than pontifical judgments. The de-

[12] Herman J. Peters and James C. Hansen, "Counseling Practicum: Bases for Supervision," *Counselor Education and Supervision* 11:82–85 (Winter, 1963).

[13] C. H. Patterson, "Supervising Students in the Counseling Practicum," *Journal of Counseling Psychology* 11:47–53 (Spring, 1964).

[14] *Ibid.*

[15] Carl R. Rogers, "Comment," *Journal of Counseling Psychology* 2:195 (Fall, 1955).

termination of the judgmental level of a statement, however, is often determined more by the degree of self-actualization of the recipient of the statement than by the one who makes the statement. The white racist may say contemptuously, to a Negro, "You are nothing but a dirty nigger." One Negro may cringe at this "judgment": another may react with violence and hatred; another may smile with sympathy, and wonder how he might help this unfortunate ignorant and fearful white man. If I am in the position of authority, namely, if I am the supervisor, then even though I may feel, quite deeply, nonjudgmental, my expression of personal feeling with regard to a certain action of the student counselor is viewed, to a greater or lesser degree, as a "judgment." The self-actualization of the student counselor has reached a high level if he can, in effect, expose himself, with risk, without being threatened. This would mean that he would no longer view "risk" as something external, which he could not control, but rather as something internal, which he could control. The risk, of course, might come from either the supervisor or his fellows in the practicum. Many student counselors view their peers as a greater threat than the supervisor. Indeed, if I am to be honest, is not my expression of feeling, to all extents and purposes, a judgment? Later on, a director of guidance may ask for my opinion regarding the effectiveness of a counselor I have had in a practicum, and who is now applying for a job. If I reflect this personal feeling in some way in a statement about the student counselor, then surely I am being judgmental. The extent to which a statement is threatening is probably less dependent on how it is put than it is on the relationship of the one who utters the statement to the other person, and the way in which the other person views the statement. I may say to a driver, "It is my feeling that you were going too fast." Exactly the same statement may be made by a traffic officer, but surely the statement will be regarded in a vastly different manner. When Carl Rogers would say to me, now, "It is my feeling that you are using words to cover up, to hide behind," I do not hear the same thing that I would have heard if he had said exactly the same words to me some years ago in Chicago. I have no question that he was then, as he is now, a warm, compassionate human being, and I may or may not have changed too much regarding my own level of self-congruence, but his relationship to me then, at least as I perceived it, was quite different. I would react in a different way today, not because he is necessarily any different, or because I am necessarily any different, but because *our relationship as I view it* is different, and this has a profound affect on my perception of what is said. This, I think, is the crux of the problem. The supervisor *is* a supervisor, and as such he carries the weight and the responsibility of judgment and evaluation on his shoulders. I have heard supervisors discussing the effectiveness of student counselors who, in turn, appear to believe that their counseling practicum is an unconditional positive acceptance, no-risk sort of human relationship. Is a supervisor being self-congruent when he develops in students the feeling of absolute freedom without risk, and later helps to determine the sorts of position that they will obtain by his statements about their counseling effectiveness, or lack of it?

There is another aspect of this problem of self-congruence and genuineness, which appears when a supervisor feels that a student counselor is ineffective in many ways, and will discuss this ineffectiveness with others, sometimes to the point of being involved in the removal of a student from a program, and yet, in the name of "unconditional positive regard," will never reveal his feelings to the student counselor himself. Is one being congruent if he *feels* "Gosh, I get the feeling that you were scared stiff of the client when he made that statement," and he *says,* "It is your feeling that you were warm and comfortable with the client," because this is what the student counselor has verbalized to the supervisor. Is, possibly, the need to be loved so strong with some supervisors that they cannot risk the loss of approbation and acceptance by the student counselor by expressing their negative feelings about his behavior? Or would some say that the supervisor, who is also a counselor, should never have any negative feelings toward anyone?

Probably no one would take issue with Anderson and Bown [16] when they say that "maximum therapeutic growth occurs within the context of free communication," but when they say that as the second stage of their supervision "the supervisor *evaluates the recording* in terms of the facilitating or inhibiting factors in the communication," they are referring to an inhibiting, but a very real, factor as far as the communicative ability and the growth of the student counselor is concerned. I would agree with Rogers that these supervisory comments are predominantly expressions of personal feeling. I would feel, however, that they are regarded as evaluative because the person who is making them is, sooner or later, very likely going to be involved in an evaluation of the student counselor. If one can be totally honest and say, as he can as a counselor, "I cannot see myself ever involved in a judgmental role regarding this other person," then, of course, we

[16] Robert A. Anderson and Oliver H. Bown, "Tape Recordings and Counselor-Trainee Understandings," *Journal of Counseling Psychology* 2:189–194 (Fall, 1955).

have a different story. Are there any supervisors who can say this about student counselors in a counseling practicum, and at the same time be consistent with their concept of their responsibility as supervisors?

A somewhat different method of reducing the evaluative function of the supervisor is reported by Truax, Carkhuff and Douds.[17] They describe how the evaluation of the trainee's behavior would be based upon "research measuring scales which have proven adequately reliable and valid rather than upon the supervisor's subjective reaction." They then go on to say that this "would also tend to remove that barrier to the communication between trainee and supervisor by removing the supervisor from the realm of evaluation." Here, instead of giving their personal feelings about the effectiveness of the student counselor (what does one do, by the way, with these feelings?), they present more objective evidence. But even if it is some instrument that, in effect, says to the student counselor that he is not indicating much ability in providing a warm and acceptant environment for the client, can the supervisor really remove himself from this evaluation? The student counselor would likely wonder, with some justification, if the supervisor agreed with the picture as presented by the evaluation scale. No matter what scales are used, the supervisor, in his human relationship with the student counselor, has an evaluative role. The stress should be on helping the student counselor to learn to be able to live, and to be honest, and to be free, in a human relationship that is therapeutic, but in which there is also an element of risk. The supervisor may be compassionate, and warm, and understanding, but openness and honesty with him *is* more risky. Self-congruence on the part of the supervisor surely demands that he not deliberately lull the student counselor into a comfortable, but false, sense of security.

When we think of the relationship between the counselor and the client, as compared with that between the teacher and the student, in the first case the verb that applies is "counseling," while in the latter case it is "teaching." The more important verb in both relationships, however, is learning, and learning occurs best in a therapeutic milieu that is acceptant and non-threatening. The supervisor, however, like the teacher, has an assessment responsibility, and this tends to lessen the security and increase the potential threat in the relationship, so that the "other person" is seen possibly more like the student than the client. The supervisory relationship should be as non-threaten-

17 Charles B. Truax, Robert R. Carkhuff, and John Douds, "Toward an Integration of the Didactic and Experiential Approaches to Training in Counseling and Psychotherapy," *Journal of Counseling Psychology* 11:240–247 (January, 1961).

ing as possible, but some student counselors may need to experience the less threatening counseling relationship so that they are able to be genuine, and grow, in the somewhat more threatening supervisory relationship.

Another major supervisory issue is related to the "cognitive-didactic" approach as contrasted with the "experiencing-feeling" approach. Advocates of both would be likely to agree that they were concerned with growth and learning and self-actualization, but they do not approach it in the same manner. A study by Walz and Roeber [18] indicated that the usual supervisory response was cognitive and information-giving, with negative overtones, and that the supervisors appeared to be more concerned with what the counselor said than with what he did, and more concerned with the content of a counselor's statement than with the relationship to the client. This might be considered as the telling approach, and would fit in rather reasonably with the supervisor who saw himself as an authority-figure teacher rather than as a counselor. For the supervisor who is a counselor, however, the cognitive-didactic-telling approach would appear to be somewhat contradictory, since most counselors, at least at a talking level, see counseling as a warm, human relationship, with the stress on process and the movement of the client toward freedom and self-actualization. Here again, however, the supervisor gets into some difficulties when he tries to function, in his supervising, as a counselor. Demos,[19] for example, points out the necessity for supervisory stress on process rather than content, and suggests as typical desirable supervisory questions such comments as, "Were you aware of the feelings and attitudes you were experiencing?"; "Were you able to experience positive attitudes toward the client?"; "Were you really listening to what the client was saying?" These questions are certainly more process- and student-counselor-centered than such statements as "Why didn't you question him about his father?" and "You sounded pretty nervous to me," but are they so different, from the viewpoint of the student counselor? One supervisor might say to the student counselor, "Were you permissive?" as above; another supervisor might have said, "I gather you have noticed that the scale tends to indicate that you were not very permissive," and another might have said "I got the feeling as I listened that you were sort of resisting this fellow." These

---

18 Gary W. Walz and Edward C. Roeber, "Supervisors' Reactions to a Counseling Interview," *Counselor Education and Supervision* 2:2–7 (Fall, 1962).
19 George D. Demos, "Suggested Uses of Tape Recordings in Counselor Supervision," *Personnel and Guidance Journal* 42:704–705 (March, 1964).

are all process-, student-counselor-centered comments, but to the student counselor the person who is uttering these words has some feelings about the "goodness" or "badness" of his statements. Sooner or later the supervisor is going to make use of his particular set of goods and bads to determine just how good or bad the student counselor might be. This vision, of course, may be dimmed or exaggerated by the person of the supervisor, but it is there. The supervisor, in a way, makes content out of process. The counselor does not, since this is not his function.

The counselor can say, with a high level of honesty, "And your feeling right now is that it is predominantly your wife who is to blame for this difficulty." The emphasis is on the client, and the client's feelings, and this is real, since the frame of reference is that of the client, not that of the counselor. A crucial difference in the supervisory relationship, however, is that in the long run the frame of reference of the supervisor, not that of the student counselor, is going to be used in an evaluative manner. The supervisor may say, with honesty, "And your feeling right now is that it is the anxiety of the client rather than your anxiety that is causing this apparent stiffness between you;" but in the total supervisory relationship, over a period of time, the supervisor is going to evaluate the student counselor on the basis of *his* frame of reference, which possibly sees the basic difficulty as the anxiety of the student counselor rather than the anxiety of the client. A few months ago I saw an example of this where the supervisor, in observing a video tape with a student counselor, indicated in a cognitive fashion that it was his impression that the student counselor was still trying to overpower the client rather than be acceptant of him. My impression of the supervisor was that he was warm and compassionate, and concerned, but by being congruent and honest he was also indicating that he did not have the much quoted "total positive regard" for the student counselor, or at least the student counselor almost certainly did not get the impression of total positive regard. When a person feels hurt, he does not usually view the one who inflicts the hurt as one who also provides "total positive regard." The supervisor could have taken the safer, but less congruent, less honest, and basically less acceptant way, by continuing to operate on the student counselor's frame of reference until the end of the year, then failing him in the practicum!

The increasing use of video tapes and movies in counseling supervision adds another dimension to the cognitive-experiencing issue. The supervisor can, like the counselor, operate almost entirely within the client's frame of reference, and it makes little difference whether he is reacting with the client to the client's experience which he has neither seen or heard, which he has seen and heard via a one-way mirror, which he has heard on a tape, or which he has seen and heard on a video tape or movie. However, the moment the supervisor begins to present his frame of reference, evaluative or no, cognitively or experientially, content or process, I would think that it tends to be interpreted by the student counselor in a content, cognitive sense. When the supervisor says, as he and the student counselor watch a movie or a video tape, "I wonder why you frowned at that moment" or "I have the feeling you were resisting the client when he made that comment," this is the supervisor's frame of reference, it is his reality. He is *thinking,* and he is likely thinking more than "I wonder why" and "I have the feeling." A comment by Pierson [20] has some bearing on this issue. He stated that the supervisor is concerned with *thinking and feeling,* and that, for the supervisor, process is not an end in itself. In this sense, then, what he says *is* content, and it is cognitive. To a much greater degree than the counselor, the supervisor is involved with *his* own frame of reference as he is "experiencing" with the student counselor.

A third issue is the personal bias and orientation of the supervisor as a counselor. The study by Walz and Roeber [21] indicated that no two supervisors reacted to the same pattern of counselor/client statements or used similar wording or meaning in their statements. The reviewers' reactions to the cases presented in Evraiff's book [22] made it abundantly clear that "good" counseling was not perceived in the same way by the different reviewers, and that each reviewer had his own perception of both the content and the process of the counseling sessions. This situation does not present too much of a problem if one views counseling in a methodological sense, and sees as the purpose of the student counselor to learn the particular method of the master. One could then agree with Patterson [23] that the student counselor should choose the supervisor whose methodology he wishes to learn, or even with Ekstein and Wallerstein [24] that the experiencing of several different methodologies might be "nihilistic in its effect." If, however,

[20] George Pierson, in a personal discussion.
[21] Walz and Roeber, *op. cit.*
[22] William Evraiff, *Helping Counselors Grow Professionally* (Englewood Cliffs, N.J.: Prentice-Hall, Inc., 1963).
[23] Patterson, *op. cit.*
[24] R. Ekstein and R. S. Wallerstein, *The Teaching and Learning of Psychotherapy* (New York: Basic Books, 1958), p. 64.

one considers counselor self-congruence and genuineness, warm, non-possessive regard, and empathic ability as basic counselor characteristics that transcend any theoretical positions, then it would seem that experience with counselors with different theoretical positions is most crucial. Only in this way could the student counselor be helped to determine just what theoretical position made most sense to him, or, indeed, whether he was able to function effectively as a counselor under any theoretical position. If a student counselor is exposed to only one theoretical position, he is very likely to adopt what is actually a most superficial position, and become quite parochial in his attitude. This has been one of the difficulties in the past in the "training" of the psychiatrist, and there are many psychiatrists who are astonishingly parochial, principally because of the "one-school-of-thought" that they have experienced in their training. I have seen many thoroughly dedicated "Rogerians" begin to wilt under the attack of a more cognitively oriented counselor, and they begin, in this way, to become more self-congruent and aware of just where they do stand. Any change is then likely to be more substantial and based more on fact than fancy. One who does not hold to a certain theoretical position, if we assume that he is a rational, reasonable and scholarly individual, is usually a better critic of that position than one who accepts it. Religion is moving somewhat out of its parochial ghetto, and some theologians are actually listening to other theologians of differing religious viewpoints. If counselors hold to a somewhat scientific point of view they should surely do the same, and the student counselor should experience differing theoretical positions. If a student counselor had the opportunity of a counseling practicum experience with Rogers, Patterson and Arbuckle, or with Rogers, Ellis and Wittaker, I would certainly recommend the latter. It might result in more confusion and uncertainty, but it would be the uncertainty of growth and movement, and this would appear to be a much better position for a counselor than the certainty of dogmatism and authority.

Again, of course, this would mean that the supervisors, as counselors, are individuals who try to help the student counselor to come to a greater understanding of who he is so that he can develop his own theoretical position at a somewhat more visceral level, and become a more genuine person who can thus develop a human relationship in which others can be helped to grow toward freedom. Even though the ultimate assessment may be from the supervisor's frame of reference, there is no reason why the student counselor should not be encouraged in every way to develop his own means of indicating to the supervisor his skills and capacities and understandings. They can hardly be effective if they are only pale carbon copies of the supervisor! Any total evaluation of the student counselor should take into account the varying theoretical positions of supervisors, and supervisors should be mature enough to distinguish between the extent to which the student counselor has internalized the supervisor's particular theoretical position, and the extent to which the student's own self-actualization has helped him to work effectively with other human beings, utilizing those theoretical concepts that are in harmony with his self.

There is still another facet in the education of the school counselor, which will probably come to the fore more in the future than it has in the past. It is likely that there will be an increasing integration of various pupil personnel service workers such as counselors, social workers, psychologists and psychiatrists as they are faced with increasing numbers of children who simply are not being effectively educated by the current school system. An increasing amount of money and time and effort is going into the attempt to solve the various difficulties that are lumped under the name of "mental health" problems, and it may be that we should look at this question of mental health and its relationship to the school, and school counselor, and his education.

For a long time, in the United States, as in other countries, a man would be considered "crazy," or "mad," or "insane," or just ordinary. There was very little of a gray area, possibly because the world was, at that time, more of a black and white, right or wrong, good or bad sort of place. People who were anxious or tense, or fearful, or lonely, or hostile, were part of the ordinary citizenry, at least until they did something that offended the mores and laws of the current culture, and then they would be dealt with harshly, as befits an absolute society. In due time, however, the gray world that is inhabited, to a greater or lesser degree, by practically all humans at different times of their lives, began to be recognized, and it is possibly unfortunate that eminent domain in this new area was taken over by the medical profession. If we can assume that Freud was the first giant figure of this century in this field, we may note that although he was a medical doctor, he was not particularly impressed by the necessity of a medical background as a prerequisite for involvement in the somewhat hazy area of the subconscious.

Medicine, nevertheless, definitely took over control of this new area of man and his behavior, and it appeared to operate on the assumption that the "psycho" aspect of man's difficulties was just as much its business as the "somatic" part. In this last decade, particularly in the United States, the term "mental health" has become a household term, and numerous misconceptions, and what at least appear to be contradictions, have grown up around it. It is dinned into us by the various communication media that some 16,000,000 of us are mentally ill, and that half of the hospital beds are occupied by people who aren't "really sick." Yet at the same time vast sums of money are being spent to build more hospitals to house more patients. It is pointed out to us that if we send enough money to cover postage and mailing we will receive a pamphlet that will help us with our mental problems, and also help us to be more effective in alleviating our neighbors' mental problems. At the same time, many other books and articles carry the very strong implication that there is not too much difference between being mentally ill and having schizophrenia. Hundreds of meetings are held around the country, by various and sundry groups, with the idea that mental health is everybody's business, and yet, at the same time, an equally strong impression is given that the whole business must, of course, be directed by a medical doctor, and that the central base of operations is an institution known as a hospital. At the same time, however, many of the medical doctors involved in psychotherapy, the psychiatrists, are moving away from a primarily medical reaction to problems of humans and their behavior, and one hears such terms as psychological growth toward freedom rather than cure and healing, inability to move toward self-actualization rather than disease and sickness, experiencing as well as knowing about, the therapist's base rather than his techniques and methods.

We may wonder, then, just how we did get into this rather confusing and contradictory situation on this whole question. I would like to question what would appear to be possible errors in our thinking, and our acting, with regard to this issue that goes by the name of "mental health." Let me then make some suggestions as to what might be done, particularly by the social organization that should have the major involvement in this problem.

Although the word "medicine" appears as a descriptive term almost as far back as written history can delve, the advent of medicine as an empirical science has been quite recent. Even at the turn of the century, organized medicine, like organized religion, was staunchly resisting any idea that implied that things could possibly be done in a more effective manner. The world of science and cognition, however, was well on the way to dominating Western thinking, and it is easy to understand how the movement in medicine became a part and parcel of empirical science. Science was investigating things and objects, and since medicine was concerned with disease, it was logical that disease should be treated as another object to be analyzed and probed and studied under the microscope of analytical inquiry. When Freud appeared upon the scene it was natural, but possibly unfortunate, that his id and ego were placed under exactly the same microscope that was involved in the study of a diseased kidney or a shattered bone. It would seem that this was at least an important milestone at which medicine, as a science, took over the study of man, his conscious and unconscious behavior, and his attitudes and his fears and his joys and his anxieties and his ecstasy. This nonphysiological part of man, this overwhelmingly basic part of man, began to be treated as a disease, and only recently have there been faint glimmerings among some members of the medical profession that possibly man, all of him, is not a disease.

Medicine, it would be fair to say, is somewhat disease-oriented, and "mental health" and its partner, "mental illness," have an obvious disease orientation. Yet, if we take the words somewhat literally, it is obvious that health and illness hardly fit the word "mental," which, we might assume, has some relationship to the various processes that take place in the mind. Actually, "brain illness" would be a more valid term, and this would refer to a disease of the brain, which would be within the realm of medicine as a science. So, too, we might refer to a healthy brain as we would to a healthy kidney or spleen. Thus the whole term is unfortunate, and probably nowhere is this seen more strikingly than in the fact that the law recognizes the right of dominance and control, by medicine, in a field that is actually quite foreign to it, and for which the acquisition of an M.D. prepares one hardly at all. The field, of course, in which man and his behavior is the center of attention is psychology, and yet psychology, striving to achieve the recent eminence of medicine, has tended to copy the scientific concepts of medicine. Thus psychology tends too frequently to treat man as a psychic problem, while older brother medicine treats him as a disease. Hovering over both is theology, which for quite some time has treated man as a soul. It is somewhat ironic that the medical doctor, even the psychiatrist, who might be considered as a "different" kind of medical doctor, quite frequently makes his decision regarding treatment on the basis of a diagnosis by the psychologist, although the law would not recognize that decision if it came from the lips of the psychologist who made it.

The education of the medical doctor in psychotherapy begins

during his psychiatric residency, and the program of the American Psychiatric Association may be taken as somewhat representative. This is a three-year program. During the first year the emphasis is on acquiring what are described as psychotherapeutic techniques through observation. During the second year the chief concern is with psychosomatic medicine, and the third year is devoted to psychotherapy, conducted under supervision, and to the study of psychodynamics. This program qualifies the candidate for examination by the American Board of Neurology and Psychiatry.

The disease orientation of medicine is difficult to dislodge, and even in the writings of some of the most liberal and least parochial of psychiatrists there would appear to be some naiveté about man, total man, and his behavior. While there is much ado about the new revolution in psychiatry, which would appear to be the actual recognition of man as a Gestalt being, not a disease, many psychiatrists do not take this very seriously, and would appear still to think of mental health and schizophrenia as almost synonymous. There is much stress, currently, on the new "community approach" to mental health, but the human being who is involved is still a patient who comes in to a hospital to see a doctor because he is sick. Some people are, of course, sick in a medical sense. But the vast majority of the people who came to see me in the psychiatric clinic of a university were not sick, and they had no disease; most individuals who have come to see me, sometimes after an unfortunate experience with another therapist, are not sick, and they have no disease; the vast majority of the children who are referred, from schools, to mental health clinics are not sick, and they have no disease; and the vast majority of those individuals who are referred to in the brochures as suffering from mental illness are not sick, and they have no disease. They do not need the medical treatment facilities of a hospital, and they do not need treatment by one who is skilled in the practice of medicine, and is known as a medical doctor. In fact, in the most forward-looking hospitals, we have the somewhat topsy-turvey situation in which at least that part of the hospital that is involved in a helping and learning relationship with the inmates does the best it can do to make itself look like anything but a hospital. On the other hand, in many other hospitals, certainly some that I have been in, the person who comes in comes in as a patient; he is considered to be sick, and it is assumed that he is in need of treatment. The treatment that is meted out all too frequently makes it clear that the inmate is considered as a disease, not even a person who has a disease, let alone a person.

Even Karl Menninger, who might be considered something of a

liberal in the field of psychiatry, indicates, if his new book is any criterion, that the position that medicine takes with regard to what it calls mental health is changing at a painfully slow rate. While he decries, and justly so, the magic in the names that have been given to various forms of behavior, he still considers them to be diseases. He talks about a "new" diagnosis, and says that to diagnose "is to differentiate, to distinguish, to designate. It is to recognize, to have knowledge of, or to come to an understanding of." [25] One might well wonder what psychiatry has been doing for fifty years if this is the "new" diagnosis! Menninger also decries the use of names, but supplies an equally questionable new set. To him, "nervousness" is a description of a form of mental illness. If being nervous makes me mentally ill, I must surely be just as ill if I am anxious, or lonely, or hostile, or fearful, or if I have any one of scores of feelings and attitudes that are a part of man and his living. We could then assume that all of us, including Menninger, are mentally ill, sick, and in need of treatment.

The human disorientation of the psychiatrist is probably accentuated by the fact that, after his medical training in diseases, he has his psychiatric internship working in hospital wards with individuals who are in an extreme stage of personality disorientation, created by, as much as anything, the abnormal life that they have been forced to endure under the name of treatment. It is easy to understand why the bright young man, fresh from his work with diseases, should assume that a person who is categorized as a catatonic schizophrenic is sick in the same sort of way that the person with lung cancer is sick. Nor is it very difficult for him to fall into the trap of assuming that everyone who comes to see him, particularly in a hospital, is suffering from that which he knows best—diseases. Thus, what the person gets in the hospital is treatment for a disease, and the myth of mental illness is perpetuated. The various human difficulties that go under this name continue to grow and expand, because our major efforts are not really being directed where they should, and we continue to operate under the fallacious assumption that we are attacking mental illness, a disease for which we must find the correct treatment.

The first step might be to take a much closer look at just who the people we refer to as the "mentally ill" might be, how they became that way, what they want to do about it, and what evidence there is that we, and they, know how to achieve any of the desired results. This would necessitate the pulling together of medical doctors,

[25] Karl A. Menninger, *The Vital Balance* (New York: The Viking Press, Inc., 1963), p. 36.

psychologists and educators, and would likely also involve members of many other obviously related disciplines such as sociologists, anthropologists, theologians, and philosophers. For a start, however, it would seem that if we are to get out of the current situation, the three key people who are involved are the medical doctor, the educator, and the psychologist. All of these terms, by the way, I would interpret in a broad sense to include most of the major personnel who are involved in the operation of a hospital and a school.

The vast majority of human beings who might be described as "mentally ill" are not in hospitals, but are going about their daily chores, possibly in a somewhat ineffective, and unhappy, way. We may note that there are at least two different reasons why some of these individuals are sent to a hospital. The major one probably is that their disorientation from self has become so severe that they cannot function independently, that they need someone to take care of them in a custodial sense. The two major places in our culture where one can receive such care are the jail and the hospital, and it is often a matter of legal determination whether a person will go to a jail or to a hospital. Another reason why these individuals go to hospitals is that they have heard that this is the place where there are people who might be able to help them. It is highly debatable whether many of the individuals incarcerated in a hospital are sick in a medical sense, and it is almost certain that most of the individuals who come to a hospital on an out-patient basis, or who come much as they would to a therapist in private practice, are not sick in a medical sense. We may note too that even those who are considered to be "very sick" are not, in the better hospitals, given "medical" treatment aimed toward a medical cure. Brain lobotomies and electric shock and even the use of insulin are no longer considered to provide a magic answer, and what is being provided is nonmedical and non-hospital. The basic care, actually, is the provision of a warm and human relationship, on all sides, individually and in groups, in which the individual may become able to grow straighter and in a direction less in conflict with his self.

But most of those who would come under the heading of "mentally ill" are not in hospitals. Where are they? If they are young, they are, of course, in schools, and those who are older were once in schools. *It is crucial to note that the school is the only social organization that for many years houses within its walls all of those individuals who might now or who will, later on, be described as mentally ill.* All of those fellow human beings who in later years will move away from us, violently or passively, sit now at their classroom desks. All of those whom in the future we will execute or incarcerate behind the walls of a jail or a hospital are being taught by some teachers, in some schools, today, as I write these words.

What is the matter with these children? Are they sick, and should we turn to medicine to find a cure? Surely the answer to this is, "No." Of course they are not sick. They are, like all of us, involved in a struggle, and I would tend to view it as the struggle and the movement of the existential self in the direction of self-actualization. It is the human struggle of the person *to be*. It is not abnormal, nor is it a sign of sickness, to be lonely or sad, or anxious, or angry; but when these feelings begin to dominate and direct the individual, it is then that he begins to lose his self. It is then, in effect, that his determined world begins to control him, and he begins to lose his struggle for the basic inner freedom. But no matter how much he loses, basically he still has the potentiality, the ability, to do and to be. He may be a young child, somewhat fearful of an aggressive teacher, or he may be a catatonic schizophrenic, curled up in a corner, immobile, but the possibility for self-actualization is still there. And for the child, the forces most involved in the process of acculturation are the home and the school. We can struggle to do something about the latter, but it is with the former that our main hope lies. We *can* do something about the school, and what happens in the home of tomorrow is determined pretty much by what happens in the school of today.

The evidence, then, would indicate overwhelmingly that those individuals who are described as "mentally ill" are not sick in a medical sense—nor are those who are on the road to belonging to this category. They are individuals who have learned to be what they now are; they have become the victims of acculturation; they have become increasingly the pawns of the culture rather than the determiners of the culture. The fact that an American child happens to have a dark skin becomes critical only when he allows that part of the culture that says, "Because of your color you are not as good as we are," to dominate and control him. As long as he can say, without bitterness, or rancor, or hatred, "That may be what you think, and this will likely mean that things will be tougher for me, but that is not what I think and feel," he is winning his struggle for self-actualization, his struggle to be.

Would it not be better, then, if we were to discard this term "mental health," and think rather in terms of growth and learning. Think, in effect, in a positive, how-can-you-be-what-you-can-be sense, rather than with the medical attitude of "you are sick and we are here to help cure you." Every human being, particularly at the period of his greatest growth, namely, his younger years, many of them spent in school, is subjected to pressures and stresses and strains of the culture and the various subcultures that surround him. Our problem is to help this individual in his struggle for self-actualization, so that for him the development of the self may be real, and he may thus come to know the joys of freedom—not outer freedom, with security, but rather that inner ingredient that demands no security, and needs no guarantee or answers. If we see this as the major struggle, and if we think primarily of the younger individuals involved in this process, who are the people who might provide the most help, and where are the logical institutions where this help might be given?

If my general reasoning is correct, it would seem that the logical result of this would be to change drastically the institutional responsibility for assistance in the movement toward self-actualization. The logical institution to direct this struggle would be the school, not the hospital, which would, in turn, become one of the peripheral institutions involved in the total problem. This would also mean a somewhat drastic change in the concept of the function of the school, and of the sort of people who are supposed to make up the staff of a school.

The school has, at best, played lip service to the concept of its responsibility for the education of the whole child, and it has ignored almost completely the environmental milieu in which the child lives and grows and learns. Action is necessary in several directions. The total curricular offering must be examined closely, and it must be geared more to the totality of the child. At the same time, the demands of the environment in which a child will live cannot be ignored. It is probably fair to say that the curriculum becomes more and more unrealistic for an increasing number of children as they move from grade to grade, until at the high school level a significant proportion of the high school population remain in school only because they must, and they are faced with unrealistic demands from both the school environment and the outer environment, including the home. There must, then, be a drastic change in the curricular offering and the curricular experience—and this experience includes the teachers, who are an important part, after all, of the curriculum. This will also necessitate more and better prepared special services people—school psychologists, school counselors, school social workers, speech therapists, remedial reading therapists (not teachers), and medical doctors. All of these individuals may have their own professional and personnel specialties in the way of skills and abilities, but they will all be involved primarily in a helping and learning relationship with the child.

They will not be teaching him; they will not be disciplining him; they will not be controlling and directing him; they will not be pressuring him to retain academic content, realistic or not. They will all be involved in the creation of a therapeutic and learning atmosphere, both in and out of the school. The school psychologist might see his function as diagnostic, in the sense of helping to provide the child with a more valid picture of who he is and what he has and does not have; the school counselor might be involved in the acquisition and provision of information of a social, educational and vocational nature; the school social worker might see her involvement as being one of attempting to help to modify in some way the child's home, the environment to which he returns when he leaves the school; the speech and reading therapists may see their function as helping the child to become more effective in his two basic communicative skills; the medical doctor will have the understanding and the skills concerned with the physiological body, and will be able to assist in the determination of the place of diseases in a medical sense as a part of the human problem. All of these individuals, however, will see their primary involvement as that of a therapeutic, helping relationship with the child, and by making use of their special skills and abilities they will help in different ways. Their function would, of necessity, be remedial as well as preventive for some time to come, but a measure of their success would be the extent to which their function became increasingly preventive in nature. All would be involved closely with the teachers and the curriculum, since this is the basic environmental milieu for the child for some years, and there would be no boss man, since excellence would be a requisite qualification for all of these professional individuals.

There are under way many rather vast projects for the development of various mental health centers. This might be a good place to begin, and some plans might be revised so that there could be developed a learning and self-actualization center, with several new schools as the center of the project, and with a hospital as an auxiliary unit. As long as we are concerned with the self-actualization of well, rather than sick, people, it would seem reasonable that the hospital be an auxiliary to the school, rather than the other way around. It would also seem reasonable that an important function of the school would be the provision of many special services, for which would be needed both special facilities and special personnel. The medical doctor, in the school, would have a key role to play in the determination of just when an individual was sick enough, in a medical sense, that he needed the services of medical personnel, and possibly hospitalization. The hospital out-patient service would be only for those who were medically sick, but the school would have as one of its services, possibly in a special building that would be part of the total school unit, a helping and learning service for those individuals who were no longer in the school, but needed this help to continue to move in the direction of self-actualization. These would be individuals who came back to the school for possible sustenance and help, but there would be no need of describing them as out-individuals. There would, in effect, be no out or in. This vastly expanded concept of the school as the basic unit involved in learning and helping would be for the whole community. Those children involved in the more academic learning would benefit from the increased services of the school, but there would also be those individuals who were no longer involved in academic pursuits but nevertheless found the school as the place where they could receive help to continue to grow.

It would seem, then, that we might consider the school as the major social unit involved in human growth and development, and that the concept of the school should not only be expanded to fit more realistically with the actuality of the children who attend the school, but should also be considered as the major community center for the continuation of learning and growth and self-actualization. Most of the individuals who are now put in the category of "mentally ill" would eventually come under the aegis of the school, not the hospital, for the very simple reason that they are not sick. The hospital would be an auxiliary unit for this expanded school, and medical doctors would be one of the many key members of the expanded special services staff. Such a new school might be called a learning and self-actualization center, and all of those people benefiting from its services would be viewed as well individuals concerned with their further growth and development and self-actualization.

What then, does all of this mean, and say, for counselor education? On the basis of past history, current movements and pressures, and some empirical evidence, it would seem that the following points identify the current status of the education of the counselor:

1. The counselor should be an educated person, and his education should therefore encompass a broad spectrum of knowledge. The counselor is a learned person, not a technician, and thus techniques and skills are of minimal importance in his education. Being a learned

person, his formal professional education does not consist primarily of the memorization of information. The suggestion by Lerner [26] that, instead of one course in occupational information, the counselor take several courses dedicated to the learning of some 203 specific items might be looked at with some horror!

2.   Both the didactic and the experiencing aspects of the counselor's education should be geared toward helping him to become a more self-actualized individual, a person with a higher level of self-understanding, a person who has moved forward to freedom, a person who is truly "becoming." His education helps him to develop his own theoretical concepts, rather than merely aping those of someone else. The evidence tends to indicate that theoretical orientation does not determine the way in which counselors respond to clients. It thus seems rather pointless to attempt to "teach" a counselor a theoretical position.[27]

3.   The second primary aspect of the counselor's education should be his personal involvement in the counseling process, with effective supervision. The didactic experience may help one to learn about counseling, but the major learning must come in the actual counseling experience. An effective counseling practicum experience requires administrative support, expensive physical facilities, effective counseling supervisors, and cooperating school systems.

4.   The didactic and the experiencing, the content and the process aspects of the counselor's education should be considered as an integrated whole, rather than as two separate parts of his education.

5.   Assessment and evaluation are a part of the counselor's education, but a major part of the assessment responsibility should rest on the student counselor as well as on the supervisor. The purpose of counselor education is to help to develop a genuine, self-actualized, empathic individual, one who really is a counselor rather than one who periodically plays the counselor's role. If he is not this sort of person, then, as Olsen [28] says, "he can only fall back upon authoritarian

[26] Leon L. Lerner, " 'Occupationology' in the Education of Counselors," *Vocational Guidance Quarterly* 10:160–163 (Spring, 1962).
[27] H. H. Strupp, "An Objective Comparison of Rogerian and Psychoanalytic Techniques," *Journal of Consulting Psychology* 19:1–7 (February, 1955).
F. E. Fiedler, "A Comparison of Therapeutic Relationships in Psychoanalytic, Nondirective, and Adlerian Therapy," *Journal of Consulting Psychology* 14:436–445 (December, 1950).
Robert W. Wrenn, "Counselor Orientation: Theoretical or Situational?" *Journal of Counseling Psychology* 7:40–45 (Spring, 1960).
[28] LeRoy C. Olsen, "Success for New Counselors," *Journal of Counseling Psychology* 10:350–355 (Winter, 1963).

behavior or the carrying out of an accepted technique. A sense of *being* someone has not been an outcome of his counselor education."

6. A two-year program of counselor education is a desirable minimal goal, and for the present a one-year program should be considered to be minimal.

7. The education of the counselor should take place only in those institutions that have shown that they have effective programs. This obviously means that a number of institutions offering what they describe as "counselor education programs" will be considered inadequate for the future education of counselors. Several smaller institutions might affiliate with a larger institution to produce jointly an effective counselor education program.

8. The graduate education of the counselor should be on a full-time basis rather than a part-time one.

9. Approval of the counselor should be primarily in the hands of the institution rather than the state department of guidance. The state department of education should insist that the institution produce evidence of the high quality of its counselor education program. Once this is done, certification should be automatic for the graduates of such a program, and no counselor who graduates from a nonapproved program should be certified, any more than a "medical doctor" who graduates from a barber shop should be certified as a competent medical doctor.

10. The counselor would be expected, as part of his education, to give some indication of his capacity to work in the milieu that will likely employ him—namely, the school—but there is no certainty that the only way to assure this is to have as student counselors individuals who have had a teaching background or to demand that students must teach for several years before they can become counselors. A New York counselor's publication, for example, states that: [29]

> Some counselors believe that qualified candidates may become effective counselors without possessing teaching experience. To test this assumption a pilot program should be established under the supervision of counselor training institutions with the approval of the State Education Department.

Some evidence, too, raises doubts as to the necessity of teaching as a prerequisite for effectiveness as a counselor. In a study reported

[29] *An Exploration of the Role and Preparation of the Counselor in the Secondary School.* A Report of the Professional Advancement Committee of the New York Counselors Association and the Professional Development and Research Committee of the New York State Association of Deans and Guidance Personnel, 1963.

by O'Hern and Arbuckle,[30] for example, the student counselors who were judged by staff members as the most sensitive in the counseling relationship were significantly younger, had attained lower educational degrees, and had been employed in their present positions fewer years than those judged least sensitive.

11.   Selection of students for counselor education should be on a continuing basis, and it should be such that some student counselors will be able to accept, for themselves, the idea that they should not be in counselor education. While the education of the counselor should be for growth, a criterion of selection should be some indication of the degree of potential for growth. The counselor-in-training should be helped so that he does not have to simulate change in accordance with the expectancies of the situation.

The preceding points may be taken as broad guide lines in the development of a counselor education program, but these are spelled out more specifically in different ways by different institutions. In the actual development of a counselor education program, three basic immediate issues must be faced.

1.   The departmental structure of the institution will obviously be a factor in the development of the program. In most institutions, counselor education is located in a School of Education, but the program has to be a rather massive one in order to have a Department of Counselor Education, and in only a few institutions does counselor education have "departmental" status. Any program is probably not too strong if it consists only of bits and pieces of other programs, but neither should it be parochial and isolated. Any counselor education program must obviously have a strong tie-in with those individuals concerned with psychology, and it would seem reasonable that a significant number of staff members should be psychologists and counselors. In the program with which I am most acquainted, one of the staff members of the Department of Counselor Education is also on the staff of the University Counseling Center, and several of the basic courses are those offered by the Department of Psychology. In addition, of course, an effective program must be part of an institution that has enough in the way of varied offerings so that the student can be exposed to a broad area of education. Certainly such areas as sociology, anthropology, philosophy, and human relations would be considered essential.

2.   The institutional degree pattern will also affect the develop-

30 Jane S. O'Hern and Dugald S. Arbuckle, "Sensitivity: A Measurable Concept?" *Personnel and Guidance Journal* 42:572–576 (February, 1964).

ment of a program of counselor education. Most institutions have on their books a one-year (more or less) master's program, and any consideration of a two-year program must take this into account. Many institutions also have some official recognition of the year beyond the master's; a fairly general title is a "Certificate for Advanced Graduate Study." A two-year program can be fitted into this degree structure, as long as it is made clear to incoming students that the institution considers the two years to be minimal, even though one may receive a master's degree at the end of the first year. Needless to say, this also assumes that the institution does have a clearly defined second year of study, and it would probably be fair to say that most current "two-year" programs consist of the original year with a few additional courses.

A related problem here is the question whether or not this second year of study would be considered acceptable as the first year of study on the doctorate for those candidates who wished to go on for the doctoral degree. Again, in the program with which I am most familiar, the second year is considered as a part of a four-year program. In the first year, the individual receives the master's degree. At the end of the second year, he receives the Advanced Certificate, and an indication that he has satisfied the institution's requirements regarding competence to function as a professional counselor. For those who wish to go on for the doctorate, there are two remaining years of work. Some individuals will come into the doctorate program after having received their master's degrees, but they will take the same second year of work and receive the same Advanced Certificate. Thus the second year is the same, although for some it may represent the second year of their two-year program, while for others it will represent the first year of their three-year doctorate study.

3. Any program must have content, and a most basic question is: What is the content of a program of counselor education? An immediate issue here is the fact that the educational institution may not always agree with the state department of education on what constitutes a required program for state certification. Not only does the institution usually conceive of the program as being longer and more intensive, but there may also be much disagreement as to the actual content of the program. This will probably continue as long as members of state departments, rather than the professional organizations, are the determiners of what constitutes an adequate program of counselor education. An example of two all too typical irritants is the situation where a course in "Psychology of Vocational Development" is not acceptable for certification—it must be called "Occupational In-

formation," and an introductory course, "Principles of Guidance," is required from a counselor who has completed the two-year program!

In the program I know best, as in many other programs, there are different areas of preparation—the student may be preparing to become an elementary school counselor, a secondary school counselor, a college counselor, a school psychologist, a rehabilitation counselor, an administrator of personnel services, or an employment counselor. There is, however, a required basic core for all students, in Year 1, in Year 2, and in Years 3 and 4. In addition, there are recommended electives in the various specialized areas, but the student is the one to determine whether or not he wishes to take these courses. These specific courses may be noted in Appendix 5.

THE COUNSELOR'S PROFESSIONAL RELATIONSHIPS

One of the signs of professional "coming of age" of any individual is his willingness to accept professional responsibility for what happens to his profession rather than passing the buck on to someone else. Instead of continually complaining to others about the sad state of his profession, he takes on some of the burden and tries to make it better. The professional counselor is willing to pay some of his hard-earned money to become a member of a professional organization, he is willing to become professionally competent in order to be considered for membership, and the question he asks is, "What can I do for my profession and for the organization?" rather than the old cry, "What do I get for my money?" The strength of a professional organization is closely tied in with the number of individuals who are willing to "put in" to the organization rather than groaning about how little they get out of it.

The acceptance of the various policy statements that have been discussed might be taken as one indication that the school counselor is coming of age. Particularly striking is the statement of the American School Counselors Association, an organization that has been in existence for only a few years, but in those few years has become the largest of the seven divisions in the American Personnel and Guidance Association. The extent to which some of these proposals are carried out within the next few years will be a still greater test of the depth of the professional attitudes of the school counselor.

The organization that would seem to be the logical Number One choice of the counselor is the American Personnel and Guidance Association. This rapidly growing organization has seven divisions, so that the counselor or guidance worker is almost certain to find one division closely related to his professional work. The National Vocational Guidance Association, the American College Personnel Association, the Association for Measurement and Evaluation in Guidance, the American School Counselors Association, the Student Personnel Association for Teacher Education, the Association for Counselor Education and Supervision, and the American Rehabilitation Counseling Association are the seven divisions. Acceptance in the American Personnel and Guidance Association may be through a division, and the admission standards of the divisions vary. It is most likely that through the years the professional standards for admission to these divisions will go up. There are many local and regional branches of the parent organization and of one of the divisions, and any group of professional counselors who do not have a local branch in their area should assume the responsibility for developing one. Thus a counselor or guidance worker living in the Boston area might belong to the Greater Boston Personnel and Guidance Association, which meets several times a year; he might also attend the annual New England Guidance Conference, which meets in a different state each year. As a counselor educator he would likely belong to the New England Counselor Educators and meet every fall at the regional meeting of the North Atlantic Association for Counselor Education and Supervision. He would also look forward each spring to the annual convention of the American Personnel and Guidance Association.

It is true, of course, that there are counselors who wish to join everything in sight so that they can add up the number of organizations to which they belong. But the responsible counselor, although he will carefully budget his time and his money, will feel that part of his professional responsibility is to be actively involved in the improvement of his profession by being an active member of his professional organization at a local, a state, and a national level.

The American Psychological Association is the other national organization with which the counselor might be most logically expected to be affiliated. This association also has numerous divisions, and the one to which most counselors belong is Division 17, the Division of Counseling Psychology. In this division, a member may have Associate or Fellow status, or be a Diplomate of the American Board of Examiners in Professional Psychology. Being Fellow or Diplomate is usually taken to mean that the individual has shown a high degree of professional training and professional competence. There are many state psychological associations, and these organizations are being increasingly concerned with the certification of psychologists to practice as psychologists. In most cases, the requirements for the professional certification of psychologists at the state level are a good deal higher than the state certification requirements for counselors.

In the long run, the state should put legal teeth into the certification requirements set up by the professional organization. It is the professionally competent lawyer or medical doctor or dentist or psychologist or counselor who knows what professional competence in his field means, and they should be the ones who determine the requirements for certification as to professional competence. Although counseling is rapidly achieving professional status, it still has a long way to go, and surely no professional counselor can feel satisfied as long as competence is measured in terms of a few semester hours of study.

On the other hand, any professional individual must be careful and deliberate when considering the motivations and the reasons for the pressures for professionalization. There are many dangers, and Stefflre issues a timely word of caution when he says: [31]

> One danger lies in assuming that constant upgrading of the occupation is motivated only by the purist altruistic concerns. It is possible that in increasing the training necessary to qualify as a school counselor we may be simply engaging in a kind of academic feather-bedding that permits us to ask for more money, prestige, and protection than we otherwise could have. And last, is it possible that as we become more professional we tend to think less about the purposes of the school and emulate more the private practitioner?

Professionalization should be a goal of the school counselor, but, like another well known historical character, he should also be sure that his heart is pure!

[31] Buford Stefflre, "What Price Professionalization," *Personnel and Guidance Journal* 42:654–659 (March, 1964).

Chapter Five

THE CLIENT

SOME COUNSELORS have been rather wary about using the name "client" to describe the person who comes to experience a human relationship with another person known as a counselor, and thus they very carefully describe him as the pupil or the student. There are still a goodly number of counselors, counselor-educators and state guidance personnel, who, despite the increasing *rapprochement* of counselors, psychologists, psychiatrists and social workers, become quite nervous when one uses such words as clinical, problems, therapy and clients, and prefer to talk about education, normal, and children. This somewhat stern and paternalistic warning, for example, was published in the Massachusetts State Department of Education *Guidance News,* Vol. 2, No. 3, 1961, and was considered to be so important that it was issued again in the May, 1963 issue of the *News:*

> Some consideration should also be given to the inference made in the wisdom of Congress as representatives of all the people that parents send their children to public schools to be educated, not to be clinically analyzed, psychoanalyzed, or therapeutically treated. Parents reserve the right to provide the foregoing services even as they reserve the right of providing medical services. These rights are carefully honored by the medical profession. The guidance profession should do no less.

This warning, and several other statements of similar ilk prompted me to write a "letter" to the editor. Part of this "letter," which was not published because of its length, commented as follows on this "commentary":

> This statement might be considered as somewhat of a warning to stay away from children, or at least to be sure that one never establishes a close and warm human relationship with them. It will be particularly confusing for the somewhat novice school counselor, who may, with his several semester hours of "professional" study, still have a very uncertain idea as to just who he is and what he is supposed to do. The implication of the use of the words "clinically analyzed, psychoanalyzed, or therapeutically treated" is that these are some dire experiences in which the counselor should never be involved. If we look at the clinical meaning of each term, it is obvious, of course, that the school can hardly be involved in the education of the child without in some way being involved in a clinical analysis of him. This is pointed out again and again in other pages of the *News*. The counselor is told, for example, that he is a member of a team whose goals are to "discover and nuture the talents of all children from an early age," and to "assist each child in overcoming obstacles to his success in work and play." One of his functions is the "early recognition of intellectual, emotional, social and physical strengths and weaknesses." Another function is to "test and observe children who are having difficulties in learning, are underachievers, show signs of emotional disturbance. . . ." It is the business of the counselor "to be aware of the kinds of behavior that indicate conflict. . . ." Surely these statements, and many others like them, would clearly indicate that the *News* is also advocating the "clinical analysis" of children and their behavior.
>
> The term "psychoanalysis," of course, describes a particular method of treatment in psychotherapy, used predominantly by psychiatrists. It is unfortunate that some guidance personnel in schools, state departments and universities appear to feel that the terms are synonymous. This is somewhat like equating a brain lobotomy with love and compassion. I have never met a school counselor who practices psychoanalysis, nor have I met one who practices heart surgery. It would seem somewhat mundane and redundant to say that this is not the function of the counselor!
>
> The term "therapeutically treated" is, however, a horse of a different color. Here again, it is surely obvious that a teacher, as well as a counselor, can hardly perform his basic function of helping the student to learn if he is not periodically involved, in a therapeutic sense, with many students or clients. This is also pointed out again and again in various other statements in the *News*. The counselor is told that he should "assist each child in overcoming obstacles to his success in work and play"; that he should "counsel children with problems when the nature of the problem and the child's maturity indicate that counseling would be helpful"; that he works with all children on "personal problems which are common among the age group with which he is working."

The evidence, surely, would indicate that the counselor *is* different from the teacher, and that the human being, young or old, who comes to see the counselor does not generally come to see him for the same reason that a student or a pupil goes to see the teacher. The child or adult who comes to see the counselor *does* have difficulties and problems and questions and anxieties and worries, and it seems rather pointless to pretend that he does not. He is, however, by no means "abnormal" or "strange" or "queer." He is primarily a human being who, for the moment, needs the help of another human being, and most of what bothers him could come under the description of "developmental." He is, above all, *not* sick, and he does not need medical treatment. The counselor should be professionally competent enough to be aware of the few times when he does, and refer him to the proper medical services. Most children who are referred, however, are not medically sick; they do not need medical treatment, and usually they do not get it. Schofield [1] discusses this subject in a somewhat different and intriguing manner.

Who, then, is this fellow who comes in to see the counselor? Who is the client? Let us look first at some theoretical and clinical versions of the client, from both school and non-school personnel, and then go on to see how the client views himself.

THE CLIENT AS OTHERS SEE HIM

Tyler [2] states that an individual becomes a client because "he must deal with a situation, or situations, for which there is some doubt as to the appropriateness of his response." Bordin [3] states that clients are likely to be looking for help, and for reassuring signs that help will be forthcoming. He also points out that almost all clients consider coming to the counselor a reflection upon their adequacy as individuals.

Whitaker and Malone, [4] on the other hand, look at this question in a somewhat different light. They point out, for example, that in seeking therapy the client tacitly blames his culture for its failure to

[1] William Schofield, *Psychotherapy: The Purchase of Friendship* (Englewood Cliffs, N.J.: Prentice-Hall, Inc., 1964).

[2] Leona Tyler, *The Work of the Counselor* (New York: Appleton-Century-Crofts, 1953), p. 69.

[3] Edward Bordin, *Psychological Counseling* (New York: Appleton-Century-Crofts, 1955), pp. 186–87.

[4] Carl A. Whitaker and Thomas P. Malone, *The Roots of Psychotherapy* (New York: The Blakiston Co., 1953), p. 71.

provide him with adequate "growth nutritional," i.e., with therapy. Thus the very act of coming to the therapist points up many of the deficiencies of the community in which the patient lives. More particularly, it implicates those members of the community who live in close relationship with him.

Sheen [5] states a theological point of view that might be unacceptable to some theologians:

> The person who seeks help with the psychiatrist considers himself "ill." He wants a cure and not a sermon. His doing of what he ought not to have done he regards as a symptom. Hence there is no sense in telling him that he sins; either he knows this, and "cannot help it," or he does not admit it and is scared away because he came to seek out the physician and not the moralist.

Rogers gives an excellent picture of the expectancies of the client: [6]

> The client may have expected the counselor to be a parental figure who will shield him from harm and who will take over the guidance of his life. He may have expected the therapist to be a psychic surgeon who will probe to the roots of his difficulties, causing him great pain and making him over against his will. He may have expected him to be an advice-giver, and this advice may be genuinely and dependently desired, or it may be desired in order that the client can prove the advice wrong. He may, due to unfortunate previous experiences with psychiatric or psychological counselors, look upon this new experience as one where he will be labeled, looked upon as abnormal, hurt, treated with little respect, and thus may deeply dread the relationship. He may look upon the counselor as an extension of the authority which referred him for help—the dean, the Veterans Administration, the court. He may, if he has some knowledge of client-centered therapy, view the counseling interview as a place where he will have to solve his own problem, and this may seem to him a positive or a very threatening possibility.

In a later article, in discussing the necessary conditions for personality change, Rogers describes the client when he says, "The first [of two persons] whom we shall term the client, is in a state of incongruence, being vulnerable or anxious." [7] Rogers thinks of incongruence

5 Fulton Sheen, *Peace of Soul* (New York: McGraw-Hill Book Co., Inc., 1959), pp. 147–48.
6 Carl R. Rogers, *Client-Centered Therapy* (Boston: Houghton Mifflin Company, 1951), p. 66.
7 Carl R. Rogers, "The Necessary and Sufficient Conditions of Therapeutic Personality Change," *Journal of Consulting Psychology* 21:95–103 (April, 1957).

as referring to a discrepancy between the actual experience of the organism and the self picture of the individual, insofar as it represents that experience.

Another description of the client is given by Ellis.[8] In a symposium on marriage counseling, he referred to the neuroticising ideas to be found in the client as:

1. The notion that it is a dire necessity for an adult human being to be approved or loved by almost everyone for almost everything he does.

2. The notion that a human being should be, or must be perfectly competent, adequate, talented, and intelligent in all possible respects; and that he is utterly worthless if he is incompetent in any way.

3. The notion that one should severely blame oneself and others for mistakes and wrongdoings; and that punishing oneself or others for errors will help prevent future mistakes.

4. The notion that it is terrible, horrible, and catastrophic when things are not the way one would like them to be; that others should make things easier for one, help with life's difficulties; and that one should not have to put off present pleasures for future gains.

5. The notion that most human unhappiness is externally caused or forced on one by outside people and events, and that, since one has virtually no control over one's emotions, one cannot help feeling bad on many occasions.

There are those counselors too, of course, who apparently never see the client as a total living person. Some of them, like some of the determinists referred to earlier, see the client as a set of behaviors or a combination of problems. Some do not even see the client as a "problem," but only as a symbol of a problem! Weitz,[9] for example, points out that:

It is important to note that (except in unusual circumstances) the counselor can never participate in or deal directly with the client's problem, or the events which initiated it, or the client's anxiety. He can deal only with the symbols abstracted from these events.

8 Albert Ellis, "Symposium on Neurotic Interaction in Marriage Counseling: Neurotic Interaction between Marital Partners," *Journal of Counseling Psychology* 5:24–26 (Spring, 1958).
9 Henry Weitz, "Counseling as a Function of the Counselor's Personality," *Personnel and Guidance Journal* 35:276–280 (January, 1957).

Esper [10] investigated the differences between junior high school students of three categories—those referred to counselors, those who were self-referrals, and those who had no contact with counselors. He found that the self-referral counselees tended to reflect a higher frequency of problems; the non-contact group seems to get the better grades, while the referral group got the poorest grades; the self-referred group were the most intelligent, the referred group the least; both referral groups displayed a higher incidence of problems in counseling regarding school; adolescent girls were more apt to be self-referred and boys were more likely to be referred for counseling.

In comparing college freshmen who utilized counseling facilities with those who did not, Mendelsohn and Kirk [11] found that the students who seek counseling score less toward the judging side, more toward the intuitive side, less toward the feeling side and more toward the introversion side. It was suggested that the customary attention to subjective experiences characteristic of the intuitive type and the greater tolerance for or enjoyment of ambiguity characteristic of the perception type predisposes such individuals to make use of the counseling approach.

Critics of school counseling, the "the kids are in school to study" type, do not always appear to realize that the personal problems that may become the business of the counselor are very much related to academic achievement in school. Taylor,[12] for example, after a survey of the literature, came to the following conclusions:

1. The degree to which a student is able to handle his anxiety is directly related to his level of achievement.

2. The value the student places upon his own worth affects his academic achievement.

3. The ability to conform and/or accept authority demands will determine the amount of academic success.

4. Students who are accepted and have positive relationships with peers are better able to accept themselves.

5. The less conflict over independence-dependence relationships a student copes with, the more effort he places on achievement.

10 George Esper, "Characteristics of Junior High School Students Who Seek Counseling," *Personnel and Guidance Journal* 42:468–472 (January, 1964).
11 Gerald A. Mendelsohn and Barbara A. Kirk, "Personality Differences Between Students Who Do and Do Not Use a Counseling Facility," *Journal of Counseling Psychology* 9:341–352 (Winter, 1962).
12 Ronald G. Taylor, "Personality Traits and Discrepant Achievement: A Review," *Journal of Counseling Psychology* 11:76–82 (Spring, 1964).

6. Activities which are centered around academic interests are more likely to produce successful achievement.

7. The more realistic the goal the more chance there is of successful completion of that goal.

In a somewhat more psychological vein, Gowan [13] states that:

> . . . . achievement is an indication that the individual has successfully transferred a large enough portion of his libidinal drives to areas of cultural accomplishment so that he derives a significant portion of his gratifications from them. We need always to consider how an individual is to receive psychological pay for tasks accomplished.

The reasons why one must become a "client" have been discussed, one might presume, since man has existed. Jung comments that "A psycho-neurosis must be understood as the suffering of a human being who has not discovered what life means for him." [14]

In an interesting discussion of Freud and Marx, Fromm [15] points out that alienation was, for Marx, *the* sickness of man. Man is independent only when he is free *to* as well as free *from,* and Freud saw the independent man as one who had emancipated himself from the dependence on mother, while Marx saw the independent man as one who had emancipated himself from dependence on nature.[16]

Mowrer, who feels that it is somewhat sinful not to be acceptant of the reality of sin, asks, "Is it any wonder that we are suffering from what Frankl calls an 'existential vacuum,' that is, *meaninglessness?*" [17]

Levitsky contrasts the two sets of forces that, he believes, exist within all of us, "as growth forces which motivate us to face anxiety and learn new ways of handling it to our satisfaction, and non-growth forces which motivate us to avoid anxiety, not to grow, or to make compromise solutions." [18]

The violence of the debate over terminology describing various kinds of human problems and difficulties has always seemed to be

13 J. C. Gowan, "Factors of Achievement in High School and College," *Journal of Counseling Psychology* 7:91–95 (Summer, 1960).
14 C. G. Jung, *Modern Man in Search of a Soul* (New York: Harcourt, Brace & World, Inc., 1933), p. 225.
15 Erich Fromm, *Beyond the Chains of Illusion* (New York: Pocket Books, Inc., 1962), p. 50.
16 *Ibid.,* pp. 70–72.
17 O. Hobart Mowrer, "Science, Sex and Values," *Personnel and Guidance Journal* 42:746–753 (April, 1964).
18 A. Levitsky, "An Approach to a Theory of Psychotherapy," *Journal of Existential Psychiatry* 4:134 (Fall, 1963).

somewhat of a tempest in a teapot since they are all, surely, from the same basic human tree. The descriptions in the previous pages apply to all of us—the difference is merely one of degree. Clients do not have a disease that the counselor does not have; the counselor has simply learned to live more effectively with what he has and with who he is. Even for those who are called mad or crazy or insane or psychotic, the human relationship still remains. In talking about insane people, Krim, who had been considered as one of them, says, "the majority had lost confidence in their own ability to survive in the world outside . . . but positively no serious effort was being made to equip them to become free and independent adults." [19] Percival, another "mad" person, in an article which first appeared in 1848, writes, "The lunatic doctors appear to think that patients do not feel their position; now I know that many lunatics are extremely sensible [sic] to ridicule; this sensitiveness is, indeed, one of the phenomena of an unsound mind." [20] Another patient, Mary MacLane, says, "Badness, compared to nothingness is beautiful." [21]

Self descriptions such as the following have been used by clients, child and adult, in school and out. Positive self statements would be:

> I am a responsible person.
> I usually like people.
> I express my emotions freely.
> My hardest battles are with myself.
> I am optimistic.
> I am sexually attractive.
> I can usually make up my mind and stick to it.
> I am satisfied with myself.
> I am relaxed, and nothing really bothers me.

Self statements on the negative side would be:

> I put on a false front.
> I often feel humiliated.
> I doubt my sexual powers.
> I usually feel driven.
> I feel helpless.

[19] Bert Kaplan, *The Inner World of Mental Illness* (New York: Harper & Row, Publishers, 1964), p. 67.
[20] *Ibid.*, p. 248.
[21] *Ibid.*, p. 279.

I don't trust my emotions.
I have a feeling that I am just not facing things.
I am no one. Nothing seems to be me.
I just don't respect myself.
I am confused.
All you have to do is just insist with me, and I give in.

These are descriptions that most of us could likely say are "pretty much like me" or "not very much like me." Probably few of us could say to any of them, "No—never—absolutely not!"

High school and junior high school counselors describe the client in the following ways:

"He is a person who is unloved and has retaliated by involving himself in norm-violating behavior."

"He is a person whose viewpoints have not been taken seriously because people have not taken the time to be interested enough in him to listen."

"He is a person whose functional effectiveness is impaired because of a lack of congruence between what he is and what he would like to be."

"He is a person who has become a victim of our societal institutions, which do not take the time to be sensitive to his needs."

"He is a person whose emotional development has been unattended because of increasingly automated human relations."

"He is a person whose individuality is usually in conflict with the demands of the group."

"He is a person who has bottled up his feelings because he feels that people will not be perceptive or understanding of his views of life."

"He is a person whose needs have been sacrificed because of the larger needs that the group has imposed on him."

"He is a person who would like to be emotionally free but has not acquired the inner conviction that he should be free."

It cannot be stressed too much that the children who are being described here, and in the pages that follow, are basically "normal," "ordinary" school children. They are not "queer" or "strange" or "deviate." They are the school children with whom the counselor works, and they are representative of the children with whom the teacher works, in a somewhat different way, with somewhat different objectives.

The recently accepted policy statement of the American School Counselors Association would appear to be acceptant of such human descriptions of "the client" when it describes the "pupil" as follows:

1. Each pupil is a unique individual. His behavior is purposeful and represents his attempt to develop in society as he sees it.

2. Each pupil has a right to acceptance as a human being, regardless of the nature and the results of his behavior, beliefs, and inherent characteristics.

3. Each pupil has a right to individual self-development and self-fulfillment. The extent and nature of self-fulfillment is directly a function of the extent to which the individual possesses real and informed personal freedom.

4. Each pupil has a right to self-direction as well as responsibility for making decisions and living with the consequences of his decisions.

THE CLIENT'S SELF-VERSION

We have talked mostly about the evidence and the attitudes of others as they view clients. Let us look now at clients as they view themselves. Often, at the beginning of a counseling session, clients do not go into any particular specific detail as to why they are coming to see a counselor. Sometimes, of course, the counselor does not give the client much of a chance. In Evraiff's book, for example, this is what happened with Carl: [22]

C1: Carl, I'm Mr. Williams.
S1: Glad to meet you, Mr. Williams.
C2: Nice to know you. I see you had a little trouble last week.
S2: Right.

When Jane's counselor, early in the first session, asked her what she would like to talk about, she replied: [23]

"I'm kind of sick of talking about myself, first of all, because I've had, I don't know what I should say, trouble, I guess, is the closest thing to it. Not with the police, not with any-

22 William Evraiff, *Helping Counselors Grow Professionally* (Englewood Cliffs, N.J.: Prentice-Hall, Inc., 1964), p. 17.
23 *Ibid.*, p. 74.

one like that, but with my own self, and maybe with my family."

Many students come to a counselor after having been told that the counselor will give them tests or supply them with information that will be helpful to them. Jack's counselor prods him with a question about his thoughts about a future job, but all he gets is: [24]

"Well, so far about, ah, the only thing I've really thought of is welding. My father's one and I can weld a little bit. Be a good job. And, ah, I've thought of flying, something like helicopters, that would be a good job."

Edna, a twelve-year-old, gives a not uncommon reaction to the counselor who presses her by asking her what she would like to discuss: [25]

"I don't know, I don't know what to discuss."

and, as her next comment:

"Well, I'll, do you want me to tell you how old I am, or where I live, or something like that?"

Richard reacts much the same way, when the counselor comes forth with the usual "would you like to tell me . . . " bit: [26]

"I don't know what to tell you."

These reactions could be expected from children who are very likely in need of help, but frequently, when the referred child arrives at the counselor's office, his immediate feeling is that he is there because someone else told him he should be there. His problem, as he sees it, is the person who referred him, rather than the issue or action for which he was supposedly referred!

On the other hand, children who are self-referrals are more likely to have already done some self-examination, or at least be somewhat ready to express what they feel as their immediate difficulty. Some

[24] *Ibid.*, p. 167.
[25] *Ibid.*, p. 227.
[26] *Ibid.*, p. 317.

self-referred junior high school children, for example, speak in this manner:

> "I thought I'd explode if I didn't talk to you."
> "Keeping things inside prevented me from doing my best work in school."
> "I don't like to be singled out for ridicule and sarcasm."
> "Nobody seems to respect me or my opinions."
> "I feel discriminated against."
> "I don't have any friends—none at all."
> "I get nervous during a test—I go blank."
> "My parents favor my youngster sister."
> "My parents are separated—and their separation just rips me inside."
> "I'm a pawn for people who use me."
> "I want to be a plumber . . . but when I mentioned it at home, all hell broke loose."
> "I'm fed up with the double standards that surround me."
> "I'm angry about the rumors that have been spread about me."
> "Everytime I try to express an opinion, he just cuts me off."
> "I wanted to develop an inner strength . . . something that would sustain me in life—and—not be washed away in the first rainstorm."

In somewhat more detail, here are some reactions of other clients to the question, "Why are you a client?":

In thinking back on why I entered counseling as a client, it is difficult for me to actually point to a particular factor or any one reason. Generally speaking, it appears that the main over-all reason for entering the counseling relationship was that I was becoming continually less able to cope with the problems encountered in every-day living; this seemingly was brought about as I began to take stock of myself, trying to find meaning and purpose in living. Actually, it seems as if a course in Mental Hygiene and a course in English Literature were the things that helped me to see the type of life I was living and the neurotic trend that seemed to be associated with it. In looking around me I could, and still can see a society that has lost sight of its end and has become painfully entangled in its means;

I felt that there must be more to life than this hopeless entanglement of means, and that in reality the fulfillment of means utilized as ends are insatiable needs that form the vicious circle which is so characteristic of neurosis. . . . . .

I'm a client because I could no longer control my actions or emotions. This was leading to excessive use of alcohol accompanied by hysteria and no knowledge of what had happened the following day. I became very depressed, because my sense of morals and a strict upbringing made me aware things had gone far beyond any sense of decency I might still have. . . . . . .

I felt that I was becoming excessively concerned with myself and my troubles and withdrawing further and further into myself and away from society. It became absolutely necessary to seek immediately some means of finding out what was wrong and to take necessary steps, at all costs, to remedy the situation. . . . . . .

I am a client because my anxieties about my work in my academic program were becoming so intense that they were interfering with my work. The study materials—books, etc.—were becoming the stimuli for so much anxiety—being, of course, a constant reminder of the subject matter that I could hardly sit down to read, or to write papers, but would become tense and fidgety—to the point of not being able to study at all. Also, my experience with some of my diagnostic test courses was stirring up a great deal of anxiety, so that I was beset by recurring thoughts of a sexual, and at times abnormal nature, which I could not inhibit. I concluded that some of my defenses were crumpling, and that the time had come to get some help. I was particularly concerned that my difficulties might affect my wife and my children, because I was also becoming irritable at home. . . . . . .

One of the main reasons I sought help was that I was (and still am, to a degree) very sensitive; had many fears and superstitions, problems with religion, and sex. I have tried to help myself with the help of Dr. Del and tried to analyze my behavior. . . . . . .

Because in recent years I have become a very miserable, despondent person within myself—*very* despondent, envious, lonely, inefficient and feel that I don't have a mind of my own any more. Always looking at everyone else and always thinking what I need, what I should do, being very unhappy generally. Everything I attempt to do is a chore and I am completely dissatisfied with life in general. I feel that I make mistakes in everything I shop for, plan for and just cannot feel at *ease* any more. I feel that making decisions has become a task —a real one. Knowing that having an interest, other than being the mother, wife, daughter, and homemaker has become one of my greatest thoughts. And from that I just flounder and flounder around—what do I want to do, what will keep me "occupied in thought" as well as time. . . . . .

I felt that at this time, when there are a *few* things about me that are disturbing, that now would be a good time to try to do something about it. This in contrast to waiting several years, when such disturbances might grow into something really serious. I also felt this to be the best opportunity—at the University, while I'm studying, early in my life and early in marriage. . . . . . .

I thought I would find a magic formula that would enable me to sleep. Since I was eighteen years old, it has been difficult to relax, and six nights out of seven I would get three to five hours a night. Basically I felt uneasy about myself—thought I was a fake and did not form relationships with people easily, although I was friendly (I thought). . . . . . .

I'm a client because I know my emotional immaturity is creating many problems for me that I wouldn't have if I could find a way to grow up. I hope that in therapy I will gain a better understanding of myself. . . . . . .

As a client I have undergone approximately twenty sessions. I feel very fortunate in having matriculated at the University, for I feel that I might not have had the opportunity to undergo counseling therapy. I spent a rather difficult first semester debating whether or not I should expose myself to therapy. After all, wasn't this admitting I was sick and unable to help myself? As I think back on this hectic period, my problems mounted increasingly; the tensions and anxieties of daily living became extremely difficult to cope with. Defense mechanisms were structured; yet nothing seemed to alleviate the fears and the tensions. One crutch after another failed; each exit became a dead end. There seemed but one unopened door—my religion. This became the only answer, this had to be it! Unfortunately, or perhaps fortunately, I twisted this excellent means to a desperate end. Consequently, more anxieties were being produced, till in complete frustration I chose to enter psychotherapy. . . . . . .

It would seem, then, that the client who comes in to see another person called the counselor about his personal difficulties, is quite often characterized by at least some of the following traits, none of which will be really modified or altered by the use of "medicine," since he is not organically sick:

1. The client is often anxious. He is anxious about failing in his courses, anxious about doing well on his job, anxious about his lack of capacity as a husband, anxious about being able to live in a new environment, anxious about deviations that he does not want to modify but that are unacceptable to society. Although anxiety, of course, is common to all human beings, the relationship between the anxiety and the object or event producing it may often be a measure of one's disturbance. Thus anxiety prior to a championship tennis match might be expected, but an equal state of anxiety before playing a friendly match with a friend might be considered unusual. A mother might be considered to be reasonably anxious about a child who is failing in all of his school work, but a similar degree of anxiety because her son received one B instead of all A's would be a somewhat different story. Then, too, the event or situation producing the anxiety may be something that will change, and so reduce the anxiety, whereas an event or situation that will remain means that the individual's reaction to it must be changed. Thus a man who is somewhat fearful for his life during a hurricane has anxiety of a short duration, but the homosexual who is anxious over the reaction of the culture to him is either going to have to adjust to such a culture if his anxiety is to decrease, or to change himself so that the reaction of the culture to him will change. Neither of these choices will be easy.

Then, too, having no anxiety might be considered more abnormal than having some anxiety. I remember an episode from Air Force days when I shared some anxiety with Air Force personnel because it appeared that the aircraft on which they were passengers was going to explode; and I can remember the irritation I shared with the others at another passenger, a fighter pilot who actually went to sleep on the floor of the plane, with the philosophical comment, "We can't do anything about it anyway, so why worry. . . ."

Clients are often extremely anxious, too, about what others would call very little or trivial things. "Will I look right?" "What will I do if I can't answer that question?" "What if it snows and I don't have my rubbers?" "What will I do if Joe doesn't meet me?" "What will I buy for Don's dinner?" Although such anxiety is out of proportion as far as the rest of the world is concerned, it is not out of proportion as far as the client is concerned. Far too often we hear such a comment as "Oh, I wouldn't worry about a little thing like that." The trouble with this statement is that "it" is little only to the person who makes the comment, not to the anxious one. It is surely, at best, a doubtful procedure to reject a client's feelings that something is big enough and

important enough to cause anxiety with an airy, "Why, that isn't anything to worry about at all." The most likely reaction to this sort of
comment would be a resigned, "Oh, well, I guess you can't blame him.
He's just like the rest of them—just doesn't understand me."

The anxiety and fearfulness of the client are very real. The fact
that what is not a threat to nearly everyone else is a threat to him
means that there has to be a modification and change in the client.
The dark room remains dark, but to the child who has grown, that
same darkness is no longer a threat. Two of my children were once
given a basement room as a bedroom when relatives were visiting, but
the night was not far along before they were squeezing into bed with
father and mother. The new room was too "spooky," they felt, and the
fact that it was the same room where they played all day did not alter
the fact that it was spooky. Their fear might even have been contagious, since neither father nor mother took their place, but all four
spent the night in the one bed!

Whatever the anxiety may appear, overtly, to be about, any
continuing stage of anxiety usually reflects an anxiety about one's self.
This anxiety may also be shown by an "I cannot understand you" or
"I cannot hear you." What these very often mean is that the person
does not want to understand or to hear because of the implications of
what might be being said, and the easiest way to avoid anxiety about
doing something is to avoid understanding or hearing, for then one
can hardly be expected to do anything.

2.   The client is often hostile, and his hostility may be shown in
a variety of ways. He may be overtly aggressive and contemptuous,
unable to accept any ideas or suggestions that might contradict his
own, or that might imply that someone else knows more than he does.
This is a difficult person to work with, particularly if one is in a supervisory position, since he will react with sensitivity to any sort of criticism, no matter how gentle (if criticism can be gentle) or constructive.
As a member of a class, he will often feel that the instructor's comments are personalized, that a criticism of some idea of his is a personal attack upon him. Similarly, he makes a difficult "boss" or teacher,
since he can brook no opposition or suggestions that a job might be
done in a different or better way than that suggested by him. No
matter what his position or role might be, he will find it difficult to
relate closely with almost anyone—other than a counselor. Other
people seldom have the patience or the understanding to attempt to
relate with such a person, a fact which in turn accentuates the difficul-

ties, since these hostile individuals are often correct in their feeling that people do not agree with them. As with other clients, it is usually only in a therapeutic relationship that the client begins to feel there is no need for the elaborate defenses he has built up. He finds, for the first time, someone who is acceptant—in a secure manner, not in a weak and passive way—of him and his hostilities.

There are many ways, of course, in which a man may express his hostility in a more socially acceptable manner; often an individual may be consciously unaware of the fact that what he is expressing is really a deeply rooted hatred or hostility toward someone. Because a woman soon learns that a mother who hates her child is an awful person, she may show her hatred by being one who loves and loves and loves her child, and indicates to all her great love for her dear darling. The philanthropist, of either the 25 cents or the million dollar variety, may be sneering at people by his donation. The comic may show his veiled contempt for his audience by getting it to laugh at him and to pay him for the privilege of laughing.

Overt or not, our hostility is usually related to our own anxiety about ourselves. Even the little child, when he says, "I hate you," to his mother, is also probably feeling, "And I hate me too." It is generally easier to assert our disdain and contempt for others than for ourselves, and perhaps to express a feeling of "I hate me" by saying, "I hate you."

Much of man's prejudice, indeed, is self-rejection rather than rejection of others. When someone else is doing something that is obviously bigger and better and superior, it is only the solid and stable individual who can say, without any twinges or negative feelings, "He is a better person than I," or "He won because he was better." Minority groups are often tolerated when they are small and pose no threat to the majority; only when they become more potent in strength and numbers, and begin to challenge the status of the majority, do they become a threat. At the same time the members of the minority group cannot afford to show their hostility, and may develop a passive aggressiveness, so that their hatreds are expressed by their meekness and humility.

3. The client often feels guilty; the more the socio-religious pressures upon him, the greater the likelihood of feelings of guilt. Much of our cultural behavior would appear to be controlled by the guilt concept, and even advertisements stress the fact that the potential purchaser would not want to be guilty of various things. The more one

learns that he "should not" do and feel, the more likely it is that he will have many feelings of guilt, since he will continue to do and feel, and it is the feelings about what has been done that cause the trouble and tension rather than the actual doing. Thus a client may feel guilty about wanting to marry someone of a different religion; he may feel guilty about speaking and acting harshly toward his children; he may feel guilty because he does not think kindly of his parents; he may feel guilty about masturbation; he may feel guilty about cheating; he may feel guilty about having sexual relations with a girl; and so on. Some would say that this is the voice of one's conscience, and that if we did not have any control by guilt we would have no social order. The trouble is that the guilt feeling itself is a contagious sort of thing that seldom changes one for the better. If an individual felt guilty only about some act that most people would agree was questionable—such as brutal treatment of one's children—and then moved ahead to a more stable attitude, and thus more positive behavior toward the children, this would be fine. That, however, is not usually what happens. If an individual is restrained from striking his children only because he feels guilty about it, then there is every likelihood that this same attitude toward his children will be expressed in an equally questionable, but possibly not equally guilt-producing manner. Thus, although guilt may repress or change or modify the act or the behavior, it does not change the attitude that produces the behavior.

4.   Low self-esteem is another overt characteristic of many clients. Such a lack of respect for oneself may show itself in statements to this effect, or by depression or general unhappiness, or it may be shown by the contempt or ridicule that the client directs toward others. Low self-esteem is also shown by a discrepancy between the individual's ideal self-concept and his actual self-concept. This discrepancy has been brought sharply into focus in research studies by Rogers and Dymond,[27] where the ideal self-concept was described as the organized conceptual pattern of characteristics and emotional states that the individual consciously holds as desirable (and undesirable) for himself. The greater the discrepancy, the more poorly he feels about himself.

5.   All of these items are, of course, related, although the inability to make a choice might be thought of as another characteristic

[27] Carl R. Rogers and Rosalind F. Dymond, *Psychotherapy and Personality Change* (Chicago: The University of Chicago Press, 1954).

of some clients. Of course, making a choice is a problem for all individuals, but a disturbed person may be completely unable to accept the responsibility for making a choice—and thereby a decision—which would then leave him subject to question and criticism. If one never makes a decision, one will never get into trouble or be blamed or criticized for making a choice. The inability of a client to make a choice of breakfast cereal might seem amusing to some, but to the person involved this choice was a major decision that she simply could not venture.

These, then, are the clients of the counselor. They are individuals who have much to contribute to the benefit of all, but their potential is hidden, and lies unused. Certainly most counselors would agree that the broad objective of the counseling process is to help the individual to clear away the entangling and hampering tentacles so that he can be what he really is, and contribute more both to himself and to his fellows.

PART THREE

BASIC ISSUES
IN COUNSELING

Chapter Six

OPERATIONAL ISSUES: I

ALL COUNSELORS doubtless have in their minds certain issues or difficulties. Some would probably see the day-to-day operational issues as paramount, while others would think of the more theoretical and philosophic issues as basic. It is unfortunate, but probably true, that a man must have some food in his belly before he can afford the luxury of pondering about why he is bothering to put food into his belly. Practical existence comes first, and counselors are no different in this respect than the rest of mankind. As they become more experienced and skilled and capable in what they are doing, the "what" and "how" begin to pose less of a problem than the "why." It is difficult, too, to sharply distinguish operational from theoretical, and a rather common method of operational escape from responsibility is to describe some suggested procedure as being "too theoretical"! In any case, several of the chapters that follow will attempt to describe what appear to be some of the more immediate on-the-job operational issues, as well as some of the more basic theoretical and philosophical issues that confront the counselor as he works with the changing person in the even more rapidly changing culture. It will be noted that there are few answers, since each counselor must devise for himself the answers that will make the most sense for him today, but quite possibly no sense whatsoever tomorrow. Unfortunately, there are probably thousands of American school counselors who are thinking of the same problems today that they thought of ten years ago. The world has almost certainly left them behind, and they are probably helping the child to prepare for a world that no longer exists.

THE SETTING FOR COUNSELING

One of the immediate problems—sometimes an overwhelming problem—that faces any counselor is the setting, the environment, the situation for counseling. Probably most schools still provide a poor setting for counseling, although the situation varies to a tremendous degree from school to school. The pressure to improve the quality and to increase the numbers of counselors is also having its impact on facilities for counseling, although we are probably getting better counselors faster than we are getting better facilities, and if we must have a choice, of course, this is the way it should be. Better a good counselor in miserable surroundings than a miserable counselor in superlative surroundings! On the whole, however, it would probably be safe to say that even in new schools the provisions that are being made for counseling facilities have not improved as much as have the facilities for other aspects of the school program, such as, for example, the teaching of foreign languages. Facilities that can be used in the education of counselors, such as counseling rooms with sound equipment for monitoring and recording, and one-way mirrors, are, other than in a few schools and laboratory institutions, practically non-existent. Many schools have reached the point where they admit the need for a counselor, but they still do not see why he has to have anything different in the way of facilities than the teacher. This is particularly so in those schools where "counseling" is still seen as a friendly chit-chat, or the offering of some advice by a person who, even though he may have the title "counselor," is still seen as a teacher, and who, in fact, very likely actually *is* a teacher masquerading in a counselor's clothes!

Every counselor should recognize this as a two-sided question, for many sincere individuals are concerned as to just how far the school should go in the provision of various services that are only indirectly related to the educational process. Actually, it boils down to one very simple and direct question: Do you believe that every American child has the right to a chance to have that educational experience which is best for him? If the answer is "Yes," then the school must also provide those personnel services which insure that the child can benefit from the educational experience that is being provided. The most crucial of these services is counseling. There is little point in providing a group of people with a plow if we forget to provide also the means for using the plow.

The attitudinal setting is usually reflected by the physical setting. The low esteem, and the complete lack of understanding of the meaning of counseling, are often reflected in some schools by the fact that there is next to nothing in the way of physical facilities. Counselors may not have offices. Often, if they do, there is no secretarial service or protection, so that privacy is impossible.

Tape recorders are still considered a luxury in many schools, and there are many school counselors who have yet to hear what they sound like, and what they say, when they "counsel."

In some schools where the actual facilities are fairly good, they are rendered ineffective by being placed cheek to jowl with the administrative offices. A student who may want to see a counselor to talk about his desire to bash the principal or perform some dastardly deed upon a teacher will naturally shy away from coming if he sees the offices together, assuming, reasonably enough, that there is a close connection between the people who are in the offices. I was once in a counselor's "office" that formerly was an anteroom to the principal's office, and the only way to the latter was to go through the former. The few clients who came to see the counselor naturally spoke in low tones, were wary of what they said, and kept a weather eye cocked on the principal's door.

If a school has a guidance or counseling suite, it should be away from the administrative offices. This is important even as a symbol of the fact that the counselor and the principal are two quite different individuals with quite different functions and responsibilities. It is important too, to have the counseling suite away from the main flow of traffic, to have a pleasant waiting room, with a secretary, to have individual counseling rooms, as well as counselors' offices, and to have at least one exit door that opens only one way. If a client has been under some stress and emotion, he naturally does not want to have to parade past many curious eyes, or to step out into a corridor swarming with fellow students.

I have recently been in several fairly new schools where the upper half of the walls of the counselors' offices were glass, giving both client and counselor somewhat of a fish in a fishbowl feeling! I have been in another school where the principal insists that the counselors keep the doors of their offices open, to convey to the students the impression of counselor friendliness!

The need for privacy, whether from other eyes or from telephones, is obvious. The office should not be austere, nor should it be a living room, although school counselors would say that while there might be some danger of the former type of office in a school, there never would be any danger of the latter type. The client, after all, will probably feel more comfortable if he has a choice of one or two comfortable chairs, and possibly even the choice of some sort of divan or couch. Some counselors, of course, particularly in schools, blanch at the very word "couch," and they immediately have sinister visions of a heavily bearded man with an Austrian accent, sitting behind the client, making copious notes and asking piercing questions about his sexual behavior. This, however, is seldom a problem, since most counselor's "offices" are hardly large enough to hold the client and the counselor!

A fairly decent office may give the client some confidence in the counselor. If all he has to sit on is a creaky chair, and all he has to look at are bare and dirty walls, he may well wonder if the counselor knows his business. One counselor has commented that he has an impressive looking library in his office so that the client may assume that the counselor is not only well-to-do but also a well educated and a well read person! In some schools, of course, the counselor would have to be wary about having too impressive an office, since this would make it stand out too much when compared with the rest of the facilities.

Thus, in a school, at least, the counselor must face the fact that he may be hired to function as a counselor in an institution that has little understanding of and even some hostility toward counseling, and in which the physical facilities for effective counseling simply do not exist. If the counselor, by being an effective counselor with students and colleagues, can come to modify the first part of this problem, then the second part may work out without too much difficulty.

The rehabilitation counselor in a state agency of a Veterans' Affairs office often has much the same impossible surroundings, in that his "office" may consist of his desk and two chairs in a large room shared with a dozen other counselors, similarly equipped. Indeed, the physical setting for so many counselors, in a variety of areas, is such that we must assume that privacy is something that many still consider an unnecessary luxury in counseling! Actually, of course, it is an absolute necessity for effective counseling, and little can be done without it.

The setting for counseling, both attitudinal and physical, is usually best in an institution where guidance or counseling or therapy is considered to be the major function. Sometimes, in a hospital setting, the attitude might be described as "Let's find out what's wrong and fix 'em," so that a therapist who does not see himself as a dispenser of medicine, information, and sage advice may find himself somewhat of an outcast. Usually, however, in a guidance, counseling, or psychiatric clinic, the prevailing attitude is therapeutic. Therapy, after all, is the purpose of the existence of the institution, and in most such situations the counselor has privacy and some sort of secretarial protection and service.

WHOM TO COUNSEL

A tacit, but questionable, policy in some school guidance departments decrees that the counselor spend practically all of his time with the college-bound youth, while the others, being apparently of less importance, are left pretty much to fend for themselves.

In some schools, on the other hand, where a real attempt is made to help all children who need help, the counselor is rendered somewhat ineffective because he has to do everything, and thus does nothing very well. Too frequently the school takes literally the idea that if a counselor "has" 500 students, then he must see 500 students; or when school people read about an ideal situation with a counselor responsible for about 200 children, they visualize the counselor spending an equal amount of time with all 200 of those children. The counselor should *know* all of his children, and they should know him, or at least know who he is and what he does, but some children he will see very often, and others he will see not at all. I cannot go along with the idea of the counselor's seeing all of the children for compulsory interviews so that they can get to know him, since very frequently they have no real reason to see him, nor do they want to see him. From the point of view of the counselor, there is no evidence to indicate that a brief interview can give a very valid picture of the client to the interviewer. Testing would surely be much more economical of both time and money as a means of helping the counselor at least to know *about* the children.

There are probably three basic kinds of counseling in the school situation. There is counseling with the students who plan to go to college after they graduate from school; counseling with students who will seek a job either before or after they have finished their schooling; and counseling with those students whose problems are of a personal and emotional nature. If there is only one counselor, then he must

simply do the best he can with all of the children, but if there are two
or more counselors, a division of labor would result in more efficiency.
In any school with three counselors, for example, it does seem a bit
ridiculous for all three to be doing everything, when there could be
a very natural division of labor.

While all counseling, is, in a sense, of course, personal, one counselor could take the major responsibility for those students who are
college bound. The odds are that this counselor would often be functioning in a guidance role rather than as a counselor, having rational
discussions with individual students or with groups of students who
are going to college. It is likely, too, that most such students would
benefit from contact with a counselor, although there will be many
who are quite capable, on their own or with the help of their parents,
of making perfectly good decisions without any help from a counselor.
Needless to say, the counselor should not go running down the halls
pursuing these students. There will, of course, be students who are in
need of therapeutic counseling who will come to see such a counselor
supposedly to talk about college plans. When such students get into
real difficulties, it would depend on the counselor's capacities and
interests whether or not he continued with them or referred them to
another colleague spending all his time with such counseling.

A second counselor could take the major responsibility for those
who will seek jobs after graduation, or those who will leave school for
jobs before graduation. Such a counselor might spend a good deal of
time in the field, getting acquainted with employers, and keeping
up to date with the rapidly changing opportunities in the community
and the surrounding area. Despite the increasing mobility of the American worker, a student who leaves school will most likely find his
employment in the same general area. Often too, this counselor might
function in a guidance role in an intellectual discussion with stable
students who are thinking logically and reasonably about their job
futures. Here, too, most of the students who are seeking jobs would
probably benefit from conversation with the counselor, although, as
before, there would be many perfectly capable youngsters with no
particular need for the services of a counselor. Some students, too, who
come for a discussion about employment would be in need of counseling, and, as before, it would be a question of referral to a colleague, or
continuing with the student as a client.

A third counselor might take as his primary responsibility counseling as it is viewed in this book; and just as some of his colleagues
would refer some of their students to him, so he would refer some of

his clients to them. This counselor would probably see the smallest proportion of the student body, but he would spend a good deal more time with individual clients. One or two discussions about colleges or job possibilities might well suffice for the majority of the students who are so concerned, but the number of sessions with students whose problems are of an emotional nature will be much greater. It is the responsibility of the school to provide such a service, and it can be effective as long as the school staff, the children, the community, and the counselor know just who the counselor is and just what he is supposed to do.

All of these counselors would, of course, coordinate their efforts, and all would work closely with the teaching staff. The relationship of the therapeutic counselor to the teacher might pose something of a problem, however, since his effectiveness as a counselor with the children depends, as has been mentioned, to some extent at least on their concept of his relationship with the administration and the teaching staff. He must be seen by the children as one who will work *for them* rather than for the teachers or the administration. On the other hand, it is essential that the teachers particularly do not feel that in working for the children the counselor is working *against them.* I know of many excellent school counselors who manage this somewhat difficult relationship. Although they work for the children, and the children know it, their relationship with the teachers is good. Even here, however, some teachers may feel that the counselor spends too much of his time with the children, and not enough with them. If there were a division of labor, however, as described above, the "college" and the "job" counselors could spend a good deal of time with the teachers without particularly damaging their relationship with the children. It is the "personal problems" counselor who will find this dual relationship a problem.

Most counselors have little or no choice as to who is going to see them, at least for the initial session. In the school situation, it is desirable for word to get around that the guidance or counseling office is a place where anyone can go and receive a friendly reception regardless of who he is or what his problem may be. Better to have the problem of wondering what to do with the large number of clients who wish to avail themselves of the services of the counseling center than to wonder why it is that everybody stays away from the counseling center as if it were contaminated.

Some students who may be in desperate need of counseling, however, do not come in to the counseling office, while other students who do not appear to have as much need for counseling want to spend most of the school day there. Being Client-centered as a counselor, however, does not mean that one is a passive creature who can never do anything about the latter type of student, although the Client-centered counselor may find this sort of fellow more of a problem than would the Napoleonic type of counselor! If counseling is effective, the client who wants to while away his time in the counselor's office can be helped to see why he does so; and he might then leave the counselor's office, or he might enter into counseling in a more beneficial way. In any counseling situation where the client seems to be actually doing nothing but wasting his own time and that of the counselor, we must, among other things, question the effectiveness of what has gone on in the counselor's office.

The client who does not come in, however, poses a different and a more difficult problem. Although it may not be the responsibility of the individual counselor, it is the responsibility of the counseling or guidance office at least to see if something can be done. The office certainly cannot pursue the client, but neither can it shrug its shoulders and watch an individual disintegrate without trying in some way to help him. Certainly the counseling office, and the individual counselors, and the teachers, can all do an effective job of helping children to feel that they are always welcome; but even so, there will always be children who will be wary of anything that smacks of authority or control, or who may be unable or unwilling to face up to their problems, or who may have learned from their parents and their culture that when you are in trouble, you keep quiet so that you won't get into more trouble. Understanding and educated teachers can often help a child to reach the point of going to see a counselor; and sometimes the teacher or principal might even make himself the "fall guy" by telling the child that he has to see a counselor—while being very careful in no way to implicate the counselor in the "you have to" deal. Thus the child may arrive at the counselor's office full of hostility toward the teacher and the school, and, possibly, the counselor. Although this is not the best situation, at least the child is in the counselor's office, and then there is a possibility that something positive might happen. The counselor may help the child to dissociate him from the authority that has commanded, "You have to see the counselor," but he cannot hold an unwilling client, and the prognosis will not be good if the client continues to feel that he is with the counselor only because he has to be there.

On the other hand, counseling with the unwilling client may

not be quite so impossible as some believe it to be. I was involved in a study where junior high school boys who were disciplinary cases were involved in an experiment where they were put into three groups. One group received the usual disciplinary action, one group had nothing at all happen to them, and the third group was required to appear before a Client-centered counselor for a minimum number of counseling sessions. Various measures were used before and after to determine differences. One of the conclusions of the study was that even when students are forced to appear for counseling, *some* of them benefit with *certain counselors.*[1]

Another example of the effectiveness of a nontherapeutic method of getting individuals into what eventually develops into a therapeutic relationship is seen in a research study in which delinquent children were paid to come to see a counselor. Practically all came with the feeling that this was a good deal, and that the counselors were really a prime lot of suckers to be taken advantage of. Yet, after a while, at least some of the children became voluntary clients in a real counseling relationship.[2]

In the long run, the crucial question regarding the unwilling client is whether or not the counselor can, with total honesty, say to the client, if need be, "I am not the one who said you *had* to be here, and you may leave here at any time if you feel that that is what you really want to do." No counselor should be placed in a position where he must, in effect, say to the client, "I am sorry that I cannot allow you to leave even though this is your wish." At the very least, every counselor should be able to say, with total honesty, "*I* had nothing to do with your having to come down here to see me. . . ." We can assume that he might also add, "but I'm glad to see you, and if there is anything that I might be able to do. . . ."

THE COUNSELOR AS A SOURCE OF ISSUES

Sometimes the counselor himself, in a variety of ways, becomes an "issue," and an ever present danger is that the counselor will become somewhat parochial, and close his eyes and his ears to new evidence and ideas that may contradict some of his more cherished

[1] Dugald S. Arbuckle and Angelo Boy, "An Experimental Study of the Effectiveness of Client-centered Therapy in Counseling Students with Behavior Problems," *Journal of Counseling Psychology* 8:136–139 (Summer, 1961).
[2] Charles W. Slack, "Experimental Subject Psychotherapy: A New Method of Introducing Intense Office Treatment for Unreachable Cases," *Mental Hygiene* 44:238, 256 (April, 1960).

concepts. A few years ago, in a famous psychiatric clinic, I heard a fine and respected elder psychiatrist say, "No, I don't know anything about Rogers and I don't want to. . . ." He almost certainly did not mean the remark as it sounded, but it was a good example of the "I don't want to hear anything that implies something I have been doing is wrong" attitude. It takes a person of high calibre—particularly a person who has been asked for the answers for years—to accept such a notion, and, of course, such notions are often presented as evidence when they are actually little more than notions.

It is probably not unfair to say that in many high schools the level of the counselor's professional education is low, and hence he operates mostly by ear. Many of the things he does he may do because of a kind heart, and he may do them almost intuitively, and the result may often be very good. But if this is true, the reverse is equally true. Many disturbed students are not receiving adequate help simply because their counselors do not know what to do. Thus when some counselors and teachers say, "I don't believe in the Freudian stuff" (or that Client-centered business or that psychological nonsense), what they are really saying is simply, "I don't know anything about it, and I'm more comfortable not knowing anything about it."

In the case of the medical therapist versus the psychological counselor, there is no question about the high level of the professional education of both; but it may be that they have come through different doors into the same room, have worked happily for a while, then suddenly discovered that another person was in the room, doing the same work, and neither one can see how the other fellow got there. Professional workers are subject to the disease of provincialism just like anyone else. We all have an unfortunate tendency to read, for example, in our own narrow sphere, with no realization that other people are involved in much the same work, using different techniques and methods and procedures, and often arriving at results that are much superior to those that we have achieved. Psychologists should read more medically oriented journals such as the *Journal of Psychosomatic Medicine,* and psychiatrists should read more psychologically oriented journals such as the *Journal of Counseling Psychology.*

There are rays of hope, however, and in some places at least provincialism is being broken down. The American Academy of Psychotherapists has as members psychotherapists with various kinds of doctorates, but they are all involved in, and all have evidence of their success in, the task of counseling and psychotherapy. There are, of course, sharp differences of opinion at their conferences and workshops, but these are professional differences among competent individuals, rather than closed arguments for a particular point of view.

Two of the visiting speakers at a recent academic year NDEA Institute on Counseling and Guidance were Albert Ellis and Adrian Von Kamm. It was interesting to note that the students, after becoming better acquainted with these two individuals, came to feel that their divergencies were not by any means as great as they had assumed. As counselors, they had much in common, and they did not allow their differences to make communication impossible.

The Psychiatric Clinic of the Harvard University Health Services is another example of an organization where psychiatrists and psychologists work together as counselors. Their capacities and skills may be different, but a patient coming to the clinic is most likely quite unaware of whether he has a psychiatrist or a psychologist as his therapist.

Although Rogers has now moved to California, his years at Wisconsin as a professor in the Departments of Psychology and Psychiatry showed that psychologists and psychiatrists could at least speak with each other! The increasing involvement, too, of the school counselor in a variety of crucial national issues—school drop-outs, poverty, juvenile delinquency, unemployment, better education for minority youth —have exerted a strong pull to get him out of any ghetto into which he might have a tendency to slip. Still, any professional counselor must continually check himself, to see if perchance he happens to be rejecting an idea or a procedure primarily because his own ignorance in the particular area threatens him, or because of his own provincialism, which may, of course, be the educated word for ignorance. There are different methods, and different counselors do use different methods; surely it is ironic if, of all people, the counselor—supposedly the most acceptant of individuals—rejects in scorn another counselor because he is not of the true orientation or school or methodology. If counselors are professional workers, then in the long run the competence of the counselor must be determined by pragmatic evidence.

The school counselor may also find himself an "issue" because of a negative identification that may have developed in the eyes of the students in the school. He can, of course, take some steps to at least reduce the likelihood of negative identification; he need not be seen as too friendly with the teachers, as having an office adjacent to the principal's, and so on. No matter what he does, however, the counselor will frequently discover that the client's picture of him may be the cause of some difficulty. The school counselor can reduce his identification with the school administration, but he will continue to be viewed by some children as the agent of the principal. He may frequently also be considered a teacher, and his clients may be somewhat disturbed when he does not "teach" them. Almost any good counselor, regardless of methodology, is going to cause some client unhappiness by not giving him the immediate answers and reassurances that are wanted. The counselor who causes all of his clients to leave his office singing his praises might be looked upon with as much scepticism as the counselor who is roundly condemned by all his clients.

The title of "Doctor" may also be a problem, although in a school it will be somewhat different from in a clinic. Not too many schools have counselors who are "Doctors," and most children know only one kind of doctor. Thus they may frequently expect that Dr. Brown, counselor, will use certain instruments in his little bag and prescribe certain medication. They may be passive, and expect the doctor somehow to examine them, tell them what is wrong, and tell them what to do. They may well be somewhat frustrated and confused when Dr. Brown does none of these things. On the other hand, in a counseling center or a psychiatric clinic the non-doctor therapist, such as a social worker, may be considered by some patients, and by some members of the staff, to be something of a second-class citizen. The Ph.D. "doctor," on the other hand, will frequently be considered by the patients as a psychiatrist, and the prescribing of medication as one of his functions.

In any case, it is likely that the biggest problem the beginning counselor has to face in this area is the fact that very often his professional approach surprises, and sometimes disappoints, the client. For instance, the client will very often push the counselor for answers. Some counselors, who answer easily all of the questions the client asks, do not realize that they are reacting purely for ego defense, and that they may quite possibly be injuring the client by their action. Such counselors, feeling that they must answer, could at least react in an honest manner and say, "I don't know"; but instead they attempt to answer such questions as, "Why am I always so fascinated by automobiles?" or, "Why must I always procrastinate so much?" or, "What does it mean when I dream of my mother with a series of breasts instead of two?" or, "Why can't I make up my mind to do something, and then go ahead and do it?" or, "Tell me why I am always afraid of these ridiculous things that I know are just superstitions?" Even the boldest of interpreters would be somewhat careful about saying what any of these questions might mean, or just what the client could do about them; and the counselor who actually tries to answer such questions is almost certainly doing so because of his own uneasiness or ignorance, or both. The basic counseling problem, after all, is not solved by answers from the counselor. Much more basic is the understanding by the client of just why he must ask such questions, and just what sort of answers he might be able to find for himself.

It is interesting to note that in the counseling literature and at various professional meetings much stress has been placed on counselor and therapist comfort. This point of view assumes, however, that it is all for the welfare of the client, and if the counselor can be comfortable only by doing something that is injurious to the client, then he is obviously in the wrong profession.

RESTRICTIONS AND CONTRADICTIONS THAT AFFECT THE COUNSELOR

Although being expected to do too much is a problem, it is not nearly so difficult as the one that faces the counselor who is supposed to perform contradictory functions. In the school situation particularly, the counselor simply cannot do some of the things the administration expects him to do without rendering himself ineffective as a counselor. Probably the most common issue in a school setting is the impossible combination of jobs, as with the principal-counselor or the teacher-counselor. In many respects the major blame for this situation lies at the door of the counselor himself, since if he does not know what he can and what he cannot professionally do, then he can hardly blame someone else for being somewhat confused on this matter. Certainly most will agree that the school principal simply cannot be a counselor. He may be an adviser, and a sage friend, and a kind person, but he cannot be the counselor, since as the principal he is primarily responsible for the welfare of all of the children and the staff. He is the person who must take disciplinary action when it is necessary. He is the top authority who can decide what will happen to any child in the school—a role that is quite contradictory to any concept of the counselor as the individual who helps the person to work out a decision for himself.

The teacher-counselor combination, is, unfortunately, still a common sight in American schools. I may be one of the culprits in this situation, since some years ago I was, I believe, the first person to write a book dealing specifically with this question, using the term "teacher-counselor." [3] Since then, however, it has become abundantly clear, to me, at least, that the two simply do not go together. This does not mean, of course, that the teacher is not a very important member of a guidance or personnel services team; but he is a member as a teacher, not as a counselor. The teacher is no more a counselor than he is a social worker, a psychologist or a psychiatrist. Since there still are so many "teacher-counselors," however, it is well to look at some of the reasons why the person who is a teacher cannot function as an effective counselor at the same time. [4] As indicated earlier, it is also highly questionable that teaching should be considered as a prerequisite experience to involvement as a school counselor.

1.   There is a specific area of knowledge that the counselor must have; knowledge that must continually be added to and modified and thrown out, and this knowledge is simply not possessed by the teacher unless he is willing to sacrifice the knowledge that, as a mathematics teacher, he must continually pursue. Contrary to what some teachers think, one cannot be an effective school counselor by only being nice to children and nodding the head at the appropriate moment. There is a vast body of knowledge that he must *know.* This knowledge is not possessed by the teacher, nor will it be, unless he abandons the mathematics or history or English or whatever it may be that used to be his particular body of knowledge. At this point, of course, he is no longer effective as a teacher of mathematics, if for no other reason than that he has forgotten all he ever knew about mathematics, and what he once knew now belongs in the prepithanthropic mathematical age!

2.   There are certain skills that must be possessed by the counselor, and these are not possessed by the teacher, other than by chance, since he has no need for them. While the line between a skill and an aptitude or a personal trait may sometimes be very thin, we can distinguish skills that are related to the area of occupational information and testing, and there is at least an element of skill related to the problem of a deep and understanding communication with another person. Thus on this count, although there may be no conflict between these skills and and those involved in teaching, the time factor is such that one person it going to find it difficult to be effective in both.

3.   There are also a number of required functions from which the teacher can never completely divorce himself, and this, more than

[3] Dugald S. Arbuckle, *Teacher Counseling* (Cambridge: Addison-Wesley Publishing Company, Inc., 1950).
[4] Dugald S. Arbuckle, "The Conflicting Functions of the School Counselor," *Counselor Education and Supervision* 1:54–59 (Winter, 1961).

any other reason, is why teacher-counselors are, at least in my observation, primarily and overwhelmingly teachers, not counselors. As teachers they manipulate and direct and control, and as "counselors" they do the same thing. As teachers they think in terms of the welfare of a group of children as taking precedence over the welfare of the individual, and as "counselors" they feel the same way. As teachers they measure, evaluate, grade, and separate the "bad's" from the "good's" and as "counselors" they do the same thing. As teachers they know and they feel that they are the authority figure in control and they are thus the ones who determine the curricular experience and practically everything else that happens to the child. There is little or no self-determination, and this person as a "counselor" shows the same level of acceptance of any concept of self-determination or freedom of choice. Finally, we might say that they are teachers, and as such are involved in the overt process of teaching something to someone; they are involved hardly at all in the learning process with another learner. As the "counselor" they are still the teacher, teaching something to someone.

Some will say that many of these functions do not have to be performed by the teacher, but that they are functioning in this way because of the sort of people they are rather than because this is something that is required of them. This is very often correct, and many of these conflicting functions can be minimized, but this often results in the teacher's being considered "not so good" by the school administrator. This raises the intriguing thought that possibly the teacher who will make a good counselor is one who is unhappy with this role as teacher, and who is not doing very well as a teacher—at least in terms of some of the traditional measures of the "good" teacher!

4. It is as risky to talk about "good" personality traits of the counselor as it is to talk about similarly "good" traits of the teacher, but one might at least raise the possibility that there are certain traits of teachers that do not appear to hinder them either in their professional advancement as teachers or in their effectiveness as teachers. But these same traits might at least be questioned as being those of the effective counselor. The somewhat overt, gregarious, slightly noisy rather than slightly quiet person is often very effective as a teacher and a leader of groups. The somewhat dominant person who feels comfortable in manipulating, directing and controlling is usually considered effective as a teacher. The somewhat conforming "let's maintain the status quo" person who tries to get children to conform and

fit into the required cultural pattern often does well as a teacher; conversely, the teacher who accepts and possibly encourages exploration and the "let's be different" attitude among children is rather rare, and may find some difficulty in getting ahead in the school system. Even the rigid disciplinarian type ("Boy, she was tough, but she was fair.") very often does well as a teacher and is quite often referred to as one whom younger teachers should emulate. From my frame of reference, at least, all of these traits and a good many others are ones that would at least be highly questionable in terms of descriptions of the sort of person with whom children would feel easy and comfortable, and be able to speak their minds on any subject that they might feel they wished to discuss. It may be the presence of these "teacher" traits, in both teachers and "counselors," that results in the depressing statistic in so many schools indicating that there is no one, either teacher or counselor, in the school to whom the children feel free to speak as they think and they feel.

Thus it would appear that every individual who has a part-time counseling function, with some other job title attached to the word "counselor," should check carefully to determine the degree to which he is being rendered ineffective as a counselor because of his other conflicting functions. He might exert every effort to see that he becomes either a full-time teacher or a full-time counselor, and we may hope that the day is not too far off when every school counselor is a fully qualified professional worker. This he can never be if he is satisfied to accept a dual role, a part-time status, which makes him an ineffective fish and an equally ineffective fowl.

There are, of course, many other contradictions that face all school counselors. "Rules and regulations" may often clash with sound professional procedures, and it is unfortunately all too rare that a counselor, or a group of counselors, takes some action about such a situation. The "counselor" who does not attempt to do something about the fact that he has to act as a hall warden, or as a reporter to the administration on the behavior of children, or as an evaluator of which children are "good" and which children are "bad," has no reason to complain, since he is probably doing what he wants to do anyway. Nor can the rehabilitation or employment counselor complain about the fact that he has to see a certain minimum number of clients, that he has to get through with them and decide what they should do, if he has not done his utmost to change such a situation. Some counselors are all too prone to say, at conventions and meetings, "Well, I certainly know that we shouldn't be doing this, but you know how it is . . ." when actually they appear to be quite satisfied to take actions that are professionally unsound.

A counselor working in a clinical or medical setting may sometimes find too that rules and regulations cause him certain difficulties. Frequently, for example, in writing a report on his "case," he may have to provide a diagnosis of the ailment at the end of each counseling session. This requirement may prove somewhat difficult to fulfill, if not impossible, particularly if he must use a prescribed set of categories. Again, however, a counselor working in such a situation should take steps toward its modification if he really feels he is doing something that is counter to his professional concept of his position.

A good example of an administrative statement that would hardly be acceptable to most counselors is one from the Veterans Administration. After discussing the responsibility of the client in a vocational counseling relationship, the statement continues: [5]

> . . . Although the counselee is to be allowed to tell his story in his own way, it is the counselor's responsibility to ensure that the conversation does not stray too far from its major purpose; in bringing it back, he must employ techniques that will not endanger the rapport that has been established.

Some counselors would feel that this is an invitation to counselee dependency; that it is just the opposite of an attempt to develop in the client the feeling that *he* can solve his own problems. It looks as if the counselor, and the U.S. Government, were saying to the client, "You can't really look after yourself, but don't worry, we'll do it for you." If this situation is not good, then it can be changed, since even the regulations of the U.S. Government are not immutable and unchangeable!

Another very obvious contradiction of roles is the decision, by the counselor, on whether the client is "well enough" to go back to college, to take a certain type of job, and so on. The counselor is placed in a conflicting situation when an administrative officer says to him, "You have had Dil in counseling for the past few months. We have a letter here from him saying that he feels he is well enough to come back to college. What do you think?" It might be that the counselor

[5] U.S. Veterans Administration, *Processes and Procedures in the Counseling Section, Vocational Rehabilitation and Education Division,* Regional Offices, Department of Veterans Benefits, Manual M-7-2, Rev. (Washington, D.C.: U.S. Government Printing Office, 1953), p. 76.

could, without revealing any particular confidential information, and with the consent of the client, give to the administrator a picture of the state of health of the client, but leave any decision on whether this is "well enough" or "not well enough" up to someone else. There should be complete frankness between the counselor and the client on this matter, so that the client knows exactly what the counselor is going to say.

A much worse situation is one where the client is coming to the counselor with the knowledge that here is the fellow who is going to evaluate his state of health, and then pass that evaluation, which will determine his acceptance to college, on to someone else. This is surely anything but a therapeutic role. The counselor is not the one to decide, for someone else, what the client can do and what he cannot do. His function is to help the client to achieve a state of health so that he can decide for himself, and there are others in the culture who can determine whether or not this state of health is good enough for the client to do what they want him to do.

THE CLIENT-COUNSELOR RELATIONSHIP

Counseling does not always proceed in a smooth and even manner, with the client doing what, according to theory, he is supposed to do, and the student counselor may often be faced with client reactions that will cause him some concern. Let us look more closely at one of these issues—namely, that of questions:

1.   There are questions that are obviously expressions of feeling rather than questions per se. When a client exclaims, "How do you expect me to go on living with her?" or, "What am I supposed to do when she tells me I'm a bum—just sit there and take it?" or, "Who is to blame anyway—me or my husband?" or, "How can you or anyone else expect me to take that job?" and so on, these are not really questions, although some student counselors might actually react to them as if they were questions demanding intellectual answers. Regardless of methodology, most counselors would feel that a proper reaction to the above statements would be either some understanding nod, or "uh-huh," or "Hmmmm . . . ," or a reflection of feeling such as, "It's pretty hard to see just how you could do that," or, "That's asking quite a bit," or, "Is it one, or the other, or maybe both of you?" or, "It's pretty unreasonable for anyone to expect such a thing of you," and so on. Thus the counselor who is alert to, and reacting to, the

expressed feelings of the client will not make the mistake of thinking that every statement that sounds as if it had a question mark after it must have an answer by the counselor.

Sometimes such a question may be a desperate request for reassurance. The counselor may feel more impelled to answer such questions as, "Surely *you* don't expect me to go ahead and do that, do you?" or, "Can't any one help me in this—must I *always* be alone?" But here again it is the feeling to which the counselor should react. The tone should be gentle and understanding, but it would seem better that the words be, possibly, "Surely there is *someone* who does not feel that you have to do this" or, "Isn't there ever *anyone* who seems to be with you?" Note here too that while the counselor may feel compelled to say, "I don't feel that way," or, "But I am with you," the real deep feeling on the part of the client that *this is actually so* will come only when he can say, maybe just to himself, maybe to the counselor too, "But there is someone—*you* don't expect me to do that" or, "Why . . . I'm not alone, I'm not alone . . . there *is* someone. . . ."

A somewhat similar sort of question may be asked when the client feels threatened by what he thinks might be a negative reaction of the counselor to something that he has said. Thus if the client, who has been talking about the stupidity of all of the people who vote the Democratic ticket, suddenly pauses and says, "By the way, are you a Democrat?" it is fairly clear that he has said to himself, "What if this guy is a Democrat?" Or it could be that this is his way of expressing his contempt for the counselor, assuming that the counselor is a Democrat. If the answer is "No," the counselor might be tempted to take the easier and safer road and say "No." If the answer is "Yes," however, he might feel that he has only a choice of lying, of telling the tension-evoking truth, or of trying to avoid answering the question either by asking some other question, or by detouring around it.

Again here, either a "Yes" or "No" answer, true or false, counselor comfort or no counselor comfort, is not really reacting to what the client is saying. A fairly safe rule of thumb in this matter is "Don't tell lies"; so we could dispense with the lie, if not for moral reasons, then for the empirical reason that when a counselor lies, it will eventually, and probably fairly soon, catch up with him. An honest reaction to the statement might be, "You mean that after all that you've said about the Democrats, you're a bit concerned about what I am. . . ." This might very well get a reaction of, "Well, yes, what are you?" which in turn might evoke from the counselor a statement such as, "This really does cause you quite a bit of concern—you've got to feel that you know where someone else stands before you speak like this . . . ," and so on. If the counselor is reacting in terms of feeling, and if this is natural and normal to him, then it will be very rarely that the client will continue to push him for an absolute answer, and even this, of course, is an exhibition of client feeling. Some counselors might feel that ultimately they might have to say something like, "Well, it doesn't really matter what I am—the way you feel is the important thing . . . ," but most would agree that this is a rather weak and unhappy reaction.

Certainly the counselor should not, at this point, answer the question, since it would not be a noncommittal answer, and it would be likely to give the client an erroneous concept of the counselor. If, of course, the counselor felt compelled to answer the question, then the client's concept might be accurate, but the effect would not be good as far as future counseling was concerned. The counselor has to build gradually in the mind of the client a picture of consistency. The counselor may sometimes be an irritating fellow, sometimes a nice fellow, sometimes a not-so-nice fellow—but he should always be consistent.

2. A second type of question is one in which there is a personal involvement of the counselor. The client is conceivably after more than just an answer when he asks, "By the way, are you married?" or "How do you get along with children?" or "Did you ever fail any subjects when you were in college?" or "Did you ever get fired?" or "Do you believe in going to church?" and so on. Personal involvement with the client is not the professional task of the counselor; indeed, it is likely that personal involvement will make counseling less effective, if not quite impossible. Unlike the previous type of question, these questions are probably asked by the client as questions to which he wants answers, possibly for reassurance, possibly to help him feel superior to the counselor, possibly to help him feel closer to the counselor. When a woman client who is having trouble with her children asks the counselor "Are you married?" a very likely next question is, "Do you have any children?" to be followed by, "How do you get along so well with them?" The development of such inquiries brings into question the effectiveness of the counselor; has he in some way given the client the feeling that he is a friendly confidante rather than a warm but professionally competent individual who is working with the client on some of his difficulties?

Whatever the reason for questions of this nature, the counselor may find "reflection of feeling" on such occasions not easy, for the very obvious reason that there is little or nothing in the way of feeling to reflect. On the other hand, avoiding the question is usually quite obvious, and a straight statement like, "It really doesn't matter so much about me . . ." may be just as threatening as silence. Many counselors feel that a brief, noncommittal, nonencouraging answer is as good a response, generally, as any; and if the question is pushed, then there is more in the way of feeling to which the counselor can react. "You really want an answer to a question like that . . . ," and so on. There would be a difference of opinion on counselor reactions to this sort of question, although there would be general agreement that the counseling session is not a question-and-answer period, regardless of who is doing the questioning and who is doing the answering. The student counselor may sometimes find himself bogged down in this sort of situation, waking up suddenly to the fact that he has become an answer man, with the questions more and more personal and his involvement deeper all the time. Even at this point, however, it is better to extricate oneself, even if it means threat to the client and possible disruption of the counseling, since what is happening is not likely to be good for either the counselor or the client.

3. Another form of question is the one that seeks an interpretation of the client's actions or thoughts or dreams. For example, a client may talk for some time, without any indication of undue stress or strain, about the difficulty of making choices, and then, in a conversational tone, ask, "What does that mean anyway? Do you know any of the possible reasons why I just seem always to shy away from making any decisions?" Or he might say, "And then one of those dreams that I always have, and have had for years, is that I'm standing on a block of ice that gets smaller and smaller and eventually disappears, and I fall into the water. What does that mean, anyway?"

Again here, there is little in the way of feeling to which the counselor may react; this is a straight question, asked as a question. There may, of course, as with other questions, be many ulterior or subconscious motives, but overtly at least these questions are asked as questions. Whether the counselor does or does not know what the behavior or the dream might mean, the Client-centered counselor would feel that it is not up to him to pass on to the client his version of its meaning. The client must come to his own interpretation, toward which an intellectual presentation is not likely to mean any more than an intelligence test score of an I.Q. of 145 to a person who considers himself stupid. A person *must be* as he sees himself, and will change only when he can accept change, not when evidence indicating that he is different is presented to him.

Usually the counselor would react to this sort of question. He might say, "Well . . . I gather it's pretty hard for you to see any meaning to this sort of behavior"; or possibly, "It's pretty important for you to find some reason behind this behavior of yours." Some might press the client with "Well, hard to say . . . what do you think it might mean for you?" There might thus be a variety of *reactions* to the question, but most counselors would agree that the counselor would not answer it.

4. Then, of course, there are noncommittal questions, in relation to which the most logical procedure is to answer them simply and briefly. A client, finding it difficult to start talking, might say, "This is certainly a cold spell that we are having, isn't it?" Although some counselors might feel that the client's uneasiness should be reflected, this would seem a somewhat cold manner in which to initiate a relationship. Why not just give a pleasant, "Yes, it really is cold weather that we have been having . . . ," and the odds are that the client will be reassured that the counselor is human, and continue in a different vein. The counselor should be consistent, and he will almost certainly be different from what the client expects, but he need not be so different as to appear abnormal. Such a result sometimes comes about when the student counselor, trying to be "Client-centered," refuses to react to any question, and the client, reasonably enough, feels that the counselor is a very queer fellow indeed!

It is true, of course, that many questions seemingly innocent enough will, if answered, be followed by a more involving type of question; but the counselor has to use his own understanding and skill to differentiate one from the other. A good general principle of operation is that the counselor should react to the *feeling* expressed in the question rather than to the question per se, and if he does react to the question, he should be brief and noncommittal.

Here are two junior high school counselors reacting to questions from self-referred students. It may be noticed that while both react to the feeling expressed in the question, one of them reacts in the first person.

Cl: Are you a member of the faculty? Do you know Mr. Jones?

Co: I'm wondering whether or not I can tell everything to the counselor. . . . I'm wondering whether I can trust him. . . .

. . . .

Cl: Are you married?

Co: It makes a difference to me if the counselor is married or not . . . it's important for me to know. . . .

. . . .

Cl: What do you think of a teacher who blames a kid for something he didn't do? Don't you think it's unfair?

Co: I'm upset because I feel that I'm being blamed for something I didn't do . . . it really bugs me because I think it's so unfair.

. . . .

Cl: How important are those tests we took last September? Do they count very much. . . . I mean do teachers use them to put you in different classes?

Co: I'm kind of concerned about those tests. . . . They worry me a little. . . . I wonder how they'll be used. . . .

. . . .

Cl: Isn't there some way you could talk to our parents and tell them how we *really* feel?

Co: We don't think *we* could get anywhere telling our parents how we really see this whole thing. . . . We're afraid to talk to them. . . . We feel they might not listen to us. . . . We want someone else to do it.

. . . .

Cl: If you're chewing gum at the end of the day . . . after school . . . can they keep you after?

Co: Someone found me chewing gum after school and kept me after. . . . It doesn't seem fair to me.

. . . .

Cl: I don't know whether I should try or give up . . . whether to try to improve or just forget the whole thing. What do you think I should do?

Co: You really can't decide if trying would be worth it.

. . . .

Cl: He has no right to play favorites . . . to let one kid do something and not allow me to do the very same thing. He has no right. Do you think he has a right?

Co: You don't feel that he's being very fair.

. . . .

Cl: Sometimes I feel awful dumb . . . real stupid . . .

like I belong in a class for slow learners or something
like that. Does my I.Q. show that I'm dumb?

Co: Sometimes you get the feeling that you're kind of
stupid.

. . . .

Cl: Can my mother force me to take a course I don't
want? I feel that it's my life and I should be able to
live it. . . . Whether or not I'm right seems unimportant. . . . I just want the right to *choose*.
Shouldn't I have that right?

Co: You want to be able to make your own decisions.

Client silences often cause some strain for the student counselor.
Many student counselors complain, in fact, that most typescripts and
tapes always seem to record clients who are very willing to talk, and
all the counselor has to do is grunt every now and then, or decide when
or where he should interrupt the client. There are several points that
might be noted on this question:

1.   The beginning counselor will likely find that client silence
poses a threat to him. As the silence lengthens, the pressure on him
to do something about it builds up—usually not for the welfare of the
client, but rather to ease his own tension. Thus, logically, we might
say that the counselor should aim for a degree of personal security such
that whatever action he takes on the matter of client silence will be
taken solely for professional reasons. Since most would agree that counselor comfort is important, and that there should be honesty in the
client-counselor relationship, it is an interesting question whether or
not the counselor who feels this uneasiness should be honest and indicate this feeling to the client. Most counselors would say "No" to this,
but some, possibly an increasing number, would say "Yes."

2.   Silences, as much as words, are indicative of feelings. The
counseler who reacts basically to client feelings might use such comments as "It's pretty difficult to get started talking . . . ," or, "This is
a real tough thing to talk about . . . it would seem easier maybe just
to let it lie . . . ," or, "It's a real nice feeling . . . ," and so on. The
counselor here must be almost intuitive as to what the client is feeling; while his words will sometimes be a fairly obvious reflection of
feeling, it may sometimes be that if the counselor is to speak at all, it
will be in the form of an interpretation.

Some counselors feel that there should be a reaction from the counselor if the silence appears to become threatening to the client, and that in some cases the counselor should thus take over the direction of the session. The Client-centered counselor would question this, feeling that the counselor reacts to the feelings, or he remains silent, maintaining his consistent feeling of the right of the client to direct the session, to talk, or, if he wishes, not to talk. When a good relationship has been established, the client may sometimes indicate that there is no need of counselor verbalization. I once interrupted a long client silence, and was gently chided by the client. She was doing quite all right as she thought and wondered silently.

3. Silence can also be therapeutic, and probably this is one of the attractions of a church. It is one of the few places where one can go and meditate quietly, without any interruptions. The counselor's office is another place where the same thing can take place. The client may be having a real therapeutic experience when he is silent, just as much, if not more, than when he is talking. Most counselors have had the experience of sharing a warm and unique silence with a client, where both client and counselor could almost feel the growth that was taking place.

Counselors who feel that they just must talk, and who feel silence difficult, might ponder over the results of a study reported by Cook.[6] He found that the lack of silence (at least 97 percent speech in a number of two-minute segments) characterized the unsuccessful counseling sessions, whereas the lesser percentage of speech tended to characterize the more successful counseling sessions.

Another reaction that may cause some counselor concern is an unexpected statement by the client, although this should occasion no despair on the part of the student counselor as long as it does not result in his anxiety. It is one thing to be surprised; it is quite another to be frightened. A beginning interview may be progressing in a conversational way when suddenly the client says, quietly, "Did you know that I was a Lesbian?" or, "By the way, I slept with the Dean over the weekend," or, "Are you nervous . . . you look that way?" and so on. As long as the counselor is a secure and acceptant individual, he does not have to worry about the long-range negative effect of his momentary loss of aplomb. Probably every counselor has his list of "bloopers," where he made statements that are obviously ridiculous to even the greenest of student counselors. I have recorded one example where

[6] John J. Cook, "Silence in Psychotherapy," *Journal of Counseling Psychology* 11:42–46 (Spring, 1964).

the client says, "Say, you look sort of puzzled . . . ," and the reply that comes back is, "Who . . . me . . . no. . . ." The client's logical reaction to this was a laugh, but the relationship at least appeared to be good, and a few minutes after this exchange the client was deeply involved in his problem. In a discussion of this example, it was suggested that *if* the counselor really was puzzled, a more appropriate answer would simply have been, "Well . . . yes . . . I am sort of puzzled." In this case, however, the reaction would not have been an honest one, since the counselor, at least during the interchange, was not aware of being puzzled; he was just surprised—and of course a counselor should *never* be surprised!

Unexpected and violent oaths, highly colored jokes, unusual or bizarre statements may, for a while, pose problems for the student counselor, but in the long run they will not be a serious issue as long as he is not actually threatened by them. If, however, he is, and if such statements are taken as a challenge, to be reacted to as a challenge, or as the sort of thing about which people simply do not talk, then the counselor is in need of some assistance to solve his own problems. Such situations as these will become counseling problems only if they represent a personal problem for the counselor.

A question that is raised by some students is, "Where do you sit, and do you look at the client all the time?" It would be safe to say that the counselor does not sit with a desk between himself and the client; a general position is one where both client and counselor can look at each other if they want to, or look away from each other without any awkwardness. A counselor has to use his own judgment as to just how consistently he looks at his client; obviously, too, this will vary with clients, and vary with the individual feelings of any one client. A counselor should be able to look steadily at the client if need be, but he should be sensitive enough not to give the impression of staring at him. The counselor's "looking at the client" should be governed by good sense and good taste.

Another possible problem for some counselors occurs when a client who seems very much in need of continued counseling decides that all is well with him, and wants to terminate the counseling sessions. The situation need not pose an immediate problem, in that a Client-centered counselor, at least, would of course be acceptant of the individual's desire to terminate counseling. On the other hand, if the evidence seems to hint strongly that the client is only getting to the point of being threatened by the uncovering of some of his basic difficulties, the counselor must sometimes wonder if the termination is in some way due to his ineffectiveness as a counselor. All would agree that when the client says, "Well, it's pretty clear that this is doing me no good, so I don't see any need to return," the counselor would not say, "Very well, let's call it quits."

There might, however, be some methodological debate as to just how the counselor should react and just what he should say. The Client-centered counselor, and probably most other counselors, would react, in varying ways, to the expressed feeling of pointlessness in continuing the counseling relationship. Some more diagnostically oriented counselors might be interpretative and present to the client their feeling of his fearfulness about what might happen if he continued the counseling relationship. Here is a good example of the difference between reflection of feeling and interpretation. It is true that the Client-centered counselor goes ahead of what the client *says,* and reacts to the feelings that are being expressed, but he does not overtly interpret for the client the meaning, or what he thinks is the meaning, of what the client is saying.

In any case, all professional counselors would probably agree that the client's initial announcement that he has had enough should not result in the immediate termination of the counseling sessions. On the other hand, the reflection of feeling by the counselor will leave the client free to decide for himself whether or not he still wants to terminate; and in some cases, he will terminate. Other counselors may feel that this is one reason why the counselor should be more interpretative. But if this procedure results in "holding" the client, he is more likely to be literally held, not because he wants to, but because he feels that the counselor wants him to stay. The Client-centered counselor does not see such a situation as an aspect of his relationship with the client. I was once told that I should have used this procedure to hold a client who wanted to leave; and yet this was exactly what had been done previously by two other therapists, with distressing results. The counselor can do only what he feels and what he believes in, and while his operational techniques will be continually modified, he cannot work against himself. Other counselors may be right in saying, "This is what I would have done," and even right that this is what the counselor should have done. But the counselor has to believe in the action himself, before he does it; otherwise he is little better than a record from which issue the words of someone else.

The complete lack of choice possible to some clients may also pose a problem. This is most obvious in the school situation, where, even though the client may be raging at the mean and miserable behavior of a teacher, he has no choice about leaving the teacher. He has to stay in school, and, more often than not, he has to go back to the same teacher. Such a lack of choice is a basic cause of many of the problems that are presented to the school counselor, and very often the fact is that the child must endure, for another year or two, an unrealistic curriculum, and quite possibly equally unrealistic and unsympathetic teachers. This is enough to test the mettle of a mature adult, and we can assume that an immature but nevertheless basically sound child is going to need some help to come through the experience a strong and stable individual.

Because youth must have practice in making its own decisions, many children would find school a better place if they were able to make the choice to withdraw from it, as they can from college, for a year or so. Their decision might be a poor one, for an unhappy school experience is not always because of a poor curriculum and poor teachers. Nevertheless, the adolescent grows up in a more realistic environment when he knows that he *can* make a choice, and that when he has made it, *he* will be held responsible for it. In our present culture, unfortunately, it almost seems that we are moving to a situation where the age of self-determination may never be reached. We may yet get to the point where, when mother has at last been removed from the picture, after the individual has been "educated" for many, many years, has been married, and has become a father, the state will take over. Then the individual may live in a happy state of irresponsibility for the rest of his days, letting someone else make his decisions for him, and thus never having to blame himself for anything that might go wrong. This state of total determinism never can, of course, be reached, and the existential, Client-centered counselor can help the child to develop the capacity for independent action, even though he may, for the moment, necessarily live in dependency. When the time comes, the child will then be capable of becoming a truly independent individual, standing on his own feet, and making his own way, and will have no need for counselors.

These are but a few of the problems that any student counselor is bound to meet. There are many others, of course, and every counselor, sooner or later, will run into problems that are peculiar for him because he is as he is. His measure as a mature and professional counselor will be determined by the extent to which he can work out answers to these problems to the greater benefit of the client, as well as his own greater growth.

Chapter Seven

OPERATIONAL ISSUES: II

THIS CHAPTER continues the discussion of operational issues, and one of the thorniest of all has to do with the meaning of words.

THE SEMANTIC PROBLEM

Many of the apparent differences among counselors are simply a lack of understanding of just exactly what one means when he uses a certain word or a descriptive phrase. Two words that still cause confusion are "counseling" and "psychotherapy," and neither really has any meaning until an individual counselor or therapist indicates what *he* means by each term. Thus we find individuals who call themselves psychotherapists doing what others would call counseling, and we find individuals who call themselves counselors doing what others would call psychotherapy. There are many differentiations between the two. One of the most common refers to counseling as dealing with a generally normal individual, and psychotherapy as dealing with an abnormal person; or some would say that counseling does not get to the same depth as psychotherapy; or some would say that counseling is concerned with the conscious, whereas psychotherapy deals with the unconscious materials. Bordin, for example, states that the counseling relationship is characterized by less intensity of emotional expression, and relatively more emphasis on cognitive and rational factors than is the case in psychotherapy.[1] Mowrer refers to counseling as a process of giving help "to persons suffering from fully-conscious conflicts which are accompanied by so-called normal anxiety." [2]

Tyler [3] thinks of the aim of therapy as some sort of personality change, while she feels that we should use "counseling" to refer to a helping process whose aim is not to change the person but to enable him to utilize the resources he now has for coping with life.

Buchheimer and Balogh [4] see the approach in therapy as historic and symbolic, relying heavily on the reactivation and consideration of unconscious materials. The content of conversation is the consideration of past experiences and the reconstruction of that which has happened and has been repressed, thus causing distortions of the present. Through the counseling conversation, on the other hand, the individual will revise his distortions and thereby alter his behavior. The emphasis is on the present, and on verbal material that is within the individual's immediate awareness or that he can easily be made aware of.

Byrne [5] sees counseling and psychotherapy as having much in common, and considers the major difference to be the degree to which psychotherapists uncover and work with hidden psychological dynamics because the individual seeking help reports a long-standing dissatisfaction with life, accompanied by long-standing ineffective or unwanted behaviors. He points out that the school counselor is not usually called upon to function as a psychotherapist, the reason lying in the relationship between function and clientele.

Then, too, some medically oriented psychotherapists would tend to feel that the practice of psychotherapy is limited to the realm of those who possess a medical degree, while what the others do is counseling. However, there are many nonmedical psychotherapists who work in certain institutions with their medical colleagues; all do practically identically the same thing, and they call it psychotherapy.

While there may be a logical difference between intellectual

[1] Edward S. Bordin, *Psychological Counseling* (New York: Appleton-Century-Crofts, 1955), p. 15.
[2] O. Hobart Mowrer, "Anxiety Theory as a Basis for Distinguishing Between Counseling and Psychotherapy," in Ralph F. Berdie (Ed.), *Concepts of Programs of Counseling* (Minneapolis: University of Minnesota Press, 1951), p. 23.
[3] Leona E. Tyler, *The Work of the Counselor* (New York: Appleton-Century-Crofts, 1961), p. 12.
[4] Arnold Buchheimer and Sarah Carter Balogh, *The Counseling Relationship* (Chicago: Science Research Associates, 1961), p. x.
[5] Richard Hill Byrne, *The School Counselor* (Boston: Houghton Mifflin Company, 1963), pp. 37–38.

guidance with a person whose stresses and strains do not control his actions, and counseling with an individual whose actions are dominated by and subject to his emotional stresses, there is no such differentiation between counseling and psychotherapy. There is not always, for example, a clear and distinct line between the conscious and the subconscious. When a person is swimming, he is partly in the water and partly out, rarely completely submerged or completely out of the water. Most professional school counselors are well acquainted with students who are pushed by subconscious pressures as causes of their difficulties; and the purpose of the counseling is to help the student to work out these parts of his totality that are only dimly, if at all, understood and accepted. Sometimes, of course, the distinction is quite clear. Nevertheless, anyone who works with people who are under stress is going to have a difficult time cataloguing what he is doing as either counseling or psychotherapy on the basis of the conscious or the subconscious.

Similarly, with regard to the depth of the process, it is probably correct to say that, traditionally, most counselors in schools have not worked with people who are completely divorced from our reality, and might thus be called psychotic, but have worked rather with those who would possibly like to be divorced from our reality, but know they are not, and might thus be called neurotic. One of the obvious reasons is that most of the former individuals are to be found in hospitals or similar institutions, whereas, until recently, counselors were to be found in hospitals only as patients.

In the last decade, however, with the advent of a high level of preparation at the doctorate and post-doctorate level for such professional workers as school counselors, counseling psychologists, rehabilitation counselors, and psychiatric nurses, it is obvious that people who may be called counselors are working with psychotic patients as are psychotherapists. On the other hand, a psychiatrist who has a private practice, or one who works in a University Clinic or a Counseling Center, most likely spends the bulk of his time with individuals who are neurotic rather than psychotic; and thus he is, if we must have a difference, a counselor rather than a therapist.

There are not only different levels of education for those who are involved in counseling and psychotherapy, there are different kinds of education as well. If we accept the definition of counseling given in this book, then it follows that those professional workers, whether called psychotherapists or counselors, are performing the same basic task, although they may be performing it in different ways because of their different educations and their different personalities. It might even be better to think in terms of psychotherapies, rather than psychotherapy. Then, possibly, psychotherapists who do different things would be more acceptable to each other, and would not threaten each other to the extent that they appear to today.

When one refers to the "practice of psychiatry," one usually means the practice of psychotherapy. Hence a psychiatrist might be described as a medical doctor who practices psychotherapy, while a psychologist is a Ph.D. who practices psychotherapy—though not all psychologists do. Psychoanalysis is generally considered by medical doctors to be a more intensive psychotherapy, although some differentiate between the two. Fromm-Reichman comments that there is no valid *intensive* psychotherapy other than that which is psychoanalytic or psychoanalytically oriented, a statement that would obviously be challenged by many psychotherapists who, though working intensively with extremely disturbed individuals, do not think of themselves as psychoanalysts.[6] On the other hand, although most medical personnel assume that only a psychiatrist can practice psychoanalysis (Freud was one medical doctor who did not see this), it is difficult for some to see just why a medical background is necessary to operate in an area that is overwhelmingly psychological in nature.

Tyler's reference to "no change" would seem to be rather pointless, since it would be impossible for one to utilize to a greater degree what he now has without undergoing any change! Nor can I see Buchheimer and Balogh's point of differentiation between the past and the present, since most individuals, when talking about themselves, mingle the past with the present. Even the school child under modest stress will be likely periodically to bring in the past as he talks about the present.

It would seem to me that the competent, professionally educated school counselor, as he goes about his daily professional tasks, is going to become involved in practically all of the human relationships that have been described by various individuals as either counseling or psychotherapy. Not in one day, or with one person, but over a period of time, with many different children, many of whom could not even be described as clients. He will work with some children almost entirely at a cognitive rational level, and with others he will spend much time in the area of feelings and emotions; with some children he may provide simple answers, which will affect their futures but create no drastic change; some children will bring much subconscious

[6] Frieda Fromm-Reichman, *Principles of Intensive Psychotherapy* (Chicago: University of Chicago Press, 1950), p. x.

material to the surface, others practically none at all; some children will spend much time on the past, which has taught them to be as they are, and others will be concerned mostly with the present. The counselor should be able to function effectively with these children, and as long as he can, it matters little whether he describes what he is doing as counseling or psychotherapy. If the term "psychotherapy" is bothersome to certain school administrators or medical personnel, the counselor might just as well refer to his function as counseling, and continue to do what he is doing anyway!

After all, the most Client-centered of Client-centered counselors is not going to "reflect feelings" when the cheery new student asks if English 3 has as its teacher Mr. Brown or Mr. Smith. If the counselor knows, he will likely say, "Mr. Brown." On the other hand, if a grim and tense student says to the same counselor, "Well, I guess you should know—which of these miserable courses in English has Smith as the teacher . . . ," the counselor will most likely react to the feeling behind the student's question, because obviously the student is not asking an intellectual question. He is expressing a feeling. Similarly, the counselor would feel that when a man quietly says, "I will kill myself tonight," the counselor reaction will not be, "Oh, you mustn't do a thing like that," because again the individual is expressing deep, intense feelings. Such a cliché as the one above would be little better than a rejection of the individual, who has possibly already been rejected by all whom he has known.

It is surely idiotic for any counselor to defend any of his actions on the basis of his supposed methodology. One does not do something, or not do something because he is a this or a that, but rather because the evidence has tended to indicate that this is the way that *he* can be most helpful with the other person, and it matters little whether he is functioning as a "vocational counselor," an "educational counselor," a "personal counselor," or a "psychotherapist." Right now I could think of several school counselors who could be described by any of these names if one happened to look through their windows at the right time!

Part of the semantic difficulty may reside in the very terms that have been used supposedly to describe different methodologies in counseling. Thus the terms "directive" and "non-directive" are unfortunate, since no counselor could avoid being directive. The very act of extreme acceptance of the client by the counselor is a means of direction of the client. There is a very definite difference in the two methodologies, but it is more in the mind and the attitude of the counselor than in the degree to which there is actual direction. Thus the question actually is, "How directive are you?" rather than "Are you directive or non-directive?"

Another term causing trouble is "Client-centered," although it is much better than "non-directive." It is hard to conceive of any counselor, professional or not, denying that he is client-centered. What else could he be—counselor-centered, culture-centered, or what? Yet again, there are differences. When one has listened to many counselors in action, it is obvious that they vary a good deal in the degree to which they are client-centered. The question is not, "Are you client-centered?" but rather, "Just how client-centered are you?" If the answer is "Not at all," it is difficult to see how such a person could be a successful counselor.

INTERPRETATION AND REFLECTION OF FEELING

As has already been indicated, words are deceptive, and two of the trickiest ones are "interpretation" and "reflection." The Client-centered counselor tends to feel that reflection of feeling is more empathic, and closer to the client's frame of reference, than is interpretation by the counselor *to* the client of the meaning of what the client is saying. Interpretation is, of course, always the counselor's version of what *he* thinks and feels that the client is communicating, or trying to communicate. Interpretation is also connected with another tricky word, "diagnosis." It would seem rather difficult to have any sort of interpretation without diagnosis, and this particular issue will be examined in the next section.

The difference between the two, however, is by no means clearcut, since the Client-centered counselor, after all, is reflecting what *he* thinks and feels that the client is thinking and feeling. The counselor is involved in both cases, and what one counselor might call reflection of feeling another would describe as interpretation. The more one empathizes with the client, the more likely it is that he can reflect accurately the deep and personal feelings of the client, and thus be close, and sensitive, to the client's frame of reference.

McKinney thinks of interpretation as the assistance that the counselor gives to the client in seeing relationships between present behavior and underlying causes or motivations. He goes on: [7]

> It is well established that an effective counselor does not interpret
> behavior until the client is *ready to grasp it and assimilate it effec-*

[7] Fred McKinney, *Counseling for Personal Adjustment* (Boston: Houghton Mifflin Company, 1958), p. 277.

tively in living. Interpretation runs the gamut. The counselor may merely repeat in an integrated manner many of the statements the client has made during the interview so that he may see their implications; or he may point out underlying repressed motives. Probably the most effective kind of interpretation consists of helping the client go just a little farther—just a little beyond where he was planning to stop.

Buchheimer and Balogh,[8] on the other hand, think of "surface" interpretation as a counseling lead, "depth" interpretation being that aspect of psychotherapy which seeks out the fundamental reasons for past and present behaviors.

One might generally describe the reflection of feeling as the attempt by the counselor to understand from the client's point of view and to communicate that understanding to him. On the one hand, one might say that there is less likelihood of counselor involvement in such a reflection than in an interpretation, and yet even here it is the counselor who is, in effect, saying, "This is the way I understand and feel you. . . ." Some would say that this differs little from skillful interpretation, since the effective counselor will never interpret too far ahead of the client. This is probably why, many years ago, Rogers had ceased talking about reflection and clarifying, and was saying instead: [9]

> [I]t is the counselor's function to assume, in so far as he is able, the internal frame of reference of the client, to perceive the world as the client sees it, to perceive the client himself as he is seen by himself, to lay aside all perceptions from the external frame of reference while doing so, and to communicate something of this empathic understanding to the client.

Hora questions the value of interpretation for another reason: [10]

> That which is, speaks for itself. That which speaks for itself is understood. What is understood needs no interpretation. What is interpreted is seldom understood.

Jung[11] gives a word of warning to dream interpreters when he says, "Do anything you like, only don't try to understand."

8 Buchheimer and Balogh, *op. cit.*, p. 54.
9 Carl R. Rogers, *Client-Centered Therapy* (Boston: Houghton Mifflin Company, 1951), p. 29.
10 Thomas Hora, "Healing or Growth," *Annals of Psychotherapy* 1:32 (Monograph 5, 1963).
11 C. G. Jung, *Modern Man in Search of a Soul* (New York: Harcourt, Brace & World, Inc., 1933), p. 12.

Even the interpretation of the analytical counselor, as he interprets the meaning of the transference relationship to the client, might be described as a reflection of subconscious feeling. This would also apply when he was interpreting to the client the possible meaning of various resistances that he might be expressing.

Thus probably all counselors, to some extent, reflect the feelings of the client—shallow and deep, conscious and subconscious, verbal and nonverbal—and what some call reflection, others will call interpretation. It is also probably correct to say that the deeper reflection of feeling, while used by all experienced counselors at some times, is used more consistently by the Client-centered counselor as his major means of verbal communication. On the other hand, far too many counselors, in the name of "Client-centered," merely repeat over and over again what the client has said, until both become fearfully bored!

Some might say that Ellis (Co), for example, is reflecting feeling in the following example.[12]

Cl: I don't know. I think it's natural being bothered by having people being disturbed and not understanding why they're disturbed. I mean, I can see why they might object, but I don't see why they don't want me to talk the whole thing out and find out why they're disturbed because I'm upset.

Co: Well, if I'm hearing you correctly you're sort of saying that—ah—that you are not objecting to their getting upset, but you at least would like them to talk it out with you.

While Rogers (Co) might appear to be "interpreting": [13]

Co: Yeah, yeah. But you felt he didn't quite understand you on that really.

Cl: I thought that he felt that I was being blunt, and that I just meant that I didn't want to talk to him any more.

Co: And I, if I sense some of your feeling now, it is, uh, a little tenseness that, that maybe he didn't really get that, he felt you were shutting him off on something.

Cl: Yes, that's what, and that isn't what I meant.

But Rogers is *the* "Client-centered" counselor, and Ellis is *the* "rational" psychotherapist!

[12] From the tape *Loretta,* American Academy of Psychotherapists.
[13] *Ibid.*

Most beginning counselors who take some pride in their "analytic" or "diagnostic" title question or probe the client to death, while most beginning counselors who fly "Client-centered" at their masthead "reflect" the client to distraction. On the other hand, it is also true that some questions demand answers, and they are certainly less centered on the client than is any kind of reflection of feeling. Carl's counselor (C), for example, is reflecting feelings and statements: [14]

C80: You feel they happen more often than they should just to be nightmares.

S81: Yes. Seems like I never dream . . . (etc.).

C82: You feel you're somewhere you really don't belong.

S83: Yes . . . (etc.).

C84: No matter how you think about it or feel about it, or try and talk about it, it seems to still be there.

S85: Yes, it still . . . (etc.).

C86: For a short period of time you feel that you are acceptable. People are not noticing you.

S87: Yes. I feel . . . (etc.).

C88: So, even being accepted now and getting away from this feeling of being alone is a problem.

Much of the superficial reflection is to ease the tension of the counselor, and there would be less direction if the counselor were merely to keep quiet, or to make understanding sounds. Jane's counselor (C), for example, by his "reflection," may encourage her to keep talking about what might be trivia: [15]

C164: You're worried about the cause of the drop.

S165: . . . . . .

C166: You're wondering if you worry more about these things than other people do.

S167: . . . . . .

C168: You feel possibly if you stopped worrying about it they might straighten themselves out.

S169: . . . . . .

C170: You feel you should do things about this, do something for it instead of worrying about it all the time.

S171: . . . . . .

C172: You feel you should be working now.

S173: . . . . . .

[14] William Evraiff, *Helping Counselors Grow Professionally* (Englewood Cliffs, N.J.: Prentice-Hall, Inc., 1963), pp. 46–47.
[15] *Ibid.*, p. 95.

C174: You feel you should be working, but you're a little too selective about the kind of job and . . . .

Nonetheless, the experienced Client-centered couneslor does tend to follow a more consistent pattern of being *with* the client, and this is usually seen verbally in a reflection or interpretation of the client's feelings and statements. It would be unlikely that the following questioning and probing would be found in a Client-centered counselor: [16]

Doctor: Tell me how you are feeling and when it started, can you?

Patient: I think so. I feel, I don't know, I feel at ease with certain people and with others I don't feel at ease. Like I'd say it started when my father got sick. I . . . I sort of took it on myself. I thought maybe it was my fault when my father got sick. I know that things have not been going too smoothly at home. I was out of work all summer, and there were many arguments, so when my father got sick I thought maybe it was my fault, but that feeling went away, of course. But my nerves haven't been the same since that.

D: Since he got sick?

P: That's right—I just seem to be ill at ease—now I mean I am talking to you—I feel natural now. With certain people I do, but at home I don't. I don't understand it.

D: You spoke before about feeling disappointed.

P: I have a depressed feeling. I—it's so hard to explain—I feel like I am waiting for something to happen, and it's never going to happen—and I feel like I gotta run away and I go out of the house and—well, I want to go right back home again. I know there's nothing out of the house. I don't have too many friends. I was going with a buddy but he's down south now and I have a feeling—and I have a lonesome feeling, to tell you the truth. (Sighs.) I don't know—I don't know what I'm looking for—forward to something that's not going to happen.

[16] Ruben R. Pottash, "A Psychotherapeutic Interview with an Adolescent," in Benjamin Harries Balster (Ed.), *Psychotherapy of the Adolescent* (New York: International Universities Press, Inc., 1957), pp. 160–164.

D: Is it dreadful do you think, what might happen, or is it pleasant?

P: Well, that's just it, I don't know. (Pause.) I've been going out very seldom now. I stay around the house all the time—I'm working in the store all the time, and well, I go to the movies, and that's all. We close now Thursday night and Sunday night, but I go to the movies or I go to a friend's house or relatives. But Saturday night was the first time for a long time that I went out since my father's been sick. That happened so suddenly. On a couple minutes' notice I went out. But when I got up Sunday morning I felt all right until I started to get a depressed feeling. I couldn't understand what it was, and I thought maybe I was sick or something—because I have had pains in my stomach all the time and my mother kept saying, "Why don't you go to the doctor," and I thought maybe I'll put it off until tomorrow and it will go away.

D: Do you have any idea what you might be depressed about?

P: I dunno. I thought it might be that I'm lonesome. You know, I feel like I'm alone. Even when I'm with a lot of people I feel like I'm alone.

D: Hasn't it always been that way?

This example would be more typical of a Client-centered counselor (T): [17]

C33:   Um-hm. So I don't know what I'll do. (Slight pause.) I usually do wait till the last possible moment, and then make a quick decision. (Laughs.) One way or the other.

T33:   You're kind of saying you won't handle it very well.

C34:   No, I won't; that's right. I'll do it the way I usually do it. Slipshod. (Pause; sighs.) Could I use a cigarette now. Oh! (Trembling.)

T34:   Right this minute, that is just what you would want.

C35:   (Sighs; tears; pause.) I guess I'm upset now. (Sighs;

[17] John M. Shlien, "Time-limited, Client-centered Psychotherapy: Two Cases," in Authur Burton (Ed.), *Case Studies in Counseling and Psychotherapy* (Englewood Cliffs, N.J.: Prentice-Hall, Inc., 1959), pp. 316–317.

pause.) Having state visitors come and visit our school tomorrow and they put up such a big show. And everyone gets very excited and . . . big fuss. (Pained, stricken look.)

T33: What—what's hitting you now?

C36: I don't know.

T36: Something upsetting, something that makes you feel like crying?

C37: (Pause; crying softly; words lost.) And I don't know why either. I just got very upset. (Still crying.)

T38: Uh-hm. Something just came over you, and you really don't know what started it.

C39: (Long pause; still crying.) I must have been getting a little too close to something—I didn't want to talk about, or something.

T39: You really don't know what made this happen. (Client looks for clock.) You've still got about fifteen minutes.

C40: (Pause; still crying.) Something hit me. (Laughs.)

T40: Hm?

C41: Something hit me.

T41: Something hurts.

Or, we may compare the personal involvement of this counselor (B): [18]

B: You were starting to say I—I did something?

T: I—sort of have a feeling that you forced some of it.

B: Oh. By what I did or by what I am as a person?

T: By, in a sense . . . uh . . . you're telling me, "Listen, you're just going around and about, now let's get to the point." And then I felt (pause) this—if I went on going around, I'd never get to the point and I'd never get well. Or—and that you would not continue therapy.

B: The fear of losing me?

T: That—that was pretty strong.

B: But I never threatened you.

T: No, I know. I don't know what it was. But I know I had that feeling.

B: Maybe you had another feeling too (pause), a feeling of a relationship with me.

[18] Arthur Burton, "Paradox and Choice in Schizophrenia," in Arthur Burton (Ed.), *op. cit.*, pp. 268–269.

T: Yes, I did—very strongly I remember until . . . uh . . . at one point when—remember when I felt you were accusing me of terrible crimes and . . .

B: Hm-mm.

T: At this point . . . uh . . . it sort of went around and I (buzzer), you became in a sense the opposite—an enemy, not as a friend.

B: At that time I was an enemy.

T: Yes, I felt very strongly that you . . . now stop wandering around and come to the point. (Laughs.)

B: Hm-m.

T: And—(pause).

B: But you wanted to be a child then. (Pause.) Your psychosis represented that, (pause). And remember I put it to you that you either take your psychosis or you take reality. It was up to you, remember?

with this experienced Client-centered counselor (T): [19]

C: Yeah. I'm afraid of being ordinary. Yet I'm afraid this is what is asked of me.

T: You want to be different and you want to—

C: (Breaking in) I want to live a life I can enjoy. And the kind of life that seems to be offered to the average man is not to me enjoyable. Sitting and watching television five nights a week. Alternating television with movies.

T: You're not contented with the lot that most people have.

C: No! I hate it!

T: Something better, and something more exciting—

C: That's right. But I don't know how to get it. That's the trouble. I feel bound—by something or other—it must be me! (Laughs.) There's nothing else that seems to be doing it. I can't blame it on anything else. But there's this knot—somewhere inside of me.

T: Feel tied up by something in you that's kind of a mystery to you.

C: Yeah! Makes me want to get mad—and cry—and run away.

T: Lots of mixed up feelings about it.

[19] Madge K. Lewis, "Time-limited, Client-centered Psychotherapy: Two Cases," in Arthur Burton (Ed.), *op. cit.*, pp. 334–335.

C: Yeah. Also feels I can never get at it the way I've been trying to get at it. . . . It's as if I can't put my attention on it.

T: Like a blind spot.

C: Yeah. I can see effects in my life I don't like; yet I can't see their cause. I must be deliberately blinding myself because it would be painful to know. But what could it be?

T: What could it be that might cause me so much hurt?

C: Yeah. Do I think I'm a failure—a ruined human being —or something of the sort? It must be something like that. That I don't feel worthy—of anything.

T: Am I flop—completely unworthy of any kind of good life?

And finally, we might compare this questioner (C), also known as a counselor: [20]

Cl: Can you tell me a little more about how you seem to be held back?

S1: Well, mathematics mostly.

C2: Mm-huh. How does that affect you?

S2: Well, I haven't done very good on the tests in taking them.

C3: Mm-huh (pause). Could you tell me a little bit about your background, where you are from, what you plan to do, and so forth?

S3: Well, I'm from (name of town).

C4: Yes.

S4: Have you ever been there?

C5: No, but I know where it is.

S5: I'm in pre-vet school. I'd like to take up veterinary medicine if I can make the grade.

C6: Mm-huh.

S6: That's my only trouble.

C7: When did you decide on veterinary medicine?

S7: Well, I've been kind of interested for some time. I live on a farm and I work with a lot of livestock.

C8: Do you know any veterinarians?

S8: Well, yes, our local veterinarian.

[20] Robert Callis, Paul C. Polmantier and Edward C. Roeber, *A Casebook of Counseling* (New York: Appleton-Century-Crofts, 1955), pp. 105–106.

C9:   Mm-huh. And you'd like to be doing the work he seems to be doing at the present time?

S9:   Yes.

C10:   You haven't worked with him, though, while he is working with animals, or anything like that?

S10:   Well, yes, I've worked some.

C11:   Have you?

S11:   Mm-huh.

C12:   What made you choose veterinary medicine as the field you wanted to go into?

S12:   Well—

C13:   (Counselor interrupts) Was it any one person or just working on the farm?

with this Client-centered counselor (Co): [21]

Cl: (Smiling) No. No. I was thinking, ah . . . that . . . sometimes . . . well, I mean I, then, ah, late, you know in the last ten years I've been . . . more tired than the average person that . . . people get tired, but, ah . . . I don't know, in fact lately it . . . seems as though I could keep on going with much less . . . sleep than I have . . . when I've felt all right . . . (smiles) . . . since I don't have very restful sleep I . . . I think I'm awake now more than I'm asleep.

Co: You mean you've always needed a lot of rest.

Cl: I've always needed a lot of rest.

Co: And you mean that you feel that you need less now than before.

Cl: Yes, I used to . . . require a good night's sleep and if I didn't have a good night's sleep I'd be . . . tired and . . .

Co: You'd have a generally tired feeling.

Cl: Yeah . . . Although when I used to take, ah, you know, those drugs . . . and . . . different things like that to get over the tired . . . feeling, but, ah, at my age . . . and I don't think, and for the little I did do, I don't think I should have been tired, as I always was.

Co: You mean you weren't particularly exerting yourself.

[21] Dugald S. Arbuckle, *Guidance and Counseling in the Classroom* (Boston: Allyn and Bacon, Inc., 1957), pp. 240–241.

Cl: Well—I, just a little bit but nothing . . . to tire me the way I . . . did get tired. And then it was probably always . . . like . . . I said in . . . my mind, and my mind was on the go a lot.

Co: Yeah. Maybe not so much the physical effort, you mean, as the . . .

Cl: Mental.

Co: As the mental thinking . . . or worrying . . . or wondering.

Cl: Yes.

Co: And that wore you out more than your physical effort.

Cl: Yeah. Uh hummm- (pause—31 seconds).

Co: And you mean you . . . don't have as much of that feeling now as you . . . used to have, ah?

Cl: No. Lately I haven't had, have had . . . have had half as much sleep as I . . . used to think that I required.

Co: And you don't feel any worse.

Cl: Oh, I feel tired, but . . . not as . . . tired . . . well, I suppose a different tired feeling.

Co: A different sort of tiredness, you mean?

And yet, even experienced counselors who see themselves as "Client-centered," and who are seen by others in the same light, vary tremendously in their degree of reflection of feeling and what would appear to be out-and-out interpretation. There would appear to be a high level of reflection of feeling, for example, in this excerpt of a session with an adult client (Cl):

Cl: . . . and if I could, I'd be more secure. . . .

Co: And this was tied in with resentment toward me. . . .

Cl: Yes . . . I was resentful of the fact that I couldn't . . . (long pause). . . .

Co: You were feeling close to me, but there was both threat and reassurance in that you could feel close to me without this sexual relationship. . . .

Cl: Yes . . . it is . . . you see . . . I've never had a relationship like this . . .

and in this one with an adult client (Cl):

Cl: Yeh—I still do—it hits me, and is gone—but why don't I remember the pleasant things . . . why . . .

> Co: A sort of a feeling . . . there *must* have been some nice things . . .
> Cl: Yeh—yeh. . . .
> Co: It couldn't always have been. . . .
> Cl: No—no—it wasn't—it wasn't. . . .
> Co: You mean it not only couldn't, it wasn't. . . .
> Cl: No—it definitely wasn't . . .

There is more of a combination of reflection of feeling and interpretation between these counselors and these junior high school clients (Cl):

> Cl: Dances, clothes, boys, parties . . . that's all they think of. . . . It's so stupid and foolish. . . . I'm glad I'm not like them.
> Co: I feel all these interests are ridiculous, but sometimes I feel, deep down, that I'd like to go to parties and dances and be popular like other girls. . . .

> . . . .

> Cl: I love animals. . . . I want to get some kind of a job later on working with animals . . . particularly horses. . . .
> Co: Animals aren't like people . . . animals are friends —they're affectionate . . . they'll return your love . . . they're loyal . . . I can trust them. . . .

> . . . .

> Cl: I'm not afraid of anyone or anything. . . .
> Co: It helps me to say I'm not afraid of anyone or anything when I'm really afraid.

> . . . .

And what would appear to be out-and-out interpretation is being given by these counselors *to* these junior high school clients (Cl):

> Cl: These women teachers bug me. . . . I get the feeling that they don't like boys because some time in their life some man jilted them.
> Co: Maybe your attitude toward them is conditioned by your attitude toward your mother. There seems to be a relationship.

> . . . .

> Cl: Becoming a veterinarian is important. . . . I think that I'd be happy at it because . . . well, for a long time I've loved animals . . . I've loved caring for

them . . . sort of makes me feel good inside . . .
kind of important.

Co: Sometimes loving animals is a lot easier than loving
people.

. . . .

Cl: I'm sort of cold toward him—it's hard to explain but
. . . well, I sort of enjoy being distant . . . sort of
testing him . . . trying to see just how much of my
coldness he'll take.

Co: The same sort of coldness that you told me exists between your father and mother.

. . . .

Cl: I find myself sort of wanting to lose my books. . . . I
doodle in book pages . . . blot out paragraphs . . .
even destroy even numbered pages.

Co: Maybe books represent infringements on your leisure
time.

. . . .

Cl: Everybody tells me I can do the work. . . . I don't
know why I'm doing so lousy . . . I . . . I just can't
seem to get myself to take an interest in school . . .
my folks are disappointed. . . . I know they're
burned and hurt and yet it doesn't make any difference . . . I just can't get going even though I *know*
I can do the work.

Co: It seems everybody says I've got the potential . . .
and I know I can do well in school . . . but maybe
I fail because it's a good way to get back at people.

DIAGNOSIS

Diagnosis may be considered as the analysis of one's difficulties
and the causes that have produced them. More clinically, it may be
thought of as the determination of the nature, origin, precipitation
and maintenance of ineffective abnormal modes of behavior. More
simply, it might be considered as the development, by the counselor,
of a deeper and more accurate understanding and appreciation of the
client.

Diagnosis of the more clinical sort has had a long and honorable
medical history, and it is directly related to prognosis and treatment.
Psychologists have generally accepted without question the need for

diagnosis, and it is even more unfortunate that many counselors apparently operate on the assumption that effective counseling without diagnosis is impossible. Many student counselors tend to take diagnosis for granted without, possibly, asking enough questions as to just what diagnosis is, why it is needed, how accurate it may be, and what one does with a diagnosis once one has it. Diagnosis provides a particularly good example of the unhappy results of assuming that the problems of the mind and the heart are the same as the problems of the physical body, even though it is rather difficult to see how those procedures that are successful in the treatment of a diseased kidney would be equally satisfactory in the treatment of fears developed in a child by insecure and frightened parents. Because the medical profession has generally taken for granted the concept that emotional disturbances are diseases, a person is frequently assumed to be a skilled practitioner in "mental health" if he possesses a medical degree, even though his psychological knowledge of personality disorders is often a good deal less than that of a student who has just been granted an undergraduate degree in psychology.

The diagnosis of a leg as inoperative because of a fracture of the tibia, caused by a sudden contact with a solid object, necessitating the setting and immobilization of the leg in a cast for several weeks may not be as complicated as the diagnosis of a pain in the belly as an inflammation of the appendix, caused by unknown factors, necessitating immediate operative procedures for its removal; but neither of these can be compared with the complexity of the diagnosis of a relatively frequent psychological problem such as that of the very intelligent boy who consistently does very poor academic work, or that of the overly aggressive child who insists on pushing other children around.

It can be assumed that the purpose of diagnosis is to develop such a picture that intelligent action can be taken on the basis of it. The easier it is to arrive at the picture, the more likely it is to be accurate, and the action taken to be appropriate. Thus a broken leg may be such that the diagnosis is quite simple, or it may be a complicated break requiring an equally difficult diagnosis. But in any case, the problem, the injury, the ailment is something that, we might say, "is there." The task of the medical doctor is, nearly always, to do something about a difficulty that "is there." When the medical doctor gets into the treatment of certain physical diseases, however, a diagnosis of, say, cancer, does not do much good, because no one knows yet what causes cancer, and thus no one knows the treatment for it. In the majority of physiological ailments and organic ailments, however, the cause is known; and once this happens, a remedy is speedily found.

With emotional disturbances, however, knowing the cause is often a rather minor matter, and not too much can be done, just as the dentist cannot do much for the rotting and decaying teeth of his patient that he knows were caused by foolish diet when she was a child. He can, however, remove her teeth and put in a false set, not as good as the originals, but still not too bad. Like the dentist, I knew with a high degree of certainty the causes of the fears of one of my clients, and in time she knew the causes too, but this did not remove the fears. Probably the basic point here is that the dentist could remove the decayed teeth and put others in their place, just as the medical doctor could skillfully set the broken bone and initiate procedures to speed its healing; but in both cases the patient was outside of this activity. Others were doing something to parts of his body. The counselor, however, cannot remove the fears of the client, and any diagnosis by the counselor *must assume that somewhere, sometime, the client is going to be able to make use of that diagnosis;* otherwise, why make it? Thus the psychoanalyst's interpretation to the client of his transference and his resistance is part of the therapist's diagnosis, being given, when the therapist feels that it is appropriate, to the client, so that he may make use of it for further development.

The Client-centered counselor tends to be more skeptical than some of his counseling colleagues about both the virtues and the necessity for diagnosis in counseling. He has some skepticism indeed about the validity of diagnosis. Many patients can vouch for the variety of ailments that they appear to have had on the basis of diagnoses by several different medical doctors who have had no contact with each other. An interesting comment on the validity of diagnosis has been made by Wittenborn: [22]

> If psychiatrists believe consistently that certain symptoms go together, the ratings which they make for their patients may reveal their belief concerning symptom-clustering. Accordingly, if syndromes are revealed among the symptoms, the possibility remains that the syndromes are more descriptive of consistencies which exist in the behavior of psychiatrists than they are descriptive of consistencies which exist in the behavior of patients.

The Client-centered counselor feels that in an understanding and acceptant atmosphere the client will come to see the "why" of

22 J. R. Wittenborn, "Symptom Patterns in a Group of Mental Hospital Patients," *Journal of Consulting Psychology* 15:290–302 (August, 1951).

his behavior, and any action that is taken will be *by him* on the basis of *his diagnosis* rather than that of the counselor. But, one might say, if the counselor is a student of psychology, he must have certain diagnostic understandings, and how can he avoid being diagnostic, at least in his own mind, even though he may not verbalize his conclusions to the client? This is a good question, and there seems little doubt that the Client-centered counselor does see a picture of the client as the counseling proceeds; but this picture is primarily one that is being developed by the client for himself and for the counselor. I find it extremely difficult, even if it were desirable, to be diagnostically minded toward either the client or myself during a counseling session. This is not the case, however, when one listens sometimes with a colleague to a tape of the counseling session. Under such conditions the counselor is certainly diagnostic with regard to himself, and with the client too, insofar as he is expressing himself during the counseling session; but he has no particular pre-planned activities with regard to where the client should go and what he should do. In the counseling session he is going to be with the client, and his intelligence and his understanding are going to be directed toward this end rather than toward the correct manner of leading or directing the client.

Diagnosis, in a way, implies the possibility of "pigeonholing" the client as belonging to a certain category or a certain type; and the implication that follows is that for a certain type there is a certain treatment. One of the most frequently quoted studies is one by Pepinsky in which he evolved a group of diagnostic categories describing various client ailments.[23] Pepinsky himself, however, never intended that these be actually used in counseling in a rigid manner, and in a later book he stated: [24]

> We are not arguing here for the use of diagnostic categories in reconstructing the learning of a client prior to his initial contacts in counseling. On the contrary, we believe that our present notions about relevant and irrelevant drives, and their associated stimulus and response events, furnish a more parsimonious and helpful account of client learning.

Nevertheless, categories are handy things to seize upon, and too frequently we see counselors who seem to operate on such concepts as: "John Smith—problem: lack of information"; "Mary Brown—

[23] Harold B. Pepinsky, "The Selection and Use of Diagnostic Categories in Clinical Counseling," *Applied Psychology Monograph*, No. 15, 1958.
[24] Harold B. Pepinsky and Pauline N. Pepinsky, *Counseling: Theory and Practice* (New York: The Ronald Press Company, 1954), p. 114.

problem: lack of assurance"; "Jim Bowie—problem: self conflict." And indeed the poor client is often categorized long before the counseling begins. The process of counselor direction has thus begun even before the client has had a chance to express himself to the counselor. On the other hand, some counselors would say that this does not necessarily apply, and that as long as the counselor is a professional and skilled therapist he will detect an incorrect or inappropriate diagnosis, and no harm will be done to the client. But counselors are human beings, and it would be a rare counselor indeed whose personal relationship with another individual would not be affected by the fact that he had already determined in his mind that there was a problem of a certain type that could best be treated in a certain manner. At best, it would seem that the open mind becomes somewhat clouded by prior diagnosis, and that a more appropriate procedure is to take the client where he is, as he is.

What happens, however, if a diagnosis is not established and the counselor starts off on the wrong foot? Aldrich expresses this danger when he says: [25]

> This case clearly illustrates the importance of establishing a dynamic diagnosis before embarking on treatment. If diagnosis is bypassed, as in this case, much time may be lost and treatment may not be used to best advantage. Fortunately for the patient in this case, the supervisor's request to discontinue the contact precipitated enough "distress" on the part of the patient that the therapist was encouraged to carry out more active diagnostic efforts. Had a dynamic diagnosis been sought for earlier in the course of the contact with the therapist, more time would have been available for a more thorough working through of the patient's guilt, and for a more comprehensive consolidation of therapeutic gains.

The Client-centered counselor, however, would not start off on the wrong foot, since he would not start off with any previous diagnostic concepts, but rather would help the client to develop these for himself as the counseling proceeded. In the above example, the reason for the inappropriate therapy, if such was the case, seems to have been that the therapist *had* established a diagnosis that was incorrect or unacceptable to the client.

In a way, the question of diagnosis brings up the earlier question of the role of the counselor as either a service individual or a researcher. The latter is primarily a diagnostician. He tries to determine

25 Aldrich C. Knight, in Stanley W. Standal and Raymond Corsini, Jr., *Critical Incidents in Psychotherapy* (Englewood Cliffs, N.J.: Prentice-Hall, Inc., 1959), p. 148.

causes. He tries to answer the question "Why?" Although certainly no one would deny his crucial role in the study of the process of counseling and psychotherapy, one may question the capacity of the person who is primarily a diagnostician to relate in a meaningful way with a client. Students will attest to the dreadful teaching that takes place when the teacher is a researcher whose specialty is, say, the human heart, but not the means by which one relates with a group of individuals so that they can learn something about the human heart. The Client-centered counselor would be even more skeptical about the capacity of a counselor to relate closely and intimately with another person, and at the same time be functioning as a diagnostician of that individual's problems and difficulties. He himself, at least, finds it impossible to be both. Thus it may surprise some of his colleagues sometimes when they refer someone to him and ask him how many data he wants on the client, to hear him reply, "I don't want any data on the client. We'll both start together when he comes in to see me."

Such an attitude may seem far-fetched and even shocking to some, and yet I have been impressed by the number of counselors of varying hues who are advocates of diagnosis, but who disregard the diagnosis of others regarding a client, and operate on the basis of their own diagnosis after they have seen him. Thus the measure of the Client-centeredness of these "diagnosticians" might come in the extent to which they were diagnostic in their relationship with the client.

The individuality of counselors, and their disagreement even among themselves with regard to professional questions, is shown in a most interesting fashion by the reactions of fifteen therapists to the question, "Do you make a diagnosis before therapy begins?" Typical of the atypicalness of the reactions are those quoted below. Ackerman writes: [26]

> My answer to this question is emphatically in the affirmative. I consider it of the utmost importance to achieve a clear diagnostic definition of the patient's disorder before making any final commitment about accepting a patient for treatment. This does not mean, however, that the diagnostic study is pursued in any routine or ritualized manner. It is not a question and answer interview. The interview itself is a dynamic, open-ended process. Its flow is determined by the perception of significant cues as to foci of pathogenic conflict and anxiety. The early interview contact, while primarily diagnostic, is simultaneously oriented to the patient's therapeutic needs. Nevertheless, a final decision as to the acceptance of a particular patient for treatment rests on a clear picture of the patient's disorder. In order to apply therapy in a

[26] Nathan W. Ackerman, in Arthur Burton, *op. cit.*, p. 70.

psychologically specific manner, one must know exactly what is wrong with the patient. The diagnostic study includes clinical psychiatrist evaluation and, wherever other examinational procedures may be indicated, psychological studies, a home visit, a medical examination, and so forth.

Szasz comments as follows: [27]

> I cannot answer this question without commenting on the word "diagnosis," which I consider to be seriously misleading if used in connection with psychotherapeutic considerations. In other words, if "diagnosis" refers to ascertaining the kind of "psychiatric disease"—such as hysteria, obsessive-compulsive neurosis, schizophrenia, and so forth—the patient "has"—then my answer would be that *I do not make a "diagnosis"* before beginning psychotherapy. If, however, "diagnosis" refers to gaining an impression of the sort of person the patient is, how he grew up, the nature of his personal relationships and his work, the degree of his freedom in the conduct of his life, and so on . . . then I would answer emphatically "Yes. *I do make a diagnosis."*

Jacobi says: [28]

> I never venture a diagnosis before working with the patient for a certain time. Even if the patient brings with him a diagnosis formulated by another analyst, I question it and wait until it is proven correct by the passage of time. If a case reveals characteristic symptoms, it can, of course, happen that I cannot avoid a diagnosis; but I always look upon it as a hypothesis as long as I am not completely certain.

Author Burton's own answer is: [29]

> I do not give much credence to formal diagnosis before psychotherapy begins. This does not mean that I do not consider the diagnosis at all. I believe every psychotherapist mulls this over in the course of psychotherapy and revises his formulation as he goes along. Formal diagnosis, as, for example, psychiatric hospital diagnosis, catches the patient at a cross-sectional period which may be not at all representative of his psyche and his functioning. These formulations then tend to become solidified and interfere with psychotherapy because of implications of a poor prognosis. The history of long-term psychoanalysis or psychotherapy is that the patient may experience phobic, schizoid, obsessive, depressed, paranoid, manic, compulsive and similar manifestations at one or another stage in the course of treatment, and of course has alternating psychotic and neurotic phases, however mild. I tend to agree

[27] *Ibid.,* p. 107.
[28] *Ibid.,* p. 139.
[29] *Ibid.,* p. 279.

with Whitaker and his school that, in treating schizophrenics at any rate, we more properly speak of a transference psychosis rather than a transference neurosis. Formal diagnosis seems at times to be somewhat a function of the training, psychiatric milieu, and unconscious needs of the one making the diagnosis rather than something indigenous to the life history of the patient. In the case presented here a diagnosis of psychoneurosis, character disorder and schizophrenia could have been made at several cross-sectional points in her illness career. All of these were correct and all were incorrect if interpreted as intellectual abstractions of some hypothetically median patient.

And John Shlien's: [30]

No. Diagnostic techniques are not sufficiently valid, for one thing. Also, they do not help; if anything, they have an adverse influence on the relationship, since they tend to categorize the client in the counselor's eyes, and give the counselor an intimidating and unwarranted "expert" status (he should be an expert, in fact, but not on that basis), and in general focus attention on artificial and impersonal issues. Finally, there is no specific treatment to be applied, so of what use would specific diagnosis be if it were accomplished? Psychotherapy is not medicine. Human misery is not an organic disease.

To clarify, diagnosis as discussed here does not mean the *judgment* exercised by the counselor at almost every step. Neither is it *prognosis,* which assesses the constructive resources and estimates the probability of achieving health. Diagnosis is the classic psychiatric classification and description which is static, and focused wholly on pathology. Therapy, in contradistinction, has a fluid tone, and anticipates change. It will encounter the pathology ("what is wrong") but can rely only on "what is right" with the organism.

We do indeed use measures of change in therapy, but these are for research to discover the facts about change in groups of clients, and these measures are not yet so keen as to be satisfactory for that purpose, much less for individual diagnosis.

Some of the more analytically oriented counselors feel that diagnosis is essential, and that our current major problem is the inaccuracy of diagnosis. They would probably agree with Mahan when he says: [31]

But the most striking result is the confirmation once again of the difficulty of predicting overt behavior from psychological test data. Pre-

[30] *Ibid.,* p. 349.
[31] Thomas W. Mahan, Jr., "Diagnostic Consistency and Prediction: A Note on Graduate Student Skills," *Personnel and Guidance Journal* 42:364–367 (December, 1963).

diction unfortunately does not follow directly from diagnosis; the "over-determination" of human behavior makes extremely hazardous the effort to isolate variables when it is the interaction of variables that is paramount. Perhaps the time has come when the training programs in school psychological services must integrate into their emphasis on individual understanding the psychological study of social situations, roles, institutional pressures, and . . . "treatments."

The answer to more accurate and empirical diagnosis, of course, is the replacement of the human being by the machine, and if diagnosis is seen as the primary function of the counselor, there would seem to be no good reason why he should not also be replaced by the machine. Meehl and Dahlstrom describe the problem of using the "too human" clinician in diagnosis: [32]

> While it would not be too surprising to find that the "clinical eye" has trained itself to recognize configurations not readily identified by conventional linear methods of statistical analysis, it might be presumed that the clinician's subjective judgment, however experienced, assigns less than optimal weights. In addition to this systematic bias, the human judge throws in some more or less random error variance due to his unreliability.

There is plenty of evidence to indicate that the electronic digital computer can carry out complex processes that are much the same as processes that may be observed in human beings who are thinking. Kleinmuntz,[33] for example, has demonstrated how the tape-recorded verbalizations of an MMPI profile analyst could be approximated by programed instructions. It is likely that an increasing number of functions that have been considered to be part of the professional responsibility of the counselor may be taken over by the machine. Robinson,[34] for example, would almost seem to be describing a day that will soon be past when he says, "A counselor attempting to analyze a client's characteristics so as to have a basis for selecting the most relevant counseling methods needs to use at least four 'diagnostic' approaches." This is exactly what the machine will be likely to do more effectively, and this may all be to the good. The hard fact is that

[32] P. E. Meehl and W. G. Dahlstrom, "Objective Configural Rules for Discriminating Psychotic from Neurotic MMPI Profiles," *Journal of Consulting Psychology* 24:375–387 (October, 1960).
[33] Benjamin Kleinmuntz, "Profile Analysis Revisited: A Heuristic Approach," *Journal of Counseling Psychology* 10:315–324 (Winter, 1963).
[34] Francis P. Robinson, "Modern Approaches to Counseling 'Diagnosis,'" *Journal of Counseling Psychology* 10:325–333 (Winter, 1963).

if a machine can do better what a certain counselor is doing, then the machine should take over. But the machine cannot establish the human relationship that is the crucial factor in counseling, and it may be that the client of the future will come to the counselor with his machine-established diagnosis and prognosis in hand. The most logical rational choice may have been presented to him by the machine, but, as a somewhat irrational human being, he will still want to see the counselor to talk about what he should do with this logical rational choice that has been handed to him!

ECLECTICISM

Some differences still exist among counselors as to the place of "eclecticism" in counseling, although, like other terms, much depends on just how one interprets it. It is interesting to note too that eclecticism is much less of an issue in current books and articles than it was in the past, and this may be some indication that counseling is outgrowing its "technique" stage. It has not outgrown it yet, however, and it is for this reason that eclecticism is still included in this book as an issue. If one thinks of the counseling process as consisting of a series of techniques, isolated from the personality of the counselor, to be used according to the client and the type of problem that he presents, then one can readily see how the counselor can be eclectic in his approach. He is eclectic in that he uses those techniques and methods that seem most appropriate for a certain client at a certain time. If, on the other hand, what are called methodologies are actually qualities of the individual counselor, it is difficult to see how the counselor could be eclectic. The counselor's sense of values, the counselor's deep feelings regarding the worth of the client, the counselor's feelings regarding his capacity and moral right to measure and evaluate, the counselor's feelings toward his basic function as a counselor—these are part of the counselor's self, and there must, surely, be a consistency of counselor self. The lack of support by the Client-centered counselor for the practice of eclecticism in counseling arises basically because he equates it with counselor self-inconsistency.

This was probably part of the thinking of Rogers over two decades ago when he challenged the generally accepted concept of eclecticism: [35]

[35] Carl R. Rogers, *Client-Centered Therapy* (Boston: Houghton Mifflin Company, 1951), p. 8.

These schools of thought will not be abolished by wishful thinking. The person who attempts to reconcile them by compromise will find himself left with a superficial eclecticism which does not increase objectivity, and leads nowhere. Truth is not arrived at by concessions from different schools of thought.

If one is to think of eclecticism in terms of superficial techniques, then every counselor must, surely, be eclectic. If the counselor who asks a question sometimes instead of never asking a question, if the counselor who sometimes gives information instead of never giving information, if the counselor who sometimes gives direction instead of never giving direction is thereby eclectic, then it is difficult to see how any counselor could possibly avoid being eclectic.

Perry and Estes have discussed this issue in an interesting manner: [36]

> Somehow recent professional literature gives the impression that if a therapist is to follow a school, be it psychoanalytic or non-directive, he must faithfully apply the same procedure to all comers, assuming his theory to be all-embracing. If he is to be an eclectic, it seems that he must apply the "appropriate" procedures to all comers, perhaps assuming *himself* to be all-embracing. Members of a school, it is true, can protend to a certain humility, because it is to a theory, not to themselves, that omnipotence is attributable. To be an eclectic, on the other hand, apparently requires utter insouciance; as one put it, in print: "The therapist must be all things to all men;" and another: "We have no hesitancy in shifting from one approach to another if the first does not produce the mutually desired results. . . ."

> It is our notion, on the other hand, that a clinician's proper task is to construct a small-scale system as a rationale for what he sees. At the present state of knowledge it has seemed to us that the clinician does well to make use of various concepts, principles, and laws, however unrelated they have claimed to be, provided only that he make a reasonable coherent synthesis. But if his rationale is to be clinically useful, he should neither claim it to be applicable to all clients nor limit it as uniquely "appropriate" to an individual. It is his responsibility to do thinking which is to a degree *ad hoc,* but the *hoc* must be general enough to include a range of cases and also specific enough to provide coherent data; it must offer a mean between the normative and the idiosyncratic. . . .

One can hardly disagree with these delightful words, and Perry himself would be one of the first to agree that the counselor cannot

36 William G. Perry, Jr. and Stanley G. Estes, "The Collaboration of Client and Counselor," in O. Hobart Mowrer (Ed.), *Psychotherapy: Theory and Research* (New York: The Ronald Press Company, 1953), p. 118.

be eclectic in his display of self, unless he is exhibiting a remarkable degree of self-inconsistency.

Williamson gives what would generally be considered a good description of eclecticism in counseling when he writes: [37]

> Counseling . . . may be thought of as embracing a wide variety of techniques, from which repertoire the effective counselor selects . . . those which are relevant and appropriate to the nature of the client's problem and to other features of the situation. . . . Each technique is applicable only to particular problems and particular students. . . . Rather, the counselor adapts his specific techniques to the individuality and problem pattern of the student, making the necessary modifications to produce the desired result for a particular student.

McKinney sees no clash in the counselor's being eclectic in that he uses various methods, and being *Client*-centered. He describes the counselor in this way: [38]

> In view of the client's maturity and emotional balance he may be directive or non-directive. He may try to prevent certain conditions from arising, or he may correct an existing condition. He may put an emphasis on immediate relief or palliation, or direct his attention to a long term attempt at enabling the individual to achieve a reorganization of his personality. He may, on the other hand, see that the client requires treatment that is beyond his training and may seek consultation or make a referral to some specialist.

Thorne has written a chapter that he entitles "Directive and Eclectic Personality Counseling," implying that there is an eclectic "method." [39] But in the first paragraph of the chapter he writes ". . . to make a definitive statement concerning the eclectic orientation that is basic for the proposed system of practice. . . ." There is a vast difference, however, between an eclectic *orientation,* which surely every professional counselor should have, and without which there will be provincialism or even downright ignorance of counseling, and an eclectic *method* of counseling.

Thus Marzolf states that: [40]

[37] E. G. Williamson, *Counseling Adolescents* (New York: McGraw-Hill Book Co., Inc., 1950), pp. 219–220.
[38] McKinney, *op. cit.,* p. 32.
[39] Frederick Thorne, "Directive and Eclectic Personality Counseling," in James L. McCrary and Daniel E. Sheer (Eds.), *Six Approaches to Psychotherapy* (New York: The Dryden Press, 1955), p. 235.
[40] Stanley S. Marzolf, *Psychological Diagnosis and Counseling in Schools* (New York: Henry Holt & Co., 1956), pp. 327–328.

> . . . the eclectic in counseling is one who is willing to utilize any pro-
> cedure which holds promise even though their theoretical bases differ
> markedly. . . . In contrast with the eclectic, the doctrinaire counselor
> resists all temptation to use any procedure, which, in his view at least,
> is incompatible with his theory. To do so would be intellectually dis-
> concerting. . . .

One could certainly agree with Marzolf that any counselor who
operated on the basis of allegiance to a theory, *per se,* would be worse
than doctrinaire—he would be plain stupid. On the other hand, the
consistency of a counselor may be the consistency of a basic approach
to a human relationship. The consistency of the Client-centered counselor, for example, comes simply because he has found, eclectically
and pragmatically, that this is the means of operation in which he
is comfortable, and in which he is most effective.

The Client-centered counselor would certainly support eclecticism in the professional educational and development of the counselor,
since without it the counselor can hardly arrive at any learned conclusions based on a great variety of evidence. Without such breadth
we have the unhappy situation where Christians assume that religion
means only Christianity, capitalists that democracy means only capital-
ism, Americans that good living means only America, and counselors
that counseling means only Freudian, or Client-centered, or psychoanalytic, or Adlerian. These are the individuals who, when they go
to heaven, will have to live in restricted areas, surrounded by high
walls, so that they may continue to live under the illusion that they
are the only people there.

Although eclecticism may appeal to the student counselor as the
democratic and broad-minded approach to counseling, if we are to
speak of it as an actual method of counseling, then there are several
serious questions as to its efficacy:

1.   It carries with it the implication that counseling is a somewhat superficial bag-of-tricks technique. The counselor, as the technician who pulls out the appropriate treatment for the particular
problem or individual, thus becomes one whose professional preparation should be a *training* rather than an *education.*

2.   Entirely apart from the question of the capacity of the individual counselor to be personally the sort of person who could wear so
many coats with ease, this view assumes an astonishing degree of
knowledge on his part. Just to know, as pure knowledge, what would
have to be known to be such an all-round eclectic, would require a
super-individual.

3. The view assumes too, generally without evidence, that there are certain techniques and procedures that for a certain individual in a certain situation are more effective and better than others. If anything, the evidence, some of which has been referred to earlier, points the other way. There certainly is serious question whether or not a student counselor should learn that this particular technique is the right thing to do, under these circumstances, with this client. Because clients are not inanimate objects, or even organs, they have a habit of contradicting the counselor who has arrived at a set concept of just what to do at a certain time with a certain type of person.

4. It would not, surely, be doctrinaire to say that an individual must arrive at some degree of consistency with himself if he is to be honest and sincere, and thereby at least have some hope of being successful in working with other individuals. If the counselor, for example, cannot completely accept a client's attacks on the counselor's religion, then in the long run he might be better off to be honest with the client and admit that this does irritate him, rather than trying to pretend that he is acceptant and understanding about something to which he is actually reacting in an emotional manner. The client, too, is going to find it difficult to relate, and to get close to an individual who appears to fluctuate and change. Probably everyone can think of some people he has known who have posed a difficulty for him; although they have been nice and pleasant, he could never feel that this was the real person speaking. The real person was never revealed, most likely because the individual could not bear to reveal the real person to himself. Teachers, too, who know the frustration and difficulty children have with authoritarian parents, know the even more difficult time the children have if their parents lack even consistency in a vice. It is easier for a child to understand, and react to, and defend himself from a brutal father, than it is to react to a father who beats his child one day, then the next day cries and gives him a dollar to make up for his miserable behavior the day before.

Eclecticism, too, gives the counselor an easy avenue of escape at all times. It is much easier for the counselor to say to himself, "I am breaking this long silence because the client seems to be blocked, and I will use a new approach . . . ," than it is for him to say, "Why am I feeling pressured to break this client silence? What is it that makes me uneasy? Am I really acceptant of this client's right to be silent, or am I breaking the silence because it is beginning to threaten me?" It is easier for the counselor to say to himself, "I have answered the client's plea for support and help by telling him that he will be all right, because this is a technique that is sometimes useful," than it is for him to say, "I have answered the client's plea for help in this way because this sort of response reassures me, although it may be worse in the long run for the client." When the client says, "Okay, so maybe I am biased, maybe I am just white trash, but damn it, don't you think that evidence shows that Negroes in the South do know less than the whites?" the counselor may find it easier to say to himself, "Well, the reason I agreed that there might be one or two studies that implied this was so was because I felt that I needed to use a technique of agreement to give him some support. . . ," than to say, "The reason I made this statement was that I share his bias. . . ."

These examples could obviously be multiplied many times. If the counselor has arrived at some level of consistency of operation, then he must give himself a close scrutiny when he departs from it, and attempt to determine the why of his departure. When he has no consistency, there is little or no need for a check on himself, since he has accepted the concept that he does what he does for professional reasons only.

5. An eclectic method of counseling is also questionable in that it is almost impossible ever to evaluate just what is happening, since nothing is happening with any degree of consistency. When one does not believe in the therapeutic benefits of prayer, or of silence, or of direct questioning, or of reflection of feeling, one cannot "use" these procedures and then say they are no good because they didn't work for him. They must be used by someone who believes in them and who uses them with some degree of consistency as part of his total make-up; and then, with suitable research controls and means of evaluation and comparison, there might be some possibility of actually determining the effectiveness of a certain procedure, as used by certain individuals. Here again, of course, we have the danger of provincialism at a more professional level. The Freudian psychiatrist who condemns Client-centered counseling, although he knows nothing about it and does not believe in it anyway, shares the same narrow bed with the Client-centered counselor who condemns Freudianism even though he knows nothing about it and doesn't believe in it. Both individuals are in need of counseling with a therapist—Freudian, Rogerian, or otherwise—with whom they are able to relate in a positive manner.

COUNSELOR DIRECTION AND COUNSELOR CONTROL

The extent to which the counselor operates within the client's frame of reference probably relates to the extent to which he is literally *client*-centered, and it is difficult to see how the counselor can operate within the client's frame of reference if there is a good deal of overt and direct counselor direction and counselor control. There is no question that counselors differ on this matter, although one may argue as to whether or not a Client-centered counselor is any less directive and controlling than any other counselor. I would think, however, that probably the major measure of the extent to which one is a Client-centered counselor would be this matter of counselor direction and counselor control. Although there must be some element of counselor direction in all counseling, there is, nevertheless, a sharp differentiation in the practice and the attitude of the counselor on this matter. Thorne seems to have little question of the directive as well as the eclectic role of the counselor when he says: [41]

> The term *directive* seemed especially appropriate to designate a system of therapy based upon a formal plan for the identification and modification of etiological factors in maladjustment. . . . Possession of such training and experience, which is more than may be expected of even the most intelligent and best-informed layman, places the basic responsibility for the *direction* of all stages of case handling with the therapist, even though he may choose to delegate some portion of this responsibility to other persons, including the client himself. . . . The general rule may be stated thus: *The need for direction is inversely correlated with the person's potentialities for effective self regulation.* . . .
>
> The significance of these facts is that the therapist is supposed to *direct* the over-all details of handling the case according to tested scientific procedures, whether he is utilizing nondirective methods or authoritarian methods in an institution. Training and experience should enable the therapist to judge when to be directive or when to be relatively nondirective. . . .

This point of view was at one time pretty much taken for granted, although few writers have used the term "directive" in describing a method or a system of counseling. Thorne himself, it has been noted, uses the term "directive and eclectic" as one description rather than two. The directiveness of counselors, too, had never been much of an issue until the advent of Rogers. As a matter of fact, little was really known about what therapists and counselors actually said until Rogers took the lead in the taping of counseling sessions, so that a discussion was not based merely on what a counselor thought he had said to a client, but on what he had actually said, and how he had said it. Every counselor will agree that there is a big difference

[41] Thorne, *op. cit.*, pp. 236–238.

between these two, although even today many therapists in various counseling centers and psychiatric clinics are shy about having anyone listen to them in action.

There is no question, however, on the directiveness of some statements that are made by counselors. One counselor, in describing what he did to a patient during a counseling session, writes, "Her general philosophy of blaming herself and others was ruthlessly revealed to her and forthrightly attacked." [42]

From notes that were used in the teaching of residents and fellows in psychiatry in a Boston hospital we note that: [43]

> The course of the therapy, and the management, is directed and controlled by the doctor. The direction is determined by an appraisal of the patient's material, but once a working hypothesis in this respect is elaborated, the doctor follows this direction until the material is exhausted or until the doctor is blocked.

In the same material, under the heading of suggested procedures for using minimal activity (sic), we note the following:

> (1) Begin by a general question which cannot be answered by yes or no. Avoid leading questions. Avoid questions which suggest the answer. Use such questions as, "How are things going?" "How do you feel?" "What's been happening?" "What are you thinking about?" "What's going on in your head?"
>
> (2) When the patient begins to talk, don't interrupt: allow him to go on. If he hesitates or stops talking, pause for a few seconds or longer and give him a chance to continue. If the silence continues, introduce another general, non-leading question as mentioned above.
>
> (3) If the patient talks about topics which do not further your goal, allow him to continue for several minutes, while waiting for him to bring up the topic in which you are interested. If he persists in talking about irrelevant topics, show no interest in the material, take no leads, ask no questions. If necessary introduce another general question.
>
> (4) As soon as the patient mentions a word or topic that you want to hear more about, hold him by one or more of the following devices in the order presented. Proceed to the use of more active techniques (d,e,f,g,h) if simpler techniques (a,b,c) do not succeed. You are trying to indicate "Go ahead, we're interested."
>
> > (a) Non-verbal activity on the part of the doctor: look up, show interest by postural change, facial expression, nodding gestures. If a glance will do, say nothing.

[42] Albert Ellis, "Symposium on Neurotic Interaction in Marriage Counseling: Neurotic Interaction Between Marital Partners," *Journal of Counseling Psychology* 5:24–28 (Spring, 1958).
[43] Unpublished material.

(b) Use sounds, conversational grunts, syllables, and ejaculations such as *ah, uh uh, hmm, so, well, really, but, and.* If a simple syllable will do, say no more. Reinforce the inflection with an encouraging look; let your voice carry along. Avoid an air of finality.

(c) If the patient stops or heads away from the significant topic, repeat the patient's last word or phrase bearing on the topic. Say it with a rising inflection as though you were asking a question: "Upset?" "Blue?" "Your heart?"

(d) If this fails, elaborate this last word or phrase with an incomplete statement: "you said . . ."; "you said you were . . ."; "you mentioned pain. . . ."

(e) If a patient persists in avoiding a topic, ask a *general* question about this topic which cannot be answered by a simple yes or no. If a general question suffices, do not make it specific. "What did you say about your headache?" "What do you mean?" "What did you mean by nervous?"

(f) In some cases, if these indirect procedures fail, you may have to resort to a direct question aimed at the pertinent topic, such as, "In what part of your head do you feel pain?" "What was the feeling in the dream?"

(g) If the patient shows overwhelming affect, you may drop the topic for the time being, and introduce another non-leading question as under (1) above, keeping alert for the charged topic later in the same interview or in a subsequent interview.

These suggestions, it may be noted, are exactly the same sort of suggestions that would be given to the medical doctor who is being told how to treat a damaged kidney. There is no question here about who is in control, and any "nondirectiveness," as indicated above, is quite obviously a technique or method being deliberately used by the therapist to get the patient where he wants him to be. The patient here would appear to be very much the same patient who lies in the bed, passively waiting for the doctors to do with him what they will.

In the following excerpts from the tape *Loretta,* already mentioned, there seems more counselor direction on the part of therapists Ellis and Felder than is the case with Client-centered Rogers.

Ellis (Co):

    Co: This group of visiting psychologists and psychiatrists from . . . have been having a workshop here, and we are seeing a few of the people like you at this hospital to see if we can understand a little about the problems and perhaps help you somewhat with them, even though we're just going to see you. I'm just going to be talking with you for this hour or so and not any longer. Now do you mind telling me what it is that bothers you most?

Cl: Well, it doesn't bother me but it does seem to bother everyone else and that is that I talk too much.

Co: All right—now what is it that bothers other people —that you talk too much?

Cl: That's what I understand.

Co: And it doesn't bother you?

Cl: Not particularly.

Co: And why do you think they may be bothered by it?

Cl: It might be the way I talk.

Co: The way you talk? What way would that be?

Cl: I seem to have a way of aggravating the situation.

Co: Yeah. Could you be a little more specific? Do you know how you aggravate the situation?

Cl: Well, I apparently—when things get a little too rough and they want to drop the subject right away, and I'm not quite ready to do that—I like to talk them out.

Co: Ah—can you remember a recent incident—such as one that might have happened today—where the situation had a . . .?

Cl: Nothing happened today.

Co: Well, yesterday, or the day before—recent, actual incidents where somebody got upset because you presumably aggravated the situation.

Cl: Well, I can think of one that had to do with meetings.

Co: All right—fine.

Cl: I can't think of . . .

Co: All right. I'm sure that one will come to you as we talk. But anyway, you are not disturbed by this normally, but other people are. Now, are you disturbed when they get upset?

Cl: It bothers me when they become upset.

Co: Now why does it bother you when they become upset? Over what?

Cl: I don't know. I think it's natural being bothered by having people being disturbed and not understanding why they're disturbed. I mean, I can see why they might object, but I don't see why they don't want me to talk the whole thing out and find out why they're disturbed because I'm upset.

Co: Well, if I'm hearing you correctly you're sort of saying that—ah—that you are not objecting to their getting upset, but you at least would like them to talk it out with you.

Cl: Yes, I would like to know what it is that disturbs them.

Co: Then if you did know it, do you think that you'd be able to change your behavior—change their behavior —or what?

Cl: I don't know.

Co: But you think it would be helpful at least to know the answers?

Felder (Co):

Co: Do you want to sit over here? Did you know we were going to see you again today?

Cl: No, I just thought it was going to be one doctor.

Co: Do you want him back?

Cl: Why, I don't care; it's immaterial to me.

Co: O.K. Ah, you knew you were coming back today, but you thought it would be the same doctor?

Cl: I thought it was just going to be one doctor.

Co: Just one time—yesterday.

Cl: I didn't know about today, no; I mean I knew I was going to talk to a doctor, but I didn't know the whole group would be there.

Co: Well, I was in the group yesterday.

Cl: I didn't have a chance to notice everyone.

Co: And I wanted to start today by telling you my feelings about yesterday. Ah, I came away from it with a headache.

Cl: I had a headache today, so I think—I tried to read a book and I couldn't.

Co: And I had two, two main feelings about yesterday. Ah, one of them is a little bit complicated. I felt you entertained us and we enjoyed it, but that, that it was kind of a dirty trick on you, for us to enjoy your entertaining us.

Cl: I'm glad you were entertained.

Co: The second feeling I had, and I would like to find some more about that today, is that you have been helped some place along the line.

Cl: I don't know. I had shock treatment. I know I have had insulin, some insulin, and deep insulin.

Co: I don't mean help in that kind of way. I meant, I had the feeling you were helped by some person, rather than some, something artificial.

Cl: I don't know.

Co: Ah, then there is something else I wanted to tell you. After they told me they wanted me to talk to you today, as I was going to sleep last night, I thought about you, and—ah—I was sort of half asleep. This was half a dream—when you're half asleep and half awake—ah, you and I were there in this place wherever it was, and I was offering you a mushroom.

Cl: Oh, dear.

Co: And I got the feeling that you were afraid to take it because so many mushrooms were poison, and then immediately you changed into a goose.
(Loretta laughs)

Co: A goose or a duck, I'm not sure which—which had two heads and two necks. And one pointed in each direction—opposite directions.

Cl: I wouldn't know what to think about that.

Co: Well, I wasn't asking you what you thought about it, I just—

Cl: I beg your pardon.

Co: Wanted to tell you about it. To sort of bring you up to date where I am with you.

Cl: Well, that's nothing. I had a dream that I was in the . . . hospital and I did. (Pause)

Co: I don't know what you're asking me. But I'd like to tell you I think you are capable of anything you, you dream.

Cl: Well, I dreamed that, ah, I had a tooth that needed to be extracted, and I didn't want it taken out, and they said: You can have it taken out of your own free will, or we'll give you shock treatment and take it out; and I said, No, I don't want shock treatment; and they said, I don't care, you're going to get it anyway. You're going to have that tooth taken out.

Co: I felt kind of mad when you were saying that.

Rogers (Co):

Co: This must seem confusing and odd and so on, but I felt really sorry that the interview had been kind of cut short, because I felt sort of, there were other things you wanted to say.

Cl: I don't know, but I am being moved right off, transferred, and I just wondered if I am quite ready for a transfer. I mentioned it was annoying that the woman talked, has been yelling like that, but I really rather liked the ward—

Co: Uh huh.

Cl: I have been helping with the . . . I had thought I could go home from there. I know being transferred means I'll probably be put to work in the laundry all day, and I don't feel quite up to that.

Co: Uh huh. So that is one immediate thing for concern, am I ready to face everything that is involved in moving away from a spot where—

Cl: You feel kind of oriented to a place when you are here—

Co: Uh huh. You get sort of used to it and . . .

Cl: Well, I meant to correct one thing. When I said "No" before, I didn't mean I was tired of talking to that doctor; I just meant "No" that I was ready—that I wondered why I couldn't go home.

Co: Yeah, yeah. But you felt he didn't quite understand you on that really.

Cl: I thought that he felt I was being blunt, and that I just meant I didn't want to talk to him any more.

Co: And if I, if I sense some of your feeling now it is, uh, a little tenseness that, that maybe he really didn't get that, he felt you were shutting him off on something.

Cl: Yes, that's what, and that isn't what I meant.

Co: Yes.

Cl: Uh, I don't know. I am wondering if the transfer is a good thing. I mean they make you feel so important around here, and still you aren't, but then when I go over to "Two" I know that's an open ward—that's a dormitory, and I have been wearing not so many of my own clothes because I didn't like to launder them. It's just—if I'm quite ready for that change.

Co: Uh huh, and—

Cl: But my father and the others don't come to visit me, or anything, and I don't get out at all on weekends, or anything.

Co: Uh huh, and that . . . in the ward where you are now that you feel they seem to make you so important, but then really you are not, is that . . .?

Cl: That's really it. I am important and I'm really not.

Co: I see. So—

Cl: I know that you are not very important when you move to that ward.

Co: So if you are not very important in the ward where you are right now, if you were transferred . . .?

Cl: I would be even less important.

Co: So that it is something that concerns you . . .

Cl: I think it means working all day in the laundry too, and I'm not quite ready for that. I mentioned earlier that I had this tickling sensation in my knees when I was on 6C, when I was getting reserpine.

Co: Uh huh.

Cl: . . . and (not intelligible) . . . I think it was, and I asked the doctor at that time if he would move me so that I could go to work and work in the laundry, and the transfer came today. I didn't ask to be transferred this time.

Co: But it troubles you whether you are really ready to face some of the things that would be involved . . .

Cl: I don't know. There isn't much to face. It's kind of confusing. I think . . .

Co: I see. It is more a question of facing the uncertainties, is that what you mean?

Cl: I don't know what I mean. I just know that . . .

Co: Now you feel kind of mixed up.

Many psychiatrists feel that therapy begins the moment a patient enters the office, and that thus the preliminary psychiatric interview is primarily therapeutic. In any case, it does set the stage; and a psychiatric interview usually reinforces the patient's original feeling that the doctor is the one who is in control, and that he is the one who will determine what is to happen in the future.

In discussing such an interview, Fromm-Reichmann states: [44]

> The first interview should begin with the patient being asked about his complaints, and about the nature of his problems and his suffering, which made him or his relatives and friends decide to have the patient ask for the advice of a psychiatrist. Coupled with this, the acute distress which has precipitated the patient's decision to see a psychiatrist should be investigated. After that, the psychiatrist wishes to clarify, as early as possible in his contact with his prospective patient, whether the patient has come on his own volition, whether he has been advised to come by friends or relatives, or whether he has been prodded into doing so against his own wishes.

Let us note the first few minutes of two such psychiatric interviews (Co indicates the therapist): [45]

Interview 1

Co: Will you sit there. What brings you here?

Cl: Everything's wrong, I guess. Irritable, tense, depressed. Just, just everything and everybody gets on my nerves.

Co: Yeah.

Cl: I don't feel like talking right now.

Co: You don't? Do you sometimes?

Cl: That's the trouble. I get too wound up. If I get started, I'm all right.

Co: Yeah? Well, perhaps you will.

Cl: May I smoke?

Co: Sure. What do you do?

Cl: I'm a nurse, but my husband won't let me work.

Co: How old are you?

Cl: Thirty-one this December.

Co: What do you mean, he won't let you work?

Cl: Well, for instance I, ah, I'm supposed to do some re-

---

[44] Freda Fromm-Reichmann, *Principles of Intensive Psychotherapy* (Chicago: The University of Chicago Press, 1950), p. 45.

[45] These excerpts are taken from two records, "The Initial Interview in Psychiatry Practice," Yale University, Department of Psychiatry (New York: International Universities Press, Inc., 1954).

lief duty two weeks, this month, next month, September, and he makes it so miserable for me that I'm in a constant stew. And he says that my place is home with the children. I agree, but I wa . . . I need a rest. I need to get away from them. I need to be with, oh with people. I can't stay closeted up in the house all the time.

Co: How many kids are there?

Cl: Two.

Co: How old are they?

Cl: Three, five months.

Co: Mmm.

Cl: Oh, it isn't only that. It's a million things.

Co: Tell me some of them.

Cl: Well to begin with, there are a lot of things I didn't know about him before we got married that I should have known—at least I feel I should have.

Co: You've been married about four or five years?

Cl: Four years.

Co: Mmm.

Cl: In November. And, I think he's a chronic alcoholic. He drinks every day, and he just can't seem to let the stuff alone. He says he can, but he can't. He never has been able to except, the one time the doctor had him on a diet. And then he ate candy bars. Candy bars, I suppose he had to have sugar. But it's just, I feel that it's, it's, either going to ruin me or the kids or all of us. It . . .

Co: What does he do?

Cl: He's a truck driver.

Co: One of these long-distance hauls or what?

Cl: No. He used to do it. He doesn't now. They just do, ah, hauling within the state. And about, mm, five or six months ago he went on trailers. Well, I know it's hard, but he comes home and he starts taking it out on all of us. He starts nagging the minute he gets in the house.

Co: Is he away a good deal?

Cl: He eats and he sleeps in the house, and that's all there is to it. And it's an insult to me naturally.

Co: Mmm.

Cl: Once in a while he's decent. I keep thinking of divorce, but that's another emotional death. And I don't want to do it with the kids right now. They're too young.

Co: Divorce is an emotional death?

Cl: I think so.

Interview 2

Co: Please sit down. You just came down here?

Cl: Yes.

Co: From the hospital?

Cl: Yes.

Co: Ah, when did you—

Cl: Oh, I went there about two weeks ago.

Co: Oh, two weeks ago.

Cl: Yes.

Co: Yeah, and, ah, do you know what the reason is you've come down here?

Cl: No, I don't.

Co: Mmm. Well, I've been asked to see you to help the doctors with—

Cl: My case. That is . . .

Co: That's right. Yes. Why, ah, what happened that you went to—?

Cl: Oh, I, I was very nervous and I didn't seem to have the desire to go anyplace. And I'd argue with my mother, and there wasn't any reason to argue with her because, ah, I don't know. Ah, I'd wake up and find my head being smashed in and everything.

Co: Your head, ah, being—

Cl: I was being molested at home. And I thought perhaps if I went some place else, I would at least be safe.

Co: Mmm. Molested? How is that?

Cl: In every way. In, in, ah, I don't know—kicking my face in and everything.

Co: Tell me about that.

Cl: Well, I can't tell you too much. I feel very ridiculous speaking about it, a little bit ashamed, I guess. But, ah, I don't know and I'd be asleep all through it.

And then, as the day progressed, I'd remember that I was. And I'd actually feel the bangs and everything in my sleep. And, ah, I find it so all the time with me. And I don't know how to explain it or why.

Co: Not . . . not—

Cl: And I'm sure there's a reason. I'm sure those people know me. And . . . ah . . . they seem familiar in a sense, but I can't replace them.

Co: The ones . . . the ones—

Cl: That are molesting.

Co: Who molest you?

Cl: Yes.

Co: Mmm.

Cl: And my memory, I don't believe it lies what little is there. And, ah, there seems to be a reason for it, but, ah, I can't remember enough as I talk to tell you. I mean, it's, it's more like stupidity and ignorance on their part. That's all—the impression I get.

Co: They do it because they're stupid, ah, not, they have no particular reason?

Cl: Well, it's theirs, no. I, I, I, it's their own, ah, ideas, I suppose. I don't know how to explain it to you. I mean it just isn't fair. I mean I haven't done anything to deserve them.

Co: It's sort of unfair . . .

Cl: And anyway, I mean, even if you are guilty.

Co: Sure.

Cl: Of something, I don't know, ah.

Co: You sometimes think you might be guilty of something?

Cl: No, I don't think I'm guilty of anything. No I wouldn't even lie if I were. I mean, I mean if you are, you seem to deserve it, and it doesn't hurt you half as much.

Co: But so, you are innocent, and yet you get all this punishment.

Cl: Yes, I do. Whatever the reason is, I don't know.

Co: That's quite real—these—

Cl: Yes.

The concept of doctor control over patient in the clinical situation differs very little from the concept of teacher control over student in the school situation. Just as the domination of the medical doctor over the patient had been pretty well accepted in psychotherapy, and still is, so the domination of the authority figure in the school, the teacher, and, too often, the counselor, over the child is taken for granted. The variation in therapist domination and control in the preceding clinical examples is no different from the variation in counselor (C) control in the following school examples: [46]

C17: (pause) You've been working for your father for some time, is that right?

S18: Mm-huh.

C18: How do you like working on the farm?

S19: Pretty well.

C19: Do you . . . (pause) . . . Are you planning to work with your father this coming summer?

S20: Yes, if I don't continue school.

C20: There is a possibility that you might stay in school this summer?

S21: Yes, sir. (pause)

C21: Well, can you tell me a little bit more about your background? Tell me something about your home life. You've lived with your parents until you came down here, is that right?

S22: Yes, sir, besides the two years I put in the service.

C22: Mm-huh.

S23: Of course, my mother—ah—deceased here a year ago.

C23: . . . (pause) . . . Was that somewhat unexpected?

S24: Well, not too much.

C24: . . . (pause) . . . How would you describe your mother? . . . (pause) . . . What was she like? (pause).

S25: Well, she liked farming and she liked associations —one thing and another.

C25: Did she have many church activities?

And another counselor (C) with thirteen-year-old Beth: [47]

C1: Tell me more about you. Where did you come from today?

S1: Um. . . . You mean from home?

[46] Robert Callis, Paul C. Polmantier and Edward C. Roeber, *A Casebook of Counseling* (New York: Appleton-Century-Crofts, 1955), p. 121.
[47] Buchheimer and Balogh, *op. cit.*, pp. 192–193.

C2:   Well, did you have time to go home before you came today?

S2:   Yes.

C3:   Oh. What time do you come home from school usually?

S3:   Well, I got out about three o'clock.

C4:   Oh, I see. That's just about a regular hour. Are you on a nine-to-three session?

S4:   Yes.

C5:   Oh. And what school do you attend?

S5:   Umm. . . . Nathaniel Hawthorne.

C6:   Oh. And does it have a number? Is it a junior high?

S6:   Yes, it's 196. Junior High School 196.

C7:   Oh, I see. What grade are you in at the junior high?

S7:   Ninth.

C8:   The ninth grade. Were you there in the seventh and eighth?

S8:   Yes.

C9:   Oh, I see. So you really know your way around in that place by now. You are an experienced ninth grader, aren't you?

S9:   (Laughs) Yes.

C10:   Oh. Well, I was just wondering had you always lived there in that neighborhood, that you know many people there, too?

S10:   Yes, I lived there ever since I was born.

C11:   Oh, really? That's just fine. That's your home town to you.

S11:   M-hm. . . .

C12:   How are you doing in the ninth grade?

And another counselor (C) with Jane, a high school student: [48]

C120:   You feel you'll take it to a point, and then. . . .

S121:   Mm-hmm. Like those clothes. I know even Betty, my best girl friend now, says that, yeah, she's looking forward to college and the few weeks before, because her mother's going to want to go out and buy her clothes, too, and she would rather just skip it.

[48] William Evraiff, *Helping Counselors Grow Professionally* (Englewood Cliffs, N.J.: Prentice-Hall, Inc., 1963), pp. 117–118.

C122: So your girl friend has the same problems about clothes, and her mother wanting to buy, as you do.

S123: Yeah, although she says that she likes her mother's taste, and she usually likes the things her mother gets her, but she doesn't like the bother of going out either. I don't like to buy a whole bunch of clothes at once because I—like when I bought this, I fell in love with it, and so I bought it, but I'd rather. . . . I like to buy underwear too. Why I don't know. Then there's no choice. You just buy some and wear it, but going out and looking for something when I have no idea what I want is too frustrating. I'd rather not do it. I don't like to be in crowds either, elbowing through Hudson's, anything like that.

C124: You find it pretty uncomfortable, going through big crowds when there seems to be no point. You're not certain what you want. You'd rather wait when you have a specific object in mind, and then go and pick it out.

S125: I suppose quite a few people feel like that. I'm not alone.

C126: You feel other people feel this way too.

S127: Sure, some must. But then there's my mother. She feels that I've got to go out and get those clothes. I'll go with her.

C128: You'll go to satisfy her.

And finally, this school counselor (Co) with an adolescent girl: [49]

Co2: Have a seat. How are things going?

Cl2: Well, they're better than they were before, I've started thinking sort of positive, instead of thinking I couldn't do things. I've started thinking that I *could* do them, and it's worked. In math I got a D last time but I said I was going to fix it, that I was going to do better, and I did it.

Co3: I decided to improve myself and make up my mind that I could do a lot better than I have.

Cl3: And it's happening in other subjects too. Like in

[49] Angelo V. Boy and Gerald J. Pine, *Client-Centered Counseling in the Secondary School* (Boston: Houghton Mifflin Company, 1963), pp. 172–173.

tests—I don't know—it just seems all of a sudden I'm starting to think I can do it. Like in science—you take notes and everything, and I didn't think I was going to do well at first because there was going to be a hard test, but I studied for it, and I said I was going to pass it, and I did, and got an A.

Co4: I used to look down on myself, but now I don't look down on myself. I just think more positively and things begin to happen and things seem to improve.

Cl4: And even at home, I find that I know more things, and I can talk about more things, and it's much better. And I'm more confident in myself, too, and the teachers have noticed it. All of a sudden something hits you, and you suddenly come out of the dark.

Co5: Suddenly you become, in a way, a new person.

One may contrast these last two examples with the counselor domination and control expressed in these words: [50]

> In the course of rational psychotherapy, the patient is not merely shown that he has such irrational ideas as these, but the therapist persistently keeps attacking, undermining, and annihilating these idiocies. Even more to the point: the therapist teaches the patient how to observe, infer, and ferret out his own illogical thinking; how to trace this thinking back to its main ideological sources; and how to question, challenge, and uproot these asinine ideologies and to replace them with realistic, flexible, more effective beliefs.
>
> . . . the therapist often actively and unequivocally forces, persuades, cajoles, or practically pushes the patient into various kinds of actions which, in many instances, serve as the very best kind of counter-propagandizing influences.

And yet, the contrast is not as simple as it may seem. The brash, noisy counselor *may* basically be more acceptant and compassionate than the quiet, verbally "Client-centered" individual. I know of at least two counselors who, on the basis of the way they describe themselves, and the way they appear to verbalize in counseling, are the utmost in Client-centered counseling. Yet their colleagues describe

[50] Albert Ellis, "Rationalism and Its Therapeutic Implications," *Annals of Psychotherapy* 1:55–64 (September, 1959).

them as autocratic and self-centered, with little concern for the welfare of their fellows. The student counselor can only answer this question by trying his utmost, possibly with some help, to reach some stage of self-actualization and genuineness so that he can accept himself, at whatever level he may be. He may then be able to evolve some methodology of counseling that will be best for him and best for those clients who relate with him, or he may, of course, also come to the conclusion that counseling is not for him. Certainly the student counselor should be wary of the counselor education program in which all the staff speak the same line—it is most unlikely that a number of genuine counselor educators who are free enough to be who they are will all be the same, smiling the same smile, frowning at the same insult, but mostly beaming brotherhood at each other and at everyone else!

Although the verbalizations of a counselor are to some degree reflections of his attitudes as a person, they themselves are less important than the attitude that causes the verbalizations—which may, after all, not always be what they seem. The Client-centered counselor believes deeply not only that the client can be, but that it is his right to be the determiner of his future; that he, the counselor, is secondary in the counseling relationship; and that the direction should therefore come from the client, not the counselor. One might well debate the empirial reality of such a belief. Some will say that this is all right with neurotic individuals, but that it can hardly be correct with psychotic individuals who are completely divorced from reality. One can well understand, too, how a therapist whose education has been in hospitals with severely psychologically maladjusted individuals might be less certain about the capacity of all people for self-direction than would the therapist whose professional education has been in a counseling center or a guidance clinic, where the majority of the clients have had emotional disturbances of a less serious nature. Yet, in some ways, this is a point that cannot really be argued. The Client-centered counselor may in some respects be like the clergyman whose parish is in an area where filth and corruption are rampant, where good deeds are few, yet who continues to see people as basically fine rather than rotten, strong rather than weak. Is he being naïve? Is he being foolish? Is he being unrealistic? Or is he, possibly, by being who he is, having a subtle and marked effect, is he really communicating in a devious manner with some, even though he will not communicate with many? Whatever may happen, this is the way he is, and this belief is reflected in his consistency of purpose and action. The Client-centered counselor is similarly consistent in his feeling that the' client must determine the direction in which he will go, even though this may mean, of course, that he may be quite ineffective in helping some clients.

ADVICE AND INFORMATION

One of the most general means by which a counselor may show that he is the controlling and directing force is by the giving of advice. In fact, this is probably why the giving of advice is so ego-supporting; it implies that the one who asks for the advice is on a lower level than the one who gives the advice. The probable satisfaction of some school counselors with their job comes from the fact that they are frequently asked, "What do you advise me to do?" The resulting counselor response may be more supportive for the counselor than it is for the client.

The school counselor, traditionally, has been an individual anything but reticent in the offering of advice. Thus the general lay concept of counseling is that it is the giving of counsel, which in turn is usually considered to be advice. Williamson probably offered as direct a statement as anyone in the field with regard to the use of advice when he said: [51]

> . . . the counselor is ready to advise *with* the student as to a program of action consistent with, and growing out of, the diagnosis. For convenience, we may summarize methods of advising under the headings, *direct, persuasive,* and *explanatory.*

Even here, however, it should be remembered that many counselors, when talking about the place of advice, are thinking in terms of guidance rather than counseling. There would obviously be much more of an argument for the offering of advice to a rational individual under no stress or strain, than for giving advice to a highly disturbed individual who might clutch it as a complete answer to his difficulties, or reject it and the counselor completely.

The psychiatric and psychological literature has generally accepted the use of advice by the therapist as part of his function, but at the same time considered it as something that should be used with care and discretion. Sullivan, for example, says: [52]

[51] Williamson, *op cit.,* p. 233.
[52] Harry S. Sullivan, *The Psychiatric Interview* (New York: W. W. Norton & Company, Inc., 1954), p. 213.

. . . Thus the advice comes in at the very end to round out the obvious. As a psychiatrist, you see, I sometimes have to round out the obvious, because there are some people, notoriously obsessionals, who are very unwilling indeed to draw a conclusion—and therefore the psychiatrist gives them the conclusion. Actually, the "advice" is for the most part an overwhelming display of the factors relevant to the problem plus a clear statement by the psychiatrist of what he firmly believes can be done about them.

Another psychiatrist, Colby, comments as follows on this issue: [53]

One type of interposition common in the beginning, as well as at other stages of the therapy, consists of advice. At times the therapist must offer practical suggestions to the patient whose reality judgment is so impaired as to jeopardize his best interests. For example, a patient whose concept of his body is distorted may be advised not to undergo the plastic surgery he has planned. Or it may be suggested that a patient change his living quarters where he is under the constant unnerving pressure of homo-sexual feeling toward a roommate. As with all advice-giving on the part of the therapist, it should be done cautiously, and in small doses. The therapist must be prepared for the prospect that often his advice will not be taken, or, even worse, that it will be followed but have bad results.

Hadley, too, accepts the use of advice as legitimate, but suggests caution: [54]

Suggestion and the giving of direct advice are techniques similar to reassurance and should be used with the greatest of caution. In nearly all counseling relationships the counselor is a figure of authority to his client. Consequently, even offhand suggestions of alternative behavior patterns or remarks not intended as suggestions may do great harm to the client if they are not carefully thought out.

Marzolf also suggests the use of advice, with caution, although he does not actually use the term: [55]

At certain times and under certain circumstances, suggestions may be made to the client without arousing resistance, a possible result of the counselor's intervention in the thinking of the client. A young client may not consider a particular course of action merely because he has never known about it or thought about it. One may also suggest sources

[53] Kenneth Mark Colby, *A Primer for Psychotherapists* (New York: The Ronald Press Company, 1951), p. 150.
[54] John M. Hadley, *Clinical and Counseling Psychology* (New York: Alfred A. Knopf, Inc., 1958), pp. 156–157.
[55] Stanley S. Marzolf, *op. cit.*, p. 552.

of information, ways of approach to teachers about situations that have confused the client, courses of study to consider, occupations to investigate, or ways to improve social effectiveness. Such suggestions should not, however, be made so freely so as to deprive the youth of all opportunity to do his own problem-solving and thus make him dependent.

All of these statements are from experienced professional counselors whose comments are to be valued. There seems to be no question in the minds of the authorities above that counselors can and should give advice, although, like certain drugs, it is something that should be given with caution. The fact that it is to be given, nevertheless, again illustrates the difference in the directiveness of such counselors, as compared with that of Client-centered counselors.

When Colby, for example, refers to advice with regard to plastic surgery, this is the medical doctor rather than the therapist who is speaking. It may be that a medical doctor should give medical advice with regard to the undesirability of plastic surgery, but this immediately establishes his relationship as one of authority. It is in such a relationship that the Client-centered counselor does not wish to be involved, not only since he does not see himself as a figure of authority, but since he cannot see himself being an effective counselor as a figure of authority.

The Client-centered counselor does not see himself as using techniques of advice any more than as using any other sort of techniques although he has many empirical reasons for not offering advice. It could be because he feels that the client might not follow his advice, or because his advice might be wrong, or because the client in following his advice might become more dependent on him. These are all valid reasons why one might be cautious about the use of advice, or not use it at all, but none of them is the basic reason why the Client-centered counselor avoids advice. The actual answer is simple. He does not offer advice because he does not have any advice to give. He feels very deeply that the basic purpose of his relationship with the client is to provide environmental nourishment so that the client may grow on the basis of his own strength rather than resting on the shoulders of the counselor.

Paraphrasing a comment by Thorne, referred to earlier, I would feel that the more a client asks for advice, the less likely it is that advice will be of any benefit to him. Theoretically, the only person who could benefit from advice would be the completely stable individual, who, since he has no need for advice, would never ask for it.

Ingham and Love express what might be described as a Client-centered point of view on the question of advice: [56]

> . . . or he could seek an answer from the counselor about whether to marry, get a divorce, or have children; about extra-marital sex experience, educational or vocational choices, or the continuation of psychotherapy. Almost any important decision that a person must make can be brought to the therapist's office. The therapist should not feel that he is in a position to know what the other should do, let alone decide for him. . . . Furthermore, even if he were right (as of course he often would be), it would ordinarily be undesirable for him to express his opinion so that it could be received by the patient as advice.

The Client-centered counselor would feel that, in the vast majority of cases, such as those examples mentioned by Ingham and Love, he would not have any opinion to express as to what the other person should do. On the other hand, one can stretch the point and say, "Well, what about the client who asks your advice on assassinating the President, or blowing up a school or raping a little girl?" The counselor here would have an opinion, it is true, that other people should not be destroyed by the client; but his acceptance of the client includes the fears and frustrations and hatreds which are a part of him, as well as the client's right to verbally express any of these feelings to him. One may push the point still further and say, "Well, what happens if the client dashes out with an obviously well formulated plan to kill the President, blow up a school, or rape a little girl?" It would seem that the only answer here would be that the counselor would have to betray the confidence of the client, and function as an agent of society rather than as the therapist of the client. There seems little difference in this situation from that of the Catholic priest who is told plans such as the above in the Confessional, although the priest would be torn between what he would feel as a sacred obligation to his God, and his obligation to his society.

The counselor should be careful to distinguish between advice and information. The latter may be thought of as objective and untouched by the bias of man; it is pragmatic and empirical. It is fact, or as close to fact as one can get. Tyler points out the basic pro and con of the use of information in counseling when she says: [57]

[56] Harrington V. Ingham and Leonnore R. Love, *The Process of Psychotherapy* (New York: McGraw-Hill Book Co., Inc., 1954), p. 22.
[57] Tyler, *op. cit.*, p. 179.

> If a client needs information in order to think soundly about something that concerns him, he should be helped to obtain it. Unfortunately . . . the questions that are brought up first do not always indicate what it is that a client really needs, and to deluge him with irrelevant information is no more helpful than to withhold essential information.

Relevant information may also be of no help. When a high school student who has been driven by compulsive parents to excel academically is provided with information that indicates that his chances of getting into a decent college are most remote, it is unlikely that he will say, "Thank you," and relax. Information may not have quite the personal sting of advice, but when it clashes with one's concept of who he is, its immediate effect is not likely to be very positive.

Information may be traumatic (what is my I.Q.?) or it may be of no particular relevance (do you like hockey?) or it may be supportive (do you have many clients like me?); but in any case it is of little help to the client in his growth toward a better understanding about himself. Several of my psychiatric colleagues feel the same way about the M.D. therapist's functioning as a medical doctor rather than a therapist, and giving medical information or advice to the patient. The medical doctor does certain things for the patient that the therapist does not do, and he gives certain things to the patient that the therapist does not give. It is difficult to be two people whose functions contradict each other.

This point is well illustrated in a comment made by Shlien. In reply to the client comment, "Okay. My eyes all red?" the counselor says, "They feel all red . . . ," and in the footnote reference Shlien comments: [58]

> Some more "directive" therapists have asked, in connection with C65, "My God, can't you even answer yes or no to *that?*" One could, but there is no point in so doing. The counselor is not needed for such information, but is much needed for understanding of the feelings about herself.

Many of the clients who come in to see the school counselor, of course, are going to be quite capable of using relevant information, *and if they want it, and if the counselor has it,* there would seem to be little reason for withholding it. Even though in the actual counseling relationship information will play a very minor role, the school counselor will periodically be called upon to supply information.

[58] Shlien, *op. cit.,* p. 319.

There would seem to be no reason why he could not do so and at the same time maintain his Client-centered relationship with the client. Generally speaking, however, he should be seen not as the giver of information, but rather as the individual who will help a person to get to the point where he can make sensible use of sensible information. In any case, in the very near future it is likely that the information-giving function of both teacher and counselor will be taken over by the machine, so that all that will remain for the counselor will be his real function—counseling.

TESTING AND MEASUREMENT IN COUNSELING

There would probably be general agreement among teachers and counselors that the purpose of testing is to provide more valid and reliable information about the individual who was tested. There may be some question, however, as to the extent to which both teachers and counselors appear to be more interested in knowing more about the student than they are in helping him to know more about himself. Information about the student may be needed for grouping and placement, and, later on, admissions officers and potential employers are also going to want to know about the student. This is a legitimate and reasonable use of information about the student, and the procuring of this information is one of the auxiliary functions of the school. This however, has little to do with counseling, and any debate over the use and place of testing in counseling should not confuse the use of testing as a part of the total school program with the use of testing in counseling.

Although not all counselors would agree as to the place, if any, of testing in counseling, the majority who do see testing as a part of counseling stress that the information that is garnered as a result of testing must be for the use of the client himself, not for the use of the counselor. In other words, the information derived from testing is for the client, and the determination as to what to do about it is the responsibility of the client. On this point, Tyler comments: [59]

> The most important principle about the use of tests in counseling . . . is that the information to be obtained is *for the use of the client himself.* . . . A test is useful for counseling purposes only if there is a considerable amount of evidence as to just what characteristic it is measuring and if the counselor can state in clear, unambiguous terms

[59] Tyler, *op. cit.,* p. 106.

what the significance of an individual's score is in relation to various life decisions.

Most counselors operate on the assumption that the more a client *knows* about himself the better he *understands* himself, and knowing is usually viewed in a cognitive sense. Byrne would reflect the feeling of many counselors when he says: [60]

> . . . the success of counseling depends partly on increasing the student's understanding of himself. In many instances growth of understanding does not require reference to cumulative record data but can be attained solely through interview processes. Usually, however, reference to appraisal data, including those obtained by testing, is fruitful.

Not only is this assumption highly questionable, but there is also something strangely contradictory in the counselor who stresses the human relationship aspect of the counseling process, and at the same time accepts easily the idea that one can change and move and grow and come to a better understanding of himself by having information about him presented to him by some other person. The extent to which I can change when I see or hear something that clashes with my concept of me must surely be related to my level of self-actualization, to the degree to which I have become a free individual. Thus it would seem reasonable to assume that only those rather solid students with a high level of self-understanding could internalize and make use of critical information about themselves.

Even more questionable, of course, is the assumption that the more a counselor knows about the client, the more effective he can be with him. Berdie, Layton, Swanson and Hagenah [61] appear to agree with this statement when they say that "no experimental evidence at present justifies the assumption that *effective counseling depends on the counselor's knowledge about his counselee. . . .*" Yet they operate on the assumption that *"the more information we have about students, the better we can work with them."* [62] And again, "Our thesis has been that test scores and other counseling information are used to help the counselor and the counselee to originate and study hypotheses concerning the counselee's future behavior."[63]

[60] Byrne, *op. cit.,* p. 129.
[61] Ralph F. Berdie, Wilbur L. Layton, Edward O. Swanson, and Theda Hagenah, *Testing in Guidance and Counseling* (New York: McGraw-Hill Book Co., Inc., 1963), p. 121.
[62] *Ibid.,* p. 11.
[63] *Ibid.,* p. 133.

The Client-centered counselor is somewhat skeptical about the validity of this assumption, and he would ask himself several questions regarding the use of tests in counseling: What would be my purpose in using tests? Why, if ever, would I use tests? If tests ever were used, what ones would I use, and how would they be selected, administered, and interpreted?

The most obvious reason why a counselor would use tests would be, as indicated, to gather more information about a client, information that he might feel that he could not obtain as accurately and as quickly in any other way. When counselors of various orientations discuss clients or patients—frequently called, not without some significance, "cases"—they normally have the results of test data, and the psychologist is often considered to be the fellow who provides the counselor with this information. The counselor who feels that he needs this information must need it either to pass on to the client or to help him in his work with the client. In any case, this is a counselor-directed procedure, in which there is no doubt that the counselor has decided that he needs to know more about the client; he determines what clients will be tested, when they will be tested, and how they will be tested.

It has already been pointed out that many counselors who see diagnosis as an integral part of the counseling process have little use for anyone else's diagnosis. Thus, even if exhaustive test data are provided by some hard working psychologists, as often as not these data are either politely ignored or thrown out the window by the current counselor. Even diagnostically oriented counselors often tend to put little weight on the results of measurement devices; they are more likely to operate with a client on the basis of their own evaluation of him, with, possibly, suggestions from several of their colleagues. A "psychiatric examination" is more often than not the pooled judgment of several therapists, or sometimes even the judgment of one therapist after a brief interview with the patient. A psychological examination usually refers to the use of standardized instruments of measurement. Whether the more subjective personal interview is any better or any worse than the standardized tests is open to debate, although some counselors would consider both of them unreliable and invalid.

The Client-centered counselor finds no particular problem on this issue. He has no need for test data, since *he* is not going to *do* something for somebody, but rather help someone to make some decisions for himself, and thus to do something for himself. He does not have to know, from test data, whether a client is an under-achiever or an over-achiever. The client who has a problem related to academic achievement will, generally fairly soon in the counseling process, present both to the counselor and to himself his picture of a person who is doing more or less than he probably could do. Although the one who is doing more might be more of a problem for himself, the academic society generally considers only the one who is doing less to be a problem. In most schools today, the guidance department will have provided the child, fairly early in his school career, with some information as to where he stands with regard to achievement tests or measures of general aptitude and intelligence. The Client-centered counselor would feel that he had no particular need for this information, and that the client would make use of it if and when he wanted to.

One might say, "Well and good, but what happens if a client describes himself an intelligent student who is doing poorly, whereas he is actually achieving at his level of capacity?" Actually, an I.Q. of 150 means nothing to a person who has come to see himself as a very dull person, with a low intellectual level. Nor does a low I.Q. mean anything to a person who has learned that he must be an intelligent person. The first individual, from an operational and a realistic point of view, has a low level of intelligence, and the second person has a high level of intelligence. The counselor does not have to know, and does not particularly want to know, before he sees the client, that there is an inconsistency between what some evidence says that the client possesses in the way of capacity and what he sees himself as possessing. If the counseling develops as it can, both the counselor and the client will come to feel, "Why must I push myself to do what I know I can't do?" or, "Why do I have to convince myself that I can't do anything, while I really know that I can do a good deal more than I have been doing?"

The Client-centered counselor operates at the level of the client, and the first individual mentioned above is, for the time, a person of low intellect because *this is what he feels himself to be;* and the second person is a person of high intellect because this is what he feels himself to be. This situation is no different from that of the client who is helped by most teachers, but feels that all teachers are picking on him, or the client who insists that the principal is out to get him, although the principal is sincerely concerned with trying to help him. Most people, however, when the threats and the fears and the pressures are no longer present, will tend to come to a better balance between what they have and what they want. The student with high intelligence may come to have less need not to do well academically, and thus will almost automatically do better. The student with low intelligence will become more secure with himself and with what he has, and will have less need to convince himself that he can do more than he actually can. The student with musical talent will feel the desire to develop and make use of his aptitude when he no longer has to show someone that he cannot do anything that that person wants. The boy who has no liking for athletics will no longer bloody himself in athletic competition, since he will be secure enough to accept the loss of the affection of a neurotic father that is related solely to athletic achievement.

It is true, of course, that the school counselor is concerned with many guidance activities other than counseling. He may be one who makes use of test data for placement and selection, but he will not, if he is a Client-centered counselor, feel any particular personal need for test data on those students who come to him as clients. One might assume, too, that the professional education of the counselor is such that he knows enough about human beings and human behavior not to need test data to give him a fairly accurate picture of this person who is called the client.

One may then ask, does this fellow who calls himself a Client-centered counselor, then, ever make use of tests? *Some* counselors would answer, "Yes, if the client wants them," although we might at least wonder here about the extent to which counselor imposition increases as he becomes more involved in the use of tests. It would probably be fair to say that, in most schools and with most counselors, the client has little or no choice in the matter of "test or no," and that the meaning of the test data is the counselor's version, presented to the client.

Patterson [64] feels, reasonably enough, that as long as tests are used to help the client to evaluate himself, they can be a part of Client-centered counseling, since the evaluative function is absent. Actually, however, this rarely happens (other than in books), and even if the counselor did present test data to the client simply as information, with no personal involvement, and even if the client was the one who determined what tests he would take, it is still the counselor who has decided what tests are available, and thereby been evaluative, since we can assume that there is no school where the client simply puts his hand in a test grab bag containing all tests, and pulls out

[64] C. H. Patterson, *Counseling and Guidance in Schools* (New York: Harper & Row, Publishers, 1962), pp. 149–151.

what he wants; and since he doesn't know much about tests, it would be rather pointless saying, "What would you like to take? You make the decision."

In the school program described by Boy and Pine,[65] the testing program is primarily the function of the teachers, with the counselors acting as advisers and consultants. Certainly achievement and intelligence testing would appear to be a rather logical function of the teacher, and one may well question whether tests of various other kinds have any place in the school, or at least in the domain of the teacher and the counselor.

Again, however, we must distinguish between the perfectly capable and rational student who wants further information about himself in the way of test data, so that he can compare himself with others as to intelligence and interests and aptitudes, and is thus in need of *guidance,* and the student under stress and strain, who sees tests as the answer to his problems. Even in these days, however, when testing, if not counseling, has become socially acceptable, the odds are that most individuals who seek testing are really in need of counseling. Although they seek testing to supply answers to their problems, tests supply only information, and few individuals under strain have their problems dissolved by the presentation of information, valid or otherwise. Thus when the client says, "Do you think that some testing might do me good?" a reply that in most cases would be fairly accurate, although maybe not appropriate, would be, "These might . . . ah . . . give you some answers that you don't have now. . . ."

In a somewhat similar situation I had a client who had been referred to me and who indicated during the session that he felt, generally, that he had things pretty well under control and could operate under his own steam. He raised the question, however, of having interpreted to him the data from tests that had been administered as part of a university experiment with which I had no connection. In this case, after some verbalizing of the client's feelings, I agreed that I would be happy to comply if the client wished. Some counselors would probably question this decision, particularly since the tests had been administered prior to the counseling, and had no relation to it; but my attitude was that my decision represented an acceptance of the feelings of the client, and that it did not involve any overt out-of-the-counseling act by me.

The counseling session might develop into a situation where a good deal of information with regard to test data would be supplied

[65] Boy and Pine, *op. cit.*, pp. 138–139.

by the counselor to the client. In more cases than not, however, the original request for testing need not actually develop into testing unless the counselor is so unskilled as to miss the feelings being expressed, and blunders ahead with a voluminous discussion of tests and testing without ever giving the client a chance to get closer to what he was trying to say when he tentatively asked the question about testing. Even when the client comes in for the sole purpose of testing, as often occurs in a vocational guidance center, more often than not the client is in need of counseling—possibly vocationally oriented, but still counseling, rather than vocational testing. The client who, after a number of counseling sessions, rather consistently raises the question of testing, may feel secure enough so that he can go to the point of taking a look at some test data; or, of course, he could, becoming more threatened, be looking for an easier way out. The good counselor, however, should be able to help the client to see just why he wants test information. When the client can see this, he may have no further need for testing; or, on the other hand, he may be even more certain, but for possibly different reasons, that it would be good for him to take a battery of tests.

Some counselors would feel, at this point, that the client should be referred elsewhere for testing, and, possibly, for test interpretation, simply because they do not see themselves as skilled in test administration and test interpretation. Others would talk to the psychologist who had administered the tests about their meaning, and then interpret the results to the client. In the majority of the schools of America, however, the counselor will have to do some testing, if any is to be done. In such a situation, it would be rather pointless to ask a client "What sort of tests would you like to have?" since this would be about the same as the medical doctor's asking the patient, "What sort of examination do you think you need?"

On the other hand, some counselors have prepared a little brochure that describes, in simple language, just what tests are available, and just what their purpose is. The counselor should bear in mind that while he may have to supply information to the client, it should be information, written or otherwise, and not advice. Once the client has had a chance to read or to discuss with the counselor just what is available and what might be expected, it is then up to him to make the choice of what he wants to take. The question, "Well, which of these two—the Kuder or the Strong—do you think that I should take?" should pose no problems to the counselor who is operating on the basis of the feelings of the client. We could assume that what the client is expressing here is, "They're about the same, and it's a pretty hard choice for someone who doesn't know anything about tests to decide which one—or maybe I should take both of them. . . ." The client must make the choice, not because the counselor is being coy, or is using technique Number 108, which says, "Thou shalt not answer questions," but very simply because the counselor does not have, for the client, an answer.

Goldman,[66] in supporting the use of tests in counseling, sees tests as providing information such as pre-counseling diagnostic information, information about the counseling process itself, and information relating to the client's post-counseling decisions. He also sees tests as having uses that do not have the element of providing information— the stimulation of interest in areas not previously considered, laying a groundwork for later counseling, and providing a learning experience in decision-making.

In the long run, the counselor must, of course, make his own choice. My own feeling on the matter is that testing certainly has a place in the total educational program of the school, although we appear to be involved now in what might almost be called a testing frenzy, and federal money could possibly be used in more effective ways than in increasing the amount of testing going on in schools. As far as counseling is perceived in this book, counselor involvement in testing would appear to be a hindrance rather than a help, a means by which the counselor will become less, rather than more, empathic with the client, and a means by which the client may possibly increase his illusion that increased knowledge about self, divorced from self, is somehow synonomous with self-understanding and growth toward freedom.

[66] Leo Goldman, *Using Tests in Counseling* (New York: Appleton-Century-Crofts, 1961), pp. 22–31.

Chapter Eight

THEORETICAL ISSUES: VALUES AND ETHICS

THOSE WHO THINK that the "why" of counseling is crucial also consider one of the major issues in counseling to be that dealing with the question of values—the values of the counselor, the values of the client and the values of the cultural milieu in which they live. Let us look, in this chapter, at this question of values, ethical behavior, and the freedom of man.

THE VALUES OF MAN

Every counselor, being a human being, has a value system on which his life is based. He may not be consciously aware of it, but everything he does is a reflection of this value system, and the value system of the counselor is obviously of critical importance, since it determines his attitudes and his actions toward the client. For the existentialist, Client-centered counselor, the basic central core of his value system is the integrity and the dignity and the rights of the individual man over all else. Fromm is saying the same thing when he writes: [1]

> Humanistic ethics, in contrast to authoritarian ethics, may likewise be
> distinguished by formal and material criteria. Formally, it is based on

[1] Erich Fromm, *Man for Himself* (New York: Holt, Rinehart & Winston, Inc., 1961), pp. 12–13.

the principle that only man himself can determine the criterion for virtue and sin, and not an authority transcending him. Materially, it is based on the principle that what is "good" is what is good for man and "evil" what is detrimental to man; the sole criterion of ethical value being man's welfare.

This, of course, is the existential view that puts man above the culture, existence above essence, individual morality above legal morality. This does not mesh with Mowrer's [2] statement that "once one has made a choice and committed himself to a given moral order or system, then he is *not* free to cheat on that system . . . ," since the existential, free man commits himself only to man, not to an order or a system. The American remains an American, but he does not kill Russians just because the system says he is supposed to; the white man remains a white man, but he does not strike a Negro because the system says he should; the business man does not cheat his customer, even though "everyone else" in the system is doing it. Man is answerable, in the long run, only to himself.

The existentialist, the Client-centered counselor, does not see a value as something that is apart from a person. Values are human products, and they exist only in a human community. Usually, a "value" implies a judgment, but the same act may have as many different values placed upon it as there are people involved in it. A generally accepted cultural concept is that certain values are better than others, and an equally acceptable concept is that values can, and should, be taught. The questionable assumption here is that the teacher somehow is the possessor of a value that is not possessed by the learner, and that it is the function of the teacher to teach this better value (his), to the learner, who either does not have this value or has a "wrong" one. This concept detaches the value from the person, so that, just as one can be taught how to drive, one can be "taught" morality, virtue and courage. This concept also makes possible the widely accepted tenet in counseling that "I like him but I don't like what he is doing." It obviously implies that the counselor should, and must, have as part of his value system a feeling of the rightness of his ways *for others,* an obligation to impose this rightness on others, and an assumption that this rightness can be imposed on (taught to) others. While these assumptions are questionable from an existential point of view, they are, nevertheless, widely held.

[2] O. Hobart Mowrer, "Science, Sex and Values," *Personnel and Guidance Journal* 42:746–753 (April, 1964).

Mueller,[3] for example, has indicated her feeling that not only can one teach ethics, but the "counselor" must teach ethics as he "counsels." She may be describing a Dean of Women, but hardly a counselor,[4] when she says: [5]

> In discipline the counselor is teaching emotional stability, moral judgment, self reliance and self control. . . . The balance between force and sympathy is achieved by first exhausting every resource of counseling and persuasion and only then turning to punitive action.

There would appear here, again, to be a concept of a detachment of the human act from the person, the idea that values are some form of appendices that one "learns" by being taught. There is an absence of the feeling that values, being a part of the person, can only come through an experiencing and a living and a human relationship. Close human contact with a patient and compassionate person may help another person to free himself so that he, too, may move in the direction of patience and compassion. He may thus "learn," from a counselor, from a teacher, from a friend, but he has not been taught. History would surely bear witness to the futility of the attempt by one person to "teach" his value system to another person.

Most counselors would probably agree with Samler [6] when he says, "It ought not to be irreligious to propose that if value commitment and promulgation work in bringing about lasting client change in desirable direction then it provides its own justification." The questions that do remain, however, are "what value commitment?" and "what desirable direction?"

Ferree [7] also leaves these questions unanswered when he raises what would appear to be a contradiction, when he calls for "a clear commitment on the part of the counselor to certain values which he in turn seeks to foster in his counselees . . . ," indicates that the counselor is to "promote in his counselee what is not already there," and states that "it may involve deliberate effort on the part of the counselor to

[3] Kate H. Mueller, "Theory for Campus Discipline," *Personnel and Guidance Journal* 36:302–309 (January, 1958).
[4] See Mary Elizabeth Reeves and Dugald S. Arbuckle, "The Counseling Attitudes of Deans of Women," *Personnel and Guidance Journal* 41:438–441 (January, 1963).
[5] Kate H. Mueller, *Student Personnel Work in Higher Education* (Boston: Houghton Mifflin Company, 1961), pp, 356–357.
[6] Joseph Samler, "An Examination of Client Strength and Counselor Responsibility," *Journal of Counseling Psychology* 9:5–11 (Spring, 1962).
[7] George Ferree, "Psychological Freedom as a Counseling Objective," *Counselor Education and Supervision* 3:13–18 (Fall, 1963).

change the basic nature of the person." Can the counselor actually have such values as "tolerance and respect for others and a capacity to listen well," and at the same time seek to foster values in his client? Can one be acceptant while he is seeking to eliminate from the individual certain values that are not of the "right" kind? It may be, of course, that Ferree, as an educational philosopher, has a somewhat hazy idea of the unique function of the counselor, and sees him somewhat as a classroom teacher. The counselor who has not moved well along the road of psychological freedom himself may have a difficult time in helping another to traverse a road that is strange to him, and the individual who sees his role as that of practically forcing his particular value system, teaching his values, if you will, to the client, is surely showing a most limited version of acceptance. The autocrat, after all, could agree totally with Samler's and Ferree's words!

In a way, Lowe has provided an answer to this question when he says: [8]

> We conclude that differences in value orientations cannot be resolved, each orientation having adherents whose beliefs should be respected. We suggest that each counselor have an understanding of the values both of himself and others and that his values be known by all who are personally affected by his professional behavior.

Simply by being the person he is, in a close human relationship, the counselor is making obvious some of his own value patterns. The fact that he is always acceptant of generally unacceptable material, the fact that he never criticizes, measures, or evaluates, the fact that he centers his complete attention on the client and never on himself, the fact that he shows unwavering patience and kindness—these are surely a display of the person, and are almost certainly transmitted in some degree to the client, who, more likely than not, will hold the therapist in trust and admiration. This situation is well described by Rosenthal: [9]

> It may be that the therapist communicates his values to the patient in many unintended, subtle ways, even when trying to avoid doing so. The patient, who is often sensitized to the therapist's every word and inflection, may be able to receive these communications, and because of his trust, admiration, and respect, may permit himself to be influenced by them.

[8] C. Marshal Lowe, "Value Orientations—An Ethical Dilemma," *The American Psychologist* 14:687–693 (November, 1959).
[9] D. Rosenthal, "Changes in Some Moral Values Following Psychotherapy," *Journal of Consulting Psychology* 19:431–436 (December, 1955).

Somewhat along the same line, Wolff [10] reported that while only 6 percent of a group of therapists who were being studied regarded change of values as a goal in therapy, 48 percent believed that therapy did directly transmit or develop value concepts in the patient.

Williamson also expresses a deterministic feeling of human limitation when he appears to view the counselor as one whose outside-of-me values control him, rather than one whose inner self is expressed in terms of his values: [11]

> Rather is counseling . . . value-oriented and not open-ended both regarding goals sought through aspirations and strivings of both counselor and student within their counseling relationship.

This concept also implies a striving by the counselor to achieve for the client something, some answer, some right path or goal that is external to the client, and possibly to the counselor. This is almost like the counselor's cheating on his income tax returns and then trying to convince the client who has been cheating on exams that the virtue of honesty is something that he should practice. Actually, this "virtue" is real for neither client nor counselor, and it is unlikely that any change is going to take place in either one. On the other hand, we might hypothesize that if the counselor is a "no-cheating" sort of fellow, in his living-being, regardless of any words, then he will see no point in trying to press this on the client. And the client, in turn, might possibly internalize, or at least let stir around inside him, the idea that this might be something worth incorporating so that it becomes a part of his being. People who believe feel no particular pressure to convince others that they should believe the same way. It is likely that the evangelist is very concerned with who he is and where he is going, and that this is why he continually tries to convince others that they should follow him. He neither respects nor trusts the other to find his own right way. If his religion includes compassion and gentleness and love toward his fellow man, he spends his time preaching it rather than practicing it.

The concept that one can separate a person from his values is a very common one in counseling. It is almost as if one could view a human act and the person who commits it as two separate entities. One might feel that the act of robbery, the taking away of another

10 W. Wolff, "Facts and Value in Psychotherapy," *American Journal of Psychotherapy* 8:466–486 (July, 1954).
11 Edmund G. Williamson, "Value Orientation in Counseling," *Personnel and Guidance Journal* 36:520–528 (April, 1958).

person's belongings so that one can further his own interests, is questionable. But when a counselor is relating with another fellow human who has committed the act of robbery, he cannot divorce the person from the act. Part of the person is the fact that he has committed a robbery, and since we accept the client as he is, the unrelated fact of robbery, or what the counselor may think about it, has no relation to the therapeutic interaction whatsoever. It is the person, all of him, with whom we are concerned, and the various bits and pieces, by themselves, mean nothing. The existential counselor, however, would not view acts at any time as detached from human beings, so that a question such as, "Well, do you mean that you don't think that robbery is bad?" really isn't a question because robbery, per se, really doesn't mean anything. It is only when it becomes a part of an individual's human behavior that it means something, and the counselor, being concerned with the person, is not particularly aware of the "goods" or the "bads" of the individual's actions.

This is probably also why practically every act that is labeled "bad" by someone is labeled "good" by someone else. Robin Hood's thieving was considered wonderful by those who were the recipients of his loot, but not by those from whom he stole! Americans think affectionately of the "robber barons" who were the ancestors of some of our most illustrious current figures, political and otherwise!

Patterson [12] expresses this somewhat separatist, and nonexistential, point of view when he states that "while the counselor may judge the attitudes, standards or actions of his client in terms of his own or prevailing standards, he does not judge the client himself. . . ."

Shoben [13] also expresses the "doing something to somebody" attitude when he comments that "the field is committed to the development of responsible individuals capable of maintaining and advancing a democratic society." The existentialist would be more concerned with helping the individual to come to be able to release and use the potential that he has, and he would have little concern about whither the "inner man" would go. He would help the person to grow to freedom, and while a product might be a "democratic society," this would be somewhat meaningless, since in today's world we have earnest people who are sure they have "democratic societies" in such countries as China, Yugoslavia, Ghana, and Russia. Shoben, of course, means *his*

[12] C. H. Patterson, *Counseling and Psychotherapy: Theory & Practice* (New York: Harper & Row, Publishers, 1959), p. 72.
[13] E. J. Shoben, "New Frontiers in Theory," *Personnel and Guidance Journal* 32:80–83 (October, 1953).

concept of a democratic society, and doubtless many of us would share this concept very closely with him. But can we not, at least in a counseling relationship, operate on the assumption that the client who has learned to be free will help to develop a society in which all may live their lives to the utmost, with respect for the rights and the integrity of their fellows, since they respect their own rights and integrity?

While we could agree that the counselor might as well admit that he has his own values, it is important to distinguish between those values that are a part of the make-up of the inner self of the counselor, and are shown in his patience, his compassion and his acceptance of the client, and values of judgment and evaluation. The counselor who feels that "robbery," per se, is "bad," is not actually very far removed from the counselor who feels that the client who has robbed is "bad," who in turn is not too far removed from the individual who feels that the person who has robbed is bad and should therefore be punished. While such individuals may be being existential in the sense that they are saying, "You, and you alone must be responsible for your deeds," they are not existential in the sense that they are not getting close to, or being understanding of, the existential self. They may be observing it, but they are not living it.

Curran expresses more of a trust in the person-in-being when he indicates that we should seek a personal integration that is also an integration with the whole civilization that has produced us. This might then: [14]

> . . . free us from the more recent, possibly Kantian, ethical concept that all personal values must be imposed from without which has come not to mean either by parents, society or even more threatening and dangerous, by the state. It would restore again the possibility of starting out . . . on a thrilling personal pursuit of oneself in a fierce and independent search for reasonable self-values and yet allow that one would ultimately come by this process, not to violent rebellion and anarchy, but to ancient and secure traditional values.

This might represent a somewhat theistic existential point of view, in that while Curran trusts the individual to determine for himself how he will move and when and where he will move, he believes that there are, somehow, already established answers and values that the individuals will come to find. The individual does not develop

[14] Charles A. Curran, "Some Ethical and Scientific Values in the Counseling Therapeutic Process," *Personnel and Guidance Journal* 39:15–20 (September, 1960).

and create his own answers, but moves toward pre-established answers. In this case, in Curran's mind, these are likely established by some deity or God. Curran also indicates the interesting concept that somehow the "ancient" values are more "secure," and, we can assume, somehow better, than more recent values. Were the ancient and traditional values of the Romans more secure, and better, than some of the values that were being advanced by a heretic named Christ? Were the ancient and traditional values of the Greeks more secure than those of the heretic Socrates? The nontheistic existentialist would probably feel, with Curran, that the individual must find his own way. With Curran, he would have faith that the individual could find his own way. But he would differ with Curran in that he would have no pre-conceived concept of where the individual might end, or what his values might become. They might be like those of yesterday, or they might be like those of tomorrow, but man lives his life, and creates his values. He never goes back to what once was, although he may become like what once was.

In a sense, Curran would seem to have his "man" attempting to discover pre-existent truths and values, to somehow become congruent with what already is, and in this sense, of course, he is expressing the view of determinism. For him, what is, was, but for the existentialist, what is, is. Life is today, now, not yesterday, and we move away from yesterday, not toward it, even though we may yearn for this return to the womb.

One cannot discuss values and freedom, and living, without also taking into consideration that closely allied experience that eventually comes to all—death. The free man of the existentialist, the human being who is never merely a victim of a pre-determined culture, the person-in-being who is the maker of his values, being free to live, is also free to die, and it would seem that no person can really be free to live if he is afraid to die. Feifel expresses this feeling when he comments that: [15]

> . . . the willingness to die appears as a necessary condition for life. We are not altogether free in any deed as long as we are commanded by an inescapable will to live. . . . Life is not genuinely our own until we can renounce it.

Sartre relates freedom with death when he says, "The very act of freedom is therefore the assumption and creation of finitudes: If I

[15] Herman Feifel, in Rollo May (Ed.), *Existential Psychology* (New York: Random House, Inc., 1961), p. 71.

make myself, I make myself finite and hence my life is unique." [16]

It is ironic, and sad, that one of the basic feelings that many individuals learn from their "religion" is fear, particularly fear of death. Feifel,[17] for example, found, in a study of his patients, that the religious person, as compared with the nonreligious person, was personally more afraid of death. There must be untold millions of Christians who spend much of their lives trying to guarantee their entry to Heaven, but, since they feel that they are not the ones who control their destiny, are never quite sure whether God is approving or disapproving. They thus seek as much as they can in the way of assurances that there is a Heaven, and that they, and a few of their chosen fellows, are the ones who will be there. The old and hoary joke about each group in Heaven having to be segregated behind walls so that they might not discover that there are other peoples in Heaven too is not a joke to many. Equally shocking to some white, male Christians is the story of the angel who, on being asked to describe God, said, "She is a negro." Many "devout" Christians cannot accept doubt and uncertainty as a part of their religion. They must know, particularly about the rewards and punishments of the hereafter, and this might logically tend to make them somewhat self-centered in their actions toward others. The one who does not know about the future, and will, with certainty, face this uncertainty, even to the point of dying to defend a fellow human, is indeed showing a far higher level of altruism and compassion.

The value system that is centered around the integrity and the individuality of man is obviously closely related with freedom, which is basic to existential thought. This may be expressed as Sartre's consciousness as freedom, Jasper's existence as freedom, Kierkegaard's self as freedom or Tillich's concept of man as freedom. It is likely that they are all saying the same thing in somewhat complicated philosophical language—that I am free, that where I go and what I do depends on me, not on the forces outside of me, or even on the forces that I may have assimilated as a part of me. I, and I alone, always have the ultimate choice, and this choice I am free to make. The very fact that one is alive means that he has the potential to be free, but one is never free to live, of course, until he is free to die.

Effectively expressing this point of view is Rogers,[18] when he talks

[16] Jean-Paul Satre, *Existenialism*, Translated by B. Freeman, Trans. (New York: Philosophical Library, 1947), p. 545.
[17] Feifel, *op. cit.*, p. 68.
[18] Carl R. Rogers, "Learning to be Free" (unpublished paper).

of freedom as essentially an inner thing, something that exists in the living person, quite aside from any of the outward choice of alternatives which we so often think of as constituting freedom. And Frankl: [19]

> . . . everything can be taken from a man but one thing: the last of the human freedoms—to choose one's own attitude in any given set of circumstances.

And Buber: [20]

> He who forgets all that is caused and makes decisions out of the depths . . . is a free man, and destiny confronts him as a counterpart of his freedom. It is not his boundary, but his fulfillment.

And May: [21]

> No matter how great the forces victimizing the human being, man has the capacity to *know* that he is being victimized, and thus to influence in some way how he will relate *to* his fate. There is never lost that kernel of the power to take some stand, to make some decision, no matter how minute.

This movement toward freedom is also the core of the therapeutic process, and May is really describing the process of counseling when he says: [22]

> The patient moves toward freedom and responsibility in his living as he becomes more conscious of the deterministic experiences of his life. . . . As he becomes more conscious of the infinite deterministic forces in his life, he becomes more free. . . . Freedom is thus not the opposite to determinism. Freedom is the individual's capacity to know that he is the determined one . . . and thus to throw his weight on the side of one particular response.

While determinism may be a fact of the physical world, it is man who completes that world, and it is man who makes of the world whatever reality he may wish it to become. Thus the growth that occurs in counseling might be considered to be the process, the experience,

[19] V. E. Frankl, *From Death Camp to Existentialism* (Boston: Beacon Press, 1955), p. 65.
[20] M. Buber, *I and Thou* (Edinburgh: T. Clark, 1937), p. 53.
[21] May, *op. cit.*, p. 41.
[22] Rollo May, "Freedom and Responsibility Re-Examined" (unpublished paper given at Chicago, 1962 APGA Convention).

the learning to be free. Rogers [23] refers to the qualities of a growth-facilitating or freedom-promoting relationship as:

1. The element of congruence—the therapist being what he is. The feelings that the therapist is experiencing are available to his awareness, and he is able to live them and be them and communicate them if need be.

2. The counselor's warmth and acceptance of what is in the client—the counselor's willingness to be whatever feeling is going on in him at the moment—the unconditional positive regard.

3. Empathic understanding—the sensing and perceiving of the feelings from the inside, as they seem to the client.

Freedom may not be the opposite of determinism, but one does not find the concept of freedom in a deterministic society. The existentialist feels that the individual may live in a physical world that is, in a sense, determined, but the human individual, the existential self, the spirit of man, is not bound by any set of determined chains. Man basically *is* free, and any man can come to learn and to grow and to become the free person he is. This is the purpose of counseling—to help the individual to loose himself from his deterministic shackles, and to come to realize and to see what he has always had—choice and freedom.

Being free is difficult, and one cannot be free without continually running the risk of losing one's person. The struggle to be free, too, is often much more intense and complicated, at the inner self level, than the struggle against overt and obvious forces of oppression. If education results in real understanding, it can widen one's horizon of freedom, and the counselor must be concerned about the extent to which the educational experience helps to free each child.

The counselor who holds to the supremacy of the individual, and his freedom, also sees the world in which we live in a relative rather than an absolute sense. He accepts the fact that what is right for one is wrong for another, and his world does not consist of neat packages of goods and bads, rights and wrongs. Any counselor who actually believes that *he* has the answers will surely almost immediately face many problems. Let us note a few of them.

1. The more one speaks in terms of absolutes, the more likely it would seem that he is dishonest, if honesty is measured by what one

[23] Carl R. Rogers, *On Becoming a Person* (Boston: Houghton Mifflin Company, 1962), pp. 61–62.

does rather than by what one says. It is often not recognized by those who speak of absolutes that they are speaking of ideals, not of reality. Unless this is recognized, the inconsistencies that exist are hard to reconcile. For example, teachers tell children that cheating in any form is bad and wrong and evil. Yet in graduate schools of education, where all of the students are teachers or teachers-to-be, there would appear to be just as much cheating as anywhere else. Christians cite the Ten Commandments as absolute rules of behavior, and yet what Christian could say that he follows them to an absolute degree? I was involved in an experience that has been common to Christians since there were Christians, namely, the education of young men with the basic purpose of teaching them how to kill their enemies more effectively and in larger numbers. Some who read these words may have medals awarded because of their accomplishments in the art of killing; in a way, then, are we not saying that the rule is not so much "Thou shalt not kill" as "Thou shalt not kill certain people, but it is all right to kill other people?" Many Catholics feel that they are perfectly good Catholics although they use contraceptive devices; many Mormons feel that they are perfectly good Mormons although they drink coffee; many Methodists feel that they are perfectly good Methodists although they quaff a frequent highball; many Jews feel that they are perfectly good Jews although they eat pork with gusto. One might assume that in each of these cases the individuals are perfectly "good" Catholics, Mormons, Methodists and Jews, although their respective churches might disagree. The setting up of an absolute rule of behavior tends to be counter to human and natural behavior; it is counter to the fact of individual differences. Thus one might say that it is counter to the law of nature. Many individuals will continue to pay lip service to such sets of rules and regulations, as long as they feel that the price they are paying is not too excessive. When they do, they may continue overtly to accept these rules, but they will pay increasingly less attention to them. Thus the counselor who states that he operates on the principle of a black and white world should search himself very carefully, and try to determine to what extent he practices what he says; or whether what he says is little more than an overt gesture to satisfy the religious and social mores that surround him?

2. It is difficult too, to see how the absolutist counselor could be acceptant and understanding of the client who almost certainly will differ from him in many ways. If the counselor believes that the American way of life is the only way, and is hurt when he discovers that not all foreigners want to be Americans, how can he understand the Indian

client who is not particularly impressed with either Communism or Americanism? The absolute counselor may listen, and he may appear to be interested and sympathetic, but how can he really believe in the client if he has no room for the feeling that some of the client's answers, although they contradict his own, may be right for the client?

3.   How can the counselor with an absolute philosophy respect the integrity of the client, if we assume that this means the acceptance of the right of the client to make decisions that may be quite contrary to those the counselor would make if he himself were in a similar situation? Maybe the right decision is to run away from school, or to get a divorce, or to leave college, or to be sexually intimate with someone else, or to kill oneself—who knows? As soon as the counselor says that he knows, we may wonder if he really means what he says when he talks about the rights and the freedoms of others. For the individual, the cultural mores are not always right; and the counselor is not the voice of society or the voice of the culture, but rather the voice of the individual. Thus the counselor may sometimes be somewhat suspect by the culture.

ETHICAL ISSUES THAT FACE THE COUNSELOR

In any close and intimate relationship between two individuals, problems of an ethical nature will arise. The counselor must frequently face such issues, and often they pose a dilemma in which he would appear to be damned if he did and damned if he didn't! While all of these issues are, of course, personal, some tend to be primarily a matter of individual decision, while others are of general professional concern.

The professional organizations most concerned with counseling are well aware of the importance to their profession of problems of an ethical nature, as they may affect both the individual member of the organization and the organization itself. The American Psychological Association's Committee on Scientific and Professional Ethics and Conduct and the American Personnel and Guidance Association's Committee on Ethics have a double function in that they protect the counselor from the public (the counselor has no protection in the matter of legal suit) and they protect the public from unethical counselors. They also have a remedial and helpful function, of course, and there are counselors and psychologists today who think of these committees as professional groups that gave them much assistance during a difficult time.

In 1960 The American Personnel and Guidance Association took its first legal step in defending one of its members. A previous circuit court decision, described below, had been appealed to the state supreme court: [24]

> The Circuit Court of Dunn County (Wis.) recently ruled that a guidance counselor had no legal responsibility for the suicide of a counselee student.
>
> Claiming their daughter was emotionally disturbed, the parents of the student in question charged the guidance counselor with negligence on three counts: failure to notify the parents of her condition; failure to secure psychiatric treatment for her; and failure to provide proper guidance.
>
> The court stated in effect, that the counselor was a teacher not a medical expert. To expect him to recognize the student's condition without benefit of necessary training and experience "would require a duty beyond reason," the court stated.

The Association then filed a brief with the Supreme Court, and it presented a significant argument that had not been raised before, namely, that a counselor cannot be held liable for an event that occurs weeks after counseling, and particularly when a medical question is involved. The result was that the original decision of the circuit court was upheld, and the Association had functioned effectively in protecting the rights of one of its members.

It is extremely difficult, however, to protect the unwary public from the various quacks who call themselves counselors and psychologists—both of these being omnibus terms that can mean almost anything. Such individuals find that the title "Doctor" gives them added authority and more business, and that it is a title easy to acquire, since few clients will ask "What is your doctorate and where did you get it?" As has already been mentioned, there are numerous institutions where one may receive a doctor's degree in wondrous and various fields by going through the motions of taking an extension course and paying a rather substantial sum. To the shame of the professions of education, psychology and counseling, there are individuals possessing high positions who proudly parade such "degrees." Certification at both the professional and state levels is one way to combat this unhappy situation, but the public has also to be educated to distinguish between a professional counselor and a quack.

Any counselor who has worked on a committee concerned with

[24] *College and University Bulletin* XII:3 (October 15, 1959) (Washington, D.C.: Association for Higher Education, National Education Association).

problems of ethical behavior soon realizes that it is a very "sticky" area where, far more often than not, there is no clear-cut indication, with no doubts whatsoever as to whether the behavior of a counselor in question was unethical or not. Any committee making a decision on the ethical behavior of a counselor must at all times be keenly aware of the ethical soundness of its own position. It may place a particular strain on a Client-centered counselor, who flies the "never judge or evaluate" standard, to find himself a member of a group that is determining the ethical fitness of one of its members, possibly on the basis of highly questionable evidence.

A committee, moreover, being made up of human beings, will not always see eye to eye on just what is ethical and what is not ethical. My reaction, for example, to a statement by Walters,[25] "How many therapists will recognize and acknowledge the error of attacking the patient's religious beliefs, as Knight did in his analysis of a minister?" is one of some astonishment. Surely this is an example of obvious unethical therapist behavior, and surely, at the very least, every therapist would "recognize and acknowledge" the error. But apparently there are some therapists to whom this would be a debatable issue. Similarly, on a tape, in discussing a patient with a group of colleagues, a therapist says that she should "keep her big fat mouth shut," a statement that some therapists would certainly regard as wholly unethical. In a professional discussion of a client with colleagues, we show little respect for him by insulting him, but, on the other hand, even some who read these words may think there is nothing very unusual about the above statement. Thus the very question, "Just what is unethical anyway?" often poses a difficult problem.

The American Psychological Association has done an excellent job in trying to answer this question by posing a whole series of questions and situations, and then giving the reactions of the committee to them.[26] Not all members of the American Psychological Association, however, agree with all of the answers as given by the committee. Every counselor, sooner or later, must face some of these ethical issues as personal problems, which he must answer for himself, to himself.

In discussing unethical practices, Schwebel makes three "assumptions": [27]

25 Orville S. Walters, "Metaphysics, Religion and Psychotherapy," *Journal of Counseling Psychology* 5:243–252 (Winter, 1958).
26 *Ethical Standards of Psychologists* (Washington, D.C.: Committee on Ethical Standards for Psychologists, American Psychological Association, 1953).
27 Milton Schwebel, "Why Unethical Practice," *Journal of Counseling Psychology* 2:122–128 (Summer, 1955).

1. Self-interest causes both unethical behavior and unethical practice. The personal profit motive may be a cause, the need for self-enhancement may be a cause, and the need to maintain security and status may be a cause.

2. Unsound judgment due to inadequate training and/or unsupervised experience, or due to ineffective selection, causes unethical practice; but since self-interest is not a primary factor, the behavior of the psychologist is not unethical. Unsound judgment may be shown in maintaining confidences in staff relations or in maintaining confidences about anti-social behavior.

3. Ignorance causes unethical practice. Here too, since self-interest is not a primary factor, the behavior of the psychologist is not unethical. Ignorance of technical information may be a cause, or ignorance on the part of the counselor of his own values, especially those that are incompatible with respect for the integrity of the individual, may be a cause.

Some readers would probably question Schwebel's statement that incorrect behavior caused by ignorance is not unethical; or some might say that while it might not be unethical of the individual, it is unethical for the employer to hire such a person without checking on his credentials; and it is unethical of the graduating institution to graduate a person who is so ignorant. It would seem that somewhere along the line, when injury is done to a patient or a client in a supposed professional relationship, then somebody, somewhere, has committed an unethical act.

Wrenn presents a few examples of ethical questions: [28]

(a) How can consultation be had with another person about the student without violating the student's confidences? (b) What is ethical for the counselor when the student, within the counseling relationship, relates wrong-doing or crime? (c) When fellow counselors, teachers, or administrators inquire about a counselee, how does the counselor keep their good-will while maintaining the integrity of his relationship with the student? (d) What does the counselor do when the problem is over his head but there is no referral agency available, or the student will not accept referral?

Warnath discusses an important point when he refers to the relationship between problems of ethics and goals to be achieved: [29]

[28] C. Gilbert Wrenn, "Status and Role of the School Counselor," *The Personnel and Guidance Journal* 36:175–183 (November, 1957).
[29] Charles F. Warnath, "Ethical Considerations of Student Personnel Work as Viewed by a Counseling Psychologist," *Personnel-O-Gram* 13:8–11 (October, 1958).

Essentially the problem of ethics is one of frame of reference. When the student personnel staff can agree on basic goals and the methods to be used in achieving the goals toward which they are moving, ethical problems will become solvable. However, so long as there is confusion in goals or discrepancies between goals and methods, the situation will remain controlled by the individuals in their separate offices, and communication will be difficult. The first step for any staff in determining the right or wrong of future activities is to admit that it is uncertain about its over-all goals and procedures. The second step is to agree on some firm philosophy of student personnel work drawing on some of the proposals which have been written up in the field. The third step is to carry on research in the areas of uncertainties about application. And finally, as the fourth step, each personnel staff must act as a group of professional people . . . mature enough to be willing to develop consistency between practices and professed goals.

Let us look now at some of the specific ethical issues that, sooner or later, will probably trouble every professional counselor.

1. The basic overriding ethical issue is related to the central core of the counselor's value system—the respect for the rights and integrity of the individual so that the counselor's primary responsibility is to the client rather than to any other individual or group—whether children as a group, teachers, parents, the community, the church, the state, or the nation.[30] The individual counselor may be able to satisfy himself that this is an ethical principle that he cannot maintain at all times; but if he must at times break it, then there should certainly be some soul searching to determine whether or not the break was necessary, and whether it was done for the good of some organization or group, or done because of the counselor's insecurity, the counselor's ignorance, and the counselor's ineptitude. This statement obviously refers to the inviolate nature of the information given to the counselor *during the counseling session.*

The question of confidentiality has become more of an issue in recent years with the vastly increased use of audio and video tapes in counselor education. While it is generally agreed that a counselor should not record, or make use of a one-way mirror or a closed-circuit television camera without the approval of the client, Marcuse, some years ago, presented an interesting defense for the use of covert recording: [31]

[30] A most interesting typescript describing the trials of a psychologist testifying in a court case appears in J. L. McCary, "A Psychologist Testifies in Court," *The American Psychologist* 15:53–57 (January, 1960).
[31] F. L. Marcuse, in "Comment," *The American Psychologist* 12:278–279 (May, 1957).

The whole purpose in covert recording, if such be indicated as required by the data, is to enable one to obtain more information, to facilitate rapport, and in the long run (it is hoped) to be of benefit to the individual therapeutically. . . .

To reiterate, concentrated sulphuric acid, a scalpel, or morphine may certainly be misused, but this does not constitute an argument against their legitimate use. . . .

Whether research is concerned with the nature of the behavior involved in jury decisions or how best to aid a patient requesting therapy, the best method for eliciting such data should be used. Doing this is both proper and needed. Covert recording can respect the patient's confidence and can be constructive.

It is true, of course, that counselors generally would consider it quite ethical to make covert recordings of children or of psychotic patients. When this is the case, one might well ask how the counselor determines whether or not the individual is old enough not to be a child, or stable enough not to be psychotic, so that he will know when to record covertly! Covert recording carries with it a good deal in the way of invasion of the privacy and rights of the individual, and it would seem that the counselor should not record unless the client gives his approval. It is true, of course, that this means that the counselor will sometimes be unable to record sessions that would have been worth while for the education of student counselors, for the education of the counselor himself, and for a greater understanding of the client.

If one is to have a recording of a beginning session, however, it must be covert in that the recorder is on when the client comes in. The counselor should, of course, immediately ask permission of the client, and then, even if he is turned down, he at least has a recording of his being turned down! Many counselors question the wisdom of recording a first session, since the client is under stress anyway, and having to begin the conversation by requesting permission to record is possibly not the best way to establish a feeling of rapport.

On the other hand, I have found that the recording even of first sessions is usually accepted with little or no concern by the client. The following conversation, taken from a tape, is typical.

Co: Hello there . . . Mary?
Cl: Yes.
Co: Come on in and have a seat.
Cl: Thank you.
Co: It's a bit cold in here. There must be something wrong

with their heating system.

Cl: Oh . . . (laughs) . . . that's all right.

Co: Do you mind, Mary, if I periodically record some of these sessions? Would that bother you at all?

Cl: No, that's quite all right . . . (pause) I really don't know how to begin except that. . . .

It is better too, if the recorder can be kept out of sight, since it is somewhat of a distraction. In the absence of better facilities, most counselors will find that a typewriter drawer on one side of the desk is a handy place to put a recorder, and all that is visible is the microphone. Once the client gives permission to use the recorder periodically, it is just as well to have the microphone always present, even though most of the time it will be "dead." The client then gets used to it; although I had a client who interrupted himself, looked at the microphone, asked the counselor if it was on, and, at the counselor's nod, requested that it be turned off, which, of course, it was.

Some counselors feel that since one never knows which sessions will be particularly good ones for the purposes of research and teaching, it is best to record all sessions, even though most of them will be erased. It sometimes happens, too, that in a certain session the counselor is faced with an unusual situation, or some challenging and threatening incident; and it is obviously beneficial if he has the session on tape so that he can study his own reactions.

A related question is the extent to which audio and video material and other data on clients should be used for teaching and learning. Most counselors would probably agree that one never uses such material unless it is with a professional group for professional purposes. Most would also agree that when audio and video tapes are used they are always edited, since not only the identity of the client is usually revealed in a counseling session, but a good deal of confidential information about other individuals as well. Most would agree, too, that a tape should not be used if the client has explicitly stated that it is not to be listened to by any person other than the counselor. On the other hand, most counselor educators probably have tapes whose use has been accepted by the client because of his trust in the counselor, but which the counselor will not use because of the possibility of identification. Thus if I had a student counselor as a client, I would never use one of these tapes, even if it had been edited, even if the student had given his consent, with any group of student counselors; I might use it with counseling colleagues, or with certain student counselors in another institution far away. In the long run, the counselor must use his own professional understanding, and his sense of decency, being always aware that the client may have given his consent only because he felt a debt of gratitude to the counselor, and that one is never quite sure how professional all members of a professional group may be.

There would seem to be little question that movies and video tapes of actual counseling sessions should be used only with the consent of the client, and that they should be shown only to those individuals whose professional status is assured. This would raise some question as to whether such movies should be shown to large classes of students taking courses in guidance and counseling. Tapes and movies of counseling sessions are for the professional improvement of counselors and student counselors, not for recreation and amusement. Respect for the individual implies respect for the confidentiality of what goes on, an attitude required of every member of a group just as much as it is of the individual counselor.

Much the same thing applies in any staff discussion of a "case" in which various records are usually referred to. The counselor discussing the client should be very careful that he does not needlessly disclose material that is confidential, although some people would say that this is greatly affected by the personnel at the staff meeting. If, for example, it happens to be a meeting of the counseling staff with certain deans, teachers, and others to discuss the problems of a certain student, it is likely that what the counseling staff will say will be a good deal more restricted than if the people at the meeting were fewer in number and limited to the counseling staff. Names of individuals other than the client should be brought in only when necessary for an intelligent discussion of the problem, and they should certainly never be brought in for "thrill" or to show off. Respect for the client should also include respect for the individuals who are involved with the client. A counselor once, in a staff meeting, elicited comment by disclosing that one of the girls involved with his client was the daughter of the principal—a disclosure showing respect for neither the principal nor his daughter, since there was no need whatsoever for their being identified.

At the university level, the presence at staff meetings of graduate assistants and fellows may also raise a problem, in that the client being discussed may well be a colleague of one of the individuals present. When this happens, it is probably just as well that the graduate student affected should leave the discussion, since he is put in an embarrassing, if not unethical, position.

2. Another ethical issue, which is also related to the individuality of the client, has to do with the use of tests. While professional counselors and psychologists may not like some of the books that are written on this subject for the general public,[32] the sales of these books leave no doubt that the public is interested. For some counselors, of course, this is no issue, in that they either use no tests whatsoever, or use them very sparingly. Whenever any test is used, however, there is still the question of its validity and reliability, and the extent to which it represents an imposition on the individual. Those counselors who make frequent use of tests might ponder carefully the extent to which such use contradicts their supposed respect for the integrity of the client.

A related question has to do with the use of test data—what information should be transmitted to what people? If tests are given to help a person to come to a greater understanding of himself, it would seem highly unethical to reveal any of this test data to such individuals as parents, potential employers, or college admissions officers. In fact, those counselors who feel that tests should be used for this purpose would surely agree that the test data is the property of the client, and no one else.

In a school system, any test data other than that from achievement tests should be available only for the counselor and the psychologist, and for the student who owns it. After all, it *is* his test data! If it is a question of no test data or test data that must be transmitted to various curious eyes, the only ethical choice would surely be no test data. This is at least one way to avoid the gross misuse of test data! If respect for the integrity of the client means anything, then it should surely mean that personal information about him, whether it comes from his voice as it is heard on a tape or from the writing on a piece of paper, is considered to be inviolate and secure.

Any state law that indicates that all school records on any child should be available for the perusal of parents or others should be questioned and challenged. And while it is being questioned and challenged, the counselor can maintain his integrity by keeping his own *private* file, if he must maintain anything in the way of records! One might hope that the amount of personal information on children

[32] Vance Packard, *The Naked Society* (New York: David McKay Co., Inc., 1964); Martin Gross, *The Brain Watchers* (New York: Random House, 1962).

on file in New York schools will rapidly diminish to next to nothing!

3. Another problem occurs when graduate students have access to records that are of a confidential, or at least a semiconfidential nature. Such a student always occupies an "in-between" status; the students see him as partially a staff member, whereas the staff people see him as primarily a student, and the poor fellow has to function as both! As much as possible, there should be a clarification of his status —to himself, to the staff, and to the students, but the problem will always remain to some extent.

4. Another ethical question concerns the extent to which the counselor should let the counselee know about any overt action that he might take on behalf of the client, if, indeed, he should take any at all without the suggestion by, and certainly the agreement of, the client. Should the counselor take steps to change what he knows to be a very negative home situation when he feels that he has a good chance of being successful, even though he also knows that the client would probably not want him to take any action at all? Should the school counselor talk to a teacher who, because of his lack of understanding of the true situation in which a boy is involved, is making things difficult for him, even though the boy is afraid that he will get into trouble if the counselor talks to the teacher? Should the counselor intervene with school authorities when he knows, from counseling sessions with another student, that a boy is being punished for deeds that were actually committed by someone else? Should a counselor talk with children who are showing a lack of understanding and acceptance of another child because of their possible misconceptions about her?

Although there are no specific answers to these and many other questions of a similar type, a general rule of thumb is that the counselor does not take any overt action unless it is requested by the client. In many cases, of course, such action should not be taken even if it is requested by the client—for example, by the client who is being charged with beating another individual and wants the counselor to appear and speak in his favor; or the boy who wants the counselor to intercede with the girl who has just jilted him; and so on. An individual who is functioning as a counselor, involved in a close and personal relationship with another person, may find his effectiveness as a counselor impaired if he begins to function in another manner—namely, as a manipulator of the environment. A certain action may be the most desirable that can be taken, but it is not the function of the counselor, not, at least, of the counselor whose full-time function is counseling.

A somewhat similar problem often occurs when the counselor works in a Health Service, a Psychiatric Clinic, or any other hospital setting. There the clients, or patients, will with increasing frequency ask for various kinds of medication to make them sleep, to keep them awake, to steady their nerves, to reduce their tension, and so on. Whether the counselor is a medical therapist or a nonmedical therapist should have no effect on the procedure in a case such as this. Since the counselor does not want to appear as the doer or giver of things, the client should be referred to medical personnel, who will make the decision whether or not the individual should have medication. In some cases there might be consultation between the medical doctor and the counselor, but it should always be the medical doctor, not the counselor, who makes the decision, even if the counselor is also a medical doctor. What sometimes happens, of course, is that the client (like one of mine) tells the medical doctor on duty that "the doctor over in the Clinic said I was to have some tranquilizers." In this case, a telephone call easily straightened the matter out, and it was the medical doctor on duty who made the decision that the client should have certain medication. The basic reason is not the somewhat out-dated fact that only the medical doctor has the legal authority to prescribe such medication—since many psychologists and other non-medical therapists have equal knowledge of such medication and its effects, but simply the fact that the act of prescribing the medication puts the counselor in a position of authority and decision.

5. Referral may also become a problem of an ethical nature. When the client wishes to be referred elsewhere, normally it raises no problem—unless, of course, the client wishes to be referred to someone who is known professionally as an unethical individual—and this would not often happen. It may happen, however, that the counselor decides that he cannot ethically continue a relationship because of his feeling of lack of capacity to work with the client, but the client refuses to be referred, insists that he is quite satisfied with the present situation, and will cease to have any counseling if the counselor refers him. Another such situation occurs when the counselor with a private practice is being paid for sessions that he feels are doing nothing for the client, and he has the choice of continuing with the client, who will not accept referral, or terminating a client who does not wish to be terminated. Still another problem comes when it is obvious that an individual should be referred, but there is nowhere to refer—although the counselor would feel that it is very rarely that understanding and acceptance are not of some help to any individual. The

reverse side of this coin, and one that frequently occurs in schools, is when a person who calls himself a counselor feels that he must refer practically every potential client who reveals anything in the way of a personal problem. When this is the case, surely the individual should be called a referral technician rather than a professional counselor!

6. The part-time counselor will soon find that the fact that he has several jobs will raise some special ethical problems for him. If he is a teacher and counselor, for example, he will find conflict between his allegiance to a group of children as a teacher and his allegiance to an individual child as a counselor. He may find that, as a teacher, he is expected to be freer with information about a child than he feels, as a counselor, he should be. He may find that parents regard him as a teacher, and he cannot, in effect, say to parents as well as to teachers and school administrators, "But you cannot expect me to do that because I am a counselor," since they will immediately reply, "But you are also a teacher, are you not?" Although this conflict of allegiance raises many difficulties for the teacher-counselor, most of them can be reduced if the teacher feels that he can function better as a teacher if he operates nearly all the time as a counselor.

These difficulties are well-nigh insurmountable, however, for the individual who is a principal. A surprising number of schools still refer blithely to the fact that their counseling is done by their principal, but this surely shows a lack of understanding of counseling and the functions of the counselor. As a principal, one owes allegiance to the teachers, and to a lesser degree to the community; and one cannot function ethically as a counselor if his primary concern is any other than the individual child. Thus, any counselor going into a new position, particularly in a school situation, should know in advance just what is expected of him, or he may find himself saddled with tasks that make his title of counselor nothing but a mockery, and he might well be accused of unethical behavior, or ignorance, or both, if he accepts such conflicting tasks. A school system needs superintendents, and principals, and teachers, and they may be fine and honorable individuals; but they do not, and they cannot, function effectively as counselors.

The counselor educator has his own particular problems; while he may not function as a counselor with any one of his students, he is, nevertheless, by his practice as much as anything else, helping the students to come to an understanding of some of the basic principles and tenets of counseling. But to what extent do students really learn and internalize the concept of acceptance rather than rejection, when the counselor-teacher functions as a critic of their counseling? To what extent do they learn acceptance without evaluation when he gives them examinations and tests? To what extent do they internalize the concept that "you are the best evaluator of you, and you are the one who must make the decisions," when the one who teaches them this sentiment indicates that he does not believe that they are capable or honest enough to do so, by grading and evaluating them, by passing some, by failing others? This state of affairs may not pose a problem for some counselor educators, but surely it must for those counselors who feel that the learning that occurs in counselor education must, in some way, be akin to the learning that occurs in the actual counseling process, in that it is internalized and really becomes meaningful in the actions and the attitudes of the learner.

7. A final question of ethics would deal with whether or not the counselor can excuse unprofessional behavior because of ignorance. His behavior might be excused by others, but the question here is whether or not the counselor can look himself in the eye and say, "There was nothing unethical about that; I was just stupid." It surely seems within the realm of ethical behavior to say that any individual is being unethical if he attempts professional tasks that he is incapable of performing because of his lack of skill and knowledge. Certainly a counselor's fellows should not condemn, but rather try to help; yet each individual counselor may wonder if he is functioning in an ethical manner when he becomes involved in a close and possibly crucial human relationship with another person, and at the same time knows that he does not know what he is doing. Any counselor, of course, no matter what his experience, is going to face situations that he cannot understand, and at times be faced with questions for which he has no answer, but this is part of his professional work, rather than an involvement in a situation about which he knows nothing.

There is usually some relationship between professional competence and the kind and extent of one's professional education. Counselor education has come a long way in the past few years, but even today large numbers of institutions with ineffective programs of counselor education continue to train (not educate) counselors. State certification in most states is still an indication of a willingness to accept mediocrity, and the professional counselor is one who does not accept state certification as an adequate indication of counseling competence. Only a handful of institutions have a well developed program of not less than two years of graduate education, and the counseling practicum is an expense that not too many institutions are willing to accept. An appalling number of current school counselors have not yet experienced a counseling practicum worthy of the name, and many counselors have yet to hear the sound of their own voices, let alone see a video tape or movie of what the client sees when he looks at the counselor! The education of the school counselor still remains one of the most critical professional ethical issues that we must face.

8. A final ethical question concerns the inconsistency of counselors rather than their ignorance. This is a particularly pertinent problem during the education of the counselor, and too frequently the assessed "effectiveness" of the student counselor would appear to depend more than anything else on just whom he happens to have as a supervisor. In Evraiff's book,[33] for example, the following comments were made by the various reviewers regarding the effectiveness of several student counselors:

The counselor of Carl, for example, had the following said about him:

From Arbuckle: You start off very dominant, but appear to become more acceptant of the client, who seems to make real progress. You tend to be too concerned with techniques and methodology.

From Stefflre: Your third interview was good, but the last was not very good. You were not "close" to the client.

From Roeber: By interview three you were doing pretty well, but you withdrew too much in the last interview—you became a silent partner. You follow the words, but not the melody.

From Dugan and Blocher: You made excellent use of techniques, and created a warm, positive relationship. In the last interview Carl was able to talk more positively about himself. You need to accept more responsibility.

Jack's counselor might have heard the following:

From Arbuckle: You have difficulty accepting Jack, and insist on dominating and controlling him. You tend to be too technique-centered. You are not too aware of "self" as yet, but you show high promise of self-understanding.

From Stefflre: You follow the "party-line," but you are on your way to becoming a competent counselor—and a free person.

From Roeber: You are too "methodology"-centered. You did

[33] William Evraiff, *Helping Counselors Grow Professionally* (Englewood Cliffs, N.J.: Prentice-Hall, Inc., 1963), pp. 366–367.

not establish too much in the way of a positive relationship with Jack.

From Dugan and Blocher: You were too "technique"-centered. There appeared to be little or no communication with Jack. You appear to have no goals.

Jane's counselor might hear:

From Arbuckle: You understand intellectually, but did not appear to get close, and to empathize with Jane. You stressed the intellectual content rather than the feelings, which were more apparent on the tape than in the typescript.

From Stefflre: You did little more than respond with statement of content. You were skilled in omission, and you appeared to avoid areas where you felt uncomfortable. I have respect for your analytic ability.

From Roeber: You appeared to be dedicated to a Client-centered methodology. You have more than the ordinary talent for counseling.

This suggests that supervisors of student counselors should be very wary of the validity of their own assessments, and it also raises a question as to the extent to which supervisors are dedicated to helping the student counselor grow toward effectiveness in his own way rather than simply becoming a pale carbon copy of the supervisor in order to receive a positive assessment. Some student counselors may never be able to determine just how effective they can be because their supervisors will never give them a chance to operate as they really are. While it may be expensive, it would seem highly desirable from an ethical point of view for every student counselor to be evaluated by several supervisors so that there might be more chance that their personal bias could be cancelled out!

EXAMPLES OF ETHICAL PROBLEMS

One of the marks of a professional counselor is the way he measures up to various ethical issues that press in upon him. Many of these issues represent, basically, assaults upon the integrity of the counselor. One school counselor, for example, has mentioned the following as examples of ethical issues that involve him:

The pressure brought on by the insecure and autocratic administrator who wants the counselor to reveal confidences.

The problem of being aware of environmental imperfections yet not being able to do anything about them because action would demand the revelation of client confidences.

The prostitution of the counselor's professional role.

The pressure brought by various people not to involve myself in therapeutic counseling.

The self-protecting reactions of decision-making groups only willing to see one side of the coin.

The protection that tenure laws afford the incompetent teacher.

The badgering of youngsters as part of the educational process.

The badgering of teachers as part of the educational process.

The badgering of offspring as an aspect of parenthood.

Another school counselor has experienced the following ethical problems:

Pressures on the counselor to reveal confidences given in the counseling relationship.

Parental perception of the counselor as an investigator and enforcer.

Parental expectation that the counselor will manipulate teachers for the benefit of the client.

Pressures that the counselor should act as a teacher—i.e., "the counselor should not listen to kids—he should explain and discipline."

Adult pressures and expectations for the counselor to act as an intermediary on their behalf—as an instrument by which some would like to control youngsters and make them conform.

The pressure exerted subtly and overtly on the counselor to help the client to adjust, but not necessarily to grow if growth and development are not in harmony with adult standards and goals.

Here are some examples of ethical issues faced by different counselors:

Example 1

John Rose saw the counselor at the beginning of his senior year in high school. He impressed his counselor as a sincere, highly motivated young man, who found in these interviews an opportunity to express himself at least partially. The counseling sessions, however, also revealed a tendency to unrealistic thinking, a strong undercurrent of anxiety, and at times some degree of confusion.

While part of John's problems were immediately connected with school, his deepest concerns were inevitably related to his home situation and background. During his childhood, from the age of about five or seven to his early teens, he had been forced to live apart from his parents as simply another member of the large family of one of his uncles, who resided in Texas. Both parents had come from lower socio-economic groups and had received but limited education. The father, a carpenter by training, had worked in mines and factories, but now made little effort to find employment, leaning on the bottle for his chief support. The mother, although still employed, had also fallen into the habit of excessive drinking. Life within the home was one of frequent arguments, discord, and nagging, with very little understanding. Basically, within his family either in the past or the present, John had found little attention, affection, or self-expression.

In the spring of his senior year, John was booked by the police on the charge of exhibitionism in the Townsville Public Library. Released with a warning, he reported his difficulty to the Guidance Office at school. Referred to the school psychologist, John's problem was diagnosed as requiring long-term treatment. Since the facilities for such treatment were not available at the time within the school structure, he was given a second referral to the hospital clinic and advised to leave school until such time as he might wish to return and at the same time could be psychiatrically cleared for further study.

In the period of a little over a year since John left school, he has returned several times for talks with his counselor, including one visit to his counselor's home. These sessions have had two main purposes from John's point of view: (1) to enable him to release some of his feelings and obtain some approval for his various efforts at obtaining personal and social adjustment; and (2) to obtain guidance and approval in his search for vocational adjustment.

During interviews John has readily admitted the fact that he has not been wholly successful in combatting the need to exhibit himself, and a number of isolated instances have occurred since his leaving school. However, he was making serious efforts to fight the need, and with some degree of success. Unfortunately, the clinic had found it impossible to admit him immediately because of case load. His counselor urged him to keep applying for early admission, but after a year of delay on the part of the clinic encouraged him to seek admission at another clinic. At this time, it would appear that the clinic at another hospital will be able to give him treatment.

The basic ethical problem is concerned with educational and vocational advisement. Following his departure from school, he took and held a factory job that offered some security but none-too-high pay and little opportunity for advancement. He is strongly motivated to rise above his present socio-economic level, but is restricted by his lack of higher education or specialized training.

(1) An additional element of his dilemma is represented, however, by the usual necessity of completing the personal history data found on most application forms for any higher level or more interesting occupational outlet. Recently he was seeking a bank job in which he was highly interested. The application form called for previous education, reasons for leaving school, and any police history. He left the form incomplete and came to see his counselor for advice. "Almost any job I really want asks these questions. I'm almost sure to be stymied in getting ahead if I tell the truth. If I don't get a better job, I'm going to be just so much more unhappy . . . and if I'm always under this pressure, I'm going to find it all the harder to keep out of trouble. What should I do? What should the counselor advise John? To tell the whole truth? Avoid jobs with such searching questionnaires? Conceal his personal history?

(2) Recently, his counselor was contacted by a representative of an agency to obtain information relative to his clearance for employment. What information if any should be released by his counselor? Should he urge the boy not to use his name as a reference? Should he inform the boy in advance as to what he would feel obligated to disclose if used as a reference? These are the specific questions asked by the representative of the agency:

1. Would you recommend John for employment?
2. Do you consider him to be a stable, well-adjusted individual?
3. Do you think that he will get along well with fellow employees?

Example 2

Bill Din is a college freshman. He seemed to have no really valid motivation for attending college other than his father's desire to have him in college. His academic record for the first semester was poor, and he was placed on probation, although all objective evidence seems to indicate that he is a student of superior ability. In working with the student to try to develop some worthwhile motivation, the counselor became involved with a friend of the father.

In time, this friend informed the counselor that the boy's mother is dead, and the father is serving a jail sentence as the consequence of some "sharp" business dealings. Thus the boy has no parental guidance or direction and is left almost entirely to his own devices, being alone at home with a housekeeper while his father is imprisoned. He is well-to-do, has a new Cadillac convertible car of his own, and spends all of his time "living a gay life."

One of Bill's instructors comes to the counselor to get some information regarding Bill. He has discovered that Bill has superior ability which is evident on the few occasions when he does some academic work. But he wonders about the boy's family situation. Why does he seem to be so poorly motivated? Under these circumstances, and with the knowledge that the counselor possesses, how much or how little should he pass on to the faculty member?

Example 3

Mary San is a college sophomore. She is friendly and pleasant in all relationships with other students and faculty. Prior to entering college, she was in Europe for three years working as a secretary. During this period of her life, she developed a keen interest in international affairs. Apparently her group there spent considerable time in the discussion of the world situation and in deciding what should be done to insure the future peace of the world. As a result, she returned to the United States critical of the way our government was handling foreign affairs and with a general feeling that the solution might be a drastic shift in social and political organization.

Although Mary came from a substantial, conservative Middle-West home background, she has always had some tendency toward inward revolt against the conservative point of view. It was interpreted by her family, however, as the "enthusiasm of youth" and since it reached only minor proportions, such as occasional family arguments, the family thought little about it. Later they became quite distressed by her activities. The time spent in Europe seemed to intensify these feelings. After returning, she worked for about a year in a textile factory before entering college. Here she became very much interested in union activities, and the excitement involved in those activities seemed to stimulate her further. She came to a conclusion that labor work would be her chosen vocational field, a decision that led to her desire for further education.

While a student, she has continued her contact with the union movement. By a fellow student with somewhat similar inclinations, she was introduced to a local "progressive" group with members from local colleges. This organization is very active and probably provides further fortification of her "liberal" or extremist tendencies.

Mary is very active in extra-curricular affairs, her interests centering mainly in student government and the school newspaper. She is also active in the political organization called Americans for Democratic Action.

About three weeks ago, an F.B.I. agent called on a routine loyalty check on this girl, who is being considered for a position of trust in the government. Since much of the preceding information had been obtained from the counselee and her parents through interviews, what is the counselor's position? What information should be given to the F.B.I. agent?

Example 4

Horace Pen established himself early in college as an unusual student. He was very able, very personable, and impressed one immediately as possessing qualities of leadership. He had had his two-year hitch in the Air Force before coming to college.

When class elections were held shortly before Christmas recess, he was elected freshman president. He quickly demonstrated his abilities both as class president and also as representative of the Student-Faculty Assembly.

A review of his two-year record—or rather of his record up to about Easter of his sophomore year—indicated the extent to which he had won not only student but faculty attention. At about Easter time, one of the departmental chairmen requested that Horace be given a work scholarship and be assigned to him. The request was carried out, and Horace began his duties. Later, by sheer accident, an instructor noticed that a boy who had not turned in a major assignment had suddenly acquired an A grade for it. A check of records indicated that not only had this change been made but that at least two others had occurred. It soon became evident that the records had been left briefly where they were available to Horace and to no other student. When Horace was interrogated about the situation, he admitted that he had made the changes.

In due course, the case came before the school department heads. They were reluctant to give the boy a dishonorable dismissal because of his previous fine record, even though it was felt that such action was indicated. Horace was finally permitted to withdraw with the understanding that application for re-admission at a future date would be denied.

About a year later, Horace applied for admission to a Midwestern university and his guidance counselor received a letter requesting information about his withdrawal.

(1) What is the counselor's ethical obligation in such a situation?

(2) Does the fact that a complete statement of the case would likely lead to rejection have any bearing on it?

Example 5

Henry Dot has completed his sophomore year at college. The victim of a broken home in his early youth, he was raised by three uncles who did what they could for him. However, he was forced to shift for himself and worked at odd jobs from a very early age. He was graduated from high school at the age of nineteen, having missed a full year of schooling because of ill health. He served two years in the Navy following high school and became interested in teaching.

Following his military service, he did various jobs and became manager of two stores. But he wanted to get a college education and train to be a school teacher. As a college student, he maintained a satisfactory record and impressed the faculty as a very conscientious, sincere, and intellectually curious young man. On his own, he visited the Counseling Center and requested assistance for some problems of personal adjustment. The school psychiatrist, feeling that he was a rather disturbed young man, suggested psychotherapy, which Henry has been receiving regularly at the V.A. Mental Hygiene Clinic. His irregular home background has probably contributed to his problems of personal adjustment, and originally there seemed to be a question of needing some help in making a more satisfactory heterosexual adjustment. Henry's counselor has worked closely with him. The psychiatrist at the Mental Hygiene Clinic feels that he has made considerable progress and now has rather good insight regarding his problems of adjustment. Some additional therapy is indicated at this time.

Henry has applied for admission as a junior to several teacher's colleges. The counselor's problem is: (1) Should he recommend such an individual for teacher-training? (2) If so, how much of this information should be passed on to the other institution or school?

Test scores indicate that he is a young man of superior ability. His interest in teaching seems to be strong and genuine. He has had valuable related work experience. But what of his own emotional adjustment at this stage? Also, is the counselor violating the student's confidence if he passes on any of this information?

Example 6

Sally Rin was probably one of the most able students in the college that she attended. All scores on the Ohio State Psychological Examination would place her at, or above, the 95th percentile, liberal arts college freshman norms. She was also one of the most confused and distressed young women ever to come to this counselor's attention.

Her family background was substantial. Her father was a medical doctor. Her mother had graduated from a well known Southern women's college. A brother was preparing for the priesthood in the Roman Catholic Church.

Sally had been sent to school in Italy for two years. While in Rome, she had observed certain things, of which her interpretations had a profound effect upon her. This was evident in her cynical attitude toward life, toward people and religion, and toward the Roman Catholic Church in particular. Her attitude was very distressing to the family.

In discussions with her counselor, the reasons back of this attitude became evident. While in Rome, Sally had seen children starving almost outside the Vatican Walls, while inside everything seemed to go on as usual. As she put it, "I could not understand how the Church could stand for Christian principles and do nothing about these poor impoverished people. I can never again swallow the stuff they put out." It was evident that a terrific conflict had been set up in this counselee's mind. Now she was disturbed by the effect that her attitudes had upon her family. Also the loss of her religious faith had taken away from her the very basis of her former stability, and she realized it. She said that sometimes the only solution seemed to be suicide.

Her parents had suggested that she take her problem to the local priest. This she refused to do, saying "What could he do except urge me to return to the Church? I would rather talk with a Protestant minister, even though I don't think that he could help me."

What should the counselor do in helping the student to solve this difficult re-orientation? With whom should the case be discussed?

Chapter Nine

THEORETICAL ISSUES: OTHERS

THERE ARE numerous theoretical "issues" that become issues for the counselor because of the very nature of his work. The first of these is an every-day aspect of living—namely, reality.

REALITY

Although there is no absolute reality, Murphy may be somewhat optimistic when he says: [1]

> The inner world has become just as real as the outer world; hardly anyone in an odd corner dares anymore to refer to the world of fantasy as "unreal." It may be called a different kind of reality, but even this does not seem coercive or constraining upon us.

It is the search, and the action and the motion that are real, rather than some preconceived "reality" that one must seek out. It is likely that Fromm [2] means this when he says, "All that the human race has achieved, spiritually and materially, it owes to the destroyers of illusions and to the seekers of reality." One might reword this slightly, and say that our debt is to those who create the new realities and are unwilling to accept the old as fixed and rigid and immutable. Sartre is looking at the same question when he comments: [3]

[1] Gardner Murphy, *Freeing Intelligence Through Teaching* (New York: Harper & Row, Publishers, 1961), p. 38.
[2] Erich Fromm, *Beyond the Chains of Illusion* (New York: Pocket Books, Inc., 1962), p. 173.
[3] Jean-Paul Sartre, *Existentialism and Human Emotions* (New York: The Wisdom Library, 1957), p. 32.

There is no reality except in action . . . man is nothing else than his plan; he exists only to the extent that he fulfills himself; he is therefore nothing else than the ensemble of his acts, nothing else than his life.

When May [4] says, "There is no such thing as truth or reality for a living human being except as he participates in it, is conscious of it, has some relationship to it," he is expressing the phenomenological concept that reality lies in the individual's experience of the event rather than in the isolated event. One might also say that there is, really, no "event," without the human individual. Hatreds and bogey men and chairs exist only as they appear to the individual as they become a part of his experiencing, his living. Thus, we may say, with the determinist, that there *is* a world of reality; but, on the other hand, it cannot be reality apart from the people who are the basic part of it. This is a problem faced by all student counselors, and even many of the more sophisticated and experienced counselors and therapists still appear to feel strongly that "reality," for them, must somehow also be reality for their client. Rather than accepting him, and thus his reality, and living through it and experiencing it with him, they sit on the outside, subtly or directly imposing their concepts upon him. They thus impede and make more difficult his growth toward greater freedom and self-actualization. It is difficult to modify or change one's reality if one is never allowed to experience deeply just what that reality might be. The insightful counselor, however, sooner or later becomes involved in asking just what reality is, anyway, or whether there is any such thing as an absolute reality. Is reality what we see, and is a wooden table therefore a hard solid piece of matter, rather than consisting of billions of atoms in wild motion, which is the way a table may be seen by a physicist? Is the "color" that a color-blind person sees not real, and the real color that which is seen by people who are not color-blind? Is the avid skier being unrealistic when he glories in the wonderful two feet of snow that has just fallen, while all his non-skiing friends groan about the miserable weather? Are the psychosomatic headaches real, or can we say to a person who moans with the pain of such a headache, "It isn't really a real headache, so you don't really feel anything"? Can we say that the handsome woman with beautiful hair, who says, "I'm a mess, and my hair is just like a mop," is divorced from reality?

This ability to live another's reality with him might be considered as a description of empathy. This also means that the counselor

[4] Rollo May, *Existential Psychology* (New York: Random House, 1961), pp. 17–18.

is one who can live certainly in a world of uncertainty, one who accepts the probability in living with security. All too frequently in counseling, it really is "cases" that we are discussing, and with which we are working, whether we are in a staff conference "case" discussion, or involved in an actual counseling session. We operate with events and problems, and questions and supposed meanings, and the real-life experiencing person, either represented (and nothing more) on a piece of paper, or the flesh-and-blood person in front of us, is ignored and unseen, and we give him little help in the struggle to see who he is, because it is not "him" with whom we are relating.

In a different way, Barry and Wolf are saying much the same thing when they discuss the myths of the vocational counselor: [5]

> The word realism is essentially a mask for value judgements about the practicality and practicability of an idea, a feeling, a plan. . . . Realism is a judgement dependent upon time and the point of view of the person making it.

It is likely that thousands of students throughout the United States have sat in classrooms and offices, today, listening to their teacher or their counselor as he said, among other things, "Now, Joe, let's be realistic about this. . . ." The counselor is indeed making a value judgment, and even worse, he is imposing an absolute reality (his) upon his unfortunate victim.

The more the counselor looks at the question of reality, which in a way is like the cultural version of truth, the more likely he is to conclude, at least temporarily, that there are two broad sets of realities. There is the reality of the group, and there is the reality of the individual. The simple but questionable way in which many people have solved this dilemma is to conclude that reality must be whatever the majority says it is; according to this view, the more the individual moves away from the concept of the group, the more odd or queer or the crazier he is. This concept might lead to only minor difficulty if one could live in a completely homogeneous society and never leave it, or never become aware that this is only one of many societies, each one having its own set of realities. The scientist may feel that he can easily avoid this difficulty by equating reality with truth. What has been proven empirically to be true is real, and, for the rest, we don't know whether it is real or not. But the "rest" is what daily surrounds almost everyone, and even scientists will haggle over their pitifully

[5] Ruth Barry and Beverly Wolf, *An Epitaph for Vocational Guidance* (New York: Teachers College, Columbia University, 1962), pp. 90–91.

small set of "truths." The clergyman may equate reality with "God's truth," but if he is an intelligent clergyman he will have to admit that there are almost as many "God's truths" as there are religious denominations, or even more. As Chenault puts it: [6]

> Consensus is not a valid criterion of truth. It ignores the very personal nature of philosophy and the freedom and right to base professional practice upon it.

For the counselor, at least, it might be best to consider the concept that while there may be a broad set of realities accepted by most of those with whom we live, each individual operates on a set of personal realities. What is real to the client, but not real to the counselor, is nevertheless, as far as the counselor is concerned, *real*. The counselor relates with his client's reality, not his own. This personal reality applies to everyone—the stable, the normally neurotic, and the psychotic; and at least the first two of this trio should be able to see it in operation with themselves, if they look carefully at any time. Unhappiness because one cannot afford two cars is just as real as a people's democracy where no one has the right to vote; fear of a dark room is just as real as a state of freedom where one does what the autocratic ruler says he must do; tension over skin blemishes that no one can see is just as real as a system of student government where the faculty determines what the students can do; student despair because of getting. a B now and then instead of all A's is just as real as the inferiority feelings of some individual because of his racial background. All of these things are real to some, unreal to others, but it is the function of the counselor to work with the reality of the client, and, if this is what he wants, to help him to come ultimately to a different concept of reality.

School counselors sometimes find it particularly difficult to move beyond their own cultural concept of reality, and they tend, too, to associate reality with things that can be seen or touched or smelled or heard. It takes time and experience before they can go beyond their primary senses and be able to accept the concept that goblins really are in that room because a child believes they are; that big blemishes really are on the adolescent girl's face because she believes they are there; that a man really is poor, although his bank balance is over $100,000; that the student with one B and all the rest A's really is doing miserable work. Client-centered counselors would generally accept this

[6] Joann Chenault, "Professional Standards and Philosophical Freedom: A Peaceful Coexistence," *Counselor Education and Supervision* 3:8–12 (Fall, 1963).

concept of reality, as, probably, would many other counselors. Some, however, like the counselor below, very likely would not. The client (P) here is described as having a moderate to severe case of mixed psychoneurosis: [7]

> T: So we know that under certain moods and emotional conditions our thinking is led to exaggerations. In depressive moods, for instance, reality is completely biased and the individual portrays himself far lower than he actually is. You see, you *are not* the way you told me just now; it is only because you are in such a mood that the exaggeration appears.
>
> P: Then I do not need to worry about the way I see myself now, since this is just the result of a mood?
>
> T: Right! And therefore you must never take such thinking seriously at such times: It is unrealistic.

It is thus quite obvious that reality is as it is perceived by the individual. Reality for me is as I perceive it for me—what is, is. For the counselor quoted above, reality is also as he perceives it, but he also apparently assumes that this same perception must be accepted by the client.

COGNITION, KNOWLEDGE, UNDERSTANDING, INSIGHT

The counselor may accept his living in a relative world, but another problem that he faces has to do with knowledge and knowing and understanding. We talk about counseling as a process, a relationship, an experiencing, but at the same time we would appear to feel that clients and counselors can, somehow, come to *know* their way out of their difficulties. Certainly no one would deny the relationship between freedom and knowledge, but one can know without being wise enough to be free. As Whitehead comments,[8]

> You cannot be wise without some basis of knowledge; but you may easily acquire knowledge and remain bare of wisdom. Now wisdom is the way in which knowledge is held.

[7] Stanley W. Standal and Raymond J. Corsini, *Critical Incidents in Psychotherapy* (Englewood Cliffs, N.J.: Prentice-Hall, Inc., 1959), p. 77.
[8] Alfred North Whitehead, *The Aims of Education and Other Essays* (New York: The New American Library, 1960), p. 41.

And again: [9]

> In a sense, knowledge shrinks as wisdom grows; for details are swallowed up in principles.

Much earlier, Cowper contributed a related thought: [10]

> Knowledge is proud that he has learned so much,
> Wisdom is humble that he knows no more.

The behavioral science concept of man has also tended to delude many counselors into the belief that by knowing about man they could also know man. One may learn about man by examining him, by studying him and analyzing him, but one may still be a long way from knowing the real man. Only by an experiencing and living-with can the counselor come to know the real person-in-being, the existential man.

Counselors have generally accepted the concept that the more we know about the client the better our chance of being effective with him. We might wonder, however, whether the material we use to get to "know" the client may possibly move us away from him, and help us to develop a highly distorted and biased picture. Each time a piece of information about one human being passes through another human being it comes out a little less like the original. Often, for example, we may have several reports from the teachers of a child, but we have no reports on the teachers or the circumstances under which the reports were made. Even when we have what might be called standardized test data we should keep in mind the fact that the people who administer the tests, and those who interpret the test data, are not standardized!

We might hypothesize, at least, that the client with whom we are working is the person who is now in the office with us, and this person may or may not bear much resemblance to the person as categorized in an information folder. We may also wonder about the relative importance of the degree to which the person present apparently differs from the test data person. In speaking to a group of psychoanalysts Hartmann was expressing the same general feeling when he said, "Despite what the great Plato thought about it, we do

---

9 *Ibid.*, p. 48.
10 James Robert Boyd (Ed.), *The Task, Table Talk and Other Poems of William Cowper*, Book VI, *Winter Walk at Noon* (New York: A. S. Barnes and Co., 1853), p. 297.

not believe in a simple correlation between the steps toward insight
and the steps to moral improvement." [11]

This scepticism about the extent to which knowledge helps us to
actually know a person is also indicated by Walsh when he says, "I
am not at all certain that the help that they receive is a direct result
of our sophisticated knowledge of the mind, unless in the process of
accumulating that knowledge we have also gained wisdom and compassion for and about people." [12] We may thus question the extent to
which human understanding, and thus human communication, is dependent on the possession of didactic information, often of a highly
questionable nature from equally questionable sources, and raise at
least the possibility that this may pose a real hindrance to the development of a deep and basic understanding between two people.

The "knowing about" is found in both the school curricular
experience and in counseling, and in schools we usually see what we
might call either an "information" counselor, or a "diagnostic" counselor. These counselors are both concerned primarily with the transmission of information *to* the client, although the typical information
counselor would probably be transmitting educational and occupational information, while the diagnostic counselor would be more
likely to be transmitting an interpretation of personal test data about
the client. Thus the first counselor would likely find communication
most difficult, since he is transmitting, at best, information that *he*
thinks the client want and needs. The diagnostic counselor, on the
other hand, is at least transmitting information *about* the client, but
it is still *from* the counselor *to* the client. Often too, of course, not
only is the information dubious and questionable, but the client is
a rather passive or even unwilling recipient of the information. Frequently, the basic purpose of this transmission of information is the
manipulation and direction of the client so that he may become more
"adjusted," more able to fit easily and comfortably into the status
quo, and a less curious, questioning, rebellious member of his society.
These counselors see the gathering and interpretation of knowledge,
and its transmission to the client, as their basic function.

The counselor who is concerned with a basic human relationship, on the other hand, is one who thinks in terms of "the client to
me," rather than "me to the client." Thus his verbal communication

---

11 Heinz Hartmann, *Psychoanalysis and Moral Values* (New York: International
Universities Press, 1960), p. 91.
12 Richard P. Walsh, "Comment," *American Psychologist* 16:712–713 (November,
1961).

is based on the client as he presents himself, rather than on the client as he is presented by others and by test data. He has no preconceived information to give to the client, unless it is information that the client desires, information that will be helpful in the process of communication. Since most communication, however, is not really very deep if it is at an information level, it is not too often that information, per se, enters into the relationship between this counselor and the client. The bare bones statistic of an IQ of 91 for a college freshman, who is being driven to desperation by the difficulty of his courses and the pressure of his professors and his family, is of no importance whatsoever to the counselor who sees himself involved in a warm and human relationship with another person, and in attempting to communicate non-verbally to that person his depth of understanding and acceptance.

If we are to think of man as a determined set of behaviors, then we could agree that ultimately every facet of man will be put under a microscope and examined, and prediction and control of the human race will become a part of an exact and empirical science. We might, on the other hand, hypothesize that one of the reasons why both psychology and medicine have never really got close to man, the total living being, is that they have fallen into the trap of empiricism. To medicine, man is a disease; to psychologists, he is a problem; to psychiatrists, he is a disease-problem; and to counselors, too frequently, he appears to be a profile of the results of various tests and examinations. Science has generally accepted the words "cognitive" and "meaningful" as somewhat synonymous. At least I think that science would probably say that the less cognitive a picture of man is, the less meaningful it is. My own perception would be that man—not man's behavior, since you cannot cut one off from the other, but man, the total existential being, if you will—is not really subject to empirical examination, and that both a human experience and a human being could mean very little in a cognitive sense, and yet at the same time could be overwhelmingly meaningful.

The empiricist would likely put knowing—cognition—above feeling, but we can know in an empirically cognitive sense without understanding in a feeling sense, and we can understand a fellow human without "knowing about" him, although we might consider "knowing about" to be more cognitive than "knowing." Menninger, in his latest book,[13] for example, shows more concern than many of his fellow psychiatrists with the total man.

[13] Karl A. Menninger, *The Vital Balance* (New York: The Viking Press, Inc., 1963).

It may also be that some counselors know much about the client, but have confused this knowing with self-understanding on the part of the client. They may then add to this confusion by "giving" the client more supposed knowledge, from some outer source, about himself. Roessler comments on this point: [14]

> But the term "cognitive," for me, denotes too much intellectual emphasis in the psychotherapeutic process . . . the process of change . . . is really more a function of experiencing oneself in totality.

As does Hora: [15]

> But if cognition, which is another word for understanding . . . if understanding, clarification, elucidation, seeing the light, seeing what one really is, if this is the focus of psychotherapy, then one would be careful not to say more, not to talk too much because it might hamper understanding. . . . So then, not the explicit, but the implicit will have the therapeutic value, and so there will be less and less talk.

Jung would appear to have been thinking in a somewhat similar manner when he said: [16]

> We appeal only to the patient's brain if we try to inculcate a truth; but if we help him to grow up to this truth in the course of his own development, we have reached his heart, and this appeal goes deeper and acts with greater force.

As does Gendlin: [17]

> Now that psychotherapy is widely thought to involve a concrete feeling process, we are less specific about the (still vital) role of cognitive symbols and exploration. . . . Apparently, any good vocabulary can be used as a symbolic tool for "working through" and interacting.

There are some counselors and some counselor educators who might say that the above words do not apply to them because they are not involved in this "personal counseling or therapy sort of busi-

[14] Robert L. Roessler, "Psychotherapy: Healing or Growth," *Annals of Psychotherapy* 4:10 (1963).
[15] Thomas Hora, in *Annals of Psychotherapy* 4:10 (1963), p. 33.
[16] C. G. Jung, *Modern Man in Search of a Soul* (New York: Harcourt, Brace & World, Inc., 1933), p. 9.
[17] Eugene T. Gendlin, "Subverbal Communication and Therapist Expressivity: Trends in Client-centered Therapy with Schizophrenics," *Journal of Existential Psychiatry* 4:105 (Fall, 1963).

ness," but rather in the "talking to, telling, information business." I would think that any form of human communication between the counselor and the client is personal, and the above words apply just as much when the client is a child who comes in to talk easily with the counselor about his job plans for the next year, as they do when the client is a child driven to desperation by his neurotic parents. They may apply even more in the former case, because it is in this talking relationship that the counselor may be most easily lulled into the false security of verbiage, just as the teacher who drones on endlessly assumes that the children *must* be learning something.

All of this, too, raises serious questions about the place of insight in the counseling process. Insight has generally been equated with self-understanding. The person who is insightful knows where he stands; he knows what he has and what he does not have. Insight usually implies, too, that not only does the individual know his assets and liabilities, but he operates with some reference to them. Thus an individual who knows that he has a low intellectual capacity but deliberately takes on a job that requires high intellectual capacity might be considered as having little insight. He knows his limitations, but he ignores them. Interestingly enough, however, despite the general acceptance of this point, it is contradicted by many school counselors who seem to feel that all that is needed for improvement is the first part of this insight—the knowing. Thus, more often than not, the use of test data in schools seems to assume that all the counselor has to do is test the students—and tell them what they have and what they do not have, and everyone will live happily ever after. Certainly for the counselor, insightfulness, if it is to be considered at all, must include the assimilation and internalization of knowledge, so that it becomes a part of the total operational individual rather than an intellectual appendage. Each of us gradually develops a basic operational self concept, and it is difficult to see how one can expect a person blithely and easily to accept a piece of information that means that this self concept has to be altered drastically.

It should be noted too, that an individual may wish, desperately, to change certain attitudes and feelings whose causes and development he has come, possibly through counseling, to understand very well. Thus the client may say, "I know all these feelings that I have are just superstitions, and that they are not really religion at all, and I know why I have believed them. But why must I still go on believing them when I don't want to and when I know they are silly?" The client must go on believing them because he still needs to go on believing them; and he will continue to believe them as long as his unaltered self has need to.

It is rather interesting to note that Munroe quotes Fromm-Reichmann as stating the role of insight for the patient as follows: [18]

> The aim of psychoanalytic therapy is to bring . . . rejected drives and wishes, together with the patient's individual and environmental moral standards, which are the instruments for his rejections, into consciousness, and in this way place them at his free disposal.

Munroe then comments on this, saying that it is this self-understanding that frees the patient not only from the limitations imposed by unconscious needs, but also from the emotional power of the transference.[19]

Fromm-Reichmann, on the other hand, uses the word "insight" because it goes beyond just understanding—intellectually, at least: [20]

> I wished to convey, by this very choice of terminology, that the intellectual and rational grasp of one interpretation of a single experience, as a rule, will be changed only by the process of "working through" into the type of integrated creative understanding which deserves to be termed "insight."

The Client-centered counselor is little concerned with insight as interpreted in terms of intellectual understanding. He is concerned if it is to be related with process, if it is to be an experiencing, a living, a being again with real and deep feelings. Thus the insightfulness of the client may include the experiencing again of the dreadful feeling of aloneness, but an aloneness that after a while is not the same, because there is someone this time who cares, someone who is concerned. Maybe it could be thought of in terms of a noun or a verb. If a noun, it doesn't matter too much; if a verb, it matters very much. If the client is now a person who no longer feels alone in a strange world, then insight, in terms of the traditional concept of understanding, is more than likely a by-product. In fact, the client might well say, "Of course, I know now that I'm not alone, but then I always did

18 Freida Fromm-Reichmann, "Recent Advances in Psychoanalytic Therapy," in Mullahy, P. (Ed.), *A Study of Interpersonal Relations* (New York: Hermitage Press, 1949), p. 122.
19 Ruth L. Munroe, "Intellectualizing Techniques in Psychotherapy," in Arthur Burton (Ed.), *Case Studies in Counseling and Psychotherapy* (Englewood Cliffs, N.J.: Prentice-Hall, Inc., 1959), p. 383.
20 Freida Fromm-Reichmann, *Principles of Intensive Psychotherapy* (Chicago: University of Chicago Press, 1950), pp. 141–142.

know that I was not alone, only I didn't believe it before." He knew intellectually, but he didn't believe what he knew. Now he believes, and we might say that it does not matter too much whether he knows or not.

This client, for example, did not have any clear knowledge about just what had happened when he said:

> The degree of trust I have in myself has a close relationship to how well I know myself. . . . I've learned something—about myself—in a tentative sort of way—that I didn't know even a few weeks ago— (pause)—maybe I'll talk about that. . . .

The more superficial concept of insight seems to be the reference point for Galdston: [21]

> Only that patient can profit by nondirective therapy who is himself therapeutically active and resourceful, and who broadly and deeply scans his past, his present, and his projected goals. Nondirective therapy is applicable only to the case wherein scanning is likely to yield the patient a deeper and more effective insight into the nature, derivation, and resolution of his difficulties.

It may be too, regarding the comment on the limitations of non-directive therapy, that one counselor does have more clients who are active and resourceful because he operates on the assumption that they are active and resourceful, whereas another counselor, operating on the assumption that clients need direction and control, finds that most of his clients are individuals who are in need of direction and control.

In the excellent book by Burton that has already been referred to several times, there is a series of questions at the end of each of the fifteen case studies.[22] One of these questions is "Do you feel that this case developed significant insight? If not, can improvement be maintained?" It is of interest to note that twelve of the fifteen answers said, in varying ways, "Yes" or "No." One, in the chapter that described Client-centered counseling, gave a reaction that was somewhat similar to that which has been presented in this book. The other two were as follows:

> If by insight is meant conscious insight, then the answer is "no." If by insight is meant unconscious, then the answer is "yes." In either case,

[21] Iago Galdston, in Standal and Corsini, *op. cit.*, p. 222.
[22] Burton, *op. cit.*

the patient has maintained her improvement for a period of five years. (*Conscious* insight has the quality of intricate fact-finding or even of simple memory of related details. Through hindsight, the patient forms such details into a significant *gestalt*. *Unconscious* insight has a quality of experiencing in the present a previously not accepted capacity. The patient may never become aware of what has occurred in him to change his behavior.) [23]

Intellectual insight is no longer a *sine qua non* of improvement in psychotherapy. It may be epiphenomenal but not necessarily causal. While we know very little about emotional insight, some such experience may take place. However, this is a function of the *Begegnung* and the change in the vector forces which come about through it. Such process is largely symbolic. (I have since regretted formulating this question for the *Addendum* except that heuristically it does reveal the present state of insight in modern-day psychotherapy.) [24]

Insight, then, would appear to be an understanding that one may gain about himself, but it is a product of experiencing more than knowing. The counselor is an individual who should have achieved a high level of self-understanding, and the evidence would tend to indicate that sensitivity to others is a function of insight into oneself.[25] Nor is this self-understanding or insight something that one acquires from someone else. As Dreikurs says, "The therapist gave her strength, but no insight or reorientation." [26]

Insight, then, is a sort of an end product. It is a deep and meaningful understanding, by me, about me, and about others. These comments, from junior high school clients, are insightful, but their cognitive respectability is of little importance compared with the fact that they are understandings arrived at by the children as a result of their human relationship with an insightful counselor:

"The more pressure a teacher puts on a kid the greater the chance that the kid will resent whatever it is that the teacher is trying to do. A kid will do anything for a teacher who respects him."

"When are people going to start putting some of the blame on the school when a kid quits? He could be quitting because he's bored right out of his skin by subjects that have been forced on him, and have no use in his life."

[23] *Ibid.*, p. 256.
[24] *Ibid.*, p. 280.
[25] See William J. Mueller, "The Influence of Self Insight on Social Perception Scores," *Journal of Counseling Psychology* 10:185–191 (Summer, 1963).
[26] Rudolph Dreikurs, in Standal and Corsini, *op. cit.*, p. 70.

"You learn more when you do something in class . . . when you're involved . . . when you're participating instead of watching and listening . . . like when you're in science and you do the experiments. . . . I really learn something."

"It's too bad the world isn't the kind of place a kid could get into trouble without getting into trouble—you know what I mean? Everybody gets so hot and bothered about delinquents and stuff like that, but if kids could have a chance to have some fun and excitement, and could do things with a little kick in them, they'd be all right. But all the adults want you to play the game with their rules. . . . The only trouble is they forget we're not adults. It's a lot more fun for us to break rules than to keep them."

EMPATHY AND CONGRUENCE

The congruent person is one who can be insightful, but the fact that he can be this way is far less important than what he is. In other words, it is his congruence, his high level of self-actualization that describes him as he is. His insight is the product of his congruence, and it is in an empathic climate that one may learn to become more congruent, more free. The empathic relationship is achieved when the counselor is able to work with the client within the client's frame of reference, within the client's reality, and is able to communicate this understanding and acceptance to the client. In describing the client, Buchheimer and Balogh say: [27]

> The way he constructs his reality and the percepts he has of himself determine the way he addresses himself to his life's tasks and the goals he formulates for his life's work. It is important therefore, that the counselor allow the person with whom he is to work freedom in self-expression as well as expression of self in relation to problems and goals.

It is in the empathic climate that this expression of self can develop, and it is through this self-expression that one gradually comes, possibly, to perceive himself in a different manner. Man has many faces, but there is one face, for each of us, that is more basic, more real, and the client comes to sense this face when he is able to accept the current face. He can say, as has been said to me, "You know, when

[27] Arnold Buchheimer and Sara Carter Balogh, *The Counseling Relationship* (Chicago: Science Research Associates, 1961), p. 3.

I actually could accept me as I was, then, right at that moment, me wasn't the same any more." As Hora puts it: [28]

> . . . if a human being attains the level of integration where he really can be what he really is, then every moment and every manifestation of his life will be a creative one.

And to be what one is, one must be a congruent, genuine, self-actualized individual. One must be able to be easily honest with oneself, and I would agree with Rosenfels that "wisdom is the product of an unfailing honesty." [29]

The congruent individual, too, is one who can perceive accurately, and Lesser [30] has reported on an interesting study, which indicated that mere feelings, by the counselor, or similarity with the client, were not conducive to counseling progress and empathic understanding. More basic was the correct perception, by the counselor, of similarity, or lack of it. In a somewhat related fashion, Buchheimer [31] has pointed out that in an empathic relationship cognitive perception of the other person becomes the capacity to perceive the counselee's frame of reference.

Thus this honesty with self, this genuineness, this self-congruence on the part of the counselor, would appear to be the crucial factor in the development of an empathic relationship in which the client also might move toward actualization and freedom. This means, too, that the counselor must be free to feel his feelings during the counseling relationship, rather than bottling them up, or presenting both to himself and to the client a blank face and pretending that he has no feelings. Since the counselor is a self-actualized individual, these feelings will be directed at himself, rather than at the client. This point is illustrated by Roessler, when, in discussing another therapist's description of his feelings during a counseling session, he comments: [32]

> . . . we could have been annoyed, irritated, and expressed this . . . the same consequences, so long as it wasn't "Damn you for behaving this

[28] Hora, *op. cit.*, p. 51.

[29] Paul Rosenfels, *Psychoanalysis and Civilization* (New York: Libra Publishers, Inc., 1962), p. 83.

[30] William M. Lesser, "The Relationship Between Counseling Progress and Empathic Understanding," *Journal of Counseling Psychology* 8:330–336 (Winter, 1961).

[31] Arnold Buchheimer, "The Development of Ideas About Empathy," *Journal of Counseling Psychology* 10:61–70 (Spring, 1963).

[32] Roessler, *op. cit.*, p. 27.

way," and instead, "I'm annoyed, I'm frustrated. Something's wrong, and something needs to be done."

This also stresses, obviously, the crucial necessity of counselor education centering on the deep and meaningful understanding *of the counselor* by the counselor, rather than on a superficial cognitive understanding of the client.

TRANSFERENCE AND COUNTER-TRANSFERENCE

Although the phenomena of transference may not be the usual experience of most counselors, particularly school counselors, as they work with their clients, they should have some awareness of what it is so that they might be more aware of its potential occurrence, and be able to differentiate it from a more psuedo sort of transference that probably occurs with all counselors. Most analytically oriented counselors would tend generally to be acceptant of the following somewhat traditional descriptions of transference. First we may note Alexander: [33]

> The principal therapeutic tool is the transference, in which the patient relives, in relation to the therapist his earlier interpersonal conflicts. Regression to the dependent attitudes of infancy and childhood is a constant feature of the transference, and, in the majority of cases, the central one. This regression in itself has a supportive effect. It allows the patient to postpone his own decisions and to reduce the responsibilities of adult existence by retiring into a dependent attitude toward the therapist which resembles the child's attitude in the child-parent relationship.

Then Hendrick: [34]

> For when a patient recounts free associations, he soon speaks of events or phantasies of vital interest to himself, and when these are told, the listener is gradually invested with some of the emotion which accompanies them. The patient gradually begins to feel that the sympathetic listener is loved or hated, a friend or any enemy, one who is nice to him or one who frustrates his needs and punishes him. The feelings toward the listener become more and more like those felt toward the specific people the patient is talking about, or, more exactly, those his uncon-

[33] Franz Alexander, *Psychoanalysis and Psychotherapy* (New York: W. W. Norton & Company, Inc., 1956), p. 154.
[34] Ives Hendrick, *Facts and Theories of Psychoanalysis* (New York: Alfred A. Knopf, Inc., 1958), p. 193.

scious "is talking about." This special case of object-displacement during psychoanalysis is called transference.

And finally, Horney: [35]

Freud observed that in the analytical situation the patient not only talks about his present and past troubles, but also shows emotional reactions to the analyst. These reactions are frequently irrational in character. A patient may forget entirely his purpose in coming to analysis and may find nothing important except being loved or appreciated by the analyst. He may develop altogether disproportionate fears about jeopardizing his relationship to the analyst. He may transform the situation, which in actuality is one in which the analyst helps the patient to straighten out his problems, into one of passionate struggle for the upper hand. For instance, instead of feeling relieved by some clarification of his problems, a patient may see only one fact, that the analyst has recognized something that he was unaware of, and he may react with violent anger. A patient may, contrary to his own interests, secretly pursue the purpose of defeating the analyist's endeavors.

The general concept held by both the medical doctor psychotherapist and the counseling psychologist is that this transference relationship takes place in psychotherapy, and that it is the working out, the explaining of these transferred feelings, including resistances and hostility, that helps the client to move ahead. It is important for the student counselor to note that when such a transference relationship does develop, it is not a case of superficial feeling, or of dislike on the part of the client for the therapist because he is like someone the client used to know. It is, rather, an infusion of feelings into the therapist, so that the therapist *is* the hated and autocratic father of twenty years ago, and the resistances that develop are as "real" as they can be. It is not that the client thinks he can now see how hostile and submissive he felt toward his father—he *is* hostile and submissive, and the therapist *is* his father. It is the gradual understanding of the why and the what and the how of this phenomenon that helps the client to greater growth. As Mowrer says: [36]

Rather does the therapist help the patient to see what he is trying to accomplish by means of his "transference" behavior which is now just as real and just as meaningful as it originally was—and to under-

[35] Karen Horney, *New Ways in Psychoanalysis* (New York: W. W. Norton & Company, Inc., 1939), pp. 154–155.
[36] O. Hobart Mowrer (Ed.), *Psychotherapy: Theory and Research* (New York: The Ronald Press Company, 1953), p. 567.

stand the circumstances in which this type of behavior originated and why it was not earlier resolved.

Thus the client comes to feel as he once felt, but there is a difference. Although he is feeling as he did before toward a superior figure, this authority figure is now one who will be acceptant of his negative feelings, and will help him to understand them rather than reject him and strengthen his basic negative feelings.

Such authority and superiority of the "doctor" or the therapist are stressed again and again in psychoanalytic literature. This reaction is easy to understand, particularly with the medical doctor therapist. Here is a person who has had a background of education and training and work where without a doubt in the vast majority of the cases he does have the answers as to what to do about the ailments of a patient —a patient who, most often, does not know what is wrong with him, and does not know what to do about it. The doctor is in authority, and he *is* the superior figure. Nor does working in a hospital tend to diminish the feeling. There the therapist is in an environment where the patients are very often psychotic, or are assumed to be psychotic, and in the staff relationship the therapist finds himself at the top of the hierarchical ladder. Although there may be frequent reference to teamwork, it is usually quite evident who is the top sergeant of the team! Thus the phenomenon of transference is very definitely related to the authority and superiority of the therapist. If the therapist did not have such authority and superiority in the eyes of both himself and his client, then we might raise the question of whether or not transference would take place. On this point Rogers writes: [37]

> For the analyst this means that he interprets such attitudes, and perhaps through these evaluations establishes the characteristic transference relationship. For the Client-centered therapist this means that he attempts to understand and accept such attitudes, which then tend to become accepted by the client as being his own perception of the situation, inappropriately held.

Thus, theoretically, at least, the Client-centered counselor feels that transference would not likely take place in his counseling relationship, because he is not in this relationship the sort of person to whom, or on whom, the client can transfer feelings of an earlier period. The client may have the feelings that are transferred in the transference

[37] Carl R. Rogers, *Client-Centered Therapy* (Boston: Houghton Mifflin Company, 1951), p. 218.

relationship, but they are not transferred to the counselor if the counselor has become to the client the sort of person that the counselor believes he really is. It is on this point, indeed, that some counselors present a most valid and reasonable criticism: can the counselor really be this sort of person, both to himself and to the client? The counselor, after all, does know more than the client about the psychology of personality disturbances. He is very frequently, in the hierarchy of values, someone who is considered to be more important than the client; and he is the one to whom the client goes to find answers, or at least to go through some experience that will make him a better adjusted person. How, then, can the counselor avoid being superior and authoritative, both in his own eyes and in those of the client?

This is a question that no counselor can answer in an absolute fashion. Certainly, more in the way of knowledge and emotional stability on the part of one individual does not mean actual or felt superiority to someone else. A Client-centered counselor feels very deeply the worth and dignity of his client. He respects him as a fellow man—not as a client, not as a disturbed person, not as a selfish creature—simply as a fellow human being. How well and how honestly does he do this? Each counselor must try to answer that for himself.

If, in either group or individual therapy, the counselor is to become completely accepted by the other members of the group (one or more), as a member of the group, it would seem that he must lose his identity as the "leader." As long as he is the leader, in the mind and in the feelings of the client or the other members of the group, he cannot be a member of the group; he remains an outsider. As an outsider he is suspect, and he is, needless to say, one on whom it would be very easy to transfer feelings. In a normal group session, for instance, a leader statement such as, "What one of you said there a few minutes ago made me feel sort of mad," would cause the defensive flags of most of the members of the group to rise. This would happen because the leader is still the leader. He is the *outside* critic.

But in some group sessions, and in some counseling sessions, the situation changes. The leader gradually disappears as the leader, and becomes rather a member of a group (of two or more), going through an exciting experience. The Client-centered counselor feels that while the counselor is the sort of person who is not very often threatened or disturbed, he is, nevertheless, a human being. If, at a certain point, as he is immersed with the client in the client's expression of feelings, he realizes, "This sort of worries me," then it may be better that, remaining at all times honest, he express his feeling to the client. If the counseling relationship has developed as it *can* develop, the client will not be threatened by such an expression of feeling on the part of this other person (not the boss, or the authority, or the head man) who is going through this experience with him. On the other hand, we can assume that if the counselor, in order to maintain his integrity and honesty, must be continually telling the client that he is worried or concerned by something in the discussion, then this person should be the client rather than the counselor!

It is likely, too, that there is a wide variance on the part of counselors in their ideas of just what constitutes transference. Might one not be liked or disliked by a client in a purely personal manner? Since counselors, after all, have had people fall in love with them (and vice versa) in a non-counseling relationship, we could probably assume that some clients might fall in love, or some reasonable facsimile thereof, with a counselor in his office as well as outside his office. On this question one therapist writes: [38]

> Much of what is cavalierly called "transference" by many therapists, and dogmatically interpreted to their patients as such seems actually to be the patient's becoming attached to the therapist on a fairly clear-cut reality basis. The therapist is, after all, usually quite intelligent; a sympathetic listener; fairly cultured; of good socioeconomic standing; and seemingly of a suitable age to many of his female patients. . . . This is not to gainsay the fact that in *many* instances patients fall in love with their therapists because the latter unconsciously represent father-figures, authority-symbols, and so forth. . . . But to insist that classic transference exists where it patently does not leads to other difficulties, including the avoidance of some of the patient's basic desires and the forcing on her of a false interpretation.

Probably most counselors would agree that what might seem to be transference has developed to some degree in one or more of their counseling sessions. Whether this actually is transference, whether it has developed because the counselor is not functioning as a Client-centered counselor, or whether it is something that would have developed with any counselor—these are good questions for debate.

These client comments, for example, were made to counselors who at least saw themselves as being Client-centered:

Client 1: People don't really care about people . . . you don't really care what happens to me . . . you're getting paid to sit and

[38] Anonymous author, in Standal and Corsini, *op. cit.*, pp. 90–91.

listen to me but you don't really give a damn whether I sink or swim.

Client 2: And then he stood there yelling at me to straighten out the wheels on the car. I clenched my fist and put it up to his face (does this to counselor) . . . and then I yelled back . . . (yells at counselor) . . . "yell at me again and I'll break your neck."

Client 3: And for that brief vacation she really filled a void in my life. . . . We talked for hours and it really made me feel as if someone cared . . . like . . . like now I know . . . I have a feeling that you care for me . . . because . . . well . . . you've given me the . . . I mean . . . a chance to talk . . . a chance not to be lonely. . . .

Client 4: And I guess maybe I love you. . . . That's all right, isn't it. . . .

Client 5: All I ask is not to be interrupted when I'm saying something. . . . If there's anything I despise it's being cut off in the middle of a sentence. . . . She always did that to me and now when you do it . . . well, just don't. . . . I won't be able to talk to you if you do.

Client 6: There are just the two of you—and I love you both, but in a different way.

Client 7: Yeh . . . I could always make him anxious . . . and right now you're anxious, aren't you?

These are certainly examples of highly personal expressions of feeling by the client toward the counselor, but the counselor would not appear in these examples to be anyone other than himself. In a way, the client feelings may be being transferred to him from someone else, but in the mind of the client he still retains his identity as the counselor, rather than becoming some earlier authority figure.

While the development of a transference relationship would appear to make the client more dependent on the counselor, the analytical counselor would say that this dependence need not continue. On the other hand, in a more Client-centered relationship, it seems that the lack of dependence on the counselor might create a more likely situation for the development of client independence, and also inhibit the development of this transference relationship.

Although Borden agrees with the concept that the therapeutic process is possible without the development of the transference relationship, his reason is quite different from that of the Client-centered counselor: [39]

[39] Edward S. Borden, *Psychological Counseling* (New York: Appleton-Century-Crofts, 1955), p. 150.

Because the counselor deals with relatively well-integrated individuals who are reasonably free of intense conflicts, his clients are not likely to exhibit many transference phenomena and will not readily develop intensive transference relationships unless subjected to quite ambiguous relationships over a relatively long period of time. Since most clients will not come with a profound therapeutic orientation, deep transference can take place in only a minority of instances.

This concept is open to some question. It is true that the Client-centered counselor tends to work with clients whose disturbances are probably less intense, on the whole, than those one might expect from clients of a counselor working in a hospital. On the other hand, many Client-centered counselors have worked, and are working, with individuals who are under severe emotional stress, including some who might be called psychotic. I am unaware of any evidence indicating that in Client-centered counseling the degree of transference, or lack of it, is dependent upon the severity of the emotional disturbance of the client.

Historically, the attention of therapists has been directed toward the behavior of their clients; thus it might be assumed that attention would be directed at the transference of the client's feelings toward the counselor rather than at the transference of the counselor's feelings toward the client. This phenomenon of counter-transference has been defined, like transference, as ranging all the way from an omnibus inclusion of all of the feelings of the counselor toward the client to the more subconscious and suppressed feelings of the counselor that may be brought out by the transference of feelings from the client.

Generally, however, as in transference, there is a differentiation between a surface relationship—such as a Baptist counselor's possible feeling of irritation toward a client who continually utters anti-Baptist statements—and the possible development of subtle but deep feelings of paternalism toward a younger male client who identifies with the counselor as an autocratic father figure. The Client-centered counselor feels that the student counselor should give priority to his feelings toward the client, and that he must work this through to a satisfactory understanding of how he himself is reacting before he can become effective in understanding the attitudes and the feelings of the client toward him. Thus for the Client-centered counselor counter-transference should not be a problem, since it should not occur. On the other hand, the more human, surface feelings that may develop between counselor and client warrant the continual attention of all counselors.

These counselors, for example, have become personally involved, and their expressions are indications of their own concern about themselves, rather than about the client. Again, these are hardly examples of counter-transference in the classic sense, although the counselor is transferring some of his personal feelings over to the client.

Counselor 1:   I can't, Martha, I can't—you must do it.

Counselor 2:   Don't you realize that I really do care what happens to my clients. I care what happens to you—I always have.

Counselor 3:   Anxious . . . who . . . ? . . . me?

Counselor 4:   Well, I wouldn't say that to him. . . . You've always been sort of meek and mild and if you ever said anything like that . . . well, he might think that I encouraged you to say it . . . that I sort of encouraged you to rebel. Saying that would only lead to more trouble for you.

Counselor 5:   It would be nice if you mentioned to your mother how much I've been able to help you in counseling.

Counselor 6:   Your search for justice may not bear fruit . . . trying to find a universal kind of justice could make a person bitter because maybe it doesn't exist.

Most counselors could probably understand, and possibly see in themselves the sort of feelings described as counter-transference by Hafner: [40]

> In this phase of treatment my counter-transference for the first time became a serious problem. After several apparently fruitless hours, I felt considerable unrest creeping up in me, since I was increasingly groping in the dark in front of my silent patient. I felt pressed to do some active analyzing, but I had to concede to myself that in this situation activity on my part might well have endangered everything that had been achieved so far. Gradually, I felt a certain resignation. I feared my treatment could fail after all. Thus I recognized aggressive impulses within myself coming up against Gisels as I anticipated the frustration of my own wish for a successful completion of her treatment. I experienced these hours that apparently had passed uselessly as a waste of time.
>
> Under these circumstances I found it difficult to carry through the treatment with a persistently friendly attitude. But it seems, after all, that I succeeded in it. . . .

Although the therapist here did not verbalize to the patient his feelings about her, the fact that he can write easily about them, the

[40] Heinz Hafner, "A Case of Pseudo-Neurotic Schizophrenia," in Burton, *op. cit.*, p. 302.

fact that he could consciously be aware of them and acceptant of them, might, in a way, be a reflection of his own honesty and security; and it was to this that his patient was reacting, so that she could feel, correctly, that he was basically being kind and understanding toward her. I would tend to think of this as a human experience. If that is what is meant by counter-transference, then it would be difficult to see how any counselor could avoid being involved periodically in such an experience.

PART FOUR

THE COUNSELING EXPERIENCE

Chapter Ten

THE BEGINNING

IN THIS FINAL SECTION of the book, the counseling process will be considered primarily by observation of what actually happened in a series of counseling sessions with a number of clients and a number of counselors. This is not a case book, but excerpts from various counseling sessions with different students and different clients will be used to illustrate certain phases and aspects of the counseling process. Extensive use will be made of John Bin, a high school client; Tom Ril, an adult client; the five clients, Carl, Jane, Jack, Edna and Richard, in Evraiff's case book; [1] and a number of other high school clients.

The clients presented here are basically ordinary, normal human beings facing problems of living. The children are in school, and if one is willing to accept the professional title of counselor, he should be professionally competent enough to work with them in a counseling relationship. The adults are individuals who were in school, and received little assistance and little help when they needed it. The counselors of Bin and Ril would consider themselves to be "Client-centered," and the others would probably attach a variety of names to describe their counseling. They would probably all say, "Of course, we are Client-centered," although there might be some discrete disagree-

[1] William Evraiff, *Helping Counselors Grow Professionally* (Englewood Cliffs, N.J.: Prentice-Hall, Inc., 1963).

327

ment on what this meant! The counselors also represent a range of experience, from those with a doctorate degree in the field and many years of professional counseling, including counseling of private clients, to student counselors who are almost at the beginning stage.

The counselors of John Bin and Tom Ril did not tape their first sessions, so we will not see them until the next chapter. This initial taping poses something of a problem for some counselors in some schools, although the major difficulty is often the counselor's own uncertainty about what to do. In clinical or laboratory situations this is less of a problem, and in an increasing number of schools taping is taken as a matter of course by the students, although, as has already been mentioned, this is an ethical issue that cannot be dismissed lightly. Many counselors, particularly in schools, do feel that a tape hinders the establishment of rapport somewhat during the first session, and will withhold the use of a tape, usually bringing up the subject toward the end of the first session, and then using it, if satisfactory to the client, from the second session on.

PREPARATION FOR THE COUNSELING SESSION

The degree of preparation for the first counseling session with a new client depends on the degree of sophistication and experience of the counselor, his own particular concept of his function as a counselor, and, of course, the amount of time available. It is also true, of course, that sometimes the counselor has no chance to prepare anything, even if he wants to, since the client appears suddenly and unannounced.

If the counselor sees himself as the interpreter of test data, we can assume that he will make himself familiar with the client's test data before seeing the client. If the counselor sees his function as the presenting of information regarding what college or what job would best fit the client he is going to see, he will probably want previous information about the client so that he can accumulate accurate information for him. If, on the other hand, the counselor sees himself not so much as the provider of information, but rather as one involved in a human helping relationship with another individual, the purpose, and the need, of information changes somewhat.

Many counselors of a more diagnostic orientation would probably feel the need of information about the client so that they could understand him better, and thereby work more effectively with him. The Client-centered counselor works with the client as he presents himself, and since he does not see himself as doing something for or to the client, he sees little or no need of previous information about him. Generally, most Client-centered counselors would feel that their understanding of the client was also based on the frame of reference as it is presented to them by the client, and thus that they needed no previous information to develop their concept of the client's frame of reference. Some of the counselors here worked with previous information, and some with none. John Bin and Tom Ril presented themselves as they were. Their counselors had no previous information about them, other than that they wanted to see them. Other counselors referred to here had perused all the information they could about the client before they saw him.

THE ESTABLISHMENT OF RAPPORT

Rapport might be described as the ideal relationship that is developed between the client and the counselor, a relationship that is easy and comfortable and free, where each person can be honest, and in which the client can learn to be. There are many factors, some out of the control of the counselor, that might affect the kind of relationship that is established:

1. Long before the counselor ever sees the client, factors are at work that may make it easy or difficult for the counselor to establish rapport with his client. In the school situation particularly, the child gradually develops a picture of the school and the people who work in it. Although it is sometimes a very positive and pleasant picture, the odds are that the disturbed children who come to see a counselor will be those individuals who have built up a picture of the school as at best a rather unpleasant place, and at worst a regular hell-hole. The people who work there may be regarded in an equally negative manner, although, over a period of time, individual teachers and counselors may gradually come to be accepted by troubled children as different from the run-of-the-mill teacher and counselor.

Generally, however, the school counselor can assume that many of the children who have problems will regard him with suspicion, and it will be the actions of the counselor, rather than his words, that may gradually dispel this suspicion. Needless to say, of course, if the school "counselor" thinks of himself as a stool pigeon for either the school administration or the culture generally, the justifiable suspicion of the child will only be reinforced. Many of the clients described here had good reason to be skeptical about the motives of anyone who was connected with the school system.

2. The establishment of rapport will also be affected by the manner in which the client happens to appear in the counselor's office. If he appears because he has something weighing on his mind, and he feels that a talk with someone in the counseling office might be beneficial, the establishment of a good relationship will be a much simpler matter than if he has been brusquely sent down to the counselor's office to be "straightened out" or disciplined in some manner. The latter sort of situation will increase the difficulties, but one must not imply that it creates an impossible situation for the counselor. An acceptant counselor can still be acceptant even in an autocratic school; and acceptance of the client's feeling that coming to the counselor's office is a lot of nonsense is no different from acceptance of the feeling that the experience might be something that would be good for him.

The client may, on the contrary, have too good an opinion of what the counselor can do for him. If he has been led to believe that the counselor is a medicine man who has all the answers to any problems that may beset him, it is likely that very soon even in the first counseling session, he will be disturbed to find that the counselor cannot do any of the things that were expected. In some respects the Client-centered counselor is in a more difficult situation in this matter, since most children have come to expect domination and control and direction from school personnel. Even in counselor education departments, most student counselors take this counselor education domination for granted, and are somewhat disturbed if it is not forthcoming. Though they may, of course, pay no attention to the attempted domination, they nevertheless expect it, and thus some students may at first find the Client-centered counselor "queerer" than the more old-fashioned Napoleonic type, because they are more accustomed to the latter. If the counselor is capable of helping the student to work through this confusion, the relationship that can then be established may be most worthwhile; but it is at this point that the relationship between the counselor and the client sometimes founders. The counselor should remember, of course, that if he has a forced clientele, the number of clients will be determined as much by the neuroticism of the teachers as by the neuroticism of the clients. A neurotic teacher will probably see a good deal of what the mental hygienist would consider normal behavior as indicative of a disturbed child; so the more disturbed the teacher, the more the counselor may expect to find healthy children trooping to his office "to have something done about their behavior."

The counselor may sometimes find himself pushed to become

"eclectic" and say and do what he does not believe in order to maintain the relationship with the client.

The counselor's problems may also be affected by the manner in which the appointment was made. If the client talked to a secretary, for example, was she kindly and understanding, or brusque and impatient? Did she give him the feeling that his meeting with the counselor would be a nice experience, or did she imply that it would be unpleasant, and probably a waste of time for both client and counselor? Did he first hear about the counselor from a friend, and, if so, what was the picture he got? If he is a voluntary client, it is likely that the picture he got was a good one—possibly too good, since if he received a negative picture he would not have come voluntarily. He may, of course, be a quite unwilling client, going to see a counselor about whom he has a very unhappy picture. He may have met the counselor in the hall, spoken to him, and formed his impressions on the basis of this brief meeting.

3. The immediate impression that the client receives when he opens the counselor's door is also going to affect him. He should see a reasonably comfortable office, with such things as curtains on the windows, pictures on the walls, comfortable chairs, some evidence of a library, and the professional competence of the counselor. He should also be able to sit down without having a desk between himself and the counselor.

Needless to say, the client will also notice the other person in the room. The greeting of the counselor should be warm, but not effusive. The counselor who rushes around the desk, seizes the hand of the client in a death grip, gives an intimate squeeze on the shoulder, and smiles his biggest smile before his "I'm AWFULLY glad to see you," would be enough to scare me as a potential client right out of the office! Overtness is next to aggressiveness, and the super-gregarious counselor must surely pose a threat to many clients. One might wonder, even, if such an individual is not in the wrong chair, and should not be coming in for counseling himself, rather than being the one who sits in the counselor's chair. On this point it is obvious, of course, that the uneasiness of the counselor is a paramount factor in the establishment of rapport with the client, and the beginning counselor, particularly, is going to experience sessions when he feels threatened and insecure. It is well if he is in a situation where he can work this out with the assistance of some other counselor, and it is nothing that need alarm him, since even the experienced counselor periodically runs into situations that shake him.

4. The client may sometimes immediately challenge his acceptance by the counselor, and what happens will have an important effect on their future relationship. A school counselor may find a client whipping out a cigarette, and the counselor's acceptance of this can be indicated by passing an ash tray to him. Obvious and studied verbal insolence is another means by which the counselor may be tested, and the counselor's capacity to accept such behavior is a good measure of his professional competence and personal security.

The highly colored, risqué, or just plain dirty joke may also pose an early problem for the counselor—again possibly a means of testing the counselor, or it may be just a part of the normal expression of the client. If the counselor has led such a sheltered life that he cannot understand the joke, then he will have his problems, although he might not be quite so badly off as the counselor who understands the joke, but is horrified that a child could come forth with such a statement. We can assume both that these individuals need some assistance if they are to become effective counselors, and that their relationship with the client is likely to be somewhat strained. The more mature counselor, on the other hand, can be acceptant of the client's feeling of humor in what he has said, and be neither frigid nor boisterous in his reaction. Nevertheless, some "jokes," such as those of an "anti" nature, may prove a problem for the student counselor, inasmuch as the client will be alert to detect any indication of approval or condemnation on the part of the counselor.

5. The more a counselor is attuned to the feelings of the client, the less of a problem the lack of understanding of the intellectual content of what he says will be. Some counselors may be somewhat disturbed when in the first few minutes of the beginning session the client mumbles several statements that are unintelligible. Generally speaking, it is better to refrain from asking for a repetition of certain statements, since the meaning of what has been said will usually become obvious anyway. If the counselor has to ask repeatedly for clarification, the counseling session will degenerate into a "teacher-asking-what-do-you-mean" sort of thing, a situation that will not usually help in the establishment of a good counseling relationship. If the client continually talks so softly that the counselor cannot hear him, the latter should gently point out that it is rather difficult to hear what is being said—although even here there is some question as to whether or not the counselor should take this step.

The counselor may sometimes hear a word, but lack the understanding of what it means. In this case, it is better to let the client continue. The counselor may eventually pick up the meaning of the word either by listening to a tape, or by hearing it again and using a dictionary. If he has to stop the client from an expression of feeling and say, "Pardon me, but what does that mean?" he is letting himself in for several potential difficulties. For one thing, the client may assume that the counselor must be a rather ignorant fellow if he does not understand the meaning of a word. It may also be that the intellectual explanation of the word will prove embarrassing to the client. Finally, an intellectual discussion is not the purpose of a counseling session, and there is no reason why an individual cannot function as a counselor, reacting to the feelings of the client, even though he does not understand the exact meaning of a word that is being used.

At the college level the counselor may sometimes have as a client a psychology student who is trying to impress himself with both the erudite state of his own mind and the lack of intelligence of his counselor; to this end he will deliberately use many long and complicated words quite new to the counselor. When this is obviously happening, the counselor may react to what is actually going on, and the verbalization may then develop into a more fruitful investigation, by the client, of just why he has to try to convince himself that he is more intelligent than the counselor. It is not, of course, of any importance whether the client actually is, or is not, more intelligent than the counselor; but it is of some importance to help the client to discover why he must feel as he does.

The counselor who must know the meaning of each word—and former teachers tend sometimes to be this way—may also find himself in difficulty with adolescent clients who insist on using a language all their own. Even if the counselor makes a valiant effort to find out just what some of the terms actually mean—and often even the adolescents themselves do not know—there will be further frustration in that the current language, like popular tunes, is in a constant state of flux. Thus the best thing the adult counselor can do is abandon any attempt to "know" the meaning, and rather concentrate on understanding the feeling behind the words that are being used. Possibly the real test comes when the counselor tries to establish a counseling relationship with a client who speaks another tongue. If these two can get together, it is certainly not on the basis of an intellectual understanding of what they are saying to each other!

All of these items may prove to be initial problems for the student counselor as he becomes involved in the establishment of rapport with the client in the initial counseling session. But in the long run the extent to which they prove to be continuing problems will be a measure of the counselor's professional competence and personal integrity. For some of the counselors depicted here, the establishment of rapport is still a major difficulty, as they struggle to find themselves, whereas others no longer have to *try*, and thus the relationship is better.

WHAT HAPPENS IN THE BEGINNING SESSION

The beginning session is more likely to be a testing ground for the client, and even for the sophisticated counselor there is the element of the unknown—neither person really understands the other, although the client may know about the counselor, and sometimes, of course, the counselor may know about the client. It is likely that some counselors want to know about the client in order to bolster their own feeling of security when, for the first time, they meet him.

Buchheimer and Balogh describe three phases of the beginning session: the statement of the problem, exploration, and closing and planning for the future.[2] These are reasonable enough, and very often do occur, although the student counselor should not assume that the client always follows this timetable! Some clients, for example, will spend more than the first session evading the problem in a variety of ways; some counselors will not give the client a chance to look at his problem, but will provide one for him; some clients will press the counselor for answers, for his version of who they are and what they should do; some clients will sit passively and take no overt action, verbal or otherwise; some clients will leave at the end of the first session without any plans for the future.

These junior high school clients (Cl) are all self-referred, and we could expect that they would wish to talk about their problems, at least as they see them, without any urging by the counselor. If, on the other hand, they had been sent to the counselor so that "he could do something about you," it is unlikely that they would have expressed themselves so easily. These are the beginning comments:

        Co: Hi, Ted, come in.
        Cl: Thanks.
        Co: What's up . . .
        Cl: Well, I wanted to see you about whether or not I should quit school.

. . . .

2 Arnold Buchheimer and Sara Carter Balogh, *The Counseling Relationship* (Chicago: Science Research Associates, 1961), p. 15.

Co: Hi, Jane, how are things going?

Cl: They're not . . . things are at a standstill . . . everything's so boring.

Co: Uh-huh . . .

Cl: Sometimes I wonder whether I'm ever going to be happy in life. I mean . . . well . . . I seem to need excitement. I can't be content with any kind of routine.

Co: Things have to be happening in my life in order for me to be content . . .

Cl: Yeh. . . . I just sort of need excitement . . .

. . . .

Cl: Hi . . .

Co: Hi, Jim . . . you wanted to talk with me . . .

Cl: Yeah . . . I want you to help me get out of the foster home I'm in. I'm just about fed up with the way I'm treated. What am I, an animal?

Co: You've just about had it, eh?

. . . .

Co: Hi, how are things going?

Cl: Pretty good.

Co: Pretty good . . . but not as good as they could be . . .

Cl: Yeah, that's right. Brother, I've gotten . . . ah . . . I've gotten into a lot of trouble and my parents are going to kill me when they find out.

. . . .

Co: Hi, come on in—have a chair . . . what's new?

Cl: Oh . . . well . . . ah . . . nothing much, I guess . . . except I'm not friendly with Ruth any more . . . we had a fight . . . I called her some awful names . . . and we really hurt each other and well . . . I . . . uhmm . . . I don't feel too good about the whole thing . . . it's stupid . . .

Co: It bothers me . . . I'm not happy about what happened between me and Ruth . . .

Cl: Yeah . . . that's why I came down to see you . . . I thought if I could talk about the fight I might feel better . . . you know . . . blow off some steam . . .

. . . .

Co: Hi, come on in. . . . You made an appointment to see
me . . . what's on your mind . . .

Cl: Well, I wanted to talk to you about math. . . . I'd
like to change my math class.

Co: Uh . . . huh . . .

Cl: I'm not doing even fair work now . . . in fact, right
now, as far as I'm concerned, math rots . . .

Co: (Silence) . . .

Cl: I'm fed up with math . . . and with . . . him . . .

Carl's counselor (C) sets the stage by directing, questioning and
dominating: [3]

Cl: Carl, I'm Mr. Williams.

S2: Glad to meet you, Mr. Williams.

C3: Nice to know you. I see you had a little trouble last
week.

S4: Right.

C5: Mm-hm. What have you been told about our counseling laboratory?

Jane's counselor (C) engages in a "getting to know you" sort of conversation: [4]

S1: It's nice in here.

C2: We've got the fan going. We're trying to make it
more comfortable.

S3: Mm-hmmm.

C4: On the sheet, as I mentioned before, you can take
that home and finish it, and, uh, if you do come
back you can bring it back or mail it back, which-
ever you prefer.

S5: Mm-hmm.

C6: Tell me, did you have a rough time getting down
here?

S7: Not rough, but whenever I ride the bus I just get all
excited about whether I'm going to get off on time
and . . .

C8: Oh, and you just made the mistake of going up on
the third floor.

Jack's counselor (C) over-elaborates on the equipment, and shows
his own nervousness: [5]

[3] Evraiff, *op. cit.*, p. 17.
[4] *Ibid.*, p. 72
[5] *Ibid.*, p. 166.

C1:   Hello, Jack; sit down. Picked a warm day to come down, didn't you?

S2:   Mm-hmm (looking around). Two-way mirror, huh?

C3:   Yeah, that's right. Did she tell you about it? So that if there are people studying to come here to observe, they can do that. That makes you a little uneasy about it?

S4:   Yeah.

C5:   Well, if there are any, there's no one around today, and if there are people who come, they will be people who are studying advanced work in college, and they're not much interested in you or me, as persons, it's just the way the counseling goes. So that's a little comfort, maybe. (Pause) It's kind of strange, isn't it, the first time?

S6:   Yeah (Pause).

C7:   Can you tell me a little about what you, ah, came down for?

Edna is not too eager to talk with her counselor (C): [6]

C1:   Hello, Edna. How are you today?

S2:   All right.

C3:   Do you mind the heat very much?

S4:   No.

C5:   Did you come all by yourself?

S6:   Yes, Ma'am.

C7:   Would you like to put your umbrella in the corner so you can be comfortable? And your purse you can put on the table or somewhere. Would you like to talk to me today about something? Would you like to discuss things with me? (Short pause)

S8:   I don't know, I don't know what to discuss.

C9:   Well, maybe you could tell me something about yourself so I'd know you better. How would that be?

S10:   Well, I'll, do you want me to tell you how old I am, or where I live or something like that?

Richard's counselor (C) pushes and probes and dominates at the start: [7]

C1:   Make yourself comfortable. Would you like to tell

6 *Ibid.*, p. 227.
7 *Ibid.*, p. 317.

me a little bit about school and the trouble you are
having?

S2:   I don't know what to tell you.

C3:   Uh-huh. You understand the set-up here at the counseling center?

S4:   Uh-huh.

C5:   Who was it that suggested that you come down?

S6:   My mother.

C7:   She's concerned about how you are doing in school?
Is that the reason she suggested it, or what?

By the end of the first session, all of these clients had indicated
their willingness to return. However, one should be cautious in interpreting just what this might mean. It could mean that the client
felt that at last he had found an adult who would listen to him, and
with whom he felt easy and comfortable, or it might mean that he
felt he had found someone who would answer his problems for him,
or it could mean that he felt he was supposed to return, and he was
willing to do whatever the authority figure suggested.

Some points that might be noted in the first counseling session:

1. The client is likely going to be testing the counselor to see if he
fits into his preconceived image of him. If he does, this may be good
or bad, depending on the image the client has of the counselor!

2. While some beginning sessions may prove to be also concluding
sessions, the counselor can usually operate on the assumption that
his primary function in the first session is to establish a positive
climate so that the client may wish to return for further consideration of his difficulty.

3. The beginning session, like other sessions. belongs to the client,
not the counselor, and the counselor's behavior should carry this
message to the client.

4. If the aim of the counselor is to establish at least the beginning of
a genuine human relationship, he will feel that he has no obligation
to any methodology or technique, that his obligation is rather to his
self integrity.

5. Toward the end of the session the counselor can indicate his interest in the return of the client without implying that the client has no
choice and should return because he, the counselor, wants him to
return. Some counselors, in the name of "Client-centeredness," give
the impression of aloofness and lack of concern, whereas others
imply that the client must return regardless of how he might feel.

Chapter Eleven

THE COUNSELING
EXPERIENCE

ONE MAY SAY that the counselor is not too obvious in the examples in the previous chapter, but this is the way, surely, that it should be. What the counselor says is not as important as the extent to which he is a genuine, self-actualized individual who can relate easily within the other person's frame of reference. On the other hand, it is also true that what the counselor says may be a very good indication—to the client as well as to a supervisor—of the extent to which the counselor really is a genuine, concerned-with-others sort of person. The counselor is very much involved in a total sense in an understanding and acceptant manner, but his manner of communication, verbal and otherwise, is one of the best indications of his effectiveness.

THE INNER FRAME OF REFERENCE

Regardless of the orientation or methodological handle of the counselor, it would seem that one of his unique characteristics should be his ability to operate within the client's frame of reference. This is particularly pertinent in a school, where many children rarely, if ever, have the experience of having a member of the school staff listen to them with attention and interest and concern.

These examples of counselor statements illustrate the counselor's involvement in the world of the client:

"You get to a point where you sort of feel like giving up—you sort of wonder if you should keep trying."

"It's confusing. . . . You feel that you don't know what to expect, and since you're not sure of what's coming, you find it more comfortable just to remain silent."

"Sometimes it's hard to grow up. You get the feeling that you should act more grown up, but still, in a way, you'd rather remain a little girl."

"One day the foster home seems OK . . . another day you hate it. You wish you could have the same feelings about it instead of one day liking it and the next day hating it."

The counselor may sometimes become so involved with the other's frame of reference that he will use the first person. Needless to say, the counselor could hardly be genuine if he was using this as a "technique":

"These tests concern me, they sort of make me worry—it seems that they might have some influence on my schooling. . . . And I'm hoping that they won't have any influence, that they won't count as much as I sometimes think they will."

"I wish that people would allow me to make my own decisions. . . . I'm old enough to decide what's best for me."

"I don't like the idea that he always has to be right. . . . Why can't I be right once in a while?"

"I have a choice. . . . I can continue to cheat on exams or I can stop. My only fear is that my honesty might result in my failing an exam."

"I just wish that he'd realize that I'm human . . . that I have feelings, and that I don't like being pushed around."

The use of the first person, however, is no guarantee that the counselor is operating within the client's frame of reference. A long counselor statement, first person or no, is more likely to be an intellectual summation from the counselor's frame of reference. For example:

"In other words it bugs me that everybody sort of thinks the worst of kids today when they aren't any different and they don't do any different than the kids of my parents' generation, or kids who even lived before that. I kind of feel there's nothing wrong in having a good time. My parents had their good times. . . . Why can't I without people getting so worried?"

Some typical comments from Tom Ril's counselor indicate his ability to be with Tom Ril:

"You were too much involved in wondering about you to be able to be stimulated or excited or feel that such an attraction was . . . well, in order to be involved in such a thing. . . ."

"It's hard to say they were pretty good . . . how could I have had three days that were pretty good. . . ."

"You mean . . . ah . . . in looking at it now, it just doesn't seem as much of a test as you thought it would be. . . ."

"And it seems to mean . . . not so much that you can trust me, but that you can trust you. . . ."

"When you become what you are, then you no longer are what you were—the very act of being means that you are changing."

"The possibility of others' suffering the pangs of hunger doesn't make my pangs feel any better . . . it's my inside that's hungry."

John Bin's counselor says:

"You feel that Miss Bel was being a little unfair with you."

"You like it now even though at times it gets a little rough."

"You kind of want to get the whole thing over with quick. You want to know where you stand."

"You want to go, but you're really worried about what might happen in court."

"You have an idea when you're going to get in trouble—you can sort of feel it coming."

"And now you feel you have a mind of your own, and you can make decisions about what you want to do."

Many counselors will fluctuate back and forth from the client's frame of reference to the counselor's frame of reference, and in this sense could probably be described as being "eclectic" rather than Client-centered. Note this counselor (C):

C1: What subject do you think you're failing in?
S2: Literature.

C3:   Would you like to talk about that or how you feel about it?

S4:   Well, I never read nothing and I don't like to read.

C5:   There's something about reading in general that has made you dislike it?

S6:   Yeah . . .

C7:   Doesn't it kind of hinder your work in school?

S8:   Well, I just read enough to get by and that's about it.

C9:   Just enough to get by.

S10:   Yeah . . .

C11:   How do you feel about that?

S12:   (Pause) What do you mean "How do I feel about that"?

C13:   About getting by all the time.

S14:   I don't know.

C15:   You don't feel anything.

S16:   Uh-hu. . . . As long as I get it done I don't care.

Certainly, C7 and C11 could hardly be called the client's frame of reference. C11 is so much the counselor's version that the client does not understand him. Did the counselor *have to* insert himself in C7 and C11? Why did he? Would it have made any difference if at these points he had nodded and grunted instead of directing the conversation as he did?

Sometimes the conversation would appear to be geared entirely to the counselor's external frame of reference. Jack's counselor (C), for example, in session eight comments as follows: [1]

C338:   I think an important thing here is that this turning it off in school, this is what happens to the school work, in some cases.

S339:   Yeah.

C340:   This is the first real talk we've ever had.

S341:   Yeah.

C342:   I wish we could go on.

S343:   I'm about talked out though.

C344:   I think you're just starting now.

S345:   Maybe we've just started on the subject, but I'm about talked out for today.

C346:   (Laughs) Yeah, I mean for today, but for the future

[1] William Evraiff, *Helping Counselors Grow Professionally* (Englewood Cliffs, N.J.: Prentice-Hall, Inc., 1963).

maybe we could find out some other ways to get rid of this tension, this anger, so that it wouldn't interfere with your school work.

So the extent to which the counselor operates within the client's frame of reference varies. The counselors of John Bin and Tom Ril functioned almost entirely within the client's frame of reference, but there are other counselors, some experienced, and apparently effective, who vary their approach considerably. The student counselor must determine what is *real* for him and *effective* for the client. If he can manage to combine these two, he is probably better off than most counselors!

LEARNING TO BE FREE

A basic and crucial part of the counseling experience is the gradual experiencing of being free. The individual can become, in an atmosphere of security, a little more honest, both with himself and with others. This learning to be free is often painful, and although it is cathartic, there may be despair and hostility and frustration. These are feelings the client comes to be able to experience, and to live with, and to go beyond. They are necessary if there is to be growth and movment. We might assume that the more a person, young or old, has lived a lie, the more violent some of these expressions will be, whereas the moderately stable, ordinary child, living through his developmental problems, periodically needs some assistance so that he can maintain his high level of honesty and genuineness. Here are some junior school children who are receiving such assistance from their counselors. They are learning to express, and to look at, their selves.

Anxiety may be detected here:

"If he ever calls my mother I'm sunk—she'll never believe it wasn't my fault."

"I just wish she'd leave me alone . . . every time I go in her room I get a feeling like . . . well, as if I had a piece of lead in my stomach."

"I just go blank. Whenever someone says tests to me I just freeze. If someone tested me on my name I don't think I'd remember it— just because it's a test."

"School is on my mind all the time. I think about it when I get up in the morning, when I go home, when I'm in bed. I'm always planning what I'm going to do the next day, or I worry if I'll pass a test or look foolish in class . . . and yet I'm doing pretty good work. I can't understand why I'm always worrying about grades, tests and school. Really, I've got nothing to worry about . . . I mean . . . I think I don't . . . I'm all mixed up."

"I wish I could stop worrying about whether the kids like me or not. I say to myself, stop worrying, don't get so bothered, the kids like you . . . and I say it over and over again . . . but it's always on my mind, even now. The kids are friendly, and they've invited me to parties, and one girl even asked me to join her church club . . . but still I worry, I don't know why."

These children express frustration:

"It's nice to be able to talk about this problem, but what can I do about it? Nobody at school can help me, you can't do anything, and I can't do anything. What's the use of even discussing it? All we're doing is running into a stone wall."

"What makes me mad though . . . the teachers just keep putting on your report card 'capable of doing better.' How do they know? That's what I can't figure out. How do they know you're capable of doing better if you think you're doing your best now?"

"I wish I could get through to him. I wish I could make him listen and understand. I keep trying to make contact with him but he doesn't seem to care. It's as if I were a chair or a lamp . . . like I'm not alive . . . and all I want him to do is pay attention, to listen and understand. Even if he can't, if he'd only try."

"How much am I expected to take? Do I go on letting him be sarcastic or do I put my foot down? The only trouble with putting my foot down is that he may react by shutting me off . . . sort of stop loving me. It's his favorite way of hurting me, and believe me, it hurts."

"I do all my homework and study for tests and still it isn't enough. What does he want—blood? I can't spend a lifetime doing homework. How much is enough? People say study but nobody tells me how much. I really don't know how much is enough. This is me in a lot of other things too . . . not just homework. I never know how much is enough."

These clients express overt hostility:

"Sometimes I wish I could choke him or push him downstairs. I sometimes just want revenge for what he's done to me."

"I'll pay her back—somehow-somewhere-sometime—I'll let her know that she can't treat me like a piece of dirt."

"Who does he think he is? If he thinks he can insult my mother like that and get away with it he's crazy. When I see him after school today I'm going to deck him. . . . I'll shove my fist right down his throat. . . . I don't care who sees me."

"I'll never respect him, no matter what he says or does. He can never mend what he's done to me. I feel broken but not broken enough so that I'm in pieces. There are a lot of different ways that I can pay him back . . . and I want to."

John Bin (Cl) expresses himself in many ways. In Session 2 he talks this way:

Co: Uh huh . . .

Cl: I don't like Mrs. Pen, I'll tell you. No, I don't like her. When I was in Grade 7, one day I was down in the gym. I used to be a wise guy—you know me—me and a few of the other guys, you know. All the little guys now, but they were big guys then. So we were all fooling around, you know, and one of them said something

(And some teachers said John couldn't reason or understand!)

to me. And I dropped a book or something. And I dropped a book on the floor and I come out with something—you know—profane language. So Mrs. Pen was standing there, and she heard it, so she said, "Who said it?" So we all just looked at her, and no one was going to tell. So she said, "If you don't tell, I'll take you all up to the office. But if you tell me, I won't say anything and I won't do anything." So I said, "Okay, I said it. I swore." So she said, "Just because you told the truth, I'm not going to take you up to the office." But the same day I had a fight with another teacher and he sent me up to the office, so I got two weeks discipline and two weeks no recess, because Mr. Dan would say, "Did you do this?" and I would say, "Yes," and he would give me two days discipline, and he'd add on every time I said something. I didn't blame him. I was being pretty wise. So then he said, "Okay, get back to your room." So this is the recess period. The next period I go into my math class with Miss Bel. What happens? I'm just sitting there, and Mrs. Pen and Mr. Dan come in. I'll never forget this, because this has bothered me quite a while. And he said, "Okay, I'm looking for a boy. All the boys in this room stand up." So I stood up and Mrs. Pen says, "That's him over there." So Mr. Dan says to me, "Take your hat and coat and get down to my office." He threw me out of school. And since that day—I don't know—I give everybody one chance. If I trust someone, I trust them. I mean it. That's the way I feel about it. I want people to trust me, and I'm here trying to get you to trust me because I want you to. That's the way I've always been. But Mrs. Pen just happened to cut my throat that day. It's not that I hold a grudge against her; it's just that I'll never trust her again.

(For far too many children, this is the dismal picture that describes "school" and "teachers.")

Co: Uh-huh . . .

Cl: And if anybody wants to blame me, they can.

Co: Uh-huh . . .

Cl: And I told her. I told her the day she got me up at the office. And I know she told Mr. Dan because I've got my own reasons, my own ways of knowing. I know everything. Believe me, Mr. Del, I know everything. I know who tells people everything in this school because—I mean—look, things get around. There's no question about that. That's something I know. So another time —you know Mr. Zol? I was walking up the stairs. I know I gave him a hard time. Then I found out the guy was okay, and now, I mean, I'm like—well, I'm close to him. I give everybody the same chance. He gave me a chance and I gave him a chance. Now I come by him and I say, "Hello, Mr. Zol." The same thing happened between me and Miss Con. I had some beefs with her until I got to know her. At lunch time I was trying to sneak into line; you know how

that line is at lunch time. And you know, I tried to
sneak in and she pulled me out. I had just said, "Hey,
Larry, I got my tickets before you." So I don't know,
I must have pushed him and she turned around. She
must have thought I was going to hit him or something. She turned around and she grabbed me, and I
felt like a nut. She grabbed me, and she said, "Get
over in that corner." And I said, "I didn't mean noth-
thing." And she said, "Get over there." So she talked
and she talked and she talked. But now the last period
she wants me to go down to her room, and she'll help
me with my work. I understand—look—I, I'm not
coming back here to fool around. I came back here to
go to school. Okay. I'll admit it. I've got a lot of
things on my mind. I'm pushing school, but it ain't
what I really can do. But I've got other things that
I just can't help. They're still on my mind, and they'll
be on my mind until they're off my mind. I know I'm
very touchy; I can't help that. You see, right now, just
by looking at me, that I'm very nervous. I can't help
the way I am. I'm just in that state, so I know that
my court case is going to go one way or the other.
But it's got to go either way, and I'm going to have
to be just the way I am now. Just keep myself out
of trouble. Just like Mr. Dan told my father, "Your
son had three or four things that could have come
out to something." I know that. Well, I know when
I'm wrong. Before—well, I don't know. I'm always
wrong when it comes to a teacher, but I know one
thing. If a teacher hits me, I'm going down to Mr.
Dan's office, and I'm going to say to him, "I came back
to school not to fool around; I came back to do some
work." I may get into beefs once in a while; that's
inevitable. I mean I might do something that will
provoke a teacher. I mean, I don't blame them. I
mean, I know myself. Like this morning I got up and
I wasn't touchy. But sometimes I get up grouchy. I
know that, so I don't blame nobody. But really, some
teachers aggravate me. Really, Mr. Del, they really do.
*(If there were more teachers like **Mr. Zol**, who would "give
a chance" to a child, there would be more children who*

would give them a chance. There are many children, too,
who actually want to learn, if the school would only provide
them with a learning environment, and some motivation for
learning.)

Co: What you want is fair treatment.

Cl: That's all. Look, Mr. Del, I want to be treated like
      other kids. That's just the way I want to be treated.
      I don't mind being here if I'm really going to learn
      something, and I've got my whole heart on that. But
      I just can't give it the extra push it needs, because I
      just haven't got it yet. But it will come, believe me,
      some day.

Co: This extra push is coming along . . .

Cl: Gosh, Mr. Del, it's got to come. . . . I've just been
      down to the office once, but I haven't got into any
      trouble over that. Mrs. Pen, she didn't want to give
      me . . . well, I just stay away from her, that's all. I
      mean, she's a nice woman and all of that, but I don't
      know. . . . I just don't trust her. I wouldn't do any-
      thing in front of her. But now take my shop teacher,
      Mr. Ton. I like him very much and I'd do anything
      for the guy. . . . I mean . . . he's nice . . . you can
      talk to him. He doesn't say, "Get out of here." He
      maybe tells you like any other teacher would, but I
      don't know . . . it's in a nice . . . in a nice way, a
      nice manner. Like I mean, if he wants you to do some-
      thing, like, "Why haven't you done your homework?"
      and he wants you to do it, you don't mind doing it.
      The guy asks you in a nice way, so you want to do it.
      But Miss Bel, if you don't get it done for her, she'll
      make you do it fifty times. I don't see that. I mean, I
      do my homework. I don't worry. It's just that once or
      twice. I've only been absent one day, but a while back
      —you know how many days I was absent—about . . .
      30 out of 35. But Mr. Del, I'm only here now to learn
      something. I know that.

Co: Uh-huh . . .

Cl: But a lot of teachers up here don't really believe it.
      They figure they have to go to work. I don't blame
      some of them, but I mean . . . but the teachers I'm
      getting to know, like the new ones, like Mrs. Non,
      and the other one—I don't know his name . . . I

just said it a little while ago . . . Mr. Zol, that's it, Mr. Zol. And that Mr. Fin, I'm back here, you know, just to blow off steam and so I won't like him a lot, he's okay. And Miss Gid. I like Mr. Hin, and now that Mrs. Il too. She's a little on the hard side, but she's okay. I like her too. I like Miss Bel . . . Miss Bel is a real good teacher. I'm really glad I have her for math. . . . I figure I'll really learn something, but I don't know, you just can't go up and talk to her like you can to some of the teachers. If you want help you go to a teacher and say something like, "I can't get this," or "Can I make up a test," but this woman . . . I get the feeling that what she wants to say is, "Get away from me." She's pretty much of an old grouch. I don't understand it. My real interest now is school, it really is. It's something that I want. I always thought that you go out into the world and make your money and figure that you were getting some place and think that you're growing in responsibility. But school is responsibility, like making sure that you've got this book. I mean, it's really nice. In a way I dislike it . . . well . . . I don't know . . . it's hard to believe, but I really like school. I really mean it. I don't understand what happened to me before, why I got into so much trouble.

Co: You like it now even though at times it gets a little rough.

Cl: I don't know, when it piles in, I just kind of let the homework slide, let it stay there, don't worry about it.

In the last few minutes of session two John Bin (Cl) talks this way:

Co: The subjects you have now you feel you must work at, and these subjects will help to give you a background for the college course.

Cl: In a way I'm glad I didn't go into the college course, because it would have been real rough. I got some friends and they would have helped me, but I don't know, you know, I really like shop . . . you know, I like that kind of work, and I've got one of my B's in it.

Co: Uh-huh . . .

Cl: I didn't do too bad in the first few months. I didn't
     do as bad as I thought I might, but I guess I didn't
     expect some of those marks either.

Co: You felt you didn't do too badly, but you didn't do
     as well as you wanted to.

Cl: Well, I wanted that B, that B in math, but she only
     gave me a C.

Co: Uh-huh . . .

Cl: I mean, I really don't blame her. The second day I
     was in school I got an 11 on a test, then I got an 80.
     I had a good average, but it wasn't good enough. I
     didn't bother to check it, because I figured I was de-
     serving of a better mark. Then there was that stupid
     notebook. She said that she couldn't read it . . . not
     that she couldn't read it; it's just that she didn't un-
     derstand what it was all about. I finally got a D, and
     I figure if I keep away from the woman I'll be better
     off, believe me, I'll be better off!

Co: You mean that if you go near Miss Bel, you'll only be
     stirring up trouble.

Cl: That's just the way I feel about it. I mean I was get-
     ting along okay with her, but I just didn't bring my
     homework in, and then she just seemed, well, I don't
     know . . . she's a funny woman. I really don't under-
     stand her. (Pause.) I know . . . well, I'll tell you the
     truth . . .

Co: Uh-huh . . .

Cl: I copied from this fellow, because I didn't have the
     first few pages . . . that was okay, and then this
     buddy of mine copied my notebook. Listen to this:
     she gave the fellow an A, she gave me a D, and she
     gave Dick an A. When I saw that, I said, "Wow—he
     copied from me word for word." I looked at both
     notebooks, and I went out of my mind. He copied my
     notebook—I get D and he gets A.

*(John does not know that many students have had this
melancholy and frustrating experience.)*

     I'll admit that I did a bit of cheating. We had two
     problems and I only had one of them because I
     wasn't in school, so I copied the other fellow's. When

I saw that A though, I laughed. What could I say? I couldn't say, "Miss Bel, I copied his notebook, but you gave him A and me D." She would have thrown me out of the room. Boy, that was funny. The whole class laughed when they saw his A and my D. You never can tell. . . . Well, I guess that bell means my time is up, Mr. Del. Can I see you next Friday at the same time?

Co: That will be fine, John . . . we'll see you then. . . .

And here in session five John Bin (Cl) shows that he is beginning to learn to be free:

Cl: I grew up too damn fast. My body matured but my mind didn't. I was easily led. I wanted to show my muscles. I wanted to show how tough I was. Sometimes I slip back, but I think . . . well . . . I think my mind is starting to understand things. I'm starting to say to myself, "Who do you think you are?" I never said that before. I always thought I was somebody.

Co: You feel that you're gaining in maturity, and this is a good feeling for you.

Cl: I'm not saying that I enjoy school all the time. I mean . . . you know . . . there are things around here that are chicken. Ah, I can never change those things . . . but I am learning. I mean I'm starting to enjoy it more than I dislike it. But the thing that I really dislike . . . you know . . . those few teachers. They think they're better than other people. They look down at me. They think they're better than everybody else. Boy, that's a bad way to feel because nobody is better than anyone else.

Co: Those teachers who feel that they're better than other people kind of bother you.

Cl: Sure they do. I can't see that. Why in hell should they think that way? What makes them think that way? One thing I don't understand is why teachers don't respect certain classes and certain kids . . . I mean, who do they think they are. . . . (Pause) . . . Well, I guess time's up for now. So long, Mr. Del.

Co: So long, John.

(The odds are that John's mind is "starting to understand

things." He is becoming involved in a warm and human relationship with another person, and movement and growth are taking place.)

And in session fifteen:

Co: You never felt really close to your mother, but lately you've been getting closer to her . . .

Cl: I never felt close to her growing up. She never wanted to do anything with me. She never wanted to do any of the things I wanted to do as a kid. Neither my father nor mother ever took me any place . . . you know, they were always too busy. Mother was always busy working, and father was always going somewhere. But my aunt taught me a lot. She took me to lots of places when I was a little kid.

Co: You felt closer to your aunt than you did to your father or mother because she took you places . . . She did things for you . . .

Cl: I've never really talked serious to my mother. If I tell her some things about myself, if there are some things that I tell her . . . well . . . she just gets mad—she just hollers and shouts at me. It's always been that way. I could never get close to her to tell her things that I wanted to tell her. I never had the confidence to do it. . . . My father, though, I could tell him anything—I always could. I never told him everything, but I could tell him more than my mother.

Co: You feel that you can tell your father things, but when it comes to your mother, you just can't seem to talk to her . . .

Cl: She yells at me—she blows her top—she gets mad. When she found out that I was going to lose my license, she really got mad. She didn't understand— she just blew her top. She just likes to talk, and as long as she's talking, she's happy. She just yells—she never gives me a chance to give my part of the story. Boy, she really gets on my neck.

Co: It bothers you that you never have a chance to give your side of the story when it comes to your mother . . .

Cl: She calls me names—all kinds of names. No mother should call her son the names that she's called me.

Co: You find it rough to talk to her. She goes on talking, and you get the feeling that she doesn't give you a chance to say what you want to say.

Cl: As long as my mother gets her way, everything's okay with her, but let me want my way once in a while, and she blows her top. She really gets mad. Why the hell should I always do the things that she wants? Why can't we do things the way I want once in a while? I don't mean all the time—I just mean once in a while. I found out about my mother when I was just a little boy. It was one summer—she'd wake me up every morning, and make me work in the house all day. I really sweated, and by the time I finished working, no one else was around. Everyone had taken off for the beach or they had gone some place, and I was alone. She used to make me feel queer. I was only a little kid, but boy, I really worked hard. She'd never let me get out of it. I had to work every day.

Co: This still bothers you. She made you work hard when you were quite young, even though you wanted to go out with the other kids and do some of the things they were doing.

Cl: I didn't mind working. I didn't mind working until noontime, or something like that, but when I had to work all day, this was a pain. And we used to rush and rush to get a job done. And even today I still rush—everything I do is in a rush. I don't want to rush any more—I want to slow down, but I just can't get over rushing. I just can't get over the idea that started when I was a little kid. But she still bothers me even now—she always has. She makes me work with her, and at my age, and in the house, and it's the same old thing—rush, rush, rush. I don't like to say "No" to her—I don't like to say that, but I don't like to work with her. After all, she's getting old, but I sure hate that rushing. She lets things go, and then she has to do something in an hour that usually takes two or three hours. And I get caught too—I have to rush along with her. I tell her, "Just because you've rushed all your life, I don't have to rush too—and that work's for girls anyway . . ."

Co: You'd kind of . . . you'd rather slow down. You don't care to rush all the time.

Cl: Even now I always find myself rushing. I rush to school, I rush to class. I rush home, I rush to work. I rush when I eat—I gobble the food down. Then at night I don't come home for supper—I just have a lousy sandwich.

Co: All this rushing started when you were a kid, and it's become a part of you, and you don't like it.

Cl: I like to take my time—I don't like to rush. You know what I've been doing mornings to slow myself down? I've been getting up early and taking a nice long walk, just so I can take it easy, so I don't have to rush. A nice easy slow walk.

Co: You're tired of all this rushing—you'd rather take your time about things.

Tom Ril has many periods when he feels despair, and hostility and frustration:

"I feel terribly defeated, especially in the morning. All the dreams one makes . . . I just have to discard them and come down to earth . . . and try to accept things gracefully and with a measure of composure. . . . I'll never be able to . . . (pause) . . . and yet, having admitted these things, you can sometimes turn around and prove them wrong."

"I guess I have to go through a period of hating her . . . and after that maybe I can see her as she was. Now I hate her guts most of the time . . . the poor, neurotic, shrill, demanding woman. She did an incalculable amount of damage, and the pathetic thing is that in a way I think she knew it."

"It's difficult not to be bitter . . . it was so wrong, so terribly wrong, so completely unjust. . . . They certainly instilled a degree of fear in me . . . a terrible fear."

"I find myself, these past few weeks—for want of a better word —drifting. Each day is conditioned by what has to be done—structured, you might say—I feel in a way—I don't mind—and yet I feel that this isn't quite right—and yet—it seems enough to be free—relatively free of tension. . . ."

"You know, this is a kind of frustrating experience for me sometimes, because there are things I think about—hard things to get a hold of, dimly perceived things which I want to get a hold of—and talk about—and I cannot . . . often I just sit here and completely block—like now—I don't understand that, I just don't."

"Some people are not haunted by their failures, but I am . . . a tremendous feeling of guilt. . . ."

"It's rough . . . I don't mean to invite your pity—but it is rough to land with your feet in the world of reality, and begin to know yourself as you are—for the first time in my entire life . . . if only it had happened years ago. . . ."

Tom Rin can also be free to be honest about his feelings about the counselor, and they are not always positive:

"I experienced a distinct chill when I left here last week. . . . (Long pause.) May I smoke?"

"If you'd been a close friend I might have said, 'He's just being bitchy, so forget it. . . .' But this is a very special relationship we have, and I'm extremely sensitive to anything you might say—quite sensitive. . . ."

And so the client comes to learn to experience his feelings, and to live with them, and after experiencing them, he learns, too, that somehow they are no longer the same. The ghosts are not quite the ghosts they were, the faces are not as threatening as they were, and the new face I see—the me—is stronger and more pleasing.

GROWTH AND MOVEMENT

As the person moves and grows, things become better—the individual himself becomes better, and somehow other people become better too. All is by no means, of course, sweetness and light, but the individual does gain the strength to be who he is. Often in the counseling hour the client may be talking, in a somewhat intellectual sense, about what has happened rather than what is happening, but often, too, what he is expressing is his feeling of an ongoing process. He is not simply saying positive words because they sound good, or because he feels this is what he is supposed to say; his words are truly expressive of what is, as well as he can perceive it, and experience it, happening.

Here are some comments from various high school students:

"I find that I'm becoming more interested in reading just because I don't have to be angry any more."

"You know, I could go on blaming others for things that have gone wrong in my life, but when I really look at it . . . I mean honestly look . . . well, I could have avoided a lot of trouble simply by using my own head."

"In the past I've always reacted with anger when somebody was mad at me . . . seems that's pretty threatening for me and I have to defend myself. It must be that I've been insecure all my life, not having any real affection or love from my dad. I just have to defend myself when I'm around him or anybody like him."

"Sometimes I think I enjoyed being afraid . . . but you know, I don't have to be scared if I don't want to. Before I thought that being afraid was the only way I could ever be."

"Let's face it—I can stand up or I can crawl. Now I figure that once I begin to crawl, that crawling becomes a way of life; but if I stand, then standing can become a way of life. Right now I prefer standing."

"Success isn't really ending up my life the way my mother wants me to. It's my life, and maybe success means sort of . . . well . . . being at ease with myself . . . sort of being satisfied with me."

"The kids aren't really as bad as I thought . . . they're OK . . . I . . . ah . . . think one of the reasons I didn't get along was . . . was . . . ah . . . ah . . . because I let them bother me . . . I mean like whenever they razz me I laugh it off now . . . before I'd get excited and mad . . . that's . . . that's why they gave me the business . . . I can't be a crybaby . . . I'm . . . I'm . . . learning to take their wise cracks and give them back to . . . I don't go walking around thinking that everybody's against me."

"I realize now that I can't have my cake and eat it too—I thought I could have the whole package . . . good times, girls, hanging around, and grades . . . now I'm beginning . . . ah . . . well . . . beginning to see that I've . . . ah . . . umm . . . ah . . . I've got to pick out what's important . . . you know . . . first things first."

"The teachers are changing . . . they don't seem to be so rough . . . but they're changing because I'm changing. . . . I used to give them a hard time, but I don't anymore . . . it's sort of . . . well . . . ah . . . I mean . . . I don't see any . . . ah . . . umm . . . reason . . . ah . . . I'm not going to get anywhere by being a wise guy— you know what I mean. . . ."

"Before I thought . . . why do this or that if I don't feel like it. . . . Now I know I can't do only those things I want to . . . I mean you've got to do some things you don't want to do . . . that's life . . . and I've got to do some things in school and even at home that I don't want to . . . the world is in enough of a mess without everybody going around doing what they want. . . ."

"You know when I talked to you the other day about my parents fighting . . . and I . . . ah . . . umm . . . ah . . . was all shook up . . . well, since I was here last time I thought a lot about what I did . . . and the more I thought about everything the more I realize that parents must fight . . . like . . . brothers and sisters fight . . . I mean right now my parents aren't fighting and I'm happy . . . but I won't be shook up the next time . . . if people have to live close together they practically got to have a fight. . . ."

"I mean . . . if I fight my brother, well . . . I consider that natural . . . well, now, I say to myself if Ma and Dad fight that's natural . . . it's not the fight but the way you look at it . . . I think . . . ah . . . grown-ups are people too . . . in other words, there must be times when they get mad . . . but the next time there's a fight at home . . . I . . . ah . . . ah . . . it won't bother me as much because I won't be the same person I was before . . . I'll . . . ah . . . ah . . . I'll be the same but I won't think the same."

Tom Ril, too, in many ways expresses his feelings of growth toward self-actualization and freedom:

"And yet for some strange reason it doesn't . . . I can . . . can feel the failure of it . . . it was a failure . . . and yet it . . . ah . . . it doesn't . . . I don't seem to have taken it as hard as I thought I was going to . . . I don't understand it . . . I wish it was otherwise . . . I don't know. . . ."

And in this exchange with his counselor (Co):

Cl: It seems to me, looking back, that I have spent an awful lot of my life defending myself—trying to be two things—to be what I thought I was and what I wanted to be, and yet to try to conform . . .

Co: Defending yourself—to you—and to others . . .

Cl: To others—and to myself too . . . it's been an appalling struggle, consuming time and energy . . . what a waste . . . a waste . . .

Co: Do I have to spend all my time defending me . . .

Cl: But I'm less so now, and the roof does not fall in—
      maybe because me as I am now is more acceptable to
      me . . . that's kind of confusing . . .

Co: You mean . . . the me that's more acceptable isn't
      the me it used to be . . .

Cl: No . . . no . . . yes, yes . . .

And again:

"Sitting right here now . . . I feel more like myself—whatever
myself is I don't know—but I and me are both right here together—
right here right now . . ."

"I don't have to go outside of me . . . I can stay right here and
be me . . . I have less faces to meet the faces . . . but you see, when
you drop the masks—and I haven't dropped them completely . . . but
enough to know what it feels like to do it . . . there is a sense of loss,
of not belonging anymore . . . my position in relation to other people is changed . . . I sort of feel . . . not all the time . . . but some
. . . something is over and done with . . . and now . . . now I can
look ahead . . . reach out. . . ."

"And so I felt that all these months had been a deception, and
so I said 'All right, this is how I feel,' but as soon as I accepted the
fact. . . that I felt that way . . . that this was how I felt, so all right
. . . as soon as that happened, something changed . . . it was never
quite the same again. . . ."

And in this exchange with his counselor (Co):

Cl: I spent most of my time growing up trying to be what
      I thought others wanted me to be . . . and I spent
      very little time listening to my inner self—listening to
      what I really was . . . and to have the courage to *be*
      what I really was . . .

Co: . . . and it was hard to ever get to the "being"
      point . . .

Cl: Yes . . . yes . . .

Co: . . . so that you could say, "I am . . . now . . . I
      am . . ."

Cl: Yes . . . yes . . . (long pause) . . . a long time ago I
      talked about preparing a face to meet the faces . . .
      that's it . . . you can sum up my whole life in that
      phrase . . . well . . . now I *don't* . . . not any more

. . . not nearly so much . . . not always maybe, but more often I am myself . . . and I'm content to be so . . .

And again:

"I've been learning to communicate more in the last few months . . . with more people . . . to take a little chance—and that pays off, you see, and you take another little chance . . . and the roof doesn't fall in on you after all . . ."

"I thought, when I came to see you that if I changed I'd be able to stand back and watch it happen, but it hasn't worked out that way at all . . . it's been slow and gradual and subtle . . . I'm only aware of change sometimes because of what doesn't happen . . . but how . . . what happened . . . where did change take place . . . (long pause) . . . and in a way that battle is over . . . I *can* check myself . . . and of all the things that have happened to me here . . . and I suppose that catharsis is one of them—to be able to tell you all the dreadful things . . . but you know to me the most significant thing is that I've been able to sit here and explore all of my self—and to test myself, in a sense—what is real, and what am I putting on . . . and I'm convinced that it is real, it is true . . . I mean the change is that I don't feel so alien any more, I'm not so different after all, I know this, I feel this . . . and I don't feel this need to *have* to prove myself. . . ."

And in this exchange with the counselor (Co):

Cl: It's always seemed to me in the past . . . when I've tried to reach out . . . just warm . . . relationships, you know . . . friendships . . . they've refused to be that way . . . it goes from a moderate to hostility . . . or to something very deep and emotional . . . I can't seem to keep it in the middle . . .

Co: It becomes a demanding sort of thing. . . .

Cl: Uh . . . huh . . .

Co: There can't be a closeness and at the same time a non-demanding on you . . .

Cl: That's right, Dr. Pin, that's exactly right . . . that's just it . . . demanding is the word . . .

And movement and growth can be painful, as in these exchanges with the counselor (Co):

Co: Are you saying, Mr. Ril, that it's difficult to feel without wondering what's behind this—why is this—and
it's difficult to accept this feeling . . .

Cl: (Long pause) . . . I guess the . . . I guess I'm crying
because one by one I've had to destroy the illusions
. . . and it's hard to give them up . . .

Co: They've been important . . . but now you're saying
good-bye to them . . .

Cl: Yeah . . . yes . . . uh . . . yes, I guess so . . .

And again:

Cl: . . . and I suppose that's why I want to cry . . .

Co: I want these big things . . . excellence . . . but I
can't. . . . I won't be in first place. . . .

Cl: No, I won't be in first place . . . there's a wide gap
between fact and fancy . . . (long pause) . . . boy,
it's a long fall. . . .

Co: . . . back to the company of other humans . . .

Cl: To hell with them . . . I don't care . . . about most
humans . . . I care about me . . .

Co: Uh . . . huh . . .

Cl: Their concern is their concern, not mine . . . (long
pause) . . . that sounds conceited, doesn't it . . . but
I don't care . . . that's how I feel . . .

Co: You care more about you . . .

Cl: I do . . . I do . . . I do . . . but I want to separate
caring from an excessive preoccupation . . . you see
. . . there is a difference there.

And again:

Cl: I just couldn't accept the whole thing, so I had to
rearrange it, didn't I, I had to reconstruct it, and
bring it here, and lie to myself, and lie to you, so that
it could become something I could accept . . . and I
felt so ashamed of myself . . . ashamed that I
couldn't listen to myself . . . ashamed that I had to
come here and lie to myself and to you . . . and I'm
frightened . . . I had to work so hard to change it
. . . it was such a feverish effort . . .

Co: You just had to make it into something good. . . .

Cl: I couldn't accept it the way it was . . . and yet, I did have to tell you . . . I couldn't conceive of our relationship as such that I could sit here and lie to you . . .

John Bin, too, moves toward growth and freedom. Here, for example, he talks with the counselor (Co):

Cl: My mother . . . well, she's a grouch and she doesn't mean anything. But my mother sometimes . . . well, she's like an animal. She's really got a lot of worries, and I don't blame her, but you know she looks at me and you know that she thinks I'm spending money and I haven't got it. She doesn't tell me to stay in, but she'd like to see me stay in a bit more, you know. She doesn't say, "Stay in this house or I'll kill you." She says it, well, in other ways . . . but boy, I know what she means. Anytime I do something wrong, she's on me. . . . But really I don't mind.

Co: You feel that although she's on you, it's just something that she's kind of going through.

Cl: She's trying to nurse me through this. She's trying harder than I am to nurse me through.

Co: You feel that she wants you to be a success even more than you do.

Cl: Boy, she really does. My mother always had ambitions for me. Always wanted to see me graduate from high school. She always wanted that, and it looks like she's going to get her wish. Boy, I quit school before, but boy, she'd shoot me if I ever tried to quit school again. I swear she'd really kill me. Last time when I quit school . . . wow! I told her and she said, "Well, go ahead. Do what you want to." Then she turned around and said, "Don't quit school . . . I'll kill you." But then, you know, she kind of let me quit, and then she didn't want to have anything to do with me. She'd always say, "Why do you want to be a dummy like me?" You know, she only went to the fourth grade, and the day I told her I was going back to school . . . well . . . she died! She said, "I don't believe it. What are you lying to me for?" So I didn't say anything to her, and then the next day, when I did go back to school, my mother thought I was kidding her, and she said, "Cut it out now, John. Are you kidding?" My father didn't believe me; nobody believed me . . . that I'd go back. I don't blame them. I used to say that I was going back to school. I used to tell my father, but he never believed me because I never did go back. But I wanted to come back. You know, I used to chicken out a lot . . . I really wanted to, but I would chicken out. But finally one day . . . well . . . I really said I was going to and I did. And then they wanted to put me back a grade, and I said, "Oh boy, I'm going to show those guys."

Co: You were so desirous of getting back into school that you'd take this just to show them that you could make it.

Cl: That's right. I really wanted school. I was going to go to prep school, but then I gave that up because of the expense. I'm wondering, Mr. Del, how many points do I need now, this year, to pass? Is it sixteen? I don't know . . . but I guess I'll get enough points. Sometimes I wonder, but I think I will. Sometimes, though, I think I would have been wiser to go to prep school . . . I'd have got better education than I can get here.

Cl: A lot of people need help . . . it's really that bad. But people, they're funny. They won't admit it. Look at me. I would never admit that I needed help. Who would I admit it to? But now I know. A person is not so big as he thought he was. You can't be so independent. Maybe some people with money, they think they can be independent, but really they can't be independent. They've got to buy friends . . . they can't trust anyone. That's why if a person can find himself, well, that's really important.

Co: You feel that it's easy to slide, but it's pretty rough to climb back.

Cl: I was doing okay. I was doing good, and then I fell apart. In a year and a half I fell so far down the hole that it took me two years to get out of it, and I'm not completely out of it yet. And just to show you how long it took me to come to my senses . . . sometimes

I wonder what happened to me in the lower grades. I
don't know, I just fell apart. I kept going down and
down and down. . . . (Pause.) . . . Boy, the summer
a few years ago, that's when it all started. I started
hanging around on the corner. I met the guys . . . I
started to smoke . . . I started to drink. I was only
about ten, eleven years old. I grew up too damn fast.

Co: And you feel that this growing up too fast has been
the cause of a lot of your troubles.

Cl: That year . . . that year really killed me. Oh boy, I
remember thinking back when I was in elementary
school . . . well, you know, I started school in the
first grade with a bunch of kids and then when we
got to third grade, they kind of split us up and sent us
to different schools, because one school was over-
crowded. Boy, I remember telling my father that I'd
never go back to school. I hated the place for what
they did. They broke up the group . . . the gang,
you know.

Co: This was upsetting to you.

Cl: It really was. I wanted to stay with those kids bad.
But boy, that third grade was rough, real rough. If I
could only have it over again. If I could only . . .
you know . . . know what I know now. I started getting really disgusted then. Started playing hookey, you
know, three or four days a week. I was a real big shot.
I could get away with everything and anything. And
the same thing happened later on. I was doing pretty
good, and I remember that the teacher was surprised
at me skipping so much, and because I skipped school
the teacher took my name off the board. Boy, I really
felt like a jerk. I settled down a little bit, but then
they just started to get on me again, so I . . . well, I
started giving them all a hard time.

Co: You were starting to come out of it, but then you
went backwards again.

Cl: That's right. You know, like I said, I was doing okay,
and when she took my name off the board, well, that
was it. I started to come back again a little bit, but
that was just too much to take. Then when I got here
. . . boy, I was a real wise guy. What an attitude

I had. I was king. I was the boss. I could push anyone around. That's just the way I felt. That's just the way it was.

Co: You kind of felt that you didn't respect school.

Cl: That's right. But there were a few that . . . well, there were a few teachers that I did. They were okay. Like Mrs. Pen, she was okay. But that Mr. Fin . . . I remember him. Boy, everytime I went by his place, he used to call me a hoodlum and things like that. Boy, he burned me up. I went in there once with my jacket on, and he told me that I was a hoodlum. He was trying to scare me, but I didn't care. He didn't scare me. I remember one day when he made me sit . . . just sit all day. Boy, I was going out of my mind. You know, just sitting . . . imagine, sitting all day.

Co: You didn't care for that feeling . . . the feeling of just having to sit there and wait and wait.

Cl: He just wouldn't let me go, but finally he did let me go downstairs to the basement . . . and to eat. Boy, he just made me sit there, and boy, I hated it. I hated every minute of it . . . and well . . . (Pause.) . . .

Co: This really bothered you.

Cl: It sure did. I counted the minutes. I counted the seconds. Boy, just sitting. Boy, was it aggravating. But boy, it didn't straighten me out. I was too big. There were times, too, when I just walked out of school. You know, just grabbed my coat and walked out. To hell with them all. That's why these kids up here who think they're doing things make me laugh. They never did the things I did. The trouble . . . they never got into the trouble that I got into. If some of these kids ever knew what I went through . . . boy, if they ever knew, it might help.

Co: You feel that your experiences might be valuable for other people.

Cl: Yeh, they sure could learn a lot through my mistakes. And the guys I used to hang around with—the guys on the corner—they die when they see me go by. They ask me, "You going to school?" and I answer, "Yeh," and they can't understand what's making me go back. They'll never understand. But a funny thing about people . . . they're all waiting for me to fall flat on my face. I know they are. They expect me to get into some real trouble . . . you know, real trouble. And then I'll be out of school for good.

Co: You want to show them that you really can last in school.

Cl: I'm going to last, Mr. Del, but I love it when people think I'm going to fail, like those people. They think I'm not going to make it. But I'll show them.

Co: You like people to think you're not going to make it, because then it'll help you to work harder to make it . . .

Cl: The more I go through with this, the more I know that I want to go through with it. It's important. I'm really going to show them. I'm really going to show them all that I can make it. Everybody's dying just waiting to see if I can't make it. Everybody except my father and mother. They know that I'm really going to . . . well, I'm really going to give it a go. But these other people . . . not them . . .

Co: You enjoyed seeing these people, and knowing what they thought about you and your future.

Cl: Look, I know all along that I'm going to make it. But these people think I'm not. And boy, I'm really going to show them. And some people that I showed my report card to . . . they flipped, they really flipped.

Co: You enjoyed showing people these marks, showing them that you could do something.

Cl: I sure did. But when I finally do make it at the end, that'll be . . . well, that'll really show them that I can make it. That I've got it inside of me to do it. My relatives, they're funny. They can't understand why I came back to school. You know why they think I came back to school? Because of my trouble. They thought that if I went back .to school, it would make me look good, and they thought this is why I went back.

And again:

Co: You feel that this is a big change that has come about in you.

Cl: It has. I don't know where it came from.

Co: You feel that you can get along with people better now.

Cl: Look, I don't care how much anybody steps on me. There'll always come . . . well, my day will come, and when my day comes, it won't be in school. It'll be out in the street. You might be stuck some night in the snow, and I'll go riding by and I'll splash you. There's always some way that I can get back at people. But why ruin my chances in school just because I have to argue with someone? Someone like you. It really isn't worth it. I come first. Before, I didn't figure it that way. Before, I used to figure I was a big shot. The teacher was just giving me a hard time, but now it's different. Now I think of myself first.

Co: You feel you've found a better way to get along with people.

Cl: Look, when people aren't honest with me, I want to get back at them in some way. If I figure that someone is ripping me apart for some reason, I don't go for that stuff. If somebody out of nowhere just starts slicing me up . . . boy, that really burns me up.

Co: You feel that you want to be treated fairly if you're going to act fairly with people.

Cl: That's right. That's why I came up here. Like when I came up here with you, I figured that maybe I'd act wise with you. But you've been okay to me, so I can be okay with you. But if you were going to give me a hard time, boy, I'd give you a real hard time in return.

Co: You feel that you can get along with people as long as they show some respect for you.

Cl: Look, I'm a person, but sometimes people forget that. You know what I mean? Like that Mrs. Non, she said to me . . . you know, I was fooling around, and she says, "Look, I don't know you, I don't know anything about you, but I want you to know that I've got a husband and children, and I'm here working at a job the same way that your parents work at their jobs." She said it was her job to see that I didn't do this and I didn't do that. She said these weren't her rules, just the rules of the school. She said there were some teachers who think they own the world, who want to throw bologna around at everybody. And she said, "As far as you're concerned, I want to be your friend, but it's up to you." Well, I said to this woman, "I want to apologize." You know, I didn't know that she was like that. She was giving me a hard time at the beginning until I got to know her. Today I go by and I say, "Hi." You know, it's different. But a teacher never said that to me before. They used to say, "Who do you think you are? Do you think I'm afraid of you? Who do you think you are? Get down to the office." They wouldn't even give you a chance.

Co: You feel that if a teacher will act right toward you, you can be friendly toward them.

Cl: Well, it's not up to them as much as it's up to me. It comes from me first.

Co: You feel that it's up to you more than it's up to the teacher . . .

Cl: It's kind of . . . well, my obligation to show that . . . you know, that I'm really not a wise guy. That I'm here to learn something.

Co: Well, then, you mean that you feel it's up to you. . . . You can start trouble or you can avoid trouble. It's kind of on your shoulders.

Cl: Right. I came in to this school a big, tough kid, and I figured that I could keep out of trouble if I just minded my own business. It's just aggravating, those teachers who . . . well, I don't know, they just don't treat me right. But then at the same time . . . well, I don't know . . . maybe it's me. I really don't know. I suppose though, that I should be . . . well, I should know how to get along with them no matter what kind they are. I mean I still fool around in school. I still sneak a smoke. I know it's against the rules, but who's going to catch me? But I know it's breaking the rules, but, well . . . I don't know . . . I mean there's something here, there's something . . . well, kids don't realize that they can get something out of school. This education's important. Well, I mean it really is. I just look at my parents, and I see what it is to be without an education.

And finally, here is a complete counseling session with John Bin. This is session seven. It is not the last session, but by now John is able to explore who he is and where he is going. He feels free to talk and think about things that he previously felt he could never face, and he expresses some feeling of astonishment that this could actually happen to him.

Session 7

Co: Hi, John . . . come on in . . .

Cl: Hi, Mr. Del, how are you?

Co: How are things going?

Cl: Have a piece of candy?

Co: No thanks, I've just had my lunch.

Cl: I thought I had 75 in my English test, but it turned out to be 90, and that makes me feel pretty good . . . I had a little argument during the math period. We had a substitute teacher, and there was a problem we couldn't agree on. We were arguing back and forth, the substitute teacher and me, so I took the problem down to Mr. Fin, and, well, he decided that I was wrong, so I guess we lost . . . or I lost. I was telling the substitute teacher, "Ya, you're crazy . . . get out of here." And I'm going to wait until tomorrow when Miss Bel gets back. I made a dollar bet with a kid. I'll pay it off tomorrow if Miss Bel says I'm wrong.

Co: Uh . . . huh . . .

Cl: I had a good week. It was okay except for the weather. I could only work two days though. I needed the money and I wanted to work more.

Co: You were kind of disappointed because you couldn't work more because of the weather . . .

Cl: Well, my uncle owed me $60 and he gave it to me this week, so that isn't so bad. I've got a job this summer where I can make up to $80 a week.

Co: Uh . . . huh . . .

Cl: I've already talked to the guy and he said that I could start it as soon as I get out of school. I just want to work so that I can save a few hundred dollars.

Co: Having a job is pretty important to you . . .

Cl: I need the job so I can have some money to run my car and take care of other expenses, get some clothes before I come back to school . . . you know. As far as school goes, I really am not where I should be. I really have got to boost it up this next few months. As each day goes by, I seem to pick up faster. Some days I'm tired, but . . . well . . . I think that altogether I'm doing better. But those days that I'm tired I can do nothing but lean back and sleep.

Co: Most of the time you're right in the swing of things, but there are just those days . . .

Cl: Well, those days . . . you know, I just haven't got it in me. It was funny this morning, my father couldn't get me out of bed. Last night I told him to wake me up early so that I could get some homework done before I went to school, but finally I did get up and I rushed through three pages of science. I had to pass them in this morning.

Co: You really had to rush, eh . . .

Cl: I sure did. I had to do the three pages in twenty minutes. It wasn't very good.

Co: You feel that if you had a chance to spend more time on it, it would have come out better.

Cl: I rushed straight through the whole chapter. Wow! I rushed right through it. I'll be able to make up for it, though.

Co: You mean that although you rushed, you'll be able to make up this work.

Cl: Oh, ya . . . although I realize I can't do good this way. I've got to spend more time on my school work at home. Oh, boy! I fell asleep today during the science period . . . I just couldn't help it. They were reading out of a book, and well . . . I just dozed off. It was real boring. If there was a bed there, I would have been out like a light. I wouldn't have gotten up. I woke up when my head slipped off my hand. I just didn't enjoy today. We had English, science, math, and social studies in the first four periods. I just didn't enjoy it.

Co: It was kind of too much subject matter . . . too much school to take . . .

Cl: Well, I'm not used to it. You know, with that week

off, it really ruined me. It made me lazy. It knocked me out. Oh, I hate to get up in the morning. It's funny though, I can get up early if I don't have to go any place, but if I have to go to school . . . wow! I just want to sack in. When I have to go to school or to work, I just make believe I'm sleeping. I just don't want to get up.

Co: You kind of feel that you want to stay in bed, rather than going to school or to work.

Cl: That's it. I just would rather stay in bed. I mean I think anybody would like to. But I don't know . . . if I stayed in bed, I'd just be a lazy old man. I wouldn't be getting anywhere.

Co: You feel that you have to get out of bed . . .

Cl: That's it. I really have to. It's kind of my duty to get out and get up out of bed. I got in this morning just as the bell rang. Believe me, I just made it. Boy, time is really flying. I can't believe the time has gone so fast. I don't know if I'm glad I'm back . . . but I don't know what I would have been doing. You know, I would have been working some place . . . cleaning cars, or something like that. It's good to be here.

Co: You feel pretty good about being in school . . .

Cl: The only thing is . . . well, you know, I'm so much older than the rest, and so much bigger . . . well, I don't know, I just don't feel right.

Co: This bothers you . . .

Cl: It's just that I feel out of place. I mean I'm getting used to it, but sometimes when I fool around with the kids in school, it's like I'm with a little brother . . . that's just what it's like . . .

Co: Uh . . . huh . . .

Cl: School is coming along okay, but I don't know . . . I just have . . . well . . . I'm going to be disappointed if I don't do as well as I want to. I really want to make it, Mr. Del, I really want to. And if I don't, I'm really going to be disappointed in myself. I really am.

Co: You'll really be disappointed if you don't make what you want to in school . . .

Cl: That's right. It's up to me. If I don't make A's, I'm

Cl: not getting the marks that I want to get and I should get. That's the way I feel. This school work is simple, Mr. Del, it really is. The only thing is . . . well . . . you've got to use your common sense. That's what you've got to do. I can sit down and use my common sense and be up for the tests. I can get A's . . . it's that simple.

Co: Uh . . . huh . . .

Cl: The tests aren't hard. It's just the idea of being home and studying for those tests . . . you know, putting in the time.

Co: You feel you can handle the work if you can just devote the time to it.

Cl: That's the idea, if I could only find the time to study. You know, it's funny . . . I think up here if you study too much, well, it's no good . . . you've got to study just enough but not too much. And you've got to be kind of smart enough to know what the teacher's going to ask on the test. Like that English test. I knew just what he was going to ask, and I was up for the test, so I got a ninety. If I put my mind to it, I can get it. But boy, when I make stupid mistakes . . . boy! If I can just stop being careless, that's what gets me into trouble. That's what gets me those lousy marks sometimes.

Co: You don't like to make these mistakes in your school work.

Cl: Those mistakes really burn me . . . like I could have got a hundred in that English test, but stupid little mistakes . . . boy . . . ten points is ten points. Boy, if I can make that kind of mistake, imagine what I can do in a real important test like a Civil Service Exam or something like that. Sometimes I make real stupid mistakes—spelling, sentences—things like that. It was a real hard test, but I guess I did okay. A lot of the other kids flunked it. It was a real complicated test. There were only four questions, but they were all long ones.

Co: But you felt real good that you did well on the test.

Cl: Oh, yeh . . . When I got that ninety . . . well, it made me feel pretty good, especially when so many other kids flunked it. A lot of kids who do good in English got fifties. I kind of think that English is my subject. You know . . . the others are okay, but I think I can do English better than the other subjects. A funny thing about science . . . you know, I got a good mark in the test the other day, and I didn't even study at all. It was funny, I didn't study, and I came out with an eighty. But I don't know . . . I got a forty-seven in the last Social Studies test. Boy, I really goofed that test up. You know . . . stupid mistakes again, carelessness. I had the right answers, I guess, but they were incomplete. I would have gotten a ninety if I gave complete answers. Oh boy, I had the right idea, but the answers . . . well, they just weren't all that he wanted.

(John, not unlike most school children—even those who have difficulties in school—must talk about school. It is an important part of his life, and it is important that he should find an understanding listener, even though some teachers, and even some counselors, might feel that what he talks about is of little importance. It may be of little importance, but it is of much importance that John should feel that he is free to talk with someone interested in him and in his conversation.)

Co: Good marks make you feel good, but bad marks due to carelessness really bother you.

Cl: When I get a bad mark I feel lousy, especially when the mark is . . . well, it's because I make stupid mistakes. You know what I mean. I don't feel right when I do bad work in school. I want to do better work. Like when I miss a homework assignment, I get nervous about it. You know . . . especially when I have to come in to school the next day not having it done. Like last night I had . . . well, I didn't do much homework, because I was working on my car, trying to get it ready. I fixed the brakes, I even skipped supper, and I was just plain tired, so I didn't get much . . . any homework done. I was so tired when I finished that I just went to bed, clothes and all. I wasn't interested in the homework, and then this morning was just rush, rush, rush, so that I didn't even get a chance to comb my hair.

Co: Uh . . . huh . . . (long pause).

Cl: I really like school, Mr. Del. I never thought I would, but I really do. I never thought I could come back, and . . . well . . . know, make it.

Co: Things have really worked out for you.

Cl: They sure have. I never expected them to. Next year I'll even do better. It's a funny thing, Mr. Del . . . you know, when you get in trouble, you've got to fight for things three times harder. One thing that people can never take away from me, and that's my education. That's why I really like school. It's something I can get . . . well . . . people can't say to me, "Why did you do that?" You know, it's a good thing. And as far as I'm concerned, I've got school beat. In fact, I've always had it beat, but I never wanted to have it beat . . . I always threw it aside . . . (pause). School really means something to me. I don't care what happens, I'm not leaving school for anything or anybody. The only way I'd leave is if my father died or something like that, and well, I had to go to work . . . (pause . . . . Mother is funny. The other night I came in about midnight, and she was really burned up because she thought I was getting back to my old ways. She almost killed me. She really lit into me. She was really mad. She told me, "Why don't you stay home and study your books? Where were you? What do you think you're doing out until this time?" Once in a while she's in that kind of a mood, and then she really bothers me. But I don't go out much. I haven't got my license back yet, so what's the sense of going out? I just kind of stay around the house. But I go out once in a while, and that's when she blows her stack, especially when I come in late. As long as I don't go out with those guys . . . you know, the guys I used to go out with before, I don't see why my mother has to worry. I can get into a lot of trouble hanging around with the guys I used to hang around with . . . (pause) . . . I don't know . . . (pause) . . . Well . . .

Co: You feel that these friends of yours helped you get into trouble in the past and you don't want it to happen again.

Cl: No, Mr. Del, that isn't it. I got myself into trouble, and now I don't want to get them into trouble, so I stay away from them. That's the way I feel, Mr. Del.

Co: You feel, then, that you get them into trouble by associating with them.

Cl: That's right. I get them into trouble, and myself. In other words, Mr. Del, if I put the blame on them, it wouldn't just be right.

(John doesn't have to say this, and there is a good chance that it is more than just a cliché offered to please an adult.)

Co: You feel that the blame doesn't belong on them . . . it kind of belongs on you . . .

Cl: There are things in my life . . . I don't know why I did them, all I know is that I did them. But I know this—no one made me do them. Nobody tied my hands, nobody stuck a gun in my back, and that's why I blame anyone but myself. That's why today I'm striving . . . that's why . . . well, if I don't make it, I'm going to break my head.

Co: You kind of feel that you control your life . . .

Cl: I control my life. There's no supernatural thing telling me to do this or do that. There's no one telling me that I've got to go out and punch someone. It's nothing like that. The only time I'll raise my hands to someone is when someone will raise their hands to me. I kind of have the green light then to go ahead and defend myself. Any man would do this. You know, Mr. Del, if I went around saying that Tom made me do this and Bill made me do that, it would soon come out that I wouldn't be able to take any blame. And when you get that way, Mr. Del, you can't stand alone. You've got to always depend on blaming someone else. If some day I . . . well . . . really got into trouble, who would I blame? You've got to be able to accept trouble and find out who's really to blame. That's why in my life I've done everything I can to make people miserable. You know I did it. And now I'm doing everything I can to kind of make up for it. And there are a lot of people in school and out who . . . well . . . they're kind of accepting it . . . that I'm trying. That's okay, that's good. But if I went around blaming other people like the policeman who picks me up . . . you know, if I blamed him for picking me up last night, and then tonight I go back and punch him in the face, I wouldn't be getting anywhere . . . I'd just be getting myself in deeper. This way, Mr. Del, by . . . you know, not blaming the others, I'm crawling out and I'm getting ahead of other people.

Co: You feel that this blaming other people is just fooling yourself. . .

Cl: Well, in other words, it's just like putting a blanket over your eyes . . . well, you know, you really can't see. I always knew that I wanted to go to school, but this blanket . . . well, it covered my eyes. I turned away from school. I didn't want it, Mr. Del, and now . . . well, it took me a long time to find out that school was what I made it, and I had to make it. And I don't think . . . well, I don't think that I can put another blanket over my eyes. I had my choice and I've got my choice now. There are two roads that I can take—the good road and the wicked road. I've been on the wicked road and I wasn't getting any place. I was spitting on myself, so I . . . well, I kind of said to myself, "John, let's go the other way." I kicked myself, and . . . well . . . here I am. And that's the best way in the world that I can explain it to you. And that's why . . . I found myself, and nobody can take that away from me, and nobody can take what I've got now, no matter where they put me, Mr. Del. Seriously, nobody can ever take away . . . well, what I know now. You know this . . . well, since . . . well . . . I know there's only one way to go and that's the right way, and nobody can ever take that away from me. Anyone who goes around blaming the people around him for the trouble he has is only fooling himself. They really don't know themselves. Look, it takes two people, Mr. Del, to make life miserable. I mean, I can't help other people to feel lousy, unless I know how to make them feel lousy . . . you know what I mean? I might not be making too much sense, but in a sense, this is what I mean

. . . in order for me to have a fist fight with you, I've
got to slap you in the face, and you can walk away
from it the same as you can slap me in the face, and
if I don't walk away, the fight starts. But you always
have to have two people to do something. That's why
if you tell someone else about me, and that person
really believes it, without really finding out about me
. . . well, that person's really stupid if he just goes
on . . . well, your opinion. And even when that person makes an opinion, it still isn't worth anything,
because they really don't know me . . . not really
know me. It's still only the other guy's opinion of me.
That's why if people in life can't go around making
up their own minds, and go where they belong and
not where someone else want them, they aren't worth
very much.

*(In this counseling relationship John can talk and think and
feel, and begin to see a part of him that he has never seen
before.)*

Co: You feel that the most important thing is to make the
decision yourself, and to stand up or fall on those decisions.

Cl: That's the way it goes, because if you can't . . . well,
in other words, if you tell me to quit school right now,
and I can't tell you . . . in other words, to go fly a
kite . . . I mean I don't belong if I just can't say
what's on my mind. How can I belong if I can't stand
up? And the people who can't stand up are the people who need the help. If you can't stand up and know
what you want, then you kind of don't belong, especially at my age. A person my age knows where he
wants to be. Either you want to be in jail, or in a
mental health place, or be in school, be something,
or be in a factory working. You know a lot of these
kids who join the service . . . well . . . they just run
away. Like Joe, he ran away from everything . . . I
mean, really, he hasn't anything. He has a car, a little
money in the bank, and a few months more left in the
service. But he hasn't got an education . . . I mean I
figure I'm better off. At least . . . well, I'm here . . .
I'm getting an education. To me that's more impor-

tant than running away, running away and hiding.
I've got a chance to make something of myself on my
own. Nobody had to teach me, I'm learning myself.
I'm learning to stand on my own two feet.

*(And once individuals get to the point where they want to
learn, they can learn, but so many teachers spend so many
fruitless hours trying to "teach" someone who does not wish
to learn.)*

Co: You found yourself.

Cl: That's right. I know what I want and I . . . well . . .
Joe, he's a kid. He doesn't know what he wants. He
still goes out and fools around and gets into trouble,
and all of the trouble . . . well, it just doesn't bother
him. The trouble I used to have didn't bother me
either, but now . . . well, I'm kind of growing up. I
mean I believe in going out and having a good time,
going out with the guys, and going to a show . . .
like last night they asked me to go out and I could
have gone out with them. But I knew where they
were going and I knew what they were going to do,
and I didn't like a couple of the guys that were there.
So I told them, "No, I don't want to go. I'm going to
stay home." And one of the kids—he was twenty-
one—he came in, and he was loaded, he was drunk,
and what was I going to do. I didn't say anything. I
just told him that I woudn't go. Look, I know that if
I go out with a couple of the guys I can have a lot
of fun with them in a nice way. I know other guys I
can go out with, and all they look for is trouble. Well,
the people that go out with them . . . well . . .
they're weak-minded. They don't want to say, "No, I
don't want to go," so what do they say . . . "Sure,
let's go," and what happens . . . trouble.

Co: And now you feel that you have a mind of your own,
and you can make decisions about what you want to
do.

Cl: Look, I know if I'm going out, and . . . well . . . I
meet this kid who wants to go some place that I don't
want to go to . . . you know he wants to get me into
trouble. Well, I can say, "No, I don't want to go . . ."
but before, I'd just go along. But now I can say, "No,

I don't want to go." And it's a funny thing . . . I tell my father where I am. Before, he never knew where I went . . . I just used to go. Now I tell him where I am. "Pa, I'm here," or "Pa, I'm there." I tell him where I'm going. It's better this way. I feel better about it. He still nags me, but outside of that . . . well . . . he's okay. My father's funny. He worries me. He thinks that I'm going to get into all of that trouble again that I got into before . . . I mean, he's scared about what I'm going to do. I mean, he really doesn't believe that . . . well . . . I'm not going to get into trouble. I think it's wrong for him to feel that way. I mean . . . now . . . I've improved in so many ways. I mean I have an argument with him once in a while because I can't stand him nagging. It really makes me nervous. Like all the questions he asks me. You know, he really can . . . he really can bug me. Every night of the week the same question, "Where are you going? What are you going to do?" The questions can drive you crazy.

Co: You feel that now that you've found yourself, other people, like your father, should be more trustful.

Cl: That's right. I don't fool around like I used to, but people . . . well . . . my father, he just doesn't think so, and sometimes my mother thinks that it's all a big act, but it really isn't. I'm not going to get into that trouble that I got into before, but my mother . . . I don't know . . . she's funny. I mean, I can talk to her, I can work around her, and I can say . . . well . . . "Hey, Ma, can I have this or that . . ." I know how to work around her, and she'll say "Sure," after a while. That's the kind of mother she is. I have to work around her.

Co: You feel that if you use the right approach with your mother, things will work out for you . . .

Cl: That's right. I've learned how over the years. But I think that my father is worse than my mother . . . I mean, he doesn't think . . . I still get the feeling that he doesn't trust me, that he doesn't really think that I've changed . . . that I've really changed. I mean . . . well . . . sometimes I do the same things . . .

not the real trouble, but the way I act with people, but I do it a lot different now. I mean it looks better, and it sounds better . . . it's not rude like it used to be. I used to be very rude to people.

Co: Uh . . . huh . . .

Cl: I was really rude with people. I didn't know how to act with them. You know, I'd say any damn thing that came into my head.

Co: You feel that now the things you say to people aren't rude like they used to be.

Cl: That's right. I mean . . . the things that I do now, I do innocently. It's not that I'm trying to hurt somebody. Before I used to try to hurt people. I mean if you're walking down the corridor and I laugh . . . before I would be laughing at you, but now I'm not. I mean it's just innocent. I mean I'm laughing at something else now. It's not that I'm blunt.

Co: Uh . . . huh . . .

Cl: But if I have something to say to you . . . well . . . I'll say it right to your face, and that's the way I've always been. I mean . . . in other words, if I thought that I couldn't like you, I wouldn't be able to sit here and talk like this. You know what I mean. In order for me to talk to a person, I've got to really have confidence in them, really trust them. But with my mother and father, and with my mother especially, I never could get close to her . . . I used to tell mother something and she'd yell at me. That's why . . . well . . . I could never really talk with her . . . she'd always end up yelling at me. She still gets mad, but I think I get along better with her, because she doesn't get as mad as she used to, although she's still . . . well . . . she's still a grouch. But I think she's on my side, because she knows . . . well . . . I'm fighting for my life now, and really, I think my mother's happy . . . I've never seen her so happy, but she has a funny way of showing it. I'm learning to understand my mother, though. She's moody . . . one day she's happy and will treat you right, and another day she just won't bother with you. I mean one day she's the best of friends, and another day she's

the enemy of somebody. That's just the way she is.
I can't explain it. She's just . . . well . . . a grouchy
old woman. I don't blame her. She's got a lot of
worries . . . bills, Pa, me . . . I mean I don't blame
her. I've caused her a lot of trouble in her life with
all the junk that I've done, and all the . . . well . . .
you know what I mean, all the trouble that I've
gotten into. That woman has gone through a lot with
me. A couple of weeks ago, though, I told her that she
was really getting unbearable, the way she was bearing
down on me . . . so a funny thing, she turned around
and said, "I'm sorry." She never did that before. She
told me that she couldn't help it. She was so nervous.
She does spiteful things . . . like maybe I'm watching TV and she comes in in a bad mood. She'll just
walk over and turn the set off. And then an argument
starts. I don't know . . . I think maybe she enjoys
starting an argument, but I don't think I deserve as
much as I'm getting. I mean . . . I know my father's
a big act . . . he'll yell and shout, but inside, I think
if I needed anything, I'd get it. I know that for a fact.
Maybe it's because I'm spoiled. I really don't know.
I admit it. Maybe I really am spoiled because I've
always had everything. Like my clothes . . . I don't
pay for my clothes, but if I want something special
and I have the money, I go out and get it. But I
think that they've always given me everything . . .
well, as far as my father could afford. He's no million-
aire, but I think that I've always had more than I
needed. I've always had everything.

Co: You feel that sometimes in giving you all these things,
they spoiled you a little bit, too.

Cl: That has a lot to do with it. Not just the things they
gave me. I had a spoiled way of acting, too. Like when
I wanted to quit school, and they wouldn't let me out
of school. Boy, was I mad. I called that Mr. Sil every
name in the book, and just to show you what kind of
a guy he is, two years later when I went to see him,
he shook my hand and said he was very happy to see
me. . . . Boy, did I feel lousy that day. I turned
purple. You know I was so ashamed. I really did feel

ashamed because I gave this guy a hard time a couple
of years before, and here I meet him again, and he
shows me that he's a real man. He didn't hold things
against me. When he shook my hand, I felt like two
cents, and I apologized to the guy for what I said to
him two years before, and he said, "That's okay, my
boy . . . go back and show them what you've got."
Imagine how I felt, Mr. Del. You should have heard
me tell him off two years before. I told him, "Who do
you think you are keeping me in school?" But two
years later I go back and the guy shakes my hand. It
told me what kind of a man he was, and that's the best
way to prove that you're a man . . . if you can sit
there and stand somebody making a jerk out of you,
and not yelling back, especially when somebody makes
a fool out of you, and well . . . that person apolo-
gizes and you accept it . . . that takes a lot of guts,
Mr. Del. Before I used to think that a person was
yellow if he took an apology . . . he'd really be
yellow to do that. In other words if I slapped you
in the face and I came back and apologized, and you
took my apology, I'd really think that you were
yellow. But really, that would take all the guts that
a person had in them . . . I couldn't understand this
before, but I think I do now. It's really funny when
I think about all the screwy ways I used to think. I
mean, I used to sit there, and if I saw someone I didn't
like, I'd tell myself that I didn't like the kid, and
before the day was over, I'd end up in a fight with
him. I mean I didn't like him, but who am I . . . I'm
not a king . . . who am I to think that I'm better
than other people . . . but that's the way I thought
. . . (pause). All I've got are my two hands . . .
(long pause) . . .

*(Mr. Sil was not a counselor, but the quiet strength that he
showed left its positive mark on John. In the counseling
relationship John can come to understand this more fully,
and can develop such strengths of his own. Mr. Sil was most
likely quite unaware of the positive effect of his understanding and acceptance of John's hostility. Schools could do with
more like him!)*

It really feels good to sit here . . . I don't know, it feels good to sit here and talk, and as I talk I think of more and more mistakes that I've made in my life. And I kind of see those mistakes, and I say to myself, "Why did I do that?" I mean it's really funny . . . like when I leave here now, I'll be walking out the door and I'll say to myself, "What did you do this for?" I'll start thinking about myself, like, "Why did I trip that kid, and try to break his head?" and I kind of think about myself and my past, and I remember those crazy things I used to do, and I really start thinking, and it's good for me. . . . This keeps me thinking; it keeps me throwing all of the trash out of me.

(John has no need to be defensive or aggressive with Mr. Del. He knows now that he is understood and accepted, completely, by Mr. Del. He can look at, and be acceptant of, parts of himself that he would previously have rejected. When he reaches this stage, the possibility of further change is good.)

Co: You feel that coming here and being able to talk gets a lot of things off your mind. . . .

Cl: It does, Mr. Del, believe me. I don't know, Mr. Del, if I ever told you before, but there are only two people that I can really sit down and talk to, and that's you and Dr. Ro. I mean I can really be free when I talk to you. I can tell you everything that happens. But I need time. I've got to get wound up. I've got to get thinking about myself. Like when I first came in here, I was trying to think about what I was going to say . . . you know what I mean. But now I'm really loose . . . I come right out with whatever I want to say. But there's one thing that I can't overcome . . . I've got to kind of get used to something before I feel free, before I can come out and say what I want to say, and I don't understand that. That's another thing that I've got to . . . I've got to be able to go into some place and start talking right away . . . you know, without fumbling to say what I've got to say . . . no hesitating, no pushing around to find the right words. If people don't like me that way . . . well, I don't

want to be blunt any more and I don't want to be
rude, but I want them to know that I'm at home.
That's the best way to feel. If you feel at home you
feel at ease, and if you feel at ease, you talk freely
and you're not ashamed of anything . . . that's just
the way I feel. If I were sneaking around here now,
thinking of words, fishing for words, when I left here
I'd feel like two cents . . . you know what I mean.

Co: Uh . . . huh . . .

Cl: But when I leave here now I can say that I've told
you everything, and I feel better about it . . . I
mean I enjoy talking to you . . .

Co: You enjoy the chance to get a lot of things off your
mind . . .

Cl: Things, Mr. Del, that I would never think of. I would
never think of things that I think about here with
you . . . I swear that the words that come out of my
mouth just astonish me when I can think of them.
They say everyone has a subconscious mind . . .
everything's back in here someplace. But when I'm
up here, I don't know . . . a drawer opens and all of
these things come flying out. And I enjoy it . . . it
makes me feel better . . . I get all of these things out.

*(What better description of the counseling process! When a
person becomes involved in this helping relationship, "a
drawer opens," and things that one had never faced before
"come flying out.")*

Co: Talking things out makes you feel better . . .

Cl: It really makes me feel clean. Really . . . like now,
I'm just about talked out, but I feel good . . . You
understand what I mean . . . everything that I could
get out, I got out . . . (long pause).

*(John feels clean, and he is clean, at least of some of the
things that previously had been held back, and had festered,
and had bothered him.)*

Cl: . . . When I think back to the years that I've wasted
. . . boy, it's funny . . . I'm glad it happened this
way, but at the same time I'm not. I think that my life
has taught me a lot, but the only thing . . . well, it's
still kind of hard being back here. . . . You know the
kids . . . it would be different if I were their size, I'm

so much bigger . . . I don't know, they act so young.

Co: Sometimes you feel uncomfortable with your classmates.

Cl: I do, I feel very uncomfortable sometimes. I don't
know . . . because I'm big, and I think people think
I'm a bully or something like that. But I'd never be a
bully, but God knows what these kids are thinking
about me. But it's not their fault . . . it's my fault
that I'm so big.

Co: Sometimes you get the feeling that your classmates
don't accept you, that they think that you're a bully
or something like that . . .

Cl: That's right. But I'm not. I mean, I still fool around,
I have some fun with these kids, but I think sometimes maybe I go too far . . . I don't know. . . .
They're decent kids. I don't know . . . maybe sometimes I don't feel so decent . . . I am, but you know
my past . . . (pause). . . . Got to go now. . . . So
long, Mr. Del . . . We'll see you again . . .

Co: Yes . . . so long, John . . .

And so John Bin, and Tom Ril, and the others, are growing and
moving. For some, the growth and the movement are not too difficult,
for they are young, and change is easier. For others, it is harder, but
all of them are going through a therapeutic experience, and none
of them is quite the same as he was before.

Chapter Twelve

THE ENDING

THE ENDING OF A SERIES of counseling sessions should, of course, be only the beginning of a newer, brighter, freer life for the person who has been known as the client. This brighter life comes to be usually because the individual has become able to do what he felt he could not do before, and he has found that he does not have to do what he once felt he had to do. The two faces have come closer together, and living with self has become easier, more comfortable, more satisfying. This can occur, in a modest and undramatic fashion, when a child sees a counselor for only a single session, as well as at the end of a long series of painful and traumatic sessions.

The ending of a single session should pose no particular problem for the counselor in that a time limit should be agreed upon, and it should be held to, except in the most unusual circumstances. In a school, a counseling period usually fits in with a class period, and most students assume that a counseling session will last the same amount of time as a class session, although in some schools the two do not necessarily coincide. The inexperienced counselor may sometimes feel pressed by the client to continue for a longer period of time, but this is usually unwise, and it is beneficial neither for the client nor for the counselor. One indication of progress in counseling might be the assumption by the client of the responsibility for indicating that the time is up, rather than waiting for the counselor to take the initiative. Often, of course, a client might be emotionally involved and quite unaware of time; in such a situation the counselor, obviously, should not cut the person off right in the middle of an expression of feeling, but somewhere within the general time limit he should take the initiative in gently suggesting that the time is just about up.

In the ideal situation it is the client who determines, correctly, that he no longer has any need of the counselor's help, and that he can get along very well without him. This, however, does not always happen, and the "ending" may come in a variety of ways. Let us note a few of these.

1.   In a school situation the counseling sessions usually end with the end of the school year. In many ways this is beneficial, in that the client knows in advance that, come May or June, he is going to have to go it alone. With some children, of course, who may be in more serious difficulties, referral would be a necessity if the counselor was not available during the summer months. Clients should know in advance if they have only a certain time available for counseling, and if a school counselor takes on a client for what would appear to be a series of counseling sessions during the month of May, he should point out that he will be available only until, say, the middle of June.

2.   In most cases, when the client indicates his desire to terminate the counseling, the counselor will see no reason why he should not be acceptant of this desire. These clients in a high school, for example, would appear to know where they are going:

"I really don't feel that it's necessary for me to come back. I feel that I'm able to . . . well . . . sort of . . . able to think for myself and decide just what I should and shouldn't do. . . ."

"Things have worked out. I went back to her and told her how I felt . . . I mean I let her know that I didn't like what was developing. After that talk things seemed to ease off . . . I sort of got it out of my system. I don't think it will be necessary for me to continue with counseling."

"I've kind of tried out this new person that I've decided to become and it feels real good. I mean I think that there's definitely a sort of a change in me . . . I don't think I'll be seeing you for a while . . . I want to be on my own. . . ."

Some counselors, after comments like these, would probably indicate their availability if and when they were needed. Others would feel that this determination should be made by the client without what might be considered as possible counselor encouragement to return for further counseling. The counselor, they would say, should not say, "Don't come back again," but neither should he say, "I'd be glad to see you again if you wish."

3. Even the most Client-centered of counselors, however, may not always honestly feel that the client is wise in terminating. If the counselor is honest and genuine, he will relate these feelings to the client. He may feel that the client is terminating because of his distaste for the counselor, and suggest another counselor with whom the client might be able to relate more effectively. He may feel that the client is terminating because of his feeling of despair that nothing is happening, or possibly because of his feeling that too much is happening. In any case, it would seem that if the counselor is to be congruent, and genuine, then his "unconditional positive regard" for the client can include his expressing his feeling that the client is unwise to choose to terminate. The final choice, of course, would be left to the client, although even here there is potentially a sticky ethical problem. What if the client has disintegrated even more, and is presenting real evidence of almost totally disorganized, psychotic behavior—does the counselor still say to the client, "The choice is yours . . . ?"

4. Some clients, of course, terminate without any previous notice or warning. They just don't come back. The counselor must be concerned with the part he had to play in this abrupt termination, and tapes of such final sessions can sometimes provide valuable leads as to why the client terminated. Some school counselors may have colleagues attempt to find out the "why" of the termination, since in such cases the client is usually still in school. Others would feel this unwise, and would not interfere with the client's right to terminate— abruptly or not.

5. Some counselors will take the initiative and pose the possibility of termination before it has been suggested by the client. Here again, if this is the honest feeling of the counselor, and if he is genuine, then it would seem that he should pass this feeling on to the client. Many counselors, of course, would say that they were simply reflecting or interpreting the feelings that the client was conveying to them. This would likely be the case, for example, with these counselors:

"It seems that there's nothing more to talk about, eh. . . . If you feel that there might be more to talk about, feel free to make an appointment."

"It appears that you're now able to handle this problem. You're free to continue with counseling if you wish . . . or you can try to get along without it . . . the decision is up to you. . . ."

"We've been getting together now for a period of four months, and you feel that you've changed . . . you don't feel the need to be angry at the world any more . . . you're able to take things in stride. You can continue to come here if you want . . . the decision as to whether or not to continue with counseling is, as always, up to you."

Sometimes, too, the counselor may feel that he is being ineffective, that he and the client are simply going around in circles, and that nothing positive is happening. Again, if he does have this feeling, and if it appears to him that the client would receive more effective help from another counselor, then he should probably pass this feeling on to the client. This may be even more of an ethical problem when this is a private situation, and the client is paying a fee. The client, of course, will not always agree with the counselor, and may indicate his feeling of satisfaction with what is happening, whether the counselor agrees with him or not. What then—does the counselor continue in a relationship that he feels is ineffective? And to what extent does this reflect on his own integrity, and on the value he places on his self?

6. Finally, realistically, it is likely that if the service was available, and if money was not a factor, there would be a large number of individuals who, periodically, off and on, would avail themselves of the services of a counselor as the pressures pushing in on them became too much to take alone. This is already happening to some degree, and as it becomes more culturally acceptable, and people can more easily avail themselves of such services without having the tab of "mentally sick" put on them, then there may be some decrease in the dreadful things that so many individuals must do to themselves, and, inevitably then, to others.

And what of the two clients to whom we have referred frequently in this section, Tom Ril and John Bin? For Tom Ril, the ending of counseling has not yet come, but he is moving in this direction, and eventually he will be able to walk alone, without the counselor. His world will not be freed of anxiety, and fear and pain, but they will mean less, because he will be stronger, and more able. He will be able to handle them—he will not let them determine him.

For John Bin, the counseling is over. In his last session he is looking ahead, and talking about what he now can do, and what he will do. This is approximately the last half of that session, and for John it is the beginning, not the ending:

Cl: I can talk free with Martha. I mean I like to do that. I don't like to hide anything. I think that when a boy takes out a girl and tries to act like a phony, he's just going to get caught; and the more he lies to her, the deeper he goes and he can never get out of it. All of his lies just mix him up—jumble him up, if you know what I mean. And with Martha it's good—I don't have to lie to her.

Co: Uh . . . huh . . . you feel that with her you can be truthful. . .

Cl: I can say anything I want to without being ashamed. I can eat any way I want to eat. If I want to eat six hamburgers, I can—Martha won't say anything. I don't have to worry if Martha will think I'm a pig, or something like that.

Co: You kind of feel free with Martha. . .

Cl: Yeh . . . I can act myself. I don't have to pretend. I don't have to be a phony. Some guys have to be phonies with their girls, but I don't have to be with Martha. I can just say what I want and do what I want and be what I want.

Co: Uh . . . huh. . .

Cl: I can trust Martha with my life. She's the only girl I could trust it with . . . well . . . besides my mother and aunt. I mean she's the only person who's not a relative, the only girl that I could trust . . . (pause) . . . I'm getting older now . . . I think about getting married—I think about having kids of my own, and I enjoy thinking about it.

Co: Marriage seems to be a part of your future—it's normal to think about it. . .

Cl: I figure I'd like to have three or four kids, and I'd like to be able to pick out a girl that I want—not have a girl pick me out, and not have anything to say about it. Maybe what I mean is this . . . maybe I want to be able to pick the girl out, and I want the girl to pick me. I want us to want each other. I don't want a girl to put a chain around my neck and drag me around.

Co: You feel that the girl should want you as much as you want her.

Cl: Martha's really okay . . . (pause) . . . I'm not going steady with her any more. I take her out once in a while, but nothing steady. She wanted to go steady, and I know that when she goes steady, she just wants to go out with me and nobody else. Well, I don't see it that way. I figure okay, I'd like to go out with Martha and I'd like to go steady, in fact. Okay, so we do go steady, but I like my freedom. I like to be able to go out with another girl when I please. I mean if I meet another girl that I like, to figure that I can take her out, and that I'm not cheating or something like that. I wanted her to go out with other guys, but she wouldn't. She said she only wanted to go out with me. So I figured that was too much. I mean she's young. I don't want to tie her down. So I told her maybe we'd better stop going steady. Maybe it's better if we just went out and didn't go steady.

Co: You don't want to go steady with Martha, because this restricts you—you still like the freedom to go out with other girls.

Cl: I don't like to lose my freedom. I like it. I like to be able to meet a new girl and go out with her. In fact, maybe I've been spoiled. I've always been able to get whatever I wanted from girls. All I have to do is call a girl up and she goes out with me. I don't know what it is, but I guess it's just been too easy for me. There's too many girls that I can take out, and I like the idea of meeting a new girl and taking her out. I like this kind of freedom. I've done a few bad things with some of the girls I've taken out, and I'd like to be able to tell Martha about it. But I'm afraid to. Sometimes I want to, and I try to, but I just can't get it out. I'm afraid to.

Co: You'd like to tell Martha about these other girls but you just can't bring yourself around to telling her.

Cl: How am I going to tell her that I was out with another girl? I just can't bring myself around to it, especially since she thinks that we're supposed to go steady. . . . But I straightened that part out—I told her that I didn't want to go steady. And I told her it's not because of me, but because of her. I tried to turn it around a little bit, but I figure this . . . she may as well go out with other boys, and then if she really likes me, she can always come back to me. And I figure I should be able to go out with other girls, and if I really like Martha, I'll come back to her. Then we'll really know that we're meant for each other.

Co: You want to tell Martha about these other girls, but still. . .

Cl: I think I'll call her up tonight and ask her to go out, and then I'll explain the whole thing to her, just what I've done, because I owe it to her. I'll feel better about it too. She'll be mad. She'll probably want to drop me, but I figure it will be better that way. I'd rather be honest with her, especially if I want to be serious about her. I'd like her to go out with other boys. I'd like her to know it's not a crime, just like I'd like her to know it's not a crime for me to go out with other girls.

Co: Uh . . . huh . . . (pause) . . .

Cl: I want to be able to bring my kids up right. I want to be able to let them make up their own minds as to what to do. I mean I can give them advice, but I want them to make up their own minds about their own lives. I just hope they make the right decisions. Like me . . . like I figure now that I'm starting to make the right decisions, and it feels good inside. It really does. Boy, I've got that confidence in me. You can't beat it . . . and it's what I need. I've got the feeling that I'm going to amount to something because . . . I don't know . . . I figure that a lot of things that were bothersome to me before, I can handle now. I want to make out good in life, Mr. Del, and I figure I can. I really do . . . I don't know . . . I've got that . . . somewhere, in my stomach some place, or in my chest some place . . . I've got that good feeling. The feeling that things are going to be okay for me if I use my head.

(It doesn't matter that John does not say, "This is what counseling has done for me. . . ." The important thing is that he has that feeling, "in his stomach," or somewhere. With Mr. Del, he has come to learn that he is somebody, and that he can do things.)

Co: You have the feeling that there's a right future ahead for you. . .

Cl: I'm in school for a purpose. I know that. I realize it, but sometimes I don't know what the purpose is. I mean I know I'm here to make something for myself. I guess that may be it, but still, I'm not sure. I don't know what I mean exactly.

Co: You feel that there's a purpose for your being here, but you're not really sure what it is.

Cl: I've got the ambition now, but I want to be sure that I use the ambition in the right way. I want to be sure that I don't . . . you know . . . go backwards again. I want to make something of myself, but I'm not sure just what. I mean I want my future to be there, but I don't know what I want it to be in.

Co: Uh . . . huh. . .

Cl: What I mean is this. I want to get something out of my education, but I'm not sure what I exactly want to get out of it. I mean I want to get a job, but I think I'd want it to mean more than just a job. I think I want something to happen inside of me. . . . That's it, I guess . . . I want to feel educated inside. I want my education to mean something to me.

Co: You want your education to do something internal, rather than just the completion of a certain amount of work.

Cl: Something like that, I guess. I want to build on what I've got now. I mean I think I know the direction that I have to go, and I want to be able to add to what I have. If I'm a good person now . . . and it's hard to say that, because I don't think I'm really a completely good person yet, but if I'm on the road, I want to keep on the road. If I'm going to get there, the only way I'll make it is to keep building . . . not to look over my shoulder, but just to look ahead. I don't know . . . I don't know if I'm making myself clear. . .

Co: Uh . . . huh. . . You feel that since you have this good feeling inside of you, you don't want to lose it. You want to hang on to it, and add to it . . . kind of build it up.

Cl: I'm going to be whatever God will let me be, but I'm going to be somebody. The only thing is that I hope that my bad record doesn't go against me. I mean I hope that if I decide that I want to become a doctor or something like that, they're not going to hold my record against me. It's stupid. I was found not guilty, but I'm afraid that some people won't understand this. They'll figure that just because I was in court on a charge, then I must be a bad kid, a bad character— that must be immoral or something like that.

Co: You feel that your bad record might be held against you some day when you're looking to further your education. . .

Cl: I hope it isn't held against me, but I just get that kind of a feeling, 'cause I know how people are. I know how they are when they hear you've been in court . . . they don't like you.

Co: You feel that people won't be very understanding.

Cl: I don't see how they can be. You don't know how those words "in court" affect people. You don't know how they act when they hear it. I mean I've seen people, I've seen how they acted when they heard about it. I'm just afraid that these people who will be making decisions about whether or not to let me into a certain place—I just hope these people won't act like the rest of the people. I hope they are older and smarter. I hope they won't hold it against me.

Co: This really worries you. . .

(The counselor does not give false reassurance to John. John's fears are well grounded, and while this counselor will help him to think things out, he is not the "things will be better" type.)

Cl: I hope that they can look at my later record and decide that I need—I mean that I deserve some sort of chance. I hope that they just don't look at certain things, and decide that they don't want me. I hope that they look further. I hope they look at what I've done this year, and what I'm going to do from now on.

Co: Uh . . . huh. . .

Cl: And another thing—I want to stand on my own two feet. I don't want to depend on anybody. I don't want you to think I'm selfish, but I just want to be able to stand up and say, "I'm John—this is me." I don't want to have to say, "This is John," and then hide my face because I'm ashamed.

Co: You want people to accept you and not to look down at you.

Cl: Nobody can change my life but me. I've made some changes so far, but I still want to make more. Nobody can do it but me. John's the only one who can do it.

Co: Uh . . . huh. . .

Cl: I just feel that there's something ahead for me. I just feel it inside of me. I mean I can come to school now and enjoy it. Don't get me wrong. I don't love school; I don't think anybody loves school. But it isn't such a hard place to take. I can get along better. I enjoy it. I'm more interested in what I'm doing.

Co: You feel better about school now than you did in the past. . .

Cl: Well, now I'm steady about school. I mean I don't have my ups and downs. Everything can go along pretty good. Like I said, I don't love it, but it isn't like before. I used to hate it, and then I'd like it and then I'd hate it, and then again I'd like it. I mean I had crazy feelings—crazy ideas about school. I mean I didn't know why I was there, and what I was supposed to do. But now I know—now I know I'm here because I want to make something of myself.

(A major task of some school counselors is to help a child to adjust to, and to live through, an unrealistic school experience, a school experience that has little or no relationship to his totality as a person, but one that he must, according to the law, endure.)

Co: Uh . . . huh. . .

Cl: I can take school now. I never could take it before.

Every little thing bothered me, but now I can take it. I don't have to be mad at the world any more; I don't have to be mad at teachers. Before, all a teacher had to do was cross me just a little bit, just enough to tip me off, just enough to let me show my temper, and boy, I'd show it. But now I figure that I don't have to show it. I don't have to prove anything to anybody. I can just—well—I guess I can just be myself.

Co: You feel more comfortable about being in school now, because you don't have to fight everything like you used to. You can just take things in stride, and be comfortable about the whole thing.

Cl: I'm dying for the next few years to go by. It's funny —I don't want them to go by, but still I do want them to. I'm dying to see what I can make of myself. I'm dying to see if that thing inside of me is real or if it's just there for a little while. I'm dying to see that I can make something of myself. There's nothing holding me back now. The only thing that can hold me back is me—myself. If I started thinking like a jerk again, then maybe I wouldn't make it. But I think that I can take care of myself. I think that I can make it. I just want to stay on an even keel, and then maybe I'll be okay. If I can just keep my mind on what I'm doing, then I think I'll be okay. I mean if I can just think before I act, then I think everything will be okay.

Co: If you can only hang on to what you've found, you feel that things will work out okay—that you'll make something of your future.

Cl: The thing to do is hang on to it, and I think I can. The more I think about it the more I can. Like I say, it depends on me. It doesn't depend on you. It doesn't depend on my aunt. It doesn't depend on my parents. It's me. If I'm going to make it, I've got to decide what I've got to do. No one can decide that for me. If my future isn't important to me, why the hell should any one else worry about it? If I'm going to have anything, I'm only going to get it because of me.

Co: You feel that your future really depends on you—you alone. It doesn't depend on anyone else.

Cl: If I said it depends on somebody else, then I'd probably never make it, but if I decide that my future depends on me, then there's a good chance that I can make it . . . because I think I can handle my future better than anyone else.

Co: Uh . . . huh. . .

Cl: Sometimes I get nervous about next year, but at other times I think of it as a challenge. I'd like to really see if what I've found out about myself is going to stick, or is it going to rub off in the first rain storm. See, I don't know—I won't really know until next year, and the year after, and so on. Maybe I'll never know. Even if I did go to college, I'd probably never really know if I made it. I don't know. How does a person know when he's made it?

Co: You feel that you may never know whether or not you've made it. . . .

(Note that even here, when both counselor and client know that their experience together is just about over, the counselor does nothing to hold the client to him; and he gives nothing in the way of nice, but possibly false reassurance. What the client has done, he has done, in a way, because of the counselor, but only because the counselor has helped him to do it himself. The counselor has respected his own integrity, and that of the client. Even here, in the last few comments, he is still saying to the client, with compassion and understanding, and with the underlying insistence on the strength of the client. "It always has been, and it still is—up to you.")

Cl: Maybe not . . . (long pause) . . . Well, I guess . . . (long pause) . . . I won't see you again, Mr. Del, for a long time . . . I'll see you to say "Hi" to, of course . . . but not like this . . . (long pause) . . . So long then, Mr. Del, and thanks, thanks for everything that you have done. . .

Co: So long, John.

And so John leaves Mr. Del. Mr. Del, being human, probably feels a bit sad, and a bit proud. For John's sake, he no doubt hopes that John will not have to see him again, and the final client comment, indicating counselor success, might well be, "Thank you—but I hope that I don't have to see you again."

The evidence, as these words are written, is that the strength that John gathered was not just a passing phase. He did become more capable of standing on his own feet; he did become more of a responsible individual, capable of standing up and answering for himself, and willing to do so. He was given no medicine, he was given no cure, but through a warm and human relationship with a skilled and educated person who respected him and understood him, he was able to marshal the strengths that he always had, and become a stronger and better person. This, then, is the experience known as counseling.

APPENDIX ONE

The policy statement of the American Personnel and Guidance Association, dealing with the education of the school counselor:

1. Counselor education should be designed to achieve carefully formulated goals based on a philosophy which reflects the highest level of professional knowledge and social concepts.

2. The counselor education staff should be concerned with the task of continually evaluating the program and searching for more adequate methods of counselor preparation. The curriculum should be sufficiently flexible and dynamic to permit revisions and adjustments as required by increasing professional knowledge or by changes in the professional responsibilities of counselors.

3. The curriculum of the counselor education program should assure that essential content and experiences are included in each candidate's program, should provide increasingly for integration of learning, and should avoid duplication of content. Each candidate's program of courses should constitute a planned sequence spiraling toward progressively more advanced work. Programs should recognize individual differences among counselor candidates (their ability, goals, educational background and experience), and should challenge each person individually.

4. Counselor education should provide experiences which are planned to contribute to the counselor candidate's growth in self-understanding.

5. The counselor education program should assure that each counselor candidate has a background in the humanities and in the social, behavioral, and biological sciences which helps him understand individuals, their behavior and adjustments; the nature of the environment and its impact on the individual, including the force which affect his personal and vocational life; and the counselor's role in a changing culture.

6. There should be provisions to promote the integration of studies in related disciplines with the professional studies in counseling in such a manner that these related studies will make meaningful contributions to the competence of the counselor.

7. The program should provide for such specialized study related to the setting in which the counselor will work as is needed to enable him to function effectively within that employment environment and to perform such duties in addition to counseling as may be an appropriate part of his professional role.

8. There should be a year-round program of counselor preparation which makes possible full-time graduate study. There also should be opportunities for additional continuing education of practicing counselors.

9. The level of competence which a counselor must achieve, and the complexity of the skills which he must master require a minimum program of two years of graduate study, a substantial portion of which should be in full-time graduate study.

To achieve the quality of professional preparation necessary for counselors, the following are recognized as essential aspects of professional studies in counseling:

1. Professional studies in counseling should provide counselors with a knowledge of counseling theory and practice, including group procedures; testing and other methods of psychological and educational appraisal; the cognitive and emotional processes of growth, change, and adjustment; the social, educational and work environment; economic, psychological and sociological aspects of work and vocational development; statistics and research methodology; and legal responsibilities and professional ethics.

2. Essential in the core of counselor preparation is supervised experience such as laboratory work, counseling practicum, and internship. Criteria for practicum and internship settings should include quality of professional supervision and of learning opportunities plus their applicability and adequacy for the employment setting

in which the counselor candidate expects to work. The candidate should work with a variety of counselees appropriate to his eventual employment under conditions which protect the interests of the counselee as well as contribute to the competence of the counselor candidate. Experiences should include related tasks which are judged to be a part of the counselor's role in that setting. There should be provision for assistance to the counselor candidate in integrating theory and practice. The experiences and the time allotment should be sufficient to enable him to grow personally and professionally, to develop an appropriate level of counseling skill, and to acquire a more meaningful understanding of the nature of the counseling relationship.

3. Counselor preparation should emphasize philosophy, theory, and scientific knowledge as well as specific techniques and procedures in a manner which assures understanding and mastery of counselor functions and which helps the counselor candidate to learn to adapt his professional self-concept and his professional skills to a variety of work situations. Learning experiences should encourage creative thinking and inquiry; the ability to use research and evaluation as a professional tool; and a recognition of the need for continued professional growth.

APPENDIX TWO

The Association for Counselor Education and Supervision policy statement dealing with the education of the school counselor:

1. The institution provides a two-year graduate program in counselor education, based primarily on the program of studies and supervised practice.
2. There is evidence of quality instruction in all aspects of the counselor education program.
3. Planned sequences of educational experiences are provided.
4. Cooperation exists between staff members directly responsible for the professional education of counselors and representatives of departments or schools offering courses in related fields.
5. Within the framework of the total counselor education program, there are available curriculum resources as well as procedures that make it possible for the counselor candidate to develop understandings and skills beyond the minimum requirements of the program.
6. The counselor education program encourages among staff and students the spirit of inquiry and the production and utilization of research data.
7. Opportunities for self-evaluation and the development of deeper self-understanding are provided for the counselor candidate.

The program of studies should provide opportunities for the development of understanding and competencies in the following:

a. The foundations and dynamics of human behavior and of the individual in his culture.
b. The educational enterprise and processes of education.
c. Professional studies in school counseling and related guidance activities:
    (1) philosophy and principles underlying guidance and other pupil personnel services;
    (2) individual appraisal, including the nature and range of human characteristics and methods of measuring them;
    (3) vocational development theory; informational materials and services;
    (4) counseling theory and practice;
    (5) statistics and research methodology, independent research, and an introduction to data processing and programing techniques;
    (6) group procedures in counseling and guidance;
    (7) professional relationships and ethics in keeping with the APGA Ethical Standards;
    (8) administration and coordination of guidance and pupil personnel services;
    (9) supervised experience.

APPENDIX THREE

The American School Counselors policy statement dealing with the education of the school counselor:

1. School counselor education is graduate education and should result in the counselor receiving as a minimum (a) a master's degree in counseling from an *accredited institution,* and (b) appropriate professional certification as a counselor from the state in which he is employed.
2. It is conceivable and reasonable that more than one level of certification can exist. It is conceivable and reasonable that more than one level of professional preparation and certification should exist. The two-year program of graduate study for counselors, including supervised counseling and pupil personnel services experiences in a school setting, is recognized as a desirable goal.
3. School counselor certification should represent legal professional status in a state and should have as one requirement the endorsement of the counselor education program in which the counselor obtained his preparation.
4. School counselor education programs should include the following components:
   (a) A core of professional study consisting of the following elements: (1) developmental and educational psychology,

(2) counseling theory and procedure, (3) educational and psychological appraisal, (4) group theory and procedures, (5) the psychology and sociology of work and vocational development, (6) the functions and methodology of research, and (7) the legal and professional ethics of counseling and education.

(b) Provision for developing a background in the humanities and the social, behavioral, and biological sciences according to the particular needs and developmental status of each counselor candidate. School counselor candidates lacking a broad under-graduate background in the physical and natural sciences, the behavioral sciences, and the humanities should correct such deficiencies in addition, rather than in lieu of, the graduate-level education referred to here.

(c) Supervised experiences such as laboratory, practicum, and internship work.

(d) Provision for developing a working understanding and appreciation of the school's curriculum and the psychological and sociological climate of in-school learning situations.

5. School counselor education programs should continue to develop and refine selection procedures reflecting the philosophical ideas stated earlier and be consistent with the intellectual and emotional prerequitites implied in the counselor competencies listed.

6. School counselor education programs should be systematic, yet planned individually in regard to each candidate's particular background and needs.

7. School counselor education does not terminate with the completion of a formal program, but continues throughout the career of the counselor. Therefore, counselors have a responsibility to plan, implement, and participate in in-service and other post-certification programs and study designed to maintain and promote professional competency.

APPENDIX FOUR

From the American Personnel and Guidance Association. Selection of counselor candidates is the responsibility of the educational institution, and counselor educators have a responsibility to state and to use efficient procedures of selective admission and selective retention.

1. Admission and continuance in a counselor preparation program should be based on evidence that the counselor candidate is a person who is likely to achieve the quality of performance necessary for excellence in counseling. Criteria should include personal qualifications for counseling, as well as the ability necessary to master academic requirements and acquire professional skills.
2. Prerequisites for entry into the counselor preparation program should be relevant and should be systematically evaluated and revised whenever there is evidence that change is desirable.
3. Procedures and standards for selection should be sufficiently flexible to recognize that there may be alternate ways of demonstrating possession of the qualities or background deemed necessary for admission.
4. Throughout the counselor preparation program, the progress of the counselor candidate should be carefully evaluated. Continu-

ance in the program should be conditional upon satisfactory growth and a continuing expectation that the candidate will achieve necessary levels of performance.

5. The institution faculty has a responsibility to indicate its endorsement or lack of endorsement of candidates completing the program. Endorsement should signify that the staff judges the counselor candidate competent to function at the level for which the program prepares professional counselors.

From the Association for Counselor Education and Supervision.

1. The institution has a procedure for identifying and selecting candidates for counselor education.
2. The institution follows a defined procedure for the selective admission of candidates to the program of counselor education.
3. The institution administers a planned program of selective retention.
4. The institution endorses successful candidates for certification and employment.
5. The institution provides a placement service.

APPENDIX FIVE

A two-year program of counselor education as practiced in one institution appears below. The basic core for Year 1 is as follows:

Counseling: Philosophy, Theory and Practice
Psychological Tests in Guidance
Principles of Psychodiagnosis
Elementary Statistics
Introductory Practicum in Counseling
Research Seminar in Counseling and Personnel Services
Psychology of Vocational Development
Field Work

The basic core for Year 2 is as follows:

Current Issues in American Education
Intermediate Practicum in Counseling
Theories of Counseling
Case Studies in Guidance
Personality Theory
Advanced Psychometrics

Recommended for those preparing to be elementary school counselors:

Guidance in the Elementary School
Group Processes in Education
Child Psychology
Seminar in Elementary School Guidance

Recommended for those preparing to work at the college level:

Student Personnel Services in Higher Education
Philosophy of Higher Education
Personnel Services in Residence Halls
Personnel Services for Foreign Students
Group Processes in Education

Recommended, and required for state certification as a school psychologist:

Education of Exceptional Children
Nature and Needs of the Mentally Retarded
Abnormal Psychology
Community Resources and Mental Health
Remedial Reading
Measurement of Intelligence
Play Therapy

Recommended, and required for state certification as a secondary school counselor:

Introduction to Pupil Personnel Services
Group Guidance
Organization and Administration of Pupil Personnel Services

Recommended for those involved in the supervision of counselors:

Supervision of Counseling

Recommended, and required for students receiving stipends from the Vocational Rehabilitation Administration:

Philosophy and Principles of Rehabilitation
Medical Orientation
Psychodynamics of Rehabilitation
Clinical Practice

INDEX

411